Cato the Younger

Cato the Younger

Life and Death at the End of the Roman Republic

FRED K. DROGULA

OXFORD
UNIVERSITY PRESS

OXFORD

UNIVERSITY PRESS

Oxford University Press is a department of the University of Oxford. It furthers
the University's objective of excellence in research, scholarship, and education
by publishing worldwide. Oxford is a registered trade mark of Oxford University
Press in the UK and certain other countries.

Published in the United States of America by Oxford University Press
198 Madison Avenue, New York, NY 10016, United States of America.

© Oxford University Press 2019

First issued as a Oxford University Press paperback, 2021

CIP data is on file at the Library of Congress
ISBN 978–0–19–086902–1 (hardback) | ISBN 978–0–19–760437–3 (paperback)

For Anne

Contents

List of Maps, Stemmata, and Figures

Maps

Stemmata

Figures

Acknowledgments

I HAVE BEEN wanting to write this book for a long time. Cato the Younger has fascinated me for years, not only because of his underappreciated role in the collapse of the Roman Republic, but also because he—more than any other man of his period—is usually remembered as a caricature. He is too often summed up as Caesar's cranky nemesis, or as the arch-conservative senator who saw the end of the Republic coming but was powerless to prevent it, or even as the Stoic philosopher whose dedication to liberty was so great that he refused to live under Caesar's domination. Cato was a major player in one of the most critical periods of Rome's history, but he is too often reduced to a symbol or an ideal. This book is my attempt to recover Cato as he was, rather than as he generally has been remembered, and to explore his role and activity—for good and for bad—in the final decades of the Republic.

I was able to begin this project thanks to the generosity of the Kommission für Alte Geschichte und Epigraphik of the Deutsches Archäologisches Institut in Munich, which provided me with a fellowship to begin my research in their library. I am particularly grateful to the directors of the Kommission, Christof Schuler and Rudolf Haensch, for their support. As the book took shape, I was fortunate to receive encouragement and assistance from Elizabeth A. Meyer and J. E. Lendon, who generously read multiple drafts and improved the work significantly with their questions, critiques, and suggestions. I am also grateful to the members of New England Ancient Historians' Colloquium, who gave many helpful comments on an early draft of the epilogue to this book, and to my editor Stefan Vranka and the anonymous readers who reviewed this book for Oxford University Press, all of whom offered many helpful suggestions.

Above all, I am profoundly grateful for the patience, assistance, and support of my wife Anne W. Drogula, to whom I offer this book—a mere token—with greatest love and devotion.

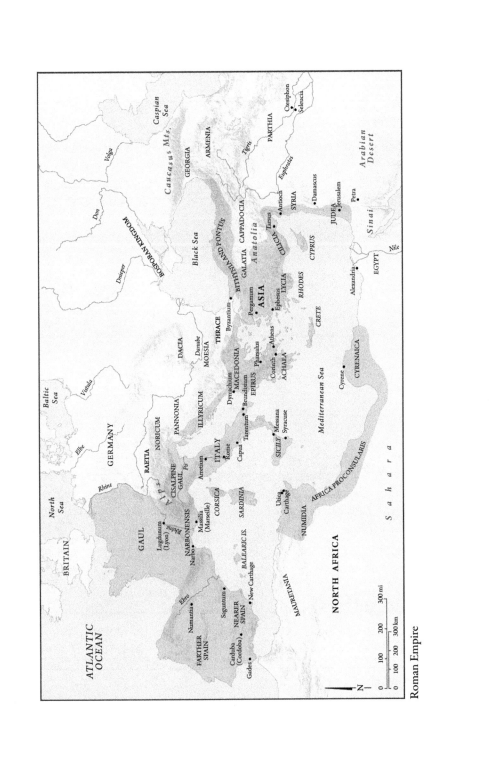

Roman Empire

Roman Italy

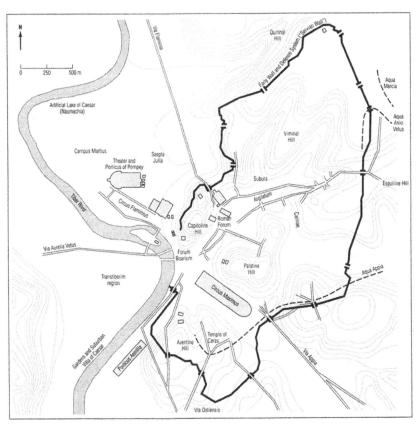

Rome in the Late Republic

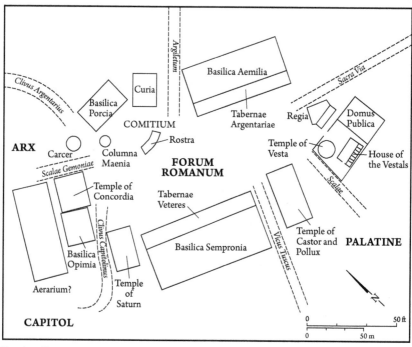

Roman Forum

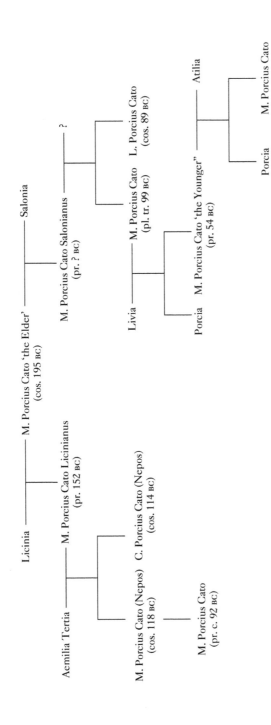

The Family of M. Porcius Cato "the Elder"

Licinia — M. Porcius Cato 'the Elder' (cos. 195 BC) — Salonia

Aemilia Tertia — M. Porcius Cato Licinianus (pr. 152 BC)

M. Porcius Cato (Nepos) (cos. 118 BC)   C. Porcius Cato (Nepos) (cos. 114 BC)

M. Porcius Cato (pr. c. 92 BC)

M. Porcius Cato Salonianus (pr. ? BC) — ?

M. Porcius Cato (pl. tr. 99 BC)   L. Porcius Cato (cos. 89 BC)

Livia — M. Porcius Cato 'the Younger" (pr. 54 BC) — Atilia

Porcia

Porcia   M. Porcius Cato

The Family of M. Porcius Cato "the Younger"

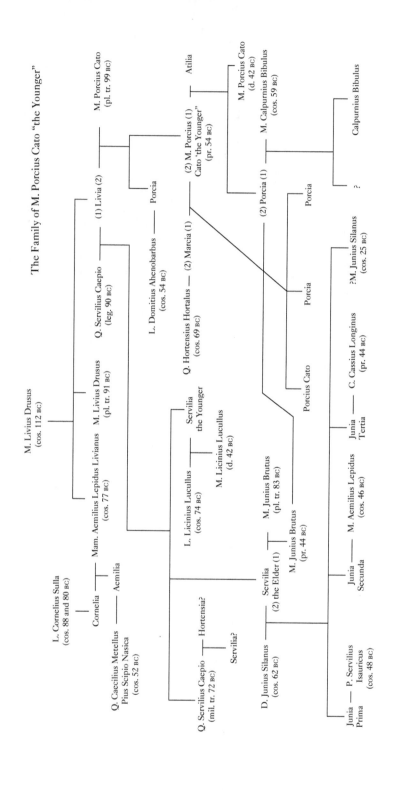

Cato the Younger

Introduction

THE HISTORIAN SALLUST had been an eyewitness to the tumultuous events of the late Roman Republic, and in particular to the civil war between Caesar and Pompey that was the death knell of the Republican government. Having known and observed the men who drove events in the final decades of the Republic, Sallust made a remarkable statement affirming that Gaius Julius Caesar and Marcus Porcius Cato were the two most outstanding Romans in living memory. That Caesar should be singled out for such high praise is unsurprising, since few would deny that he was one of the most important men in the late Republic, if not *the* most important man. Caesar outclassed his opponents throughout his career, and his very name became synonymous with power and authority. Yet Sallust insisted that Cato had been Caesar's equal in merit and virtue. This comparison may strike many readers as odd and surprising, because it is not immediately obvious why Cato—whose accomplishments are rarely (if ever) mentioned by historians—should receive such high praise. Cato never reached the consulship or led Roman legions in battle, he did not have great wealth or throngs of clients to do his bidding, and he is more often recalled as an obstinate crank than as a great statesman. So why does he rate higher in Sallust's estimation than great men like Marius, Sulla, Pompey, Crassus, and Lucullus? How is Cato more deserving of praise than Cicero or Brutus? Sallust's quote is worth citing in full:

> But within my own memory there have been two men with exceptional virtue, albeit with differing characters: M. Cato and C. Caesar. . . . Their birth, age, and eloquence were very nearly the same, they had the same greatness of spirit, and their glory was evenly matched, although different to each. Caesar was held to be great because of his benefactions and munificence, but Cato for the integrity of his life. The first became famous for his mildness and mercy, while severity added distinction to the latter.

Caesar obtained glory through his giving, his assisting, and his pardoning, while Cato achieved this by engaging in no amount of bribery. The one was a shelter for those suffering, while the other was a bane for evil-doers. The courtesy of the first was praised, but the constancy of the second. Finally, Caesar had trained his mind to labor and to be alert, to focus on the business of friends and neglect his own concerns, and to refuse nothing that was worth giving. He hoped for himself a great command, an army, and a new war, where his bravery would be able to shine. But for Cato was the pursuit of restraint, of dignity, and most especially of severity. He did not contend with the wealthy in wealth, nor with the partisan in partisanship, but with the vigorous in virtue, with the restrained in decency, and with the upright in integrity. He preferred to be good rather than to seem good, and so the less he sought glory, the more it attended on him.[1]

Sallust identifies many of Cato's admirable traits in this passage, but the comparison of him with Caesar is awkward—why did Cato's austere virtues make him a match to Caesar? The virtue or merit of each man is defined in drastically different terms, but it is not immediately clear why Cato's austerity made him Caesar's equal in fame and glory, especially since Cato is rarely included among the important figures who directed major events in his lifetime. He lacked all of the usual sources of power in the Republic: he was no military commander; his father's family was recently undistinguished and had all but disappeared; he had neither great fortune nor an army of clients; he never advanced high enough on the political ladder (the *cursus honorum*) to acquire the imposing authority of a consul; and his own political allies often found him a liability. By the political metrics of the time, therefore, Cato—for all of his virtues—should not have been particularly important, and yet Sallust was right: Cato became a leading figure among the Senate leadership and was able to marshal enough influence to stand toe to toe with Caesar in a political battle for control of the Republic. Cato was able to transmute his virtues into political power.

Cato's influence came from his deft manipulation of tradition. The Romans were a naturally conservative people who looked to their ancestors for examples of proper values and actions, and senators tended to be even more conservative than the general population, since their collective authority and influence arose primarily from their claim that their families had always been the leaders of the Republic and the fathers of the state. Their families had done great and many

---

1. Sall. *Cat.* 53.6–54.6. All translations of Greek and Latin authors in this book are my own unless otherwise stated. The abbreviations in this text may be found in the fourth edition of the *Oxford Classical Dictionary*, edited by S. Hornblower, A. Spawforth, and E. Eidinow (2012).

services for Rome over the centuries, and in return they deserved to be seen as the natural leaders of the state. Roman voters responded positively to these claims, and they showed willing deference to senators whose ancestors had established the Republic and built Rome's empire. Thus senators established and maintained their claim to be Rome's "best men" (*optimates*) according to Rome's traditional values, forming a meritocracy that deserved to lead the state. This deep and widespread respect for ancestral custom (the *mos maiorum*) usually enabled the Senate to control the voters by combining and directing the massed influence of its members. Although the citizens occasionally threw their backing behind a populist politician (a *popularis*) who sought widespread support by promoting policies that were favorable to the people (and usually at the expense of the elite classes), their deferential nature and innate respect for tradition normally inclined them to follow the lead of the Senate. Cato was one of these tradition-minded senators, but he used new and innovative ways to promote his conservatism in order to gain influence and status rapidly. Knowing that he lacked the advantages and resources necessary to become a leading member of the Senate according to the prevailing political calculations of his day, he instead found unusual and even radical ways to promote himself as the man who best embodied the *mos maiorum*. Exploiting the malleable nature of tradition, he adopted a number of old-fashioned practices and mannerisms that appeared to have been drawn from Rome's archaic past, and promoted his own particular interpretation of what Rome's ancestral customs had been (or—he thought—should have been). Many of these habits were long out of date, and some may never have actually existed, but Cato deftly used them to present himself as a man uniquely connected to Rome's hallowed ancestors. Using aggressive and eye-catching methods, he promoted and popularized the idea that he was the most conservative and traditional man in the state, which turned out to be a potent political tool among the deferential Romans. Thus it was his deft and highly calculated appeal to an imaginary past, in a society with a fathomless reverence for the past, which allowed him to cast what was nearly a magical glamor over the so-often cynical senators of Rome.

His unusual tactics were very successful, and Cato became the living voice of Rome's ancestors, an identity he used to acquire considerable influence and standing rapidly among the leadership of the Senate. While his self-promotion as *the* archconservative in Rome made him a figurehead for the senators, it also tested the limits of the Romans' reverence for tradition. Cato was not merely conservative; he fashioned himself into his own particular interpretation of ancestral custom, and this interpretation was often too inflexible or unrealistic for many of his contemporaries. The people had great respect for the tradition Cato embodied, but his extreme interpretation of that tradition often offended the voters, who were not always prepared to revert back to the "ancestral values" they admired. Thus Cato reveals the complexity of the Romans' engagement with their own traditions. This was particularly visible among the leading senators, who saw in Cato a very useful champion of the traditional prerogatives of the Senate, but who frequently found his inflexible insistence upon old-fashioned morality to be a liability. Cato was very successful in uniting groups of senators with calls to defend tradition, but he was often frustrated to find that the Romans were not willing to go as far as he was in the defense of tradition, or that they had other priorities that were equally important to them. So while the Romans admired Cato deeply, they offered him little support when he tried to reach the consulship or pass major legislative reforms.

Yet Cato was a primary mover of events in the late Republic despite his political setbacks, and Sallust was right to recognize that his personal virtues were the foundation of his importance. Like Caesar, Cato understood the complex and mercurial world of the Roman Senate, in which blocks of senators were constantly shifting and realigning themselves depending upon which issues were at stake. Far from being a unified, policy-driven aristocracy, the matrixes of alliances within the Senate shifted regularly according to the priorities of each elite family, so holding a leading position in the Senate meant knowing how to navigate among (and influence) a large number of changing factions or alliances. Cato's virtues and his unique, self-made identity as the voice of the ancestors often enabled him to unite critical masses of senators at key moments to oppose the daunting power of great men like Pompey and Caesar. Sometimes he was able to push senators into active opposition to the great men, and other times he was able to reduce the political support of his opponents. He was not the head of anything like a modern political party, but he was often successful in uniting a large number of senators to support him on certain issues, or at least in influencing them not to support his opponents. Some may have shared Cato's values, while others may have been reluctant to be seen opposing Rome's champion of tradition, but his influence enabled him to be a driving force in politics. He appears time after time at the center of those critical events or decisions that gradually pushed the Republic toward civil war. He played a central role in alienating Caesar from the leading men in the Senate; he was a chief architect of attacks on Caesar, Pompey, and Crassus that resulted in the formation of the First Triumvirate; he repeatedly scuttled attempts by Caesar and his allies to come to compromises with the Senate; and he supported and influenced the tactics that ultimately pushed Caesar into marching on Rome. Cato frequently appears at linchpin moments in the history of the late Republic, sometimes as a major player, and other times as the driving force that pushed others to act. So while Cato was not solely responsible for the actions that determined the fate of the Republic—such as the formation of the Triumvirate, or Caesar's decision to cross the Rubicon—he did play a decisive and even essential role in creating the conditions that made those decisions possible and even probable. Indeed, it is one of the great paradoxes of Roman history that Cato's efforts to protect the Republic unintentionally but directly contributed to the collapse of the Republic.

In addition to being a critical player in Republican politics, Cato provides a particularly good window through which one can study the Roman engagement with ideas. His promotion of himself as the champion of ancestral tradition, and his efforts to assert the superiority of his interpretation of that tradition, reveal how flexible the idea of ancestral custom was in the minds of the Romans, and how the manipulation of ideas could be used as a political weapon. And because Cato's political influence was so closely tied to his self-identification with Rome's ancestral values, his successes and failures illustrate the strengths and weaknesses of appeals to tradition in late Republican politics. So the Romans admired Cato's own antique austerity and honesty, but they rigorously rejected his attempts to curb electoral bribery, since it would deny them needed (but illicit) income. Likewise, Cato was often very successful at using appeals to core values such as *libertas* (liberty) and hatred of tyranny to build opposition to Caesar and his allies, but the limits of such appeals became evident on occasions when the voters nevertheless threw their support behind Caesar's popular proposals. Cato viewed and presented his opposition to Caesar in cultural terms as a battle for freedom in opposition to tyranny, but the very flexibility of the tradition that he championed meant the Romans could engage with those ideas in a variety of ways, which often limited Cato's effectiveness.

Cato is also a potent example of the personal nature of Roman politics. He goes down in history as a determined champion of the Republic who opposed Caesar's tyrannical aims, but he actually began attacking Caesar very early in their careers, long before Caesar gave any clear evidence that he would attempt to challenge the Senate. Indeed, when Cato was demanding the death penalty for the Catilinarian conspirators in 63 BC, he tried to implicate Caesar falsely in their crime, which—if successful—would have resulted in Caesar's execution before he had held a major magistracy or taken up his first military command. This extreme animosity may have arisen from a prescient understanding that Caesar would someday aim at a tyranny, but it was more likely the product of a personal feud that Cato conducted with Caesar. The origins of this feud are murky, and it is not even clear that Caesar reciprocated the hostility, but some personal motive drove Cato to attack Caesar relentlessly from the start of their careers. While such feuds were not unusual among Roman aristocrats, Cato's feud would have the critical consequence of alienating Caesar from the senatorial leadership at a time when he might have been incorporated into their fold. Caesar was certainly ambitious, but the Senate had managed to accommodate and even use the ambitions of many talented senators in the past, and it might have found a way to work with Caesar had it not been for Cato's relentless hostility, which drove Caesar to advance his career through extraordinary measures that often ran contrary to the Senate's interests. Had it not been for Cato and his feud with Caesar, therefore, Caesar might have built a political career as a leader and champion of the Senate.

This book is not a comprehensive history of the late Republic, but rather a portrait of Cato's career and what it reveals about Roman society in the last decades of the Republic. Cato is the main subject, and therefore the narrative follows his life and career closely, giving less attention to events in which he was not directly involved. This will necessarily result in a different kind of account of the late Republic: instead of focusing on the great military commands—Pompey in the East, or Caesar in Gaul—this inquiry examines Cato's personal life and his early career, his political activity in Rome, his engagement with other senators, his special commission to Cyprus, his legislative initiatives, his role in bringing about the civil war, and his activities in that war. Events are presented in a chronological narrative, but with frequent digressions to explore how Cato's activities reveal the inner workings of Roman politics, how the Roman people engaged with the ideas that Cato championed, and how he was instrumental in driving major events of the period despite not being a great military commander. The chapters that make up this narrative attempt to recover Cato as he truly was, which requires filtering out the many exaggerations and misinterpretations that were connected to him by later authors, who wished (for their own purposes) either to lionize or condemn him.[2] An epilogue examines how the legend of Cato quickly developed and changed after his death, transforming him from a man of his times into a Stoic hero and a symbol of freedom and Republican virtue. This revised, idealized Cato has been celebrated for two millennia, but it is the real, impatient, unbending, and often unreasonable Cato who is the subject of this book; the man who fought to save his vision of the Republic, and who—as much as Caesar or Pompey—contributed to the collapse of that Republic.

The principal sources on Cato and his career are often a challenge. A single letter to Cicero is all that remains of Cato's own writings, so he must be recovered through the writings of others. This is not easy, because in life Cato was a polarizing figure whose actions could cause frustration at one moment and admiration the next, and after his death he became a revered symbol of Roman liberty,

---

2. The biases in the sources have challenged many historians who have studied Cato. See discussions in: Taylor (1949), Fehrle (1983), Goar (1987), Marin (2009), Morrell (2017), and the popularizing book by Goodman and Soni (2012).

so all of the primary sources must be approached with some caution. Cicero is our best contemporary source and mentions Cato in a large number of speeches and letters, but his opinion of Cato shifted many times over the years, oscillating between respect and utter exasperation. Given the shifting nature of Roman politics, Cicero and Cato were sometimes allies and sometimes opponents, and Cicero was occasionally even jealous of Cato's powerful influence over the leadership of the Senate, so the wealth of information we receive from him must always be scrutinized. Other contemporary authors, such as Caesar and Sallust, offer good insights and details into certain episodes of Cato's life, but neither is entirely trustworthy: Caesar was Cato's archenemy and even wrote a propagandistic pamphlet against him after his death, and Sallust had been one of Caesar's partisans during the civil war. Beyond these contemporaries, a great deal of our information about Cato comes from authors who lived much later. This is a problem because, as will be argued in the epilogue, Cato's legacy was substantially reimagined and revised in the years and decades following his suicide, and through that process of revision Cato the Roman senator was transformed into Cato the Stoic sage. Plutarch is the most important of these sources. His biographies of Cato and of other contemporary figures provide a wealth of information, but they mislead as well as inform. On the one hand, Plutarch was a serious scholar and writer, and he had access to many sources of evidence that are now lost, including the biography of Cato written by his contemporary and friend Munatius Rufus, as well as treatises on Cato by Brutus, Cicero, and Caesar. On the other hand, as a biographer, Plutarch was keenly interested in explaining how his subject's morals and character influenced his actions and shaped his career. This often leads Plutarch to organize his biographies around his own selection of central themes and moral principles, which can shape how he understood and reported the actions taken by his subjects.[3] As a result, his biography of Cato—which is by far the fullest surviving account of Cato's life— can often be slanted to emphasize the moral lessons Plutarch wanted to make. Finally, Plutarch and other writers in the high Roman Empire were heavily influenced by the powerful symbolism that was made out of Cato's suicide in 46 BC. As will be argued, Cato was reinterpreted by those who survived the collapse of the Roman Republic; his embrace of extreme Roman conservatism was later explained as philosophical asceticism, and his defiant suicide was transformed into a Stoic statement on liberty and equated to Socrates's own famous death. Cato was made into a symbol of the lost Republic, and the idealization and

---

3. Plutarch's style as an author (including in his biography of Cato) has been well discussed. See Fehrle (1983) 1–21, Duff (1999) 13–98 and 131–60, and Pelling (2002) 1–44 and 237–51.

romanticism that tend to accompany such symbols quickly obscured the real Cato from view. The later authors who wrote about Cato tended to see him through such idealized lenses, but careful readings of their texts can still recover the real Cato, who was not a Greek philosopher, but a thoroughly Roman aristocrat who strove to save his own idea of the Republic.

I

Family

Cato the Elder and His Descendants

The recorded history of Cato's family begins with his great-grandfather, Cato the Elder, also known as Cato the Censor. Like many of Rome's aristocracy, Cato the Elder belonged to a Latin family that had gained Roman citizenship and had risen to prominence in the mid-Republic. According to tradition, the Porcian clan or *gens Porcia* originally lived in Sabine territory, northeast of Rome, but at some point in the late fourth or early third century BC, the clan moved to the Roman *municipium* of Tusculum, where it took up residence and obtained Roman citizenship.[1] It is not clear how early the clan moved to Tusculum, but the *gens Porcia* had probably possessed Roman citizenship for several generations by the birth of M. Porcius Cato the Elder in ca. 234 BC.[2] At least three branches of the *gens Porcia* are known, but this work will focus only on one: the *Porcii Catones*.[3] This family retained close connections with its Sabine roots, and even drew income from an estate in Sabine territory.[4] It had a tradition of producing brave soldiers,

---

1. Plut. *Cat. Mai.* 1.1. Tusculum was said to have become Rome's first *municipium* in 381 BC (Cic. *Planc.* 19, Livy 6.26.8, Dion. Hal. 14.6.6). See Salmon (1970) 49–50.

2. The year of his birth and his age at his death in 149 BC are not clear. Cicero (*Brut.* 61, 80, *Sen.* 10, 14, 32) suggests he lived to be eighty-five years old (and thus was born in 234 BC), while Livy (39.40.12) and Plutarch (*Cat. Mai.* 15.4) record that Cato lived to be ninety years old, which would put his birth in 239 BC. Astin ([1978] 1 n. 1) points out that this earlier year is impossible because Cato himself stated (Plut. *Cat. Mai.* 1.6) that he was seventeen when Hannibal first invaded Italy (ca. 217 BC), which makes ca. 234 BC the likely date of his birth.

3. Members of other branches of the *gens Porcia* achieved political success at roughly the same time as Cato the Elder: two members of the *Porcii Licini* branch reached the praetorship in 207 and 193 BC, the latter of whom reached the consulship in 184 BC, and one member of the *Porcii Laecae* is known to have held the praetorship in 195 BC. See Astin (1978) 9.

4. Plut. *Cat. Mai.* 1.1.

but M. Porcius Cato (the Elder) was the first member of the clan to gain political distinction and achieve high office in the Roman state.[5] According to Plutarch, this M. Porcius originally had the *cognomen* "Priscus" ("elder" or "ancient"), but later received instead the *cognomen* "Cato" ("wise" or "experienced"), and therefore was the first M. Porcius Cato of his clan.[6] By all accounts, this Cato and his family adhered closely to Roman traditions: he was a brave soldier, he worked his farm with his own hands, and he lived in a simple and somber lifestyle. He took as his role model the great Roman hero M'. Curius Dentatus (cos. 290 and 275 BC), who had three times been honored by the state with a triumph for the military victories won under his command. Dentatus was famous for his austerity, and for stating that good citizens should be content with only seven acres of land.[7] Cato lived near the farm that had once belonged to Dentatus, so he probably grew up hearing stories about the great commander's character and exploits, which would have had a strong influence on the younger man.

Cato the Elder worked hard to develop his powers of oratory, and he acted as an advocate for any of his neighbors who needed legal assistance. This helped him gain prominence and a reputation as a public man, and also helped him build a base of clients who owed him future support in return for his aid. As a young man he fought in the campaigns in Italy against the Carthaginian general Hannibal, and his military bravery brought him to the attention of the famous Q. Fabius Maximus Verrucosus, hero of the Second Punic War.[8] His bravery and virtues also gained him the support of the patrician senator L. Valerius Flaccus, whose land was not far from Cato's home.[9] With the support of these powerful patrons, Cato began his climb up Rome's political ladder, known as the *cursus honorum* ("race of honors"). Early in his career he served as quaestor under Scipio Africanus in Africa, a campaign that Fabius Maximus had strenuously opposed. This appointment is surprising, because Fabius was politically and personally opposed to Scipio. He disapproved of Scipio's embrace of Greek culture, and he resented the younger man's rapidly growing military reputation. Much more important, Fabius vigorously opposed Scipio's plan to launch an invasion of Africa, thereby expanding the war against Carthage. For these reasons, Cato probably found it

---

5. For a detailed discussion of the life and career of M. Porcius Cato the Elder, see Astin (1978).

6. Plut. *Cat. Mai.* 1.2. It is more likely that the *cognomen* "Priscus" was only later attributed to this Cato in order to distinguish him from his great-grandson, Cato the Younger (one cannot have an "elder" without a "younger").

7. Plut. *Cat. Mai.* 2.1–2.

8. Plut. *Cat. Mai.* 2.3.

9. Astin ([1978] 9–10) discusses the relationship of Cato and Flaccus.

difficult to serve under Scipio. Although most quaestors enjoyed a strong bond of loyalty with the consuls they served in war, Cato criticized Scipio's Hellenistic learning and customs, and complained that Scipio's military discipline was lax and contrary to Roman custom.[10] These accusations suggested that Scipio was not only a bad commander, but a bad Roman who did not lead his men with traditional Roman discipline. Cato thus presented himself as the champion of true Roman virtues. For a quaestor to challenge his commander in such a way was highly unusual, and Cato was released from service and returned to Rome, but it is not clear whether this was voluntary or whether he was sent away by Scipio. In most cases, such rude treatment of a consul would have ended a quaestor's political career, but the bitter feud between Fabius and Scipio gave Cato cover, since his powerful patrons protected him from any serious ramifications. With Fabius and Valerius, Cato continued to attack Scipio and any other senator he deemed un-Roman or tainted with Hellenism by bringing charges against them in court, including important men such as M. Claudius Marcellus, T. Quinctius Flamininus, L. Cornelius Scipio Asiagenes, Q. Minucius Thermus, and M'. Acilius Glabrio. Public prosecutions like this were an effective way for Roman aristocrats to enhance their own reputations while punishing their rivals, and throughout his life Cato would remain an active litigant and a tenacious foe in the courtroom, thereby enhancing his credentials as a true Roman by acting as a scourge of un-Roman activities.

As praetor in 198 BC, Cato performed his duties with traditional strictness and austerity. He was sent to take command of Sardinia, where he kept his expenses to a minimum and used harsh measures to root out money-lending in the province, which he considered to be un-Roman.[11] As consul in 195 BC, Cato was drawn into a debate among the plebeian tribunes over the *lex Oppia*, a law restricting displays of wealth by women, which had been enacted in 215 BC after a string of devastating Roman losses to Hannibal. Since the war was long over, the women of Rome persuaded two tribunes to propose the law's repeal, but other tribunes used their power of veto to block this motion.[12] For days, women took to the streets entreating the magistrates and voters for the law's repeal. Cato was outraged by this unusual display of political activity by the women, and Livy records him giving a speech castigating the women's behavior and arguing against the repeal of the law. In this speech, Cato attacked the very idea of repealing a piece of duly passed legislation, and railed against the extravagance of his fellow citizens that

---

10. Plut. *Cat. Mai.* 3.5–6.

11. Livy 32.27.2–4, Nep. *Cato* 1.4, Plut. *Cat. Mai.* 6.1–3.

12. Livy 34.1.2–4.20, Val. Max. 9.1.3, Zon. 9.17.

he compared to a disease harming men and women alike. In this address Cato is said to have been particularly harsh toward Rome's women, and Livy writes that one of the bill's proposers reprimanded him for being more interested in rebuking Rome's women than in arguing the legal merits of the bill.[13] In this way Cato appears more interested in moralizing and defending tradition than discussing the merits of the proposal, and even the opposing tribunes were eventually convinced to end their obstruction and allow the law's repeal. In this way, Plutarch makes Cato look principled but unrealistic in pushing for his own beliefs about what Roman tradition was, and what moral standards should be enforced. This may reflect his own attitudes, but it may also be foreshadowing of the younger Cato's career a century later.

As his consular command, Cato received the war in Spain, where he is said to have treated his soldiers with stringent discipline and his defeated enemies with cruelty. He lived simply as a common soldier, avoiding the ostentatious expenses and displays for which he had faulted Scipio.[14] He proved to be a capable commander, and in one year he conquered many towns and tribes, frequently using wholesale slaughter to solidify Rome's control over its possessions. He also shared a greater amount of the plunder with his soldiers than was common for aristocratic commanders, and prevented his staff from excessive profiteering. He probably hoped to have his Spanish command extended for an additional year in order to accumulate more glory and spoils of war, but Scipio had been elected to a second consulship for 194 BC, and in retribution for Cato's previous attacks, he arranged to have Cato removed from Spain as early as possible. Nevertheless, Cato returned to Rome laden with treasure, and he received the honor of a triumph, which he celebrated with due ceremony in 194 BC.[15] Three years later he accepted a position in the army of the consul M'. Acilius Glabrio, who was sent to fight Antiochus and the Aetolians in Greece. His position in this campaign is disputed: most sources refer to him as a military tribune, but this would have been an unusually low position for a senator of consular rank.[16] Since military tribunes of new consular legions were elected officers, it is possible that Cato accepted the lower position out of respect for the voters, although in describing this campaign Livy refers to him as a legate (a lieutenant chosen by the commander),

---

13. Livy 34.5.3, *qui tamen plura verba in castigandis matronis quam in rogatione nostra dissuadenda consumpsit.*

14. Plut. *Cat. Mai.* 10.1–5. For further discussion of this campaign, see Knapp (1980) 21–56.

15. Plut. *Cat. Mai.* 11.1–3. For a discussion of Scipio's actions, see Astin (1978) 51–2.

16. Cic. *Sen.* 32, Plut. *Cat. Mai.* 12.1, Front. *Strat.* 2.4.4, App. *Syr.* 18, Auct. *Vir. Ill.* 47.3.

which seems much more appropriate given Cato's high rank and experience.[17] He executed his duties with his usual bravery and tactical savvy, and contributed significantly to Glabrio's victory in the Battle of Thermopylae (191 BC).

After these years of military service, Cato became a leading voice in the Senate and in the courts. He continued to attack Scipio and his family, as well as other senators he thought tainted by un-Roman customs. Fabius Maximus had died in 203 BC, but Cato maintained his fervent political opposition to Scipio and his clan, and he became the most outspoken champion for traditional Roman values, opposing the introduction of foreign customs into Rome. To this end, he sought election to the censorship in 189 BC, but was defeated through the influence of Scipio and his allies, who no doubt feared what Cato would do with the power of that office. Yet popular support for Cato and his old-fashioned morals was high, and when he tried again five years later, he was successfully elected to the censorship for 184 BC.[18] The aristocracy had once again worked to prevent his election, and had put up seven rival candidates to appeal to the voters, but they nevertheless elected Cato and his friend L. Valerius Flaccus. The people may have supported him out of respect for his close adherence to Roman traditions, but they may also have looked forward to watching the senators squirm under his severe review of their order. His work as censor was famous for its harshness: he revised the membership of the Senate and expelled seven senators, including the consular L. Quinctius Flamininus (cos. 192 BC), and rather than allow the expelled senators to slink off as usual, he gave speeches reviling them and their un-Roman habits.[19] He also deprived L. Cornelius Scipio Asiaticus (cos. 190 BC) of his horse in the review of the equestrian order, a strong insult to the hated Scipio clan.[20] He also staunchly opposed the influence of untraditional ideas. He objected to the Greek manners and styles that were gaining traction in Rome (especially among the aristocracy), and he raised taxes dramatically on luxury objects—including on young slaves—in an effort to prevent their popularity.[21] Cato ordered that pipes bringing water to private houses should be cut, raised the rents on public lands, commissioned several construction projects for public works, and he even

---

17. Livy 36.17.1. Astin ([1978] 56) accepts that Cato was a military tribune, but remarks that this was "a most unusual position for ex-consuls."

18. Nep. *Cato* 2.3, Livy 39.40.1–44.9, Val. Max. 2.9.3, Plut. *Cat. Mai.* 16.1–19.6, Auct. *Vir. Ill.* 47.4, 53.2.

19. Livy 39.42.5–7, Plut. *Cat. Mai.* 17.1–5.

20. Livy 39.44.1, Plut. *Cat. Mai.* 18.1.

21. Livy 39.44.2–4, Plut. *Cat. Mai.* 18.2–4.

expelled one senator for embracing his wife in public.[22] Despite his severity, he
does not seem to have been entirely scrupulous or disinterested in the execution
of his duties: the Senate strongly (but unsuccessfully) opposed his use of public
money to commission a new basilica that would bear his name in the Forum. Yet
Cato became famous for his activity as a censor, and was often referred to by later
Romans as the Censor.

Cato spent the rest of his life aggressively championing those values he
considered to be traditionally Roman, and opposing luxury and other vices that
he believed undermined those values. In 181 BC he supported the *lex Orchia* that
restricted the number of guests one could invite to dinner (thus suppressing large
dinner parties), and sometime later he supported the *lex Voconia*, which sought
to reduce sharply the amount of wealth and number of luxurious items a woman
could possess.[23] He opposed an effort by some senators to start what he considered
to be an unjust war against Rhodes, and even in his old age he joined the prosecution of a praetorian commander who had massacred some Lusitanians in Spain
after pledging not to do so.[24] More than a century later, Cicero knew of 150 different speeches that Cato had delivered during his career, demonstrating what an
active speaker he was in political debates, and also how he had carefully preserved
his speeches to ensure they had a wider audience.[25] He similarly became an active writer, composing everything from histories to agricultural treatises, and this
body of written work played an important role in the development of Roman
prose writing.[26] He was devoted to making money, which was not in itself inconsistent with the *mos maiorum*, but he went so far as to invest in cargo ships, which
was considered sordid and shameful business for a senator.[27] He never ceased
participating in government, however, and in his eighties he helped drive Rome
into the Third Punic War, which started in the year of his death, in 149 BC.

Cato was particularly known for opposing Greek practices. The Greek cities
in southern Italy had fallen into Rome's power early in the third century BC, and
many Romans had embraced the resulting influx of Greek culture and ideas. The
Scipionic circle, for example, cultivated Greek thinkers and their culture, drawing

22. Livy 39.44.5–8, Plut. *Cat. Mai.* 17.7, 19.1–2.

23. *Lex Orchia*: Macrob. *Sat.* 3.17.3, Fest. 220L., *Lex Voconia*: Cic. *Balb.* 21, Livy *Per.* 41, Plut. *Cat. Mai.* 18.1–2, Gell. 6.13.3, 17.6.1.

24. Livy *Per.* 49, Gell. 6.3.7, and Val. Max. 8.1.abs.2.

25. Cic. *Brut.* 65.

26. Plut. *Cat. Mai.* 25.1. On Cato's influence, see Astin (1978) 182–266, Gruen (1992) 52–83, Courtney (1999) 41–91, Sciarrino (2011) 117–60.

27. Plut. *Cat. Mai.* 21.5–6.

Cato's contempt. He was said to have been entirely opposed to Greek philosophy, and when a distinguished group of Greek philosophers arrived in Rome as ambassadors, he did everything in his power to hasten their departure from the city, fearing that the youth of Rome would be damaged by their influence.[28] Greek doctors also drew his ire.[29] According to Pliny the Elder, Cato believed the Greeks were a depraved and ignorant race (*nequissimum et indocile genus*) that threatened to corrupt traditional Roman society, so he regularly advocated for the removal of all Greeks from Rome and even from Italy.[30] As a consequence of such testimony, he was long seen as an enemy of Greek culture, but this is not quite correct. He actually indulged in Greek literature and learning, and accepted some aspects of Hellenic culture easily, while bitterly rejecting others.[31] Rather than rejecting Greek culture outright, therefore, his attitudes toward Hellenism were complex; he believed that Roman culture and values were superior, and wanted his countrymen to behave as Romans.[32] Thus Cato was not an enemy of the Greeks and was not absolutely opposed to their culture, but his writings were intended to show his fellow Romans in general—and his own children in particular—the importance of Rome's own values and national character. This shows that he was particularly devoted to Rome and its *mos maiorum*, which he did not wish to see diluted by foreign customs. So Cato's view of Hellenic culture was nuanced, and he could attack fellow Romans for adopting some foreign customs while overlooking and even appreciating other cultural borrowings that he felt were acceptable, or at least were not a threat to Roman culture.

This flexibility is also visible in Cato's view of the *mos maiorum*. Roman ancestral custom was not a fixed set of immutable rules engraved in bronze, but rather the widely accepted understanding that certain practices had been (or could be) designated as "ancestral" on account of their long habitual usage. These time-honored customs were so ubiquitous, and so universally recognized and accepted, that they often took on the weight of law.[33] Yet because the *mos maiorum*

---

28. Plut. *Cat. Mai.* 22.1–23.4.

29. Plut. *Cat. Mai.* 23.3–4.

30. Pliny *NH* 29.14 (cf. 7.113).

31. Astin (1978) 157–81.

32. Gruen (1992) 52–83.

33. Hölkeskamp ([2010a] 17–8) describes the *mos maiorum* very well: "Its range of reference and meanings was almost unlimited and indeed, as it were, defied limitation: any modern attempt to narrow it down must fail to grasp its true constitutive importance. This notional stock of time-honored principles, traditional models, and rules of appropriate conduct, or time-tested policies, regulations, and well-established practices not only prescribed social behavior in 'private' life, but also regulated all criminal and 'public' law, the state religion as well as

was made up of customs rather than statutes, there existed significant flexibility for Romans to interpret or reinterpret what was or was not truly in accordance with ancestral custom. So the *mos maiorum* changed and evolved over time, and at any moment different Romans could define tradition in different ways, and interpret the examples (*exempla*) of the ancestors to suit their own positions. The *mos maiorum* always harkened back reverently to the actions of earlier generations from Rome's hallowed past, but individual aristocratic families had their own distinct traditions and legends of their forefathers' exploits, so men from different families could have different ancestors in mind when they referred to ancestral custom. So while some Romans could see the adoption of foreign customs as being a part of Roman tradition—they had indeed adopted a great deal from the peoples they encountered—others could see the influx of Greek practices as a dilution of the *mos maiorum*. Ancestral custom was therefore a flexible concept that could be adjusted or slanted, depending upon the views and goals of a speaker. Roman politicians could use this flexibility to their own advantage by claiming that their own practices and positions flowed from the *mos maiorum*, while those of their rivals were violations of tradition and therefore bad. Cato the Elder was a master of this tactic, positioning himself as the great defender of the *mos maiorum*, and using that position to attack his political enemies—especially the Scipionic clan—by alleging that their behavior was contrary to tradition and therefore un-Roman, which was a potent charge because it was very hard to disprove. So Cato was not a blind hater of all things Greek; he appreciated some Greek practices—especially their literature[34]—that did not notably transgress his understanding of the *mos maiorum*, but he rigorously opposed Greek practices that seemed contrary to Roman custom, or that he wished to present as being contrary.

Cato's reputation, therefore, was closely linked to his self-identification as a leading advocate for traditional Roman values. He did this not only by speaking against the popularity of Greek culture and showing the superiority of Roman values, but also by living in a manner that ostentatiously embraced what he thought were the "old virtues" of Rome's ancestors. He became famous for his extreme moderation and frugality by modeling for his countrymen how a true

the military system, the ways and means of running politics at home and abroad. Last but not least, *mos maiorum* also included what one might call the 'constitutional conventions.'" See Lintott (1999a) 4–8, Bettini (2000) 303–52, Blösel (2000) 25–97, Pina Polo (2004) 147–72, Wallace-Hadrill (2008), and van der Blom (2010) 12–25 for a detailed study of the evolution of the term *mos maiorum*.

34. On Cato's appreciation for Greek literature, see Astin (1978) 157–81.

patriotic Roman—according to his interpretation—should live. Plutarch writes of Cato's own manner of living:

> He says that he never wore clothing that was worth more than one hundred drachmas, that he drank the same wine as his workmen, even when serving as praetor and consul, and that for his dinner he prepared dishes worth thirty asses from the markets, but this he did for the sake of the city so that he might strengthen his body for serving in the army. He also says that, having come into possession of a many-colored Babylonian drapery through an inheritance, he straightaway sold it; that not one of his country houses was plastered; and that he had never purchased a slave for more than fifteen hundred drachmas, wanting not dainty nor youthful slaves, but hard-working and solid types, such as horse grooms and ox-drivers. And when these became old, he thought it was important to sell them and so not feed the useless. On the whole, he thought nothing superfluous was cheap, but that anything that was not needed was expensive, even if it was sold for a single as. He owned arable land and pastures, rather than sprinkled and cleaned lawns.[35]

This description reflects not only a man who was dedicated to avoiding the luxurious habits that were taking hold of Rome's wealthy citizens, but also a man who worked very hard to promote himself visibly by making sure that his fellow citizens knew that he was living in a different and more truly Roman lifestyle—a lifestyle more in tune with Rome's austere past and the *mos maiorum*. Plutarch thought that Cato went too far, and that his disregard for his old slaves and animals—which were sold off rather than cared for after their years of service—was callous and cruel.[36] He notes that many thought Cato was miserly and ungenerous, but that others recognized that his unusual lifestyle was meant to set him apart from other wealthy Romans; his old-fashioned behavior was meant to be noticed and compared (favorably) to the behavior of others.

While Cato's unusual behavior may in part reflect his own opinions and values, it was also an important political tool for him. He was a new man (*novus homo*), which meant that none of his ancestors had ever reached high office in Rome. This was a serious social and political disadvantage, because Roman voters had special reverence for men whose families had led the state for generations. Whereas other senators could point to a long and glorious lineage of ancestors

---

35. Plut. *Cat. Mai.* 4.3–4.

36. Plut. *Cat. Mai.* 5.1–2.

who had reached Rome's highest offices, and could claim that this heritage conferred upon them the special status of being a noble (*nobilis*) and endowed them with the collected moral authority (*auctoritas*) and rank (*dignitas*) of their ancestors, Cato was the first member of his family to reach high office. Unable to claim inherited nobility, he compensated by adopting and emphasizing old-fashioned, blue-blooded aristocratic values and behavior—that is, his extreme parsimony was to some extent affected for social and political purposes; by acting as a senator of ancient Roman lineage, he hoped to be treated as one. He adopted an austere lifestyle that harkened back to Rome's revered ancestors, thereby presenting himself as a man uniquely in tune with the *mos maiorum*.[37] This gave him considerable influence among the Romans, who were culturally predisposed to show great deference and respect to men who best embodied the customs and attitudes of Rome's glorious forefathers. Indeed, the authority of Rome's ruling aristocracy was in large part based upon their claims to be the inheritors of the values, traditions, and glory of their ancestors, who had built the city and established the Republic. Imitation of Rome's ancestors implied that the imitator would be as successful and as beneficial to the state as the ancestors, and that the imitator would enjoy the same divine favor that the gods had shown to Rome's forefathers.[38] Senators were expected to be the champions of the *mos maiorum*, so Cato's austere lifestyle was certainly intended to enhance his status by making him the living embodiment of Roman tradition, and the inheritor of the virtues that had built Rome's empire. Plutarch seems to have recognized how Cato skillfully crafted his own image, and even thought him something of a hypocrite for having championed frugality and attacked money-lending as a means to acquire rank and status as a younger man, but once he had climbed the political ladder and achieved his goals, he often sought to enrich himself through money-lending, and he often hosted fancy dinner parties once his successful political career had brought him wealth.[39] This suggested that Cato's forceful advocacy for tradition was at least partly a façade or political tool. Despite this criticism, his strategy worked with the tradition-loving Romans: by behaving as a man whose

---

37. Reay ([2005] 331–61) has convincingly argued that Cato deliberately used his lifestyle and writings to make himself an exemplar to the Roman people by fashioning himself as a self-conscious throwback to the days of their ancestors (their *maiores*). Hölkeskamp ([2010] 19–20) has similarly pointed to Cato as a self-promoter, who used his speeches to claim for himself a place among Rome's blue-blooded aristocracy, while Sciarrino ([2011] 117–202) points out that Cato's written work was a strategic attempt to overcome the disadvantages of his status as a *novus homo*.

38. Van der Blom (2010) 14.

39. Plut. *Comp. Arist. Cat.* 4.4–6 and *Cat. Mai.* 21.3–7.

ancestors had ruled Rome for centuries, he came to be recognized as a man who belonged among Rome's leadership. So while there is little doubt that he genuinely respected the values he championed, at the same time he compensated for his status as a *novus homo* by fashioning himself into the foremost representative of the *mos maiorum*.[40] In this he was a success, and he became one of the most famous men of his generation.

Cato the Elder had two sons, each by a different wife, and these two sons established the two branches of the *Porcii Catones* that existed in the late Republic (see Stemma 1). The elder son, M. Porcius Cato (later known by the *cognomen* Licinianus), was born from his father's first marriage to Licinia. He died as praetor-designate in 152 BC, which (assuming he obeyed the age limits established by the *lex Villia annalis*) means he was born in or before 191 BC, not long after his father's return from Spain. Like his father, Cato Licinianus made a name for himself as a soldier. He first appears in 173/2 BC in the army of the consul M. Popilius Laenas, who outraged the Senate by notoriously rounding up and selling into slavery large numbers of peaceful provincials (the Statelliates), and then by ignoring senatorial instructions to undo this scandalous action.[41] What Cato Licinianus thought about his commander's actions is not recorded, but when Popilius disbanded the legion in which Licinianus was serving, the young man immediately volunteered to re-enlist in the consul's other legion, reportedly eager to win a reputation for military valor. According to Cicero, on this occasion Cato the Elder wrote his son and instructed him to take the military oath a second time upon re-enlisting, in order to be entitled legally to act as a soldier (he had been released from his original oath upon the disbanding of his previous legion).[42] A few years later, Licinianus served under L. Aemilius Paullus (Macedonicus) at the decisive Battle of Pydna in 168 BC. During this battle Licinianus lost his sword in the fighting, and after begging his comrades for their assistance, he plunged back into the thick of the fighting, jeopardizing his life and sustaining many wounds in order to recover his sword and thus avoid the shame that would have come from returning from battle without his weapon.[43] He retrieved his sword and won great glory and a reputation for bravery from the fighting. When Licinianus was honorably dismissed from the army to recover from his wounds,

---

40. See van der Blom (2010) 152–65 for discussion of Cicero emphasizing Cato the Elder as an *exemplum* of the new man who succeeds in politics by championing the *mos maiorum*.

41. Cic. *Off.* 1.36, Livy 42.7.3–9.6. Astin ([1978] 104 n. 1) argues that this is an error, and that Licinianus did not serve under Popillius Laenas.

42. Cic. *Off.* 1.36–7.

43. Plut. *Cat. Mai.* 20.7–8 and *Aem. Paul.* 21.1–5.

his father once again cautioned him that—having been discharged—he was no longer legally permitted to act as a soldier.[44] These repeated paternal admonitions to follow the law precisely may reflect the litigious nature of the elder Cato, who continued to attack political enemies in the courts—and was attacked by them in turn—into his ninetieth year.[45] He may have assumed that rivals were searching for new ways to attack him and his family, and therefore cautioned his son to follow the laws scrupulously. Licinianus won a great reputation in this campaign, and even impressed his commander Aemilius Paullus, who offered the young man his daughter Tertia as a wife when they returned to Rome.[46] This was an illustrious match, showing the increasing status of the *Porcii Catones*.

Licinianus became a celebrated jurist back in Rome, wrote several important legal treatises that were long remembered, and was elected to the praetorship of 151 BC, although he died before taking office.[47] He left behind him two sons. The elder son, M. Porcius Cato (Nepos), reached the consulship in 118 BC but died in office, probably in Africa on a mission to establish the succession of the Numidian kingship.[48] He was survived by a son, M. Porcius Cato, who reached the praetorship around 92 BC, but who seems to have died in Narbo.[49] The younger son was C. Porcius Cato (Nepos), a contemporary and friend of Tiberius Gracchus, the famous plebeian tribune of 133 BC who was murdered for advancing land reform legislation. This C. Cato (Nepos) reached the consulship in 114 BC and received a command in Macedonia, where he suffered a humiliating defeat at the hands of the Scordisci (a powerful northern tribe) and afterward returned to Rome, where he was prosecuted and fined for extortion.[50] Five years later, he was prosecuted and condemned by the Mamilian commission for collusion with Jugurtha, the king of Numidia, and went into exile in Taracco.[51] To the best of our knowledge,

---

44. Plut. *Rom. Q.* 39.

45. Plut. *Cat. Mai.* 15.4–5.

46. Plut. *Cat. Mai.* 20.8, 24.1, *Aem.* 5.6. Astin (1978) 104–5, and Fehrle (1983) 50–51.

47. Livy (*Per.* 48) and Plutarch (*Cat. Mai.* 24.6) record that he died as praetor, but Cicero (*Tusc.* 3.70) and Gellius (13.20.9) say that he was praetor-elect. On Licinianus's activity as a jurist, see: Gell. 13.20.9, Fest. 144L., *Dig.* 34.7.1–5, 45.1.4.1, 50.16.98.1. His father is said to have given him a very modest funeral ceremony—see Astin (1978) 105.

48. Vell. 1.15.5, 2.7.8, Val. Max. 5.10.3, Plin. *NH* 2.99, Gell. 13.20.10.

49. Gell. 13.20.12 and Münzer (1999) 302–3.

50. Cic. *Verr.* 2.3.184, 2.4.22, Livy *Per.* 63, Vell. 2.8.1, Flor. 1.39.4.

51. Cic. *Balb.* 28, *Brut.* 128, Eutrop. 4.24.

therefore, this branch of Cato the Elder's family seems to have died out or faded into obscurity by the start of the first century BC.

A second branch of the *Porcii Catones* arose when Cato the Elder at age eighty married Salonia, the daughter of one of his scribes. According to Plutarch, the aged Cato—who was now a widower—had been indulging his sexual appetites with one of his slave girls, but when he realized that this annoyed his adult son Licinianus, he decided to remarry and selected Salonia, who was said to have been the daughter of one of his clerks.[52] This union produced the son M. Porcius, called Salonianus to distinguish him from his older half-brother. Born in 154 BC, Salonianus was barely two years old when Licinianus died as praetor-elect in 152 BC, and he was about five years old when his father died in 149 BC. Little is known about Salonianus, except that he had two sons and that he died while holding the praetorship at an unknown date.[53] Of his two boys, the younger son, L. Porcius Cato, was probably praetor in 92 BC, and as consul in 89 BC he died fighting against the Marsi during the Social War (Rome's war against its Italian allies from 91–87 BC).[54] Salonianus's elder son, M. Porcius Cato, was plebeian tribune in 99 BC and a friend of the dictator Sulla.[55] This M. Cato entered into his tribunate in December 100 BC, and—according to Orosius—he immediately promulgated a bill to recall Metellus Numidicus from exile, which was a bold challenge to the retiring consul Marius, who was the bitter enemy of Numidicus.[56] This opposition to Marius—a powerful *popularis* politician who was holding his sixth consulship—demonstrates Cato's staunch identification with the traditional aristocratic leadership of the Senate (the *optimates*). Sometime after his tribunate, this Cato married Livia, who was the daughter of M. Livius Drusus (cos. 112 BC) and the sister of the famous M. Livius Drusus, who would be assassinated while tribune in 91 BC for trying to enfranchise Rome's Italian allies. This Cato died

52. Plut. *Cat. Mai.* 24.1–2 (cf. Gell. 13.20.7–8, Pliny *NH* 7.61–2). Licinianus was not particularly pleased with his father's second marriage, or at receiving a new stepmother. See Astin (1978) 104–5 and Churchill (2001) 106.

53. Gell. 13.20.14, Plut. *Cat. Mai.* 27.5. This may be the praetor who promulgated the *lex Porcia* of 101 or 100 BC. See Drogula (2011) 281–2.

54. Livy *Per.* 74–5, Vell. 2.16.4, App. *BC* 1.50. Orosius (5.18.24) claims that this Cato was killed by the son of Gaius Marius, because Cato compared his campaigns to those of the elder Marius, but the earlier sources do not support this.

55. Plut. *Cat. Min.* 3.2.

56. Oros. 5.17.11. Since tribunes take office in the middle of December, this M. Cato (trib. pl. 99 BC) took office in the final two weeks of Marius's consulship in 100 BC. Numidicus had been forced into exile for refusing to take the legally mandated oath to support agrarian legislation backed by Marius. Cato's proposed recall of Numidicus was vetoed by another tribune (Oros. 5.17.11). For discussion of this branch of the family, see Münzer (1999) 270–5 and 303.

while a candidate for the praetorship sometime before 91 BC, leaving behind a daughter named Porcia and a son, M. Porcius Cato "the Younger," the subject of this book.[57]

Despite his undistinguished beginnings, therefore, Cato the Elder raised the status of his family and established a clan that was important and powerful throughout the second century BC, with four *consulares* as well as members who reached the praetorship but died before they had the opportunity to stand for the consulship. He had been a *novus homo*, and therefore had been outside the traditional aristocratic elite, but early on he connected himself to tradition-minded leaders in the Senate and shared their distaste for cultural innovation. His descendants in the second century BC seem to have shared his traditional aristocratic principles, but are not known to have adopted his unusually austere lifestyle, no doubt because they did not feel the need to augment their status by promoting an image of being particularly strict adherents to tradition. Whereas Cato the Elder had needed an extra advantage to advance in politics, his sons and grandsons were the progeny of a famous consul, and so they did not need to embrace the *mos maiorum* and reject foreign customs quite as fiercely and publicly. That is, once Cato had established the nobility (*nobilitas*) of his family, his descendants became accepted members of the ruling aristocracy, becoming insiders rather than outsiders.[58] They grew up surrounded by visible signs of the wealth and international power that Rome rapidly acquired in the decades after its victory over Carthage in the Second Punic War, so foreign influence probably seemed less alien to them than it had to Cato, who had been raised on a modest Italian farm. Although he was said to have educated his sons to emulate his own values and adherence to the *mos maiorum*, there is nothing to indicate that they sought to struggle against luxury and Hellenism as he did. While they were reliably conservative in their viewpoints, therefore, Cato's descendants do not seem to have been substantially different from their contemporaries, because—with their *nobilitas* established—they did not need to resort to his strategy of presenting himself as the "most Roman" man in Rome.

---

57. Gell. 13.20.14, Plut. *Cat. Min.* 1.1. Szymanski ([1997] 384–6) argues that an extra generation has been wrongly added into this line, and that Salonianus's son (not grandson) was Cato the Younger.

58. See Hopkins and Burton (1983) 107–19 for discussion of how the Roman nobility was periodically renewed as less successful families failed to maintain their status, and as new families entered the ruling class.

2

Early Years

Cato's Youth and Character

Although the family of the *Porcii Catones* had many important members at the end of the second century BC, they were all gone before Cato the Younger emerged from childhood. Cato was born in 95 BC, and by his sixth birthday all of the previously mentioned *Porcii Catones* were dead or in exile.[1] So Cato had a noble name, but he grew up without much of the infrastructure that maintained an aristocratic family's prominence and importance in Rome. From early childhood, he was effectively cut off from his own family line, and so did not grow up under the living influence of the *Porcii Catones*. Although the date at which he and his sister Porcia were orphaned is unknown, the fact that they were taken in by their maternal uncle M. Livius Drusus—who was murdered while tribune of the plebs in 91 BC—indicates that their parents were dead before Cato was four years old. When their father died, Cato and his sister remained with their mother Livia instead of going to their paternal uncle, L. Porcius Cato (cos. 89 BC), who was still alive at the time, but who does not seem to have sought guardianship of his nephew and niece. Livia moved into her brother's house after her husband's death, and when she died shortly thereafter, her children must have fallen into the guardianship of their uncle Livius.[2] When Livius was murdered in 91 BC, Cato and his sister probably became the wards of their mother's other brother, Mamercus Aemilius Lepidus Livianus (cos. 77 BC), who was the full brother of Livius, but had been adopted into the illustrious *Aemilii Lepidi* clan.[3] Growing

---

1. The cousin C. Porcius Cato (cos. 114 BC) had been in exile in Tarraco in Spain since 110 BC.

2. See Harders (2010) 62.

3. That Mamercus assumed guardianship of Cato and his sister is not certain. Only a tutor named Sarpedon is named as a caretaker for the young Cato (Plut. *Cat. Min.* 1.5, 3.2–4), but it is impossible that the orphan children of two illustrious families would have been left without

up among his mother's family, Cato would have learned about his father's clan through stories and family histories, in which the most prominent member was certainly his great-grandfather, Cato the Elder. As later events would demonstrate, the stories of his famous great-grandfather made a deep impression on the young Cato and shaped the way he looked at the world, and he no doubt studied his famous ancestor's numerous writings. Thus he grew up having to look back in time for examples of his father's family and its traditions, which may have instilled in him the habit he would later display for looking into Rome's past for examples of proper behavior and values.

Many stories are told of Cato's childhood, but these have the scent of invention by later authors who were anxious to suggest that he was predestined for greatness, and that he had the same personality as a child that he would have as an adult. For example, Plutarch writes that in childhood Cato was the leader of his troop of boys, and that he used to be chosen to act as judge over the behavior of his friends, but Plutarch says such things about many of the famous men whose biographies he wrote. More interesting is his observation that Cato was not particularly imaginative, but stuck to his opinions no matter what:

> . . . he was dull and slow to learn things, but learning something by rote he held it fast and had a good memory. This is certainly natural, for some, being naturally clever, are more able to recall things readily, but others remember things only after engaging in toil and hard work, and each of the things they learn is like something branded into their mind. And so it seems that Cato's intractability made his learning much more laborious.[4]

This description is somewhat surprising, since it undermines Cato's later reputation as a philosopher, and even suggests that he was not particularly intelligent.[5] Plutarch's biography of Cato is generally very complimentary, so these comments about his intelligence may have been intended to prepare the reader for the stories of Cato's amazing resolve and fixedness of purpose. Of course, it also suggests that his famous steadfast tenacity was in reality the result of a lack of imagination, and

---

a guardian. The fact that his uncle Mamercus was married to Sulla's daughter Cornelia, and that Sulla apparently took an active interest in Cato and invited him to discussions at his house, suggests that Cato was under Mamercus's care. Harders ([2010] 62–4) points out that there is no mention of Cato's father's family in stories about Cato's upbringing.

4. Plut. *Cat. Min.* 1.3–4.

5. For example, Tatum ([2010] 196) remarks of Cato, "pertinacious and brave, his nobility and his traditional, uncomplicated politics more than compensated, amongst his peers, for his lack of intelligence."

an unwillingness (or inability) to consider other points of view. In this respect, Plutarch implies that Cato was not reflective or particularly insightful, which may be foreshadowing of the role he would play in the collapse of the Republic.

Plutarch gives two other stories from Cato's youth to illustrate his character. First, when he was only four years old and newly installed in the house of his uncle M. Livius Drusus, Pompaedius Silo—a high-ranking Italian who was visiting Livius—playfully asked him whether he would support his uncle's legislation proposing the enfranchisement of the Italians.[6] Cato only glared at Pompaedius angrily and refused to answer, so Pompaedius picked him up and threatened to throw him out the window unless he pledged his support to the legislation, but the young boy continued to hold his silence. If this story happened as Plutarch tells it, then Pompaedius was surely jesting: Cato's uncle Livius was powerful and friendly to the Italians, so it is unthinkable that his Italian guest would offer any serious threat to his family. Indeed, Pompaedius is said to have admired the boy's spirit and determination, and put him down without harming him. The second story took place a few years later, when Rome had fallen into a civil war between Marius and Sulla (and their partisans). Countless Romans died in this war, and the still-young Cato first watched Marius and his supporters slaughter their political enemies in 87–86 BC, and then witnessed Sulla's vengeance in 82–81 BC when, after seizing the city and making himself dictator, he published lists of thousands of wealthy Romans who were to be hunted down and killed. Sulla confiscated the property of the proscribed citizens, and paid bounties to the murderers who produced the heads of their victims. Cato's family was on friendly terms with Sulla—his father had been Sulla's friend, and his uncle Mamercus had married Sulla's daughter—but upon seeing the murders of so many distinguished men, Cato is said to have asked his tutor Sarpedon why no one undertook to kill the dictator. When the tutor replied that the Romans feared him, Cato asked for a sword so that he might do the deed himself.[7] Sarpedon believed that he was serious, and kept a close watch on him lest he carry out his threat. While the veracity of these early stories is questionable, they were told by those who knew Cato's character as an adult and wanted to show that it had been established in childhood.[8] Plutarch in particular wanted to show that Cato's nature was innate and untutored, and his habits were not a result of study or philosophical

---

6. Plut. *Cat. Min.* 2.1–4, Val. Max. 3.1.2a.

7. Plut. *Cat. Min.* 3.2–4, Val. Max. 3.1.2b.

8. On Plutarch's interest in fleshing out the personalities of his subjects with stories of their youth, see Pelling (2002) 301–38.

belief, but rather fundamental qualities of his character.[9] In this light, Plutarch demonstrates a man who was fearless in the defense of his country and unshakable in his convictions, but who did not allow for reconsideration or for the possibility of compromise. In this respect, the traits that made Cato stand out among his peers also limited his ability to accept any opinion or position other than his own.

As a very young man, Cato was made a member of the *quindecimviri sacris faciundis*, the board of fifteen priests in charge of sacred rituals, especially the consultation and interpretation of the Sibylline Books—ancient prophetic scriptures that dated back to the monarchy.[10] When this happened is not recorded, but Plutarch places it shortly before Cato received his inheritance, which should have happened when he reached adulthood (around age sixteen), so he probably became a *quindecimvir* around 79 BC. This was a significant honor for one so young, and it raises the question of why he was selected. It is possible that his conservative values were already apparent as a teenager, but the help of a powerful patron such as his uncle is a more likely explanation. Mamercus may have used his influence to secure the priesthood for his nephew, perhaps in an effort to raise the status of his sister's child, the orphan of a noble family.[11] Sulla held the dictatorship until the middle of 79 BC, and he is known to have been well disposed toward the young Cato, so this connection also may have facilitated his selection as *quindecimvir*.[12] This was a great honor, and certainly involved a degree of religious training, but the *quindecimviri* performed their religious duties only rarely. Their priestly college guarded the prophetic Sibylline Books, but they were only to consult those books when instructed to do so by the Senate, which did not happen often.[13] If Cato did receive the priesthood on account of Sulla's favor, it would have brought him to the particular attention of Sulla's lieutenants, who

---

9. Swain (1990) 199.

10. Plut. *Cat. Min.* 4.1. Fehrle (1983) 67–8. Plutarch says Cato was made a priest of Apollo, which is generally understood to mean a member of the *quindecimviri sacris faciundis*, who helped supervise Rome's annual festival for Apollo (Livy 10.8.2). Plutarch was himself a priest of Apollo at Delphi (Plut. *Mor.* 792f), so his inclination to associate the *quindecimviri* as priests of Apollo is understandable. Lewis ([1955] 86) specifically identifies Cato as a *quindecimvir*. On the identification of the *quindecimviri* as priests of Apollo, see Miller (2009) 239–42.

11. Julius Caesar had similarly been designated *flamen Dialis* at a very young age when his uncle Gaius Marius controlled Rome in 87 BC (Vell. 2.43.1, Suet. *Iul.* 1.1). Gelzer ([1968] 25) suggested that Mam. Aemilius Lepidus likewise used his influence with the Senate leadership to get the young and still-promising Julius Caesar co-opted as a *pontifex*.

12. Plut. *Cat. Min.* 3.2.

13. Cic. *Div.* 2.112.

would hold tremendous power in Rome for the next twenty years. Indeed, given that there were no *Porcii Catones* left to help ease his introduction into Roman politics, Cato's priesthood may have been his most important introduction to a powerful circle of influential senators. On the other hand, since he is said to have been angry at Sulla's execution of their fellow citizens, he may have avoided too close an association with the dictator's henchmen.

Shortly after his sixteenth birthday and his entry into the *quindecimviri*, Cato took possession of his inheritance, presumably from his father who had died over a decade earlier. Plutarch writes that Cato received one hundred and twenty talents, took a house of his own, and began to live even more simply than he had before.[14] One hundred and twenty talents was a great deal of money; it amounted to 2,880,000 *sestertii*, which easily placed Cato within the equestrian order—the highest of Rome's wealth-based census classes.[15] Yet this was not a great fortune relative to some of Cato's contemporaries: in 62 BC Cicero would buy a house on the Palatine Hill for 3.5 million *sestertii* (it was not his only property); a year later M. Valerius Messalla bought a house for 13.4 million *sestertii*; and in 58 BC the flamboyant P. Clodius bought a house for a whopping 14.8 million *sestertii*.[16] Julius Caesar was said to have incurred debts amounting to 25 million *sestertii* in his pursuit of the consulship, and senators such as Lucullus, Hortensius, Pompey, and Crassus also had vast sums at their command.[17] So while Cato's inheritance made him wealthy in absolute terms, and enabled him to pursue a career in politics, his financial resources were probably modest compared to those of the leading senators of the day, such that Valerius Maximus even expressed surprise that Cato became so important considering his small patrimony and other limitations.[18]

Cato took a house of his own soon after receiving his inheritance, which seems strange given his youth—he had not yet started his military service, and therefore must have been around sixteen or seventeen years old. It is possible that this was expected of elite children raised by extended family, and that, having been

---

14. Plut. *Cat. Min.* 4.1.

15. Equestrians needed to show property valued at 400,000 *sestertii* (Plin. *HN* 33.32, Dio 54.17.3). We do not know whether there was a separate property qualification for senators before Augustus (see Lintott [1999a] 71). One talent was worth approximately 6,000 *denarii* or 24,000 *sestertii*.

16. Cic. *Fam.* 5.6.2, *Att.* 1.13.6, Plin. *HN* 36.103.

17. App. *BC* 2.8.

18. Val. Max. 2.10.8. Jehne ([2016] 188–207) discusses the importance and use of wealth on a senatorial career.

recognized as an adult and having received his inheritance, he was expected to relieve his uncle Mamercus of the financial burden of his upkeep. Yet his uncle's house must have been a hub of political activity around this time: Mamercus was very wealthy, was praetor in or shortly before 81 BC, was a close friend of Sulla and had married Sulla's daughter, was influential enough to secure the dictator's pardon for the young Julius Caesar, and reached the consulship in 77 BC.[19] Mamercus was extremely important and influential, so it would have been an advantage to remain living in his house. It is possible that Cato did not like his uncle's connections with Sulla, or he may have wanted the freedom to live differently than he had in his uncle's house. Plutarch hints at this by suggesting that Cato began studying Stoicism at this time under the philosopher Antipater.[20] Stoicism was a philosophical school of thought that taught adherents to seek happiness by living in accordance with nature (which is guided by divine reason or fate), to be free from strong emotions (to achieve *apatheia*), and to be indifferent to things that are subject to chance and so cannot be controlled, such as pleasure, pain, wealth, and poverty. Stoicism was popular among Roman elites, and it was not at all unusual for aristocratic youths to include Stoic philosophy among the wide range of things they might study. Yet Cato did not limit himself to the Stoic School; he also studied with the Epicurean Philostratus and the Peripatetic Demetrius, taking in a range of philosophical schools of thought.[21] At the same time, he dedicated himself to mastering "warlike" oratorical skills, which were appropriate for swaying the opinions of crowds, but were highly unusual for a student of Stoic philosophy.[22] Stoics normally used an austere and plain style of rhetoric, so Cato's study of different styles suggests that he pursued the normal education and training for a young aristocrat who was ambitious for advancement.[23] His study of Stoicism was only one piece of his education, but Plutarch emphasizes it here to foreshadow later events in his life. Of course, Cato could have pursued these studies in his uncle's house, so his decision to move out probably had little to do with his interest in Stoicism or study. As events would

---

19. Mamercus's wealth: Cic. *de Off.* 2.58. Caesar had angered Sulla by refusing to divorce his wife (the daughter of Cinna) as the dictator had commanded. Caesar had fled Rome and was living in hiding in Sabine country until powerful friends—Mamercus in particular—secured a pardon (Suet. *Iul.* 1.2–3, and see Gelzer [1968] 21).

20. Plut. *Cat. Min.* 4.1.

21. Plut. *Cat. Min.* 57.2, 65.5, 67.2, 69.1, and 70.1. Fantham ([2003] 99) refers to Cato's adherence to philosophers of the Academy.

22. Plut. *Cat. Min.* 4.2 (μάχιμον).

23. On Stoic styles of rhetoric, see Stroup (2010) 26–8.

soon prove, he wanted to establish himself as a very particular kind of public figure, and he wanted to take on behaviors and customs different from the mainstream aristocratic culture that prevailed in his uncle's house.

In these early years between reaching adulthood and starting his military service, Cato adopted some very unusual mannerisms that distinguished him from other aristocrats. These behaviors were not merely old-fashioned, they were archaic and reached far back into Rome's fabled past, creating a strong relationship between Cato and the founding fathers of the city. Romans were generally very conservative, but Cato embraced eccentric and even bizarre mannerisms that reflected an almost fanatical devotion to tradition. He traveled long journeys on foot even when his friends rode on horseback, he walked around the city barefoot and wrapped only in his toga—forgoing the tunic that a Roman man normally wore underneath his toga—and he favored a darker and more old-fashioned hue of senatorial purple on his clothing, rejecting the rich crimson worn by his contemporaries.[24] In all of these cases, he was following very ancient practices and fashions that the Romans had abandoned long ago; he was not reaching back one generation, but many generations into Rome's distant past. This was no display of philosophic asceticism; Cato did all of this in a deliberate effort to appear very closely linked to the oldest interpretation of the *mos maiorum*. Asconius makes this point clearly, stating that Cato stopped wearing undergarments and footwear in imitation of statues on the Capitol and on the Rostra that portrayed kings Romulus and Tatius, and the republican hero Camillus (early fourth century BC), wearing togas as their only clothing:

> Because the trial was being held in summer, Cato the praetor presided over it without a tunic, wearing only a loincloth under his toga. He also came down into the Forum thus dressed and pronounced his judgment. He claimed it followed an old custom, since the statues of Romulus and Tatius on the Capitol, and the statue of Camillus on the Rostra, showed the men wearing togas without tunics.[25]

---

24. Plut. *Cat. Min.* 5.3, 6.3–4. Horace (*Epist.* 1.19.12–4) jokes about a barbarian attempting to imitate Cato by wearing a grim expression, going around barefoot, and wearing a skimpy toga (*exigua toga*). See Olson (2017) 29 on Cato choosing an old-fashioned style.

25. Ascon. 29 (cf. Val. Max. 3.6.7). This was the trial of M. Scaurus. Plutarch (*Mor.* 276 c–d) writes that Cato claimed that this was the appropriate style of dress for a Roman candidate soliciting votes from the people, but this cannot be correct, since Asconius, Valerius Maximus, and Plutarch himself all remark on how unusual his style of dress was, and all attest that Cato dressed in this manner even when not a candidate for office.

As this makes clear, he was not displaying Stoic austerity or any other philosophic principle with his unusual dress; he was purposefully copying the style of dress found on statues of Rome's earliest heroes. This was more than simple conservative values; he copied the style of dress he saw in these statues because he wanted to create a visual association between himself and Rome's ancient founders; he wanted to be seen as the living embodiment of the *mos maiorum*. There is no obvious reason why Cato should have adopted this type of behavior as a young man—none of his recent relatives is known to have used such self-consciously archaic mannerisms, and he was raised in a wealthy aristocratic house that is not known to have departed from mainstream contemporary culture. He made a deliberate decision to break with the norms of his peers and adopt characteristics and habits that he drew out of Rome's past; his display of extreme conservatism was as manufactured as it was ostentatious.[26] Beyond simply holding conservative values and pursuing traditional policies, he wanted to make a public display of himself in ancient garb, a visible statement that no one could miss.

Cato's unusual clothing and mannerisms were not simply reminders of the good old days. Roman senators were the keepers of the *mos maiorum*, and those who best exemplified ancestral customs held considerable influence and moral authority over the tradition-loving Romans. Cato the Elder had understood this, and had used his writings to make himself appear to be the most authentic Roman in the Senate, a perception that made his words weightier and harder to ignore. Cato the Younger seems to have taken his great-grandfather's tactic further, and began his career by adopting clothing and habits that marked him out as a champion of the *mos maiorum*, as someone whose ancient *auctoritas* gave him an innate right to be a leader of the state. Since all of his close relatives among the *Porcii Catones* were long dead, Cato could reinvent himself and take on mannerisms that evoked the popular reputation of the most famous member of his family, Cato the Elder, who had championed Roman tradition and resisted foreign influences.[27] Although he was not the *novus homo* that his great-grandfather had been, Cato the Younger nevertheless faced daunting challenges in his intended political career, so he leveraged his strongest asset—his great-grandfather's reputation as a champion of tradition—to enhance his own status. Yet he was not only copying his famous ancestor; he was using the flexibility of the *mos maiorum* to fashion himself into his own interpretation of what an authentic, traditional

---

26. Plut. *Cat. Min* 6.3, "Cato believed it was necessary for him to follow a path that was the opposite of the lifestyles and customs of his time, since they were bad and needed a great change." Flower ([2010b] 145) pointed out: "Cato's antiquarianism was essentially artificial."

27. Ancient authors noted that Cato emulated his great-grandfather Cato the Elder (Cic. *Mur.* 66, Plut. *Cat. Min.* 8.1, Dio 37.22.1). See van der Blom (2010) 17–24 and 154–5.

Roman leader should be. His great-grandfather had been known to wear sleeveless tunics when working on his farm, but Cato the Younger was making a much more dramatic statement by wearing no tunic at all, even in the city, and even as a candidate and a magistrate.[28] So he was not projecting a particular period in Rome's history, but crafting his own unique amalgam of ideas and customs that he believed would catch the popular imagination and mark him out as a man uniquely in touch with the *mos maiorum*.[29] By adopting the archaic style of dress found on statues of Rome's ancient heroes, he sought to present himself as the ideal of Roman virtue. This presentation of tradition was sure to appeal to the conservative senators who ran the state, but there was also a strong popular appeal in Cato's unique behavior, since all Romans had at least an outward respect for tradition. Although he never was nor would be a *popularis* (a politician who wields power primarily through popular support in the voting assemblies), his visual display of ancestral clothing and mannerisms was sure to have a magnetic appeal on the Roman citizenry, who cherished and revered their ancestors, as did the senators.

Cato reinforced his association with his great-grandfather by publicly opposing a proposed change to the Basilica Porcia, the public building that Cato the Elder had commissioned as censor in 184 BC. The basilica was in the center of the Forum, and it had become the regular meeting place for the plebeian tribunes, who were required to be readily available for any citizen who needed their help. When Cato was still a young man, the tribunes proposed moving a column that was in front of their seats and so impeding their view of the Forum.[30] It seems unlikely that they wished to move a structural column, so this probably refers to a commemorative column associated with the basilica but not structurally a part of it.[31] Cato took umbrage at this proposed alteration of his family monument, and delivered a powerful and skillful speech that won his case and prevented the change. It is difficult to know what to make of this incident. Public buildings such as the Basilica Porcia were prized heirlooms that perpetuated a family's fame and greatness, so men could be expected to defend their family monuments. At the same time, it is not clear that the column that

---

28. Plut. *Cat. Mai.* 3.2.

29. Kenty ([2016] 429–62) has demonstrated how appeals to the *mos maiorum* could be used in flexible ways to have a strong emotional influence on the Romans.

30. Plut. *Cat. Min.* 5.1–2. We do not know when this happened or how old Cato was, but Plutarch describes the event taking place before Cato joined the army of L. Gellius Publicola in 72 BC, which would make Cato at most twenty-three years old. See Fehrle (1983) 68–9.

31. Lehmann-Hartleben ([1938] 286–7) suggested this may have been the *Columna Maenia*.

the tribunes wanted to move was actually part of the basilica, which raises the
possibility that Cato seized upon the proposal as an opportunity to make a very
showy entrance into public life by appearing to defend his family's honor and
reputation, a public statement that he was the new head of the *Porcii Catones*.
Ambitious young aristocrats often sought out opportunities to introduce themselves to the citizens with showy speeches—Caesar had done the same[32]—so
Cato may have been thinking more about starting his career than defending the
monument. This not only would gain him a reputation for the all-important
quality of familial respect (*pietas*), but also would connect him in a very public
way with his most famous ancestor.

   Cato decided to marry in his early twenties,[33] and selected his cousin Aemilia
Lepida, the daughter of his uncle Mamercus Aemilius Lepidus. She was certainly
a good catch, since her father was a recent consul and a leading figure among the
most senior and important senators (the *nobiles*), but Cato was already related
to Mamercus, and it is not clear that marrying Aemilia would have improved his
political connections or his relationship with his uncle (who had probably raised
him from a very young age).[34] The normal goal of aristocratic marriages was to
expand one's political alliances and gain resources, but it is not clear that this
marriage would have brought Cato any new support. He may have been in love
with his cousin, or he may have been interested in her dowry, which was probably very large. Aemilia previously had been engaged to Q. Caecilius Metellus
Pius Scipio Nasica (cos. 52 BC), who called off their engagement sometime before
the wedding, so Cato also may have engaged himself to Aemilia in an effort to
protect her honor.[35] It is even possible that he saw himself renewing his great-
grandfather's feud with the *Cornelii Scipiones* by marrying a woman rejected by
a scion of that clan. Whatever the reason, he was shocked when Scipio again
changed his mind, and wanted back the fiancée he had jilted. When Aemilia (or
more likely, her father Mamercus) decided that a marriage alliance with Scipio
was more desirable, Cato was angry and fought for the girl, denouncing his rival
in poetic verses using the rude, mocking style of the Greek poet Archilochus, although it is unlikely that he indulged in the full obscenity that was normal in this

---

32. Julius Caesar used the occasion of his funeral speech for his aunt Julia in 68 BC to remind
the audience of his family's heritage, thereby advancing his own reputation (Suet. *Iul.* 6).

33. The exact year is uncertain. Cowan ([2015] 37–8) argues that 70 BC is probably the latest the
marriage could have occurred, given the timeline of Cato's daughter Porcia.

34. See Münzer (1999) 289.

35. Plut. *Cat. Min.* 7.1–3.

genre.[36] He was even going to take the case to court to assert his right to marry Aemilia (presumably, to enforce the engagement), but his friends were able to dissuade him from this course. This means that Cato had been contemplating suing his uncle, who alone had the authority to determine to whom he would give his daughter.[37] Since Mamercus was probably his most important and influential living relative, and had likely raised him from childhood, Cato appears imprudent, reckless, and ungrateful to have even considered bringing a lawsuit against his uncle. Had it not been for the intervention of his friends, Cato's impulsive and extremist nature could have alienated him from his mother's powerful family before he had even begun his career.

Deprived of his first fiancée, Cato instead married Atilia, the daughter of an Atilius Serranus. The identity of this Serranus is not known. He may have been the C. Atilius Serranus who was consul in 106 BC and was murdered by Gaius Marius and L. Cornelius Cinna in 87 BC, and whom Cicero called "the most stupid man."[38] If so, the choice is interesting. The *gens Atilia* dated back to the Republic's early history and boasted of a long line of consuls, but the family seems to have diminished by the end of the second century BC, and it produced no consuls until the clan was resuscitated by the emperors in the Imperial Era. Thus the *gens Atilia* was a noble family in decline, much like the *Porcii Catones*. Cato may also have felt a close connection to *gens Atilia* because C. Atilius Serranus had shared the consulship of 106 BC with Q. Servilius Caepio, a relative of Cato's half-brother and half-sisters, who was a notable optimate politician and opponent of the *popularis* Gaius Marius. So Atilia may have represented a link with Cato's family, and the marriage must have brought him sufficient political connections and wealth to be attractive. He would have two children with Atilia: a girl named Porcia and a boy named M. Porcius Cato (see Stemma 2). In addition to making this good connection, he also arranged to secure an excellent connection through his older sister's marriage to L. Domitius Ahenobarbus (cos. 54 BC), a man of such lineage that Cicero described him as being designated to the consulship from

---

36. Robert Cowan (2015) 9–52 argued that Cato was probably too prudish to use the full obscenity and childishness of the genre, and suggests that one of Catullus's poems (#56) may be a response to Cato's misuse of the genre.

37. The year of Mamercus's death is not known, so it is possible he had died recently, which would mean that Cato and Scipio were particularly interested in marrying Aemilia because she was now an heiress. If this was the case, then Cato probably intended to sue the relative to whom the guardianship of Aemilia had fallen.

38. Cic. *Planc.* 12. Münzer ([1999] 304–5) suggests that Atilia may have been the granddaughter (rather than the daughter) of the consul of 106 BC.

infancy.[39] This was a very important connection, demonstrating that Domitius and his family saw an advantage in making an alliance with Cato.

Beyond his sister, Cato's closest relations were his half-brother and two half-sisters, the progeny of his mother's first marriage to Q. Servilius Caepio.[40] This Caepio divorced Cato's mother Livia sometime before 97 BC on account of a feud he was having with her brother Livius Drusus, and she subsequently married Cato's father.[41] Although children were normally kept by the father after an aristo-cratic divorce, Plutarch indicates that Livia kept her three children from her first marriage, and when she and her second husband died, both sets of Livia's children were raised by her brother Livius Drusus until his death in 91 BC, after which they were all presumably raised together by Livia's other brother Mamercus.[42] The children were very close, and Cato was particularly devoted to the elder Servilia and to his half-brother Caepio.[43] Sometime before 85 BC—when Cato was younger than ten years old—the elder Servilia married M. Junius Brutus (trib. pl. 83 BC), whose family claimed descent from the legendary founder of the Republic, and together they had one son: M. Junius Brutus, the future assassin of Julius Caesar. Despite these blue-blooded credentials, in 77 BC Servilia's husband joined M. Aemilius Lepidus (cos. 78 BC) in his effort to reverse the optimate leg-islation of the recently deceased dictator Sulla. This was an explosive issue, and the two sides rapidly resorted to Rome's armies. In the battle that ensued, Sulla's lieutenant—the young Pompey (Cn. Pompeius Magnus [cos. 70. 55, 52 BC])—captured Brutus and treacherously killed him at Mutina, leaving Servilia a widow

39. Cic. *Att.* 4.8a.2, Plut. *Cat. Min.* 41.2. When Porcia was married to Domitius is not known, but their son was consul in 32 BC, which means he was born at least forty-two years earlier, as-suming he observed the normal age requirements for office. Cicero (*QF* 3.6.5) mentions that in 54 BC he wrote a eulogy for Domitius to deliver at the funeral of a son named Serranus, which may be another son of Porcia and Domitius, who had been adopted by Serranus, perhaps to keep the family name alive. See Münzer (1999) 303–5.

40. This Q. Servilius Caepio probably was not the praetor of 91 BC who was killed at the out-break of the Social War, but the homonymous legate who served under Rutilius Rufus in that war and was killed fighting the Marsi. It was once believed that Caepio was Livia's second hus-band (after M. Cato, the tribune of 99 BC), but the relative ages of Cato the Younger and his half-siblings show that this was an error, and that Livia was married to Caepio first.

41. According to Pliny (*NH* 33.21), their feud started because of a dispute over a ring at auction. Since Cato was born in 95 BC and his sister Porcia was at least one year older, Livia must have married Cato (trib. pleb. 99 BC) no later than 97 BC. Caepio (pr. 91 BC) died fighting in the Social War in 90 BC (Livy *Per.* 73, Eutrop. 5.3.2, Oros. 5.18.14). See Fehrle (1983) 53–8.

42. Plut. *Cat. Min* 1.1. See Münzer (1999) 273 and Harders (2010) 62–4.

43. Plut. *Cat. Min.* 3.5–6, *Mor.* 487C.

with her young son Brutus.[44] She remarried after a few years, taking D. Junius Silanus (cos. 62 BC) as her husband, and having three daughters with him and perhaps a son, D. Junius Silanus (cos. 25 BC).[45] Sometime before his death in 67/66 BC, Servilia's brother Caepio formally adopted her son Brutus, although Cato was said to have exercised a strong influence over Brutus's upbringing.[46] At some point, Servilia also became the lover of Julius Caesar. Cato's other half-sister, the younger Servilia, would marry the great optimate commander L. Licinius Lucullus (cos. 70 BC) sometime after his return from the East in 66 BC, although she became notorious for licentious behavior and was eventually divorced.[47] Thus Cato's half-siblings made excellent marriages to other elite families, helping him develop his network of political allies.

In 72 BC Cato's half-brother Caepio became a military tribune in the army of the consul L. Gellius Publicola, who was dispatched to suppress the slave revolt led by Spartacus. Cato—now roughly twenty-three years old—was so devoted to Caepio that he joined Publicola's army as a volunteer. This was surely not Cato's first campaign, since he had already been eligible for military service for several years (his later reputation as a soldier was excellent). Although he is reported to have fought very well in this campaign, the army in which he served was twice routed by Spartacus's forces, so the Senate stripped the consul of the command and transferred it to M. Licinius Crassus (cos. 70, 55 BC), who was ultimately successful in defeating Spartacus.[48] Despite this turn of events, Cato's valor in the campaign had caught the attention of his senior officers, but when Gellius attempted to present him with much-coveted military awards, Cato refused to accept them, claiming that the symbols of honor and bravery had not been earned.[49] For a private soldier to question a consul's judgment and reject status-enhancing military decorations was extraordinary, and those who witnessed it found this behavior inappropriate and strange.[50] Indeed, it must have embarrassed the consul to have his evaluation of military bravery repudiated by a young man. Military glory and bravery were two of Rome's most respected qualities, and

---

44. Plut. *Pomp.* 16.4–5, *Brut.* 4.1–2, Livy *Per.* 90, Val. Max. 6.2.8.

45. See Tatum (2008) 110–11.

46. Cic. *Att.* 2.24.3 (cf. *Phil.* 10.26, Plut. *Brut.* 2.1–2). See Harders (2010) 64–6.

47. Plut. *Luc.* 38.1. See later in this chapter for further discussion of Lucullus's decision to marry Servilia.

48. Livy *Per.* 96–7, Plut. *Crass.* 9.7–10.1, *Cat. Min.* 8.1.

49. Plut. *Cat. Min.* 8.2, οὐκ ἔλαβεν οὐδὲ προσήκατο.

50. Plutarch (*Cat. Min* 8.2) uses the word ἀλλόκοτος to express the strangeness of the refusal.

Cato had—in the judgment of his commander—earned the prizes he was offered. It is possible that he truly had not deserved the awards, and that Publicola was offering unearned awards in an attempt to flatter a youth from a noble family, or perhaps Cato did not want awards for serving in a twice-routed army. He would later criticize M. Fulvius Nobilior (cos. 189 BC), who was said to have bestowed military awards on soldiers simply for building military camps well, so Cato may have thought that Publicola's standards had not been high enough.[51] He may also have been imitating the strict standards of his great-grandfather, who once gave a speech attacking those who exaggerated their military accomplishments (*De Falsis Pugnis*).[52] Whether or not one of these was the case, Cato seized the opportunity to reject the awards, demonstrating the type of old-fashioned severity that had made his great-grandfather famous. In this very public way Cato advertised that his standards for military accomplishment were much more stringent than the consul's, and the strangeness of this act was so shocking that it was talked about and remembered back in Rome. Indeed, his rejection of the awards was so unusual and surprising that it seems to have enhanced his reputation more than accepting the awards would have done.

Cato continued to demonstrate this type of unusual behavior when he sought election to the post of military tribune for 67 BC. A law (perhaps a *lex Fabia*)[53] had recently been passed that forbade candidates from using *nomenclatores*—slaves who whispered to their owner the names of those he met—when canvassing for votes, but this law seems to have been widely ignored. Indeed, Cato was the only candidate in this campaign who actually followed this law, making a very public demonstration of his old-fashioned discipline and doing his best to remember people's names without help.[54] People are said to have respected him for following the law in such a precise and unbending way (even a law that everyone else ignored), but he also gave offense to the other candidates, who were not willing or able to emulate his extreme adherence to the law. To them, Cato's behavior was more a disruption of normal processes than a praiseworthy display, especially since the law he was so ostentatiously observing may not have truly been a law: the absence of references to this legislation in other sources suggests

51. Gell. 5.6.24–6.

52. Gell. 10.3.17.

53. Cicero (*Mur.* 71) cites a *lex Fabia* that limited the number of followers or attendants that could accompany a candidate for office, and this may have also prohibited the use of *nomenclatores*. See Gruen (1974) 216, Ferrary (2001) 169–72, and Rosillo López (2010) 60 and 221.

54. Plut. *Cat. Min.* 8.2.

that it may have been only a proposal that was never approved or ratified.[55] If true, it would further emphasize the strangeness of Cato's display and the aggravation of his rivals, since he was receiving credit for following a mere proposal that had not been ratified by the people, and so was not required of the candidates. Given how little we know about this so-called law, one can only wonder where it came from, and whether Cato received (or took) credit merely for observing ancestral custom by avoiding innovations such as *nomenclatores*. Whether or not this was the case, he apparently changed his mind later in his career and began using a *nomenclator* as did other senators, enabling Cicero to chide him for hypocrisy in 63 BC.[56] At the time, however, Cato won the election.

Cato served bravely as a military tribune in the army of the propraetor M. Rubrius in Macedonia, earning the respect of his soldiers by living like them, treating them justly, and sharing all of their labors. Despite being a high officer in the army, however, he continued his unusual habit of walking everywhere instead of riding a horse.[57] This must have seemed very strange; military officers did not ride horses only for comfort and distinction, but also to improve their field of vision, to enable better mobility in communicating with their men, and to be visible to their men. Thus Cato sacrificed certain important tactical advantages in order to display his extreme old-fashioned virtue. Equally strange, he permitted his friends and servants who accompanied him on the campaign to ride on horseback, and on the march he would awkwardly carry on conversations with them as they rode and he walked on the ground. If his purpose had been to reform the behavior of the Romans, then surely he would have encouraged his friends and dependents—and certainly his servants—to follow his example. Instead, he was content to be the only one displaying such adherence to ancient custom. Of course, it is not clear that this actually *was* a Roman custom. The only (remote) precedent for this odd behavior was the archaic and now-defunct law that prohibited Roman dictators from mounting a horse, which Cato seems to have adapted—like his habit of modeling his clothing from old statues of ancient kings—as a means to display an extraordinary connection with the *mos maiorum*.[58] Yet the reality of this ancient practice was not important—it had the appearance of being antique, which advanced his reputation as the voice of tradition. His goal, therefore, was to promote his own self-fashioned image as an authentic, old-fashioned Roman.

55. Ferrary ([2001] 170) suggested that the *lex* in question had merely been proposed, and either was not voted upon or failed to be approved by the people.

56. Cic. *Mur.* 77.

57. Plut. *Cat. Min.* 9.2.

58. Livy 23.14.2 and Plut. *Fab.* 4.

He created a shocking and eye-catching image—a military tribune marching on foot while his friends and servants rode—that served no real purpose except to get people talking about how Cato embodied the *mos maiorum* better than any other Roman.

While serving as a military tribune, Cato was entitled to take a two-month furlough during this campaign, presumably in the winter of 67/66 BC. He decided to visit Pergamon in Asia Minor, which was fairly close to Macedonia, and was a favorite among Roman aristocrats for its luxury and learning. It was there he met the Stoic philosopher Athenodorus, who is probably the same Athenodorus whom Diogenes Laertius (citing Isidorus of Pergamon) described as the librarian at Pergamon who was discovered excising from the texts of Zeno those passages to which he and like-minded Stoics objected (upon discovery, the excised passages were replaced);[59] that is, he sought to edit the fundamental texts on Stoicism to make them reflect more closely his own ideas about Stoic principles. Cato had already developed an interest in Stoic philosophy, and Athenodorus's uncompromising approach may have appealed to his own (by now) famous inflexibility. To both men, excision was preferable to compromise. The two men formed a close friendship, and although Athenodorus had previously rejected invitations from governors and kings, he accepted Cato's invitation to travel first to the Roman military camp in Macedonia, and from there to Cato's house in Rome, where he remained until his death.[60] Although the Roman Senate had once banned philosophers from living in Rome (in 161 BC), in the late Republic it was fairly common for interested Roman elites to host philosophers in their homes. Stoic philosophers were common, as were masters of other philosophical schools: Scipio Aemilianus had welcomed the Stoic philosopher Panaetius, Cicero entertained the Stoic Diodotus, Brutus housed the Academic Aristus, and M. Piso hosted the Peripatetic Staseas.[61] It was also common for Roman elites to select such philosophers as traveling companions: Lucullus took the Academic philosopher Antiochus to his eastern command, and Crassus took the Peripatetic philosopher Alexander on his travels.[62] In hosting Athenodorus, therefore, Cato indulged in contemporary practices rather than maintain his great-grandfather's famous position against Greek philosophers.

---

59. DL 7.34. See discussion in Schonfield (1999) 8–10.

60. Plut. *Cat. Min.* 10.1–2, Strabo 14.5.14.

61. Banning of philosophers: Suet. *de Rhet.* 1, Gell. 15.11.1–5; Scipio: Cic. *Mur.* 66, *Fin.* 4.23, *Tusc.* 1.81; Cicero: Cic. *Brut.* 309; Brutus: Plut. *Brut.* 2.3; Piso: Cic. *Or.* 1.104, *Fin.* 5.8. See discussion in Clarke (2012) 74–6.

62. Plut. *Crass.* 3.3.

During his military service in Macedonia, word reached Cato that his half-brother Caepio had grown very ill in Aenus, a town in nearby Thrace. Caepio had been en route to Asia, probably to take up an appointment under Lucullus or Pompey in the eastern campaign against Mithridates, the king of Pontus. Cato immediately set out by boat during a dangerous storm, but by the time he arrived Caepio had already died.[63] Cato's grief was profound and—according to Plutarch—excessive for one who studied Stoic philosophy. He lost control of his emotions, lamenting his brother and clinging to his corpse. He spent lavishly on the funeral, paying for expensive incense and valuable clothing to be burned with the body, and constructing a costly monument of polished marble to be set up in the marketplace of Aenus. Cato was co-heir of Caepio's property along with Caepio's daughter, but Cato bore the full cost of the extravagant funeral himself and did not deduct it from the estate. The extent of his grief for his beloved brother is one of the most humanizing moments of Cato's life, but it also reveals the limits of his internalization of Stoic philosophy, since his extreme and public suffering was a dramatic rejection of the core Stoic principle of *apatheia* or "living without passions."[64] This was one of many occasions on which Cato paid little attention to Stoic values.

At the end of his service as military tribune, Cato took some time to travel through Asia in order to learn about the different peoples and lands there, and also to spend some time with Deiotarus, the king of Galatia, who had been a friend of his father.[65] Such travel was not unusual for a member of Rome's aristocracy, but whereas most elite Romans flaunted their status and made heavy demands for service and hospitality from provincials, Cato traveled in such a quiet and unassuming way that he was often mistaken for a man of low status. Yet this did not mean that he was actually humble or disinterested: if he received no reception at all from locals, he would chastise their magistrates and warn them to be more hospitable to Romans, who had the power to take what was not offered. On the other hand, when at Antioch he discovered a great multitude of citizens lined up outside the city to receive one of Pompey's freedmen, he lamented the servility of the city.[66] So while he demanded comparatively little from provincials,

---

63. Plut. *Cat. Min.* 11.1–4.

64. Münzer ([1999] 307) points out that Cato's friend and later biographer, Munatius Rufus, had accompanied Cato to Macedonia, and therefore was an eyewitness to Cato's extreme displays of grief. See further discussion of Cato's relationship with Stoicism in later chapters.

65. Plut. *Cat. Min.* 12.2–5. See Fehrle (1983) 73 and Bellemore (1995) 376–9.

66. Bellemore ([1995] 376–9) has argued persuasively that—based on what is known of Pompey's movements and the length of time Cato spent in Asia—this happened at Carian or Pisidian Antioch, but not at Syrian Antioch.

he did expect them to show proper respect for his status. Of course, one can also ask how fair Cato's rebuke was: if he did not act like other Roman elites and telegraph his high status, how were provincials to recognize him as someone deserving of particular attention? Thus he expected provincials to show proper deference and hospitality to their Roman overlords, but he also expected Romans to act with moderation and self-control.

While on his eastern tour, Cato had an unusual encounter with Pompey (Figure 2.1) at Ephesus. Pompey was then at the height of his reputation, having cleared the Mediterranean Sea of pirates in 67 BC, and now was completing Rome's war against Mithridates in the East. Despite Pompey's current fame as Rome's greatest commander, Cato had strong personal reasons to dislike him: he had been one of Sulla's henchman and had killed noble Romans, including M. Junius Brutus (trib. pl. 83 BC)—the first husband of Cato's half-sister Servilia—and Cn. Domitius Ahenobarbus, the brother of Cato's brother-in-law L. Domitius Ahenobarbus (cos. 54 BC). Cato also would have loathed Pompey's

FIGURE 2.1. Bust of Gnaeus Pompeius Magnus (Pompey the Great), Augustan copy of a ca. 70–60 BC original, Museo Archeologico Nazionale di Venezia.
Source: Wikipedia.

past use of *popularis* tactics to build his career: he had pushed the Senate to give him an available command in Spain in 77 BC despite being a private citizen and too young to hold the consulship legally; as consul in 70 BC he had joined with M. Licinius Crassus (another of Sulla's lieutenants) to restore the full powers of the plebeian tribunate, which Sulla had sharply limited; and in 67 BC Pompey's lieutenant, the tribune A. Gabinius, had sponsored a law deposing the senior senator L. Licinius Lucullus from the command of the Mithridatic War, and the following year Pompey himself took over the command and worked to steal all credit for the war from Lucullus. Cato surely resented all of this, most especially Pompey's shabby treatment of Lucullus, whom Cato respected (a few years later the two would become linked by a marriage alliance). In light of this, it seems strange that he would take the time to call on Pompey. Perhaps he thought it appropriate because Pompey was a Roman proconsul, or perhaps he wanted to size the great man up, or even create a contrast between the wealth of Pompey's council and his own austerity and old-fashioned virtue. According to Plutarch, Pompey leapt up upon seeing Cato and rushed forward to greet him, praising his virtue so all could hear.[67] This was quite a welcome from Rome's leading general, especially considering that Cato had not yet begun a political career. Pompey may have remembered him as the young man whom Sulla had favored many years earlier, or his exuberance may have been intended to smooth over the fact that he had killed two of Cato's in-laws. He may even have hoped that showing outward respect to Cato would smooth over his rocky relationship with the Senate leadership. Indeed, when he returned to Rome a few years later, Pompey sought a marriage alliance with him, no doubt hoping to improve his relationship with Cato and the powerful senators with whom he was associated. All of this was probably political maneuvering, since Plutarch makes it clear that Pompey had little genuine interest in Cato, and that his warm welcome had only been for show—he wrote that Pompey was happy to be seen admiring Cato for a short time, but that he was also very pleased to see Cato leave. Of course, Plutarch likely exaggerated the warmth of Pompey's welcome in order to build up Cato's status in his narrative, and to develop the biography's theme of Cato's legendary virtue.[68] His family was certainly famous and worth being connected to if possible, but he himself had not yet held the quaestorship or entered the Senate, so it is difficult

---

67. Plut. *Cat. Min.* 14.1–3.

68. Kit Morrell ([2017] 16–7) has argued this point: "Plutarch or his source has shaped the story in line with Cato's later opposition to Pompey and the theme of Cato's virtue as a source of shame to others."

to imagine that Pompey would have shown the extreme respect that Plutarch imagines Cato commanded even as a young man.

On this trip Cato also visited King Deiotarus of Galatia, who was a faithful Roman ally, a friend to Pompey, and a friend of Cato's father. Such a visit to foreign royalty was not unusual for young Roman aristocrats, who sought to cultivate foreign friendships and clients, especially with persons as important as Deiotarus.[69] Yet Cato's behavior on this trip was far from normal. Instead of allowing himself to enjoy the luxuries and pleasures made available to Roman dignitaries in the eastern courts, he seems to have gone out of his way to avoid and even snub the splendor offered him. He not only refused the rich presents Deiotarus offered, but when pressed to accept them he abruptly departed from the king's city. Deiotarus was perplexed at this unusual behavior, and his surprise indicates that Cato's rejection of the offered gifts diverged considerably from the usual behavior of Roman aristocrats, who were normally eager for presents from foreign rulers. Deiotarus even thought that he had insulted Cato by offering subpar gifts, and so quickly sent even better and richer presents, begging him to give them to his retainers if he would not keep them for himself. Much to the chagrin of his friends, Cato refused to do even this, and sent all the gifts back. Once again, his behavior stood in stark contrast to the prevailing norms of his contemporaries, but it is not enough to interpret this behavior entirely as the product of great virtue. As a private citizen visiting a family friend, he was perfectly entitled to accept Deiotarus's gifts, and those gifts should have been anticipated, since royal gift-giving in the East was as ancient as Homer. Gift-giving was normal and acceptable, and therefore it should not have contravened the *mos maiorum*. To Deiotarus, the presentation of gifts was probably intended to forge a personal connection with a future Roman senator, and Plutarch emphasizes that the aging king wanted to commend his children to Cato's future care.[70] Furthermore, Deiotarus was the client of a number of Roman senators, indicating that Cato was rejecting normal practice by refusing to accept the gifts.[71] It is possible that he was trying to avoid the bad reputation that Julius Caesar had acquired years earlier when he spent too much time at the court of King Nicomedes of Bithynia, generating rumors that he had prostituted himself to the king, but if this was his concern, he handled the situation very badly, mystifying and wounding his host Deiotarus.[72] Cato may

---

69. Plut. *Cat. Min.* 15.1–3. See Fehrle (1983) 75.

70. Plut. *Cat. Min.* 15.1.

71. See Gelzer (1969) 91.

72. Suet. *Iul.* 2.1 and 49.4. See Paterson (2009) 135–6.

have believed that this customary gift-giving was nothing more than bribery, but even so, his reaction seems extreme: refusing the gifts of a family friend without explanation, departing from a host's house suddenly and without taking his leave, and refusing to allow even his friends to have the gifts. The degree of Cato's reaction does not seem appropriate, especially since he can hardly have been surprised that Deiotarus offered him gifts. As had been the case with his refusal of military awards, his surprising departure from normal, accepted practice suggests a deliberate effort to build a reputation for old-fashioned values. Indeed, the substantial attention given to this episode by later writers shows that his extreme (even excessive) display of virtue in the East was widely discussed and remembered, indicating that he succeeded in enhancing his reputation through such dramatic and public displays of old-fashioned virtue.

Cato's Entry into Politics

Shortly after this incident, Cato returned to Rome fairly early in 65 BC, bearing the ashes of Caepio with him. He was eligible to stand for election to the quaestorship of 64 BC, which was the first rung in the *cursus honorum* and would confer membership in the Senate. According to Plutarch, Cato took the time to study the duties of the quaestor carefully before standing for election.[73] He not only read the relevant laws relating to the office, but also questioned former quaestors to make sure he understood the power and scope of the office. Apparently, this degree of preparation for the quaestorship was highly unusual, and Cato is not recorded as preparing in a similar manner for other offices. It may be that he really did not understand the responsibilities of the quaestor fully, which would be understandable because quaestors performed a wide range of duties depending upon which assignment they received: some quaestors managed the granaries in Rome's port city of Ostia, some managed the state treasury, and one was assigned to each consul and praetor as a financial officer for his army.[74] It is also possible that Cato undertook these studies for a more specific purpose. Given his later actions, he was clearly concerned about the regular operation of the state treasury, and it may have been his intention to bring about reforms as far-reaching as the

---

73. Plut. *Cat. Min.* 16.1.

74. See Lintott (1999a) 133–7. If the consul or praetor was prorogued in office and became a proconsul or propraetor, it was normal for their quaestor to remain with them as a proquaestor.

powers of his office would permit. Given his connections and growing reputation, he won election without any difficulty, and took office on December 5 of that year.[75]

Sometime shortly before or after Cato took office, L. Licinius Lucullus—one of the greatest *nobiles* in the Senate—approached him and expressed an interest in marrying his younger half-sister (or perhaps it was his niece) Servilia.[76] Lucullus was another of Sulla's lieutenants and had held the vast eastern command against Mithridates from 74 to 66 BC, until Pompey's ally, the plebeian tribune A. Gabinius, promulgated legislation stripping Lucullus of the command. This *popularis* tactic of using the popular assembly to remove a leading optimate senator of his command outraged many in the Senate, but Pompey went even further by arranging for his political allies to block Lucullus's request for a triumph when he returned to Rome in 66 BC. Lucullus had won many victories in the East and therefore had earned a triumph, but Pompey's friends managed to delay the authorization of the celebration in hopes that Pompey might return to Rome and take all of the credit for the victory. Lucullus was stymied, but rather than admit defeat, he remained outside Rome's sacred boundary (the *pomerium*) in order to retain his military authority and therefore his ability to hold a triumph if and when the political landscape shifted in his favor.[77] During this time he also divorced his wife Clodia—sister of the infamous P. Clodius Pulcher—for infidelity, and expressed a desire to marry Cato's half-sister.[78] Servilia certainly had wealth and family connections that made her a desirable match, but Lucullus was already fantastically wealthy, was one of the leading men in the state, and was probably already politically allied to her influential uncle Mamercus Aemilius Lepidus Livianus and his family (both men had been fellow lieutenants of Sulla). Indeed, the main benefit that Lucullus seems to have acquired from this match was a close connection with Cato, who was only a quaestor-elect, but whose good military reputation, solid conservative values, and eccentric behavior made him stand out as an up-and-coming young senator who would eventually wield considerable *auctoritas*. Lucullus probably saw great potential in an alliance with

---

75. In the late Republic, quaestors took office on December 5 (*RS* 14 ll. 7–31, Cic. *Verr.* 1.30).

76. Plut. *Luc.* 38.1, *Cat. Min.* 24.3, 29.3. The ancient sources suggest that this Servilia was Cato's half-sister, but Harders ([2007] 43–61) has argued persuasively that Lucullus married Cato's niece.

77. Ryan ([1995] 293–302) discusses the chronology of Lucullus's efforts and of the opposition to him by Pompey's lieutenants.

78. Cic. *Mil.* 73, Plut. *Luc.* 34.1, 38.1, *Cic.* 29.5, *Cat. Min.* 29.3. The marriage would not last, because Lucullus found this Servilia to be corrupt and scandalous.

Cato, and may even have hoped that the younger man could help him achieve his longed-for triumph. Pompey had certainly shown Cato outward respect when they met in the East, and Plutarch says that Q. Lutatius Catulus, yet another of Sulla's lieutenants, who surpassed even Lucullus in *dignitas* and *auctoritas* and was elected censor in 65 BC, specifically commended Cato's way of living.[79] All of this demonstrates that Cato—despite his junior rank—had caught the attention of senior men in the Senate, and that *nobiles* like Lucullus and Catulus identified him as a good political prospect. Indeed, his technique of building up a cult of personality around his extreme conservatism made him a very good ally to counter Pompey's use of populist tactics. Second—and more immediate—Cato was a quaestor-elect, had a reputation as an effective speaker, had good reasons to dislike Pompey, and had demonstrated an aggressive and confrontational nature, all of which would make him a very effective ally in breaking down resistance to Lucullus's bid for a triumph.

When Cato took office as quaestor, the purpose behind his careful study of the magistracy became clear. The operations of Rome's state treasury (*aerarium*) were remarkably complex, but the laws that regulated it were not easily collected and understood, and there was money flowing into and out of so many different accounts that it was impossible for the average disinterested Roman aristocrat to comprehend.[80] For this reason, quaestors had long abdicated their supervisory roles to the professional clerks who worked in the treasury, which had resulted in widespread corruption that was difficult to weed out. In addition to maintaining the fiscal accounts, the state treasury also served as the storehouse for senatorial decrees, and corrupt clerks could be bribed to edit those decrees or even introduce false decrees.[81] As soon as he took office, therefore, Cato threw himself into the job and wrested control of the finances away from the clerks, who struggled against his authority. By prosecuting the worst of them and subduing the rest, he overhauled the operations of the entire treasury. He collected long-overdue debts, paid those owed money, imposed reforms to reduce corruption in the future, and established new procedures to ensure that documents were not altered or otherwise forged. In all of this, he aggressively promoted his old-fashioned honesty, advertising himself as an incorruptible Roman who best embodied ancestral virtue. Plutarch emphasizes that Cato's supervision of the treasury made

---

79. Plut. *Cat. Min.* 16.4.

80. Plut. *Cat. Min.* 16.2–18.5. Nicolet ([1991] 149–206) gives a full discussion of the Roman treasury.

81. Gruen (1974) 254 and Yakobson and Horstkotte (1997) 247–8.

him very popular with the people, so by his outstandingly scrupulous behavior, he won fame and reputation from the very first step of the *cursus honorum*.[82]

Cato was the first senator to gain fame for his careful administration of the treasury, so some of his actions deserve special attention. First, when he was prosecuting a clerk guilty of fraud, none other than the sitting censor Lutatius Catulus came forward to defend the clerk.[83] This was powerful assistance, because Catulus wielded both his personal *auctoritas* as a leading *nobilis* and the considerable *auctoritas* of his office, but the clerk's guilt was obvious, and Catulus was forced to beg the jurors to acquit his client as a favor. Before the jurors could be swayed, however, Cato interrupted Catulus and prevented him from speaking further, threatening to have him hauled out of the court if he continued asking for the acquittal of an obviously guilty man. According to Plutarch, Cato warned the very senior senator, "it would be disgraceful for you, Catulus, who are censor and sit in judgment of our lives, to be thrown out by our attendants."[84] In a superb moment of theater, Plutarch records Catulus and Cato locking eyes across the courtroom, but Catulus was the first to blink, and left the courtroom stymied and perplexed. As he walked away, two questions were surely running through his mind: why had his vast *auctoritas* failed to secure the acquittal of his client, and why had Cato, who so clearly *seemed* to be a kindred conservative optimate, rebuffed him unnecessarily? In traditional Roman politics, Cato as a junior senator should have been eager to do favors for a leading senator like Catulus, but instead he unyieldingly enforced the letter of the law, allowing no compromise. That he had rebuffed Catulus so publicly, and had refused to recognize the greater *auctoritas* of the senior *nobilis*, must have seemed more appropriate for a *popularis* politician than for the scion of a famously conservative family. Indeed, although Plutarch portrays Cato's action as virtuous and honest in his biography, in his *Moralia* he calls the threat to Catulus "severe and presumptuous," indicating that the threat may have appeared more harsh than virtuous at the time.[85] But Catulus was not done: when the jury voted at the end of the trial, there was one more vote for condemnation than for acquittal, but one juror was absent on account of illness and so had not cast his ballot. Catulus had the man carried into the court on a litter in order to cast his vote for acquittal, but Cato refused to count this late vote, and so the clerk lost his job and his pay.

---

82. Plut. *Cat. Min.* 18.1 (cf. Cic. *Off.* 3.88).

83. Plut. *Cat. Min.* 16.4–6.

84. Plut. *Cat. Min.* 16.5, cf. *Mor.* 808e.

85. Plutarch (*Mor.* 808e [cf. 534d]) uses the phrase βαρέως καὶ αὐθάδως to describe Cato's actions.

Second, as quaestor Cato is said to have pursued men who had received money from the state for killing fellow citizens during the murderous proscriptions when Sulla was dictator. Sulla had unleashed a bloodbath by publishing lists of citizens who could be killed with impunity, and he had the state treasury pay bounties to the men who produced the heads of the proscribed. Cato used his quaestorship to scrutinize past activities of the treasury, and in particular those relating to Sulla's proscriptions, which had so angered him as a youth. He seems to have produced the record of men who received payment from the treasury for delivering the heads of proscribed citizens, and he demanded repayment of those funds. As Plutarch describes it,

> There were men to whom Sulla himself had given twelve thousand drachmas as a reward for killing each of those people who had been proscribed, and everyone hated them as being cursed and polluted, but no one dared to punish them. Cato exacted punishment upon them, citing each one for unjustly having public money, and simultaneously decrying the profanity and illegality of their action in an angry speech.[86]

Cato is credited with recovering the money, but how he achieved this is not clear. The murderers had been acting under the authority of a dictator, and Sulla had exempted these men from the murder laws in his *leges Corneliae*.[87] Plutarch suggests that Cato used his reputation for old-fashioned morality and his powerful rhetoric to shame the men into repaying the money voluntarily, but one may fairly doubt that men who had killed fellow citizens for cash two decades earlier would simply give the money back to the treasury. Instead, he may have had some unwelcome help. At the same time that he was demanding back the blood money from these men, Julius Caesar became interested in prosecuting them for murder.[88] Caesar had been *curule aedile* in the previous year, and acting as either a specially appointed judge (*iudex quaestionis*), or as a *quaesitor* or *accusator* in another's court, he decided the time was right to challenge the legal immunity of Sulla's henchmen. Like Cato, Caesar was building his career, and he seized upon the opportunity to gather public accolades for prosecuting hated men who had profited from the murder of citizens. It may well have been

---

86. Plut. *Cat. Min.* 17.4–5, cf. Dio 47.6.4. Gelzer ([1934] 74) suggests that Cato's prosecution of Sulla's henchmen was meant as a criticism of Sulla's dictatorship.

87. Suet. *Iul.* 11.1.

88. Cic. *Lig.* 12, Suet. *Iul.* 11.1, and Dio 37.10.1–2. See comments by Gruen (1974) 76 n. 124 and 277, Brennan (2000) 2.421 and n. 298, and Goldsworthy (2008) 115–6.

this prosecution that forced Sulla's henchmen to repay the money to Cato in the treasury—either in the form of fines or in confiscation of property. While this was good for the treasury, Cato may have resented Caesar's involvement, since the prosecution of the murderers surely received more glory and attention than the mere repayment of money—Dio emphasizes that Caesar's activity was seen at the time as being most important.[89] There is no reason to suspect that Caesar was deliberately trying to overshadow Cato in this event—he may have been oblivious to Cato's aims, or may even have resented that Cato seemed to be claiming glory for collecting fines that had resulted from Caesar's successful prosecution of the assassins. This was the first recorded occasion on which their political paths crossed, but both men were simply attempting to increase their political profile and visibility by pursuing Sulla's henchmen.

On the last day of his quaestorship, when Cato had left the treasury and had gone home accompanied by a procession of his supporters praising his fine work, he received word that one of his colleagues named Marcellus had remained in the treasury and was being pressured by friends and influential men to enter false remissions of debts into the state records.[90] This Marcellus was described as an old friend of Cato, and he may have been M. Claudius Marcellus, the future consul of 51 BC who would collaborate closely with Cato in their efforts to bring down Julius Caesar. Plutarch says Marcellus was weak and therefore entered the false records into the state accounts at the behest of his friends, and this was doubtless the type of favor that powerful elites normally did for one another to ensure their mutual benefit. Yet Cato stormed back into the treasury, erased the false records Marcellus had made, and led Marcellus away from the pressure of his friends. This no doubt frustrated Marcellus and his friends, who were accustomed to getting their way, but Cato had invested a great deal of time and effort to make his supervision of the treasury remarkable and memorable, and he was not about to permit any last-minute corruption under his watch. He kept an eye on the operation of the treasury even after he left office: he had copies made for himself of all treasury accounts from the time of Sulla down to his own quaestorship, for which he paid the huge sum of five talents (roughly four percent of his inheritance), and he regularly dispatched slaves to make copies of new transactions.[91] Perhaps he anticipated that future quaestors would ignore his example and allow confusion and corruption to once again take over the treasury, and so wanted his own set of records to facilitate the prosecution of future wrongdoers. Cato did a great

---

89. Dio 37.10.2.

90. Plut. *Cat. Min.* 18.3–4.

91. Plut. *Cat. Min.* 18.5.

service for the state by taking such care of the treasury, but he also served his own ambitions: he became the first person to acquire such tremendous fame and reputation from the management of state finances.

At some point during the latter half of his quaestorship—or perhaps early in the following the year—Cato turned his attention to helping his new brother-in-law Lucullus obtain a long-awaited triumph for his victories in the East. As discussed earlier, Lucullus had won many victories during his years in command, but Pompey was determined to claim all of the credit for winning the Mithridatic War, and therefore his agents in Rome obstructed all efforts to recognize Lucullus's achievements through the awarding of a triumph.[92] Plutarch writes that Cato was driven to help Lucullus by his moral scruple and his indignation at the unjust treatment of a great aristocratic commander, but his assistance only came in the second or even third year of Lucullus's struggle, which suggests that it was Lucullus's marriage to Cato's half-sister (or perhaps niece) that really drew him into the fight.[93] He was morally obligated to help his new brother-in-law, but it also served his own interests, since he surely expected that his own climb up the *cursus honorum* would benefit from Lucullus's considerable influence as a leader of the *optimates* or *boni*. Rome had no political parties in the modern sense, identifiable by particular platforms or ideologies, but the Senate leadership was generally dominated by the *consulares* (senators who had held the consulship) and by other high-ranking men from old aristocratic clans. Each of these nobles or *nobiles* had his own ambitions and goals for his family, and so pursued his own interests, but the majority of senators usually aligned to protect the special status and privileges their elite families had enjoyed for generations. All senators were generally conservative, but the terms *optimates* and *boni* are usually used to refer to those senators who took a particular interest in preserving the customary practice of politics, which had enabled a relatively small group of elite families to dominate the state through their influence, wealth, and political connections. This was not a political party in any sense, but *optimates* could usually be counted

---

92. Only one of Pompey's agents (C. Memmius) is named, but the year of his tribunate is disputed. See Fehrle (1983) 84 n. 3, Ryan (1995) 293–302, and Bellemore (1996) 504–8 for discussion. Regardless of the year of his tribunate, he and others of Pompey's supporters worked together to block Lucullus's triumph until 63 BC. Hillman ([1993] 216) suggests that Lucullus's triumph may have been approved by the Senate, but tribunes friendly to Pompey had blocked the actual celebration of the triumph. See Keaveney (1992) 129–36 for discussion of Lucullus's activities during this period.

93. Plut. *Cat. Min.* 29.3–4. On the other hand, Keaveney ([1992] 241–2 n. 11) suggests that Cato may have also worked to bring about the triumph of Q. Caecilius Metellus Creticus (cos. 69 BC), whose application for a triumph over Crete was similarly being blocked by Pompey's agents. On the identity of Lucullus's wife, see earlier discussion.

upon to unite against men such as Pompey, who used populist or *popularis* tactics to accumulate unprecedented honors, influence, and commands, usually at the expense of the Senate's dominance over the state. Just as Cato the Elder had advertised himself as an old-fashioned Roman in order to secure his place among the senatorial elite, so his great-grandson sought to gain a position of prominence among the *optimates*, who worked to build up the Senate's authority (and so their own ability to lead the state). By making an alliance with Lucullus and helping him gain a triumph, therefore, Cato joined these *optimates* in their opposition to Pompey, which suited his personal distaste for the man and helped him gain the support of powerful *nobiles*. Displaying his usual energy and capacity for confrontation, Cato led a political assault on Pompey's agents, browbeating them into withdrawing their threat of prosecution and lifting their obstruction of Lucullus's triumph.

The timing of this victory is difficult to establish. Plutarch says that Pompey's supporters retaliated by making many slanderous accusations against Cato, and they even tried to have him ejected from his office because he was exercising "tyrannical power," a potent charge tapping into Rome's deep cultural hatred of kings and tyrants.[94] This suggests that Cato was quaestor at the time, but Lucullus did not actually triumph until late in 63 BC, which seems very long time to wait if the triumph had been approved almost a year earlier.[95] Perhaps he began pushing for the approval of Lucullus's triumph during his year as quaestor, but only succeeded—probably with the help of the consul Cicero—in the following year.[96] It is also possible that Plutarch has overstated Cato's role in an attempt to further lionize his subject. Lucullus certainly had a number of supporters assisting him, but Cato would repeatedly prove to be a vocal and bellicose participant in political battles, so there is every reason to believe that he fought tenaciously to support his new relation, and so drew the particular ire of Pompey's supporters. Although little is known about how he helped Lucullus overcome the

---

94. Plut. *Cat. Min.* 29.4 (τυραννίδος). Bellemore ([1996] 507) suggests that the accusation of tyrannical action may mean that Cato interrupted the voting on Lucullus's triumph in the Tribal Assembly in order to influence the vote in Lucullus's favor. This is only speculation, but it certainly fits with Cato's later behavior in the public assemblies (see later discussion).

95. Lucullus triumphed around the time of the consular elections for 62 BC, which had been delayed to October on account of the threats posed by the revelation of the Catilinarian conspiracy (Cicero notes [*Mur.* 37 and 69] that Lucullus's soldiers were in Rome for the triumph during the time of the elections). See Hillman (1993) 211–28 and Ryan (1995) 293–302.

96. MacDonald ([1977] 171) suggests that Cicero as consul threw his full weight into getting Lucullus's triumph approved, because doing so would bring Lucullus's soldiers to Rome around the time of the consular elections. Those soldiers would likely vote for Murena, and thereby help secure the defeat of Catiline in the elections.

obstruction of Pompey's friends, it must have been the case that they built a sufficient consensus among senatorial factions to make resistance untenable. Cato would later show a talent for building support in the Senate, and his forceful advocacy no doubt earned him the special attention and gratitude of Lucullus's circle, including many of the great *nobiles* who formed the Senate leadership.

This event helps to clarify why Cato was held in such high respect by his peers despite his relatively low status as quaestor: he possessed greater energy, tenacity, and single-mindedness than any of the senators who coalesced around Lucullus, Catulus, and the other great *nobiles*. It was also an advantage that he was entering political life during a rare and unusual "changing of the guard" period in the Roman Senate, which enabled him to acquire far greater *auctoritas* than his current rank in the *cursus honorum* would traditionally have conferred. Normally, the dual consulship produced enough *consulares* to give considerable depth and stability to the Senate's core leadership, and because consular rank could be achieved as young as age forty-two, many men spent fifteen or even twenty years as *consulares* in the Senate.[97] This normally meant that a large body of *consulares* was available to satisfy the need for leadership among the aristocracy, but the Social War between Rome and its allies (91–87 BC) and then the Civil War between Marius, Sulla, and their partisans (88–79 BC) had been bloodbaths for the elite classes, and an entire generation of senatorial families had been devastated.[98] As a result, the leadership of the Senate—the *consulares* who held the greatest status and influence, and whose opinions held sway over the great majority of senators—had grown very thin. Most of the men who held the consulship in the 80s BC were killed in the Social War or in the Civil War, so that there were only five *consulares* left in 81 BC, and by 70 BC the leading senators were Q. Caecilius Metellus Pius (cos. 80 BC) and Q. Lutatius Catulus (cos. 78 BC), and the senior senator (the *princeps senatus*) was Cato's uncle Mamercus Aemilius Lepidus Livianus, who had only been a *consularis* for seven years.[99] By 65 BC, the leading *consulares* of the Senate comprised a fairly small group, including Q. Caecilius Metellus Pius (cos. 80 BC), Q. Lutatius Catulus (cos. 78 BC), L. Licinius Lucullus (cos. 74 BC), M. Terentius Varro Lucullus (cos. 73 BC), Cn. Pompey Magnus (cos.

---

97. One famous example is M. Aemilius Scaurus, who held consular rank for twenty-five years, and Cicero had been a *consularis* for twenty years before his premature death.

98. See Syme (1939) 22–4, Meier (1966) 243, 268–9, Gruen (1974) 7–12. Sulla had increased the size of the Senate following the civil war, but these new men were on the whole less prestigious than the scions of ancient families who had died in the wars (see Santangelo [2014] 12–3).

99. See Santangelo (2014) 13 on the *lectio* of 81 BC. Ryan ([1998] 194–6) discusses the debate on when Livianus was named *princeps senatus*. For a full discussion of the Roman nobility, see Gelzer (1969) 27–53.

70 BC), M. Licinius Crassus (cos. 70 BC), Q. Caecilius Metellus Creticus (cos. 69 BC), Q. Hortensius Hortalus (cos. 69 BC), and M'. Aemilius Lepidus (cos. 66 BC).[100] Although these men were impressive, influential, and respected, their small number meant they would have difficulty controlling and unifying the Senate. Traditionally, the senior leadership of the Senate had been able to direct the decisions of the entire body, but this depended upon having a large enough core of *consulares* to influence or overawe the rest of the senators. Not only was the core of *consulares* small in the late 60s BC, but powerful men like Pompey and Crassus were using their wealth and influence to acquire personal advantage through *popularis* measures, which fractured the cohesion of the Senate, making it harder for the more conventional (optimate) Senate leadership to develop a consensus among the senators. As a result, few of the tradition-minded *nobiles* still had the stomach for leading bold and aggressive opposition to Pompey, preferring instead to lead a quiet life in wealthy semi-retirement, further depleting the Senate's leadership.[101] In this atmosphere, Cato—who was only thirty-one or thirty-two years old when he finished his quaestorship—was exactly what the *optimates* wanted and needed: he shared their traditional, conservative views about the primacy of the Senate and its elite leadership, and he had the tireless energy and the oratorical skills to contend against Pompey's agents in the Senate and in the assemblies. Since the *optimates* were not a political party, Cato was not joining a specific group of senators linked by a particular social or political outlook, but was claiming a prominent place among those who championed the traditional conduct of politics and the Senate's claim to lead the state. Like all senators, he was primarily focused on his own priorities, and would form alliances if and as needed to pursue his goals, but it became clear that he would take an active role in opposing men who—in his view—threatened the conventional order of the Senate, and the "shallow bench" of the Senate's conservative leadership enabled Cato to gain prominence rapidly. In the absence of a strong core of *consulares*, therefore, he was able to assume a leading position quickly among the *optimates* despite his junior status in the *cursus honorum*.

While the leanness of the conservative leadership was one factor that explains Cato's dramatic rise to prominence, another was his great success in fashioning himself as the living embodiment of tradition through his archaizing habits and mannerisms. While his dedication to the *mos maiorum* was certainly genuine,

---

100. These men are found on the lists of distinguished witnesses who testified against C. Cornelius in 65 BC (Ascon. 60) and for the poet Archias in 62 BC (Cic. *Pro Arch.* 6). See discussion in Taylor (1949) 27, 119, and 221–2, and Gruen (1974) 50 and 262–8.

101. Cicero (*Att.* 1.18.6, 1.19.6–7, 2.9.1) would lament that many senior *optimates*—including Lucullus and Hortensius—preferred their fishponds to politics. See Syme (1939) 22–4.

there can be little doubt that many of his bizarrely old-fashioned mannerisms were deliberate contrivances rather than learned modes of behavior. To the best of our knowledge, he grew up in senatorial houses that embraced the range of customs of contemporary elite society: his uncle Livius Drusus (trib. pl. 91 BC) was famous for breaking with tradition by trying to enfranchise the Italians, and Dio noted that Cato had a much better Greek education than his great-grandfather had possessed.[102] Anecdotes relating Cato's strangely archaic behavior do not start until he had reached manhood and had begun his public career, and many of those habits contrasted so sharply with contemporary norms that they seem specifically intended to generate public chatter about his extreme commitment to the *mos maiorum*. Plutarch also saw that Cato's behavior at times seemed contrived, and he attempted to defuse this suspicion by saying of his refusal to wear footwear or any clothing under his toga, "he was not chasing popular repute from these novel behaviors, but rather was accustoming himself to feel shame in shameful things alone, and to despise disreputable things."[103] This is nonsense— Cato was not forgoing underwear and footwear in an effort to learn about shame; he did it because he wanted to dress like the kings and heroes of early Rome.[104]

Attempts to attribute Cato's behavior to Stoicism ignore the more powerful cultural significance of his behavior. He was certainly interested in philosophy and gave time to reading and study, but his strange habits did not emerge from his philosophic principles.[105] Riding a horse, accepting gifts, wearing a contemporary shade of purple, and wearing footwear and a tunic under his toga were not inconsistent with Stoicism. Cicero and the emperor Marcus Aurelius were famous Stoic philosophers, and they had no problem following the behaviors that Cato eschewed.[106] As Plutarch—a great admirer of Cato—pointed out, he did not have a particularly nimble or insightful mind; he learned things by rote, and he maintained without compromise or question the opinions he had formed.[107] This does not seem like a description of a philosopher, but rather of a politician who used certain convenient principles of Stoic philosophy to support his political

---

102. Dio 37.22.1.

103. Plut. *Cat. Min.* 6.3–4.

104. Ascon. 29 (see earlier discussion).

105. Valerius Maximus (8.7.2) mentions Cato reading Greek texts before Senate meetings.

106. Syme ([1939] 57) clearly stated the issue: "Stoic teaching, indeed, was nothing more than a corroboration and theoretical defense of certain traditional virtues of the governing class in an aristocratic and republican state. Hellenic culture does not explain Cato; and the *virtus* about which Brutus composed a volume was a Roman quality, not an alien importation."

107. Plut. *Cat. Min.* 1.3.

views. With certain exceptions, the Romans were not great admirers of philosophy or philosophers, and they did not accord much respect to a man simply because he adhered to a particular philosophical school. Romans admired men who excelled in Roman cultural values, which could be reinforced by Greek philosophical ideas, but did not originate in philosophical schools. Thus the ideas of the Stoics probably influenced Cato's thinking, but they do not explain the old-fashioned persona that he cultivated and presented to the Roman people.

As is obvious from the attention he received from those around him, Romans identified Cato's behavior as representing a much older code of Roman values. He made himself into a living example of the old-fashioned Roman; he made himself into a living ancestor. Like the *flamen Dialis*, the priest of Jupiter who stood out in a crowd because he was required to follow certain archaic rules of dress and behavior, Cato made himself into a representation of Rome's legendary heroes.[108] This was certainly strange, but it tapped into the deep vein of patriotism and conservatism that ran through the blood of every Roman citizen. His archaic behavior would cast an almost magical glamor over his fellow citizens; agreeing with Cato—the living embodiment of tradition—seemed to show support for the *mos maiorum*, whereas disagreeing with him seemed to be a rejection of Roman tradition and therefore of Rome itself.[109] In this way, his self-fashioning as the voice of the ancestors enabled him to push or shame others into agreeing with his opinions. This gave him considerable influence and compensated for his disadvantages, which Valerius Maximus summarized clearly: "his patrimony was poor, his habits were bound tight by moderation, his clientage was modest, his house was closed to those canvassing for office, he had only one famous ancestor in his paternal line, his countenance was not very agreeable, but his virtue was complete in all categories."[110] Cato harnessed and manipulated Roman respect

---

108. Gellius (10.15.1–25) discusses the various restrictions placed on the *flamen Dialis*.

109. Gruen ([1974] 49–50) properly noted that, whereas most senators built up their standing and influence through a nexus of political relationships, Cato achieved his position through personality and vigor (and only afterward acquired a nexus of supporters). Stemmler ([2000] 141–205) has explored the power that *exempla* of ancient virtue had on the Roman mind, and emphasized the importance of reception and recognition of a particular individual as an *exemplum*, while Treggiari ([2003] 139–64) has shown how Roman senators carefully crafted their self-presentation in order to shape public perception and gain political advantage, and Kenty ([2016] 429–62) has demonstrated how Cicero skillfully used references to the *mos maiorum* to exert a powerful emotional influence over the Romans.

110. Val. Max. 2.10.8. See Jehne (2016) 188–207 for a survey of the role and importance of money in enabling men to pursue a senatorial career.

for tradition so effectively that Cicero later wrote that he conferred more glory on his father than his father had given to him.[111]

His unbending dedication to tradition could also make him a difficult ally because his extreme interpretation of Roman conservatism gave him little room to compromise without seeming to abandon his principles. This was compounded by his naturally inflexible nature, which made it impossible for him to make concessions. As a result, Cato was much admired for his devotion to the *mos maiorum*, but his own allies often had trouble enduring his extreme positions.[112] Many times he would frustrate his political allies by putting the letter of the law ahead of practical governance, and many thought he cut a poor figure as praetor and disgraced the majesty of the office by wearing his usual bizarre costume when presiding over court cases.[113] Cicero summed the problem up well, saying that he loved Cato, but that his spirit and integrity often harmed the Republic (*nocet rei publicae*) because he spoke as if he was living in Plato's Republic rather than in Romulus's cesspool.[114] This illustrates a problem Cato would have throughout his career: his methods of winning influence could also alienate political allies.

---

111. Cic. *de Off.* 3.66.

112. Cato's friend Curio expressed the hope that Cato would visit Asia while serving as military tribune in the East, so that he might become a more agreeable and pleasant man (Plut. *Cat. Min.* 14.4: ἡδίων γὰρ ἐπανήξεις ἐκεῖθεν καὶ μᾶλλον ἥμερος).

113. Plut. *Cat. Min.* 44.1.

114. Cic. *Att.* 2.1.8.

3

Cato the Tribune

The Tribunician Elections of 64 BC and the Trial of Murena

Following his highly successful performance as quaestor in 64 BC, and his role in helping his brother-in-law Lucullus gain a triumph later in 63 BC, Cato is said to have planned to take a break from political life in order to study philosophy. Although he was eligible to stand in the mid-year elections for the plebeian tribunate of 62 BC, popular tradition says that he planned to forgo that opportunity and instead retire to a country estate in Lucania for an extended period of study.[1] On the road, however, he crossed paths with a long convoy of pack animals and servants carrying the baggage of Q. Caecilius Metellus Nepos, one of Pompey's legates, who was returning to Rome to seek election to the tribunate. Recognizing that an unchecked Nepos would use his office to advance Pompey's interests in the capital, Cato is said to have immediately canceled his philosophic retreat and returned to Rome to seek election to the tribunate as well.[2] This story of Cato rousing himself from private life to serve the state seems far too romantic to be true, and is probably a fable that developed years later, intended to equate him to legendary heroes such as L. Quinctius Cincinnatus, who was famously summoned from his plow in 458 BC to become dictator and save the state in Rome's hour of need. Several years later, when Cato was a candidate for

---

1. Yakobson ([1999] 167) suggests that Cato planned to delay holding the tribunate until there was a more interesting year when he could make better use of the tribune's veto. It is not known when Cato's family acquired this estate, but Kay ([2014] 136) points out that Cato the Elder had acquired several small, scattered estates during this lifetime, and that Roman aristocrats started building many villas in Lucania after the Second Punic War, so this estate may have been part of Cato the Younger's inheritance.

2. Plut. *Cat. Min.* 20.1–3.

the consulship, he similarly explained that he was seeking the office in order to save the state, once again presenting himself as an unwilling hero and protector of Rome.

There is every reason to believe that Cato always intended to stand for the plebeian tribunate of 62 BC. In the first place, it seems unlikely that he would have left Rome for an extended sabbatical in Lucania while he was supposedly undertaking great efforts at the time to support Lucullus's claim on a triumph. Second, another of his relations—his brother-in-law D. Junius Silanus, the second husband of the elder Servilia—was a candidate in the consular elections that year, and it would have been a considerable dereliction of familial duty for Cato to leave Rome and thus refuse to support his relation, especially since Servilia reportedly exercised great influence over her half-brother.[3] Third—and most obvious—it would have been very odd for him *not* to stand for the tribunate in 63 BC. Although later folklore portrayed him as a man who generally avoided magistracies except when called to them by the state, this is a romantic reworking of his legend that does not hold up to scrutiny.[4] He followed the usual pattern of ambitious aristocrats by seeking election to offices in the earliest years possible: he sought the quaestorship as soon as he reached the minimum age for that office, he stood for the tribunate as soon as he was eligible after his quaestorship, and he would also seek the praetorship as soon as he reached the minimum age.[5] There was special prestige for a man who won an office in the first year he was eligible—in "his year" (*suo anno*)—and Cato seems to have contended for this honor with each office. And despite his claims of disinterest, he campaigned rigorously and may even have invested his own money in winning the election: archaeologists have discovered a terracotta bowl (Figure 3.1) advertising Cato's campaign for the tribunate.[6]

---

3. See Syme (1939) 23. Dragstedt ([1969] 76) suggested that Cato supported Sulpicius Rufus, rather than Silanus, in the consular election, but this seems an error based upon Cato's later cooperation with Sulpicius to prosecute the winners of that election (except Silanus) for electoral bribery (see later discussion). Gruen ([1974] 130 n. 34) argues that Cato did not support Sulpicius in the election.

4. Geiger (1971) and van der Blom ([2012] 47) emphasize that the presentation of Cato's popular support in this campaign is exaggerated with romantic and rhetorical flourishes.

5. Cato was probably twenty-nine years old when he stood (in 65 BC) for election to the quaestorship for 64 BC. Although there is some debate over the minimum age for the quaestorship, twenty-nine (when Cato stood for election) and thirty (when he actually held the office) are the two generally accepted ages. See Astin (1958) 49–64 and Lintott (1999a) 145.

6. *CIL* VI 40904 = *AE* 1979, 64. The bowl reads: *M(arcus) Cato quei petit tribun(at)u(m) plebei* ("Marcus Cato, who is seeking the tribunate of the plebs"). This type of campaign token

FIGURE 3.1. Cato propaganda cup, 1st century BC, CIL VI 40904 = AE 1979, 64, from Museo Nazionale Romano - Terme di Diocleziano, Rome.
Source: Wikipedia.

The authenticity of this bowl is not certain, but if real, it may be that it and many others like it were filled with food or drink and were distributed to citizens in an effort to win over their votes for Cato's campaign, which would indicate that he expended significant sums to promote himself and to win popular support for his candidacy. So with his sterling reputation and the help of his influential friends among the Senate leadership,[7] he was victorious in the tribunate elections for 62 BC.

At some point in this year (63 BC), Cato gave his first speech (that we know about) in the Senate. Since Pompey's eastern campaign was coming to a close and the great commander was expected to return to Rome soon, many senators were positioning themselves to benefit from Pompey's influence. Two tribunes, T. Ampius Balbus and T. Labienus, promulgated a law that would confer extraordinary honors upon Pompey, including the right to wear a laurel wreath at all public games, and triumphal garb at all horse races.[8] Caesar spoke in favor of this proposal, and he may well have been a driving force behind the tribunes' promulgation of the law. Cato is the only senator named as speaking against the proposal,

---

was not unusual: L. Cassius Longinus paid for the distribution of similar bowls supporting one of L. Sergius Catilina's consular campaigns (*CIL* VI 40897 = *AE* 1979, 63).

7. Yakobson ([1999] 167) discusses Cato's support from the *optimates* in this election.

8. Vell. 2.40.4 and Dio 37.21.4.

although there must have been others, such as Lucullus.[9] Although most junior senators would have thought it foolish to provoke unnecessarily Rome's greatest general and potential bestower of favors, Cato made a powerful, public statement of his opposition to Pompey and to the *popularis* tactics he had used in his unusual climb to power. These were undoubtedly his own political views, but they may also have been calculated to reinforce his support with the *optimates*, who opposed populist practices that undermined the influence of the aristocratic clans. It was an opening shot, and suggests that he had already decided to advance his career by opposing Pompey's further ambitions.

Cato was elected in July and would take office in December, but he was able to use his status as tribune-elect to his advantage even before entering office. Magistrates-elect were normally given higher speaking priority in the Senate than their achieved rank conferred; in his case, being a tribune-elect meant that he was recognized to speak right after the *consulares* and *praetores*, and he would use this advantage to his immediate benefit.[10] During these later months of 63 BC, Catiline's conspiracy against the state came to light. Frustrated by his failures in the consular elections of 64 and 63 BC, and facing political extinction as his family fell into debt, the patrician senator L. Sergius Catiline had formed a conspiracy of men who hoped to profit from an overthrow of the state. The consul Cicero (Figure 3.2) discovered and revealed the conspiracy in mid-October, and in early November Catiline fled from Rome to take command of an army raised by his co-conspirators. Despite this national emergency, however, Cato as tribune-elect focused his interest on the consular elections for the following year. Electoral bribery (*ambitus*) was both common and illegal, and as tribune-elect he made a public speech condemning this corrupt practice and promising to prosecute any candidate for the consulship whom he thought guilty of bribery, excepting only the candidate D. Junius Silanus, who was his half-sister's husband.[11] As events turned out, Silanus and L. Licinius Murena were elected, and—true to his word—Cato joined with one of the defeated consular candidates, Serv. Sulpicius Rufus, to prosecute Murena under a bribery law passed earlier that year in Cicero's consulship.[12] Many of Rome's leaders were exasperated by this action,

---

9. The fact that he had the opportunity to speak probably means that Cato was already tribune-elect, since senators were called upon to speak according to their seniority.

10. See Pina Polo (2016) 66–72.

11. Plut. *Cat. Min.* 21.2.

12. Cic. *Mur. passim, Flacc.* 98, *Fin.* 4.74, Quintil. *Inst. Or.* 6.1.35, 11.1.69, Plut. *Cat. Min.* 21.3–6. Sulpicius was the main prosecutor, and Cato his assistant (*subscriptor*), but Ayers ([1954] 248) argued that Cato was the prime mover in the prosecution. They were joined by two others in the prosecution: C. Postumius and Serv. Sulpicius (the latter probably a younger relation of

FIGURE 3.2. Bust of Marcus Tullius Cicero, 1st century AD, Palazzo Nuovo, Musei Capitolini, Rome.
Source: Wikipedia.

since Murena's proven military skills were much needed to confront Catiline's army on the battlefield. The trial was held in November, and Murena (who probably was guilty, since bribery was not unusual) was defended by three leading orators of the day: Cicero, Hortensius, and Crassus.

This case was remarkable, because all parties involved should have been on friendly terms with one another, if not actually aligned politically: Murena had been the legate of Cato's brother-in-law Lucullus, Cicero had strongly supported Sulpicius's candidacy for the consulship, and Cato was in other ways supportive of Cicero as consul. The jury unanimously acquitted Murena, perhaps because there was insufficient evidence to demonstrate his guilt, but more likely because Cicero convinced the jurors of the ridiculousness of prosecuting an experienced general

Serv. Sulpicius Rufus). For a discussion of the entire trial, see Alexander (2010) 121–7, Fantham (2013), May (1988) 58–69.

and consul-elect during a national crisis.[13] Seen in this light, Cato's grandstanding in issuing a blanket threat of prosecution ended up endangering the state, because he could not retract that threat without undermining his reputation as the unswerving champion of traditional values. Whatever the jurors thought about him personally, they refused to cast even a single vote for his prosecution.

Although Cato's speech in this trial does not survive, it is possible to recover some of his points by looking at Cicero's defense speech. Regarding the charge of bribery (*ambitus*), Cato accused Murena of violating the law in three ways: paying crowds of people to welcome him when he returned to Rome from his recent province; hiring a large crowd to follow him around the city and attend on him during his campaign for the consulship; and bribing voters in their tribes with free performances and meals.[14] Cicero pointed out that there was no evidence at all that Murena had committed the first two crimes, and he simply denied the third charge outright. Murena may well have been guilty, but bribery was a very difficult thing to prove. Perhaps anticipating this difficulty, Cato also attacked Murena's character, calling him a dancer (*saltator*) and claiming that the reputation he had won fighting Mithridates in Asia was unmerited, because the enemy army had been nothing more than little women.[15] The charge of being a dancer or performer was a common slur on an opponent's character, and may have been accompanied by other such character attacks.[16] On the other hand, the claim that Murena fought only little women in the East is surprising, since Murena fought under the command of Lucullus, the great *nobilis* and Cato's new brother-in-law. Indeed, Lucullus seems to have been present for Murena's trial, so this attack on Murena was also a slur on Lucullus's reputation. Given his recent efforts on Lucullus's behalf, one wonders whether Cato was carried away with emotion during his speech, and so unthinkingly insulted his brother-in-law as well as Murena, or whether his efforts to attack Murena blinded him to the blows his words might deliver to his friends.[17]

---

13. Cic. *Flacc.* 98.

14. Cic. *Mur.* 68–72.

15. Cic. *Mur.* 13 and 31.

16. See Fantham (2013) 8, 102–3.

17. Ayers ([1954] 250) points out that Sulpicius had tried in his speech to undermine Murena's military reputation by claiming he accomplished nothing important in the East, but Cicero's colleagues in the defense refuted this claim so thoroughly that Cato was forced to change his line of attack by minimizing the quality of Mithridates's army. Cicero (*Mur.* 20) mentions Lucullus's presence at the trial.

In addition to these accusations, Cato also attacked Cicero in an effort to undermine his anticipated defense speech on Murena's behalf. Cicero was not only Rome's leading defense advocate, but also a sitting consul, giving him considerable influence over the jurors. Cato tried to shame him for using the dignity and influence of his office to win a court case, and he tried to embarrass Cicero by reminding the jury that the consul had himself promulgated the anti-bribery law (the *lex Tullia*) under which Murena was being tried.[18] Yet this attack does not seem to have been effective, probably because it was not true; sitting magistrates could and did appear in courts as advocates.[19] Cato also suggested that defending a base criminal like Murena was contrary to the high principles that had thus far characterized Cicero's consulship, which is only an effective criticism if one already assumes that Murena was guilty, since there could be no shame in defending an innocent man.[20] Finally, Cato seems to have used part of his speech to address the state of the Republic (*de re publica*), which probably means he tried to paint Murena as being responsible (in part) for what he saw as the decline of the state.[21]

Cato's speech was certainly effective, not only for the arguments he made and the character attacks he launched against Murena and Cicero, but also for the great weight his own *auctoritas* gave to his claims, as one who spoke with the authority of Rome's revered ancestors (*maiores*). To emphasize this, he invoked the memory of his great-grandfather, reminding the audience that Cato the Elder's antique virtue flowed down the ages to his great-grandson.[22] Indeed, Cicero was particularly concerned about Cato's influence and moral authority; although he could dismantle the arguments constituting the prosecution's case, he worried aloud that Cato's influence alone could sway the votes of jurors. He voiced this fear to his audience, saying,

> Now I come to Marcus Cato, because he is the foundation and strength of the entire prosecution, who moreover is so weighty and forceful a prosecutor that I fear his moral authority (*auctoritas*) much more than the indictment.... For if someone should by chance say this—that Cato would not have undertaken the prosecution if he had not first made a ruling on the case—it would, judges, establish an unjust rule and miserable

---

18. Cic. *Mur.* 3 and 67.

19. Ayers (1954) 249.

20. Cic. *Mur.* 6 and 67. See May (1988) 58–9.

21. Cic. *Mur.* 54.

22. Cic. *Mur.* 66.

circumstances for men in a trial, if that person thinks the judgement of the prosecutor ought to prevail against a defendant as some kind of pre-judgement.[23]

Cicero feared that the jury would be swayed by Cato's unique moral authority, so to get his client acquitted, he needed to undermine Cato's influence over the jurors.[24] Yet this was difficult and dangerous: Cato's famous virtue made him a difficult target to attack with invective, and Cicero certainly feared making an enemy of the pugnacious Cato. In an attempt to escape this dilemma, Cicero adopted a clever strategy: instead of attacking Cato the man, he would attack his use and understanding of Stoic principles, and he would make Stoicism—rather than Cato—look foolish to the jurors. It seems clear that Cato made use of Stoic principles in his speech, no doubt using certain maxims about the importance and inflexibility of justice to argue that it was a moral necessity for the jurors to vote for condemnation. Cato was known for his aggressive style of oratory, and he no doubt hoped that these uncompromising philosophical arguments would influence the jurors, even those who were not conversant with Stoicism but might be impressed with its high-minded principles. Cicero—who was well trained (and probably better trained) in philosophy—made Cato's use of Stoic doctrines the linchpin of his defense strategy; he contorted those principles and made them appear laughable and alien to Roman values.[25] In this way, he deflated the force of Cato's moral condemnation of Murena without launching a personal attack against Cato himself. Quintilian recognized and praised this skillful strategy:

> Moreover, he handled Cato with such a soft touch! While admiring his nature greatly, he wished it to be seen as having become harsher, not through his own fault, but through certain elements of the Stoic school of thought, so you would have thought that it was a scholarly debate taking place between them and not a forensic argument.[26]

---

23. Cic. *Mur.* 13, 58–60. See May (1988) 64–5.

24. See Craig (1986) 230, "[Cato] could make clear to the jury that an acquittal would bring upon them the stigma of having disregarded justice and of holding in contempt the traditional Roman values for which he spoke."

25. May ([1988] 65) explains this tactic well: "when taken out of context, dissected, and exaggerated, Stoic virtues and their chief exponent become caricatures at which, despite all their value, we (and even the Romans) can only chuckle."

26. Quint. 11.1.70. Plutarch (*Cat. Min.* 21.5) also mentions Cicero's attacks on Cato's use of Stoic principles. See May (1988) 65–6.

In this way, Cicero undermined the weight of Cato's influence by making his use of Stoicism seem inconsistent with the *mos maiorum*. As discussed earlier, Greek philosophy was never seen as a particularly Roman occupation (although it was widely studied among the elites), so Cicero attacked the philosophy rather than the man. In doing so, he suggested that he understood the *mos maiorum* better than Cato, and that, while Cato was indulging in strange and foreign ideas, he (Cicero) was the true Roman, who was acting to save Murena and the Republic. Thus he blunted the force of the prosecution by making the audience laugh at Stoicism.[27]

Cicero's speech also provides helpful insight to understanding Cato, especially since it is an early firsthand presentation of Cato's character and demeanor.[28] He addresses Cato directly in the speech, saying,

> . . . you are the kind of man that seems to need a little correcting rather than changing. For nature itself has shaped you for honesty, seriousness, self-restraint, greatness of mind, justice, and moreover for all virtues of a great and eminent man. Yet a learning has been added to this that is neither moderate nor mild, which seems to me too harsh and callous for either truth or nature to endure.[29]

Cicero then describes principles set down by Zeno of Citium (335–263 BC), the founder of the Stoic school of philosophy, which are made to sound unreasonable and inappropriate for Romans:

> His sayings and teachings are of this type: the wise man is never moved by gratitude, never pardons anyone's offense; no one is sympathetic except the fool and the fickle; it is not right for a man to be won over or to be appeased; wise men alone are attractive, even if they are very deformed, they are rich even if greatly impoverished, and they are kings even if they labor in servitude; they say that we who are not wise men are fugitives,

---

27. Craig (1986) 231, ". . . the humorous treatment of Cato's Stoicism does more than simply puncture Cato's moral authority. Cicero also wins from his opponent the immense advantage which comes from the appearance of a proper alignment with the *mos maiorum*." Van der Wal (2007) 188, "here he provokes laughter to turn attention away from the actual charges, pretending to uphold Cato's authority and his appeal to ancient Roman morality and tradition, while in fact humorously undermining this position."

28. For general discussion of this speech, see Ayers (1954) 245–53, Nelson (1950) 65–9, Craig (1986), May (1988) 58–6, Alexander (2002) 121–7.

29. Cic. *Mur.* 60.

exiles, and indeed even insane; all crimes are equal; every defect is a wicked crime, nor does he commit any less a crime who throttles a rooster without need than he who strangles his father; the wise man supposes nothing, regrets nothing, errs in no matter, and never changes his mind. Marcus Cato, a most talented man, convinced by such erudite writers, has seized upon this learning, not for the sake of debate as most people do, but for the sake of living in this way.[30]

While Cicero's focus is on Zeno's teachings, the characterization of Cato is biting: he is not only unreasonable and unfair, but his dedication to justice is so extreme that it becomes unjust, and his refusal to compromise is presented as un-Roman. Cicero instructs the audience on the many ways these Stoic ideas could be faulty, and suggests that Cato would benefit from studying Platonic and Aristotelian philosophy, which allow for reconsideration, reflection, exceptions, and for a man to change his mind. He adds: "Cato, if some chance occurrence carried you, together with that nature of yours, to these teachers, you would not indeed become a better man, nor more resolute, nor more self-controlled, nor more just—for such you are not able to become—but you would become a little more favorably inclined towards mildness."[31] This is a friendly statement full of outward praise, but it contains a strong jab that probably exploits a wider recognition of Cato's extreme inflexibility. Cicero then suggests that Cato has been enflamed by his youthful studies, and needs time and age to mellow him. He instructs Cato that there are exceptions to every Stoic principle, and that the wise man needs to recognize that absolute convictions are not wise.[32] Cicero undermines him by saying his inflexible attitude is in direct contrast to ancestral tradition, and argues that Cato is actually endangering the Republic by allowing his uncompromising attitude to take precedence over national interest.[33] As a final shot, Cicero takes over Cato's own invocation of his great-grandfather, pointing to the elder Cato's sense of fairness and justice, saying:

> Cato, do you regard anyone to have been more pleasant, more courteous, and more orderly in all patterns of human feeling than your great-grandfather? . . . if you sprinkle his kindness and good nature on your

---

30. Cic. *Mur.* 61–2. See Fantham (2013) 168.

31. Cic. *Mur.* 64.

32. Cic. *Mur.* 64–6.

33. Cic. *Mur.* 75, 78.

seriousness and severity, these qualities of yours, which are now the best, will not become better, but certainly they will be made more agreeable.[34]

Cicero was here using the legend of Cato the Elder to undermine his great-grandson's reputation as an authority on the *mos maiorum*.[35] And by claiming (perhaps incorrectly) that Cato the Elder had been an affable and agreeable man, Cicero suggests that the famously inflexible Cato the Younger is not quite living up to his great-grandfather's reputation; the younger Cato's interpretation of the *mos maiorum* is not quite right.

We must, of course, allow that Cicero is trying to win his case here, and so he probably tailored his arguments to undercut Cato's influence and sway the jurors. Years later, he would even admit that he had played to the jurors when defending Murena.[36] This does not mean that what Cicero had said was a lie: the power of humor is the way it comments on the truth, and the picture Cicero paints of Cato is largely consistent with that of Plutarch and other authors: he was dedicated to the ideal of justice, but his inability to compromise, to make exceptions, and to revise his own thinking made him difficult as a friend and fearsome as an enemy. He was blind to his own shortcomings in this trial, and was causing the Republic to come into danger rather than yield his point. The speech also shows that Cato was familiar with Stoic principles and liked to use them in his oratory, but Cicero's ease at dismantling his prosecution suggests that Cato may not have had a full or nuanced understanding of Stoicism.[37] Despite Plutarch's statements that he was a devoted Stoic, Cato does not seem to have been able to deploy Stoic ideas to good effect, which is surprising given his high reputation as a great orator. Cicero once mentioned that Cato's style of oratory was unlike that of the Stoics (he thought Cato was a more effective speaker), which suggests that he adhered too closely to Roman practices to accept the Stoic style of rhetoric.[38] Cato—who was not eas-ygoing or forgiving—does not seem to have taken offense at Cicero's lambasting of Stoicism, which would seem strange if he had based his life around those Stoic principles that Cicero had publicly derided. His life was defined by his interpre-tation of the *mos maiorum*—and not by Greek philosophy—so Plutarch records

---

34. Cic. *Mur.* 66. See May (1988) 65–6, Bücher (2006) 264, van der Wal (2007) 188, and van der Blom (2010) 154–5.

35. Christopher Craig (1986) makes this point clearly. See also Treggiari (2003) 157.

36. Cic. *Fin.* 4.74.

37. See Craig (1986) 229–39.

38. Cic. *Parad.* 1–3. Donald Ayers (1954) 248 suggests that Cato was "too much a Roman" to follow Stoic principles closely.

that he just laughed off Cicero's attacks, calling him a humorous consul.[39] Cicero's speech proved very effective, and the jurors unanimously acquitted Murena.[40] In the end, his strategy was a success: he knew that Cato's attachment to Stoicism was not particularly deep, so the twisting of Stoic maxims would undermine Cato's arguments without offending him personally.

Cato had made a big splash with his broad threat to prosecute the winners of the consular election, but his effort to suppress bribery fell flat, and even backfired on him. It is likely that his threat had been aimed primarily at Catiline, since Silanus was family, Sulpicius was a famous scourge of electoral bribery, and there was no previous animosity between Cato and Murena.[41] When Silanus was elected consul, however, Cato was in an uncomfortable position, since he had to exempt his brother-in-law from his threat, which may have caused some tongues to wag about whether he was truly as dedicated to justice as he claimed. Many Romans would have understood the need to overlook the faults (and even crimes) of family members, but Cato's particular promotion of himself as the champion of traditional values made his inconsistent application of those values conspicuous.[42] Of course, Murena was not an ideal target either; he was supported by Lucullus and Cicero, and Catiline's insurrection had made Murena's acquittal a matter of national security. Another man would have let the matter drop, but Cato could not retreat from the position he had taken and the threat he had made. Constancy (*constantia*) was a traditional Roman virtue, and it was probably an essential quality for Cato, whose special status derived heavily from his moral authority. He no doubt felt that he could not abandon his threat of prosecution without damaging his *constantia* and *gravitas*. Yet his decision to take a secondary role (*subscriptor*) in the prosecution and to encourage Sulpicius to be the lead prosecutor may suggest a lack of enthusiasm for the prosecution, although it may also be that Sulpicius insisted on taking the leading role, since—as a defeated candidate—he had the most to gain from a successful conviction. Had Cato been less prone to taking inflexible positions, however, and more willing to compromise as situations changed, he might have avoided partaking in a prosecution that failed to receive a single vote from the jury.

---

39. Plut. *Cat. Min.* 21.5 (γελοῖον ὕπατον). See van der Wal (2007) 188–9.

40. Ayers ([1954] 253) suggests that Cato would have won the case had it not been for the danger posed by Catiline, and the need to have Murena in the consulship to defend Rome from Catiline's army.

41. Gruen ([1974] 130 n. 34) makes a good case for this interpretation.

42. Fantham (2003) 101, "another recurring aspect of Cato's politics was his inconsistency of principles where his kin were concerned."

Cato's Role in the Catilinarian Debate

Cato's most famous action as tribune-elect in 63 BC was certainly his speech in the Senate demanding the death penalty for P. Lentulus Sura and the other Catilinarian conspirators who had been captured in Rome.[43] After Catiline had fled the city, Cicero's careful administration had arrested these co-conspirators and had acquired clear evidence of their guilt. Cicero as consul had convinced the Senate of the conspirators' guilt, but he faced a dilemma: he wanted to restore peace in the city by executing the conspirators, but his magisterial authority did not empower him to ignore a citizen's right to appeal, or his right to a trial before the people. Of course, consuls had killed seditious (or at least dangerous) citizens without trial in the past, but only during times of national emergency when armed violence had broken out inside the city walls, and nothing of that sort had yet taken place under Cicero's watch. The Senate had already passed its so-called final decree—the *senatus consultum ultimum*—authorizing the consuls to take whatever steps were necessary to defend the Republic, but like all *senatus consulta*, this did not have legal weight and could not in itself protect Cicero from prosecution if he executed citizens illegally.[44] So Cicero wanted clear instructions and the full backing of the Senate—which he probably thought would transfer responsibility to the Senate as a whole—before he would order the execution of the conspirators. He therefore convened the Senate and, calling on the senators in order of seniority, he asked them what they thought should be done with Lentulus and the others.

The consul-elect D. Junius Silanus—the husband of Cato's half-sister Servilia—was the first to speak, and he is said to have advocated the "severest penalty," which he did not define, but was generally understood to be the death penalty.[45] The next senators whom Cicero called upon to speak all agreed with Silanus, and their *auctoritas* might have carried the discussion had it not been for Julius Caesar (Figure 3.3), who—when called upon as praetor-elect to speak—urged instead that the conspirators should merely be held in custody until such

---

43. For more on this debate, see: Sall. *Cat.* 50.1–53.1, Plut. *Cic.* 20.4–21.5, *Caes.* 7.5–8.3, *Cat. Min.* 22.1–23.3, Suet. *Iul.* 14.1–2, App. *BC* 2.5–7. Modern discussions include: McGushin (1987), Drummond (1995), Tannenbaum (2005) 209–23, Odahl (2010), and Levick (2015).

44. Sall. *Cat.* 29.2–3. See discussion in Drogula (2015) 121–5.

45. Sall. *Cat.* 50.4 (. . . *D. Iunius Silanus . . . supplicium sumundum decreverat . . .*) and App. *BC* 2.5 (τοὺς ἄνδρας ἐσχάτῃ κολάσει).

FIGURE 3.3. Green basalt bust of Gaius Julius Caesar, early 1st century AD, from Egypt. Altes Museum, Berlin.

Source: Shutterstock.

time as Catiline's military forces could be destroyed and the entire matter could be considered most carefully.[46] Caesar's speech was eloquent and effective; not only did those who spoke after him endorse his suggestion, but Silanus and those who had spoken before him changed their minds and supported incarceration over execution. Thus the *consulares* seem to have supported Silanus's initial proposal, but when the more numerous *praetores* (including Caesar) voiced opposition to his position, Silanus lost his nerve and sided with the growing majority.[47] This was possible because in 63 BC the *consulares* were not as numerous or influential as they usually were—their numbers had been greatly

---

46. Sall. *Cat.* 50.5–51.43, Suet. *Iul.* 14.1, Plut. *Caes.* 7.8–9, *Cic.* 21.1, *Cat. Min.* 22.4, Dio 37.36.1–2. Appian (*BC* 2.5) records that this opinion was first given by Ti. Claudius Nero (the grandfather of the future emperor Tiberius), but Drummond ([1995] 23–6) has argued that this is a mistake.

47. Ryan (1998) 318.

thinned by the Social War and the Civil War, so the senior leadership of the Senate was less able to influence the opinions and votes of their juniors. Some approved the humanity of Caesar's proposal, others did not want to become vulnerable to prosecution for executing citizens without trial, while still others feared that Caesar was secretly allied with the conspirators and might resort to violence to protect them. Without a strong bloc of *consulares* to unite the senators, a consensus was very difficult to reach. When Cicero saw that Caesar had dissuaded the senators from supporting execution, he interrupted the discussion to deliver what is now his fourth Catilinarian speech, which urged immediate action.[48] Yet this speech by Rome's great orator apparently failed to persuade the senators, and Caesar's suggestion continued to gain support. Then it was Cato's turn as tribune-elect to speak, and he gave a powerful oration calling for the execution of the conspirators. Velleius presents him as the first to speak against Caesar's proposal of leniency, but Plutarch in his biography of Cicero says that Catulus was the first to oppose Caesar's opinion, and that Cato followed and supported Catulus, which should be correct since one would expect a senior consular like Catulus to be called upon to speak before the tribune-elect Cato.[49] Whether or not Catulus spoke first, Cato's speech was so forceful that it won over the majority of the Senate, even those who had previously supported Caesar's more merciful suggestion. The *consulares* praised Cato's bravery, and Cicero put his motion to a vote. When the motion passed, Cicero had the conspirators put to death, and was hailed by his colleagues with the honorific title *pater patriae* ("father of the fatherland"). Cicero wrote that it was Catulus who first bestowed this title upon him, but later authors said it was Cato, which probably reflects their intention to build up his early importance and prominence in the Senate.[50] Another senator of consular rank—L. Gellius Publicola (cos. 72 BC)—proposed that Cicero should receive the civic crown for saving his country, and the Senate proposed a *supplicatio* in Cicero's honor.[51] Cato supported both motions.

---

48. Heyworth and Woodman ([1986] 11–2) and Pelling ([2011] 166–9) point out that the sequence of speakers in Sallust's account is strange, and suggest that Cicero's speech may have cut off a first round of speeches, and may have started a second round of speeches with the *consulares* speaking a second time.

49. Vell. 2.35.3, Plut. *Cic.* 21.4. Years later, Cicero would confirm that Cato was not the first to argue for the death penalty (Cic. *Att.* 12.21.1). See Odahl (2010) 66.

50. Cic. *Pis.* 6, *Sest.* 121, Plut. *Cic.* 23.6, App. *BC* 2.7.

51. Civic crown: Cic. *Pis.* 6, Gell. 5.6.15; *supplicatio*: Cic. *Sull.* 85, *Cat.* 3.15, 3.23, 4.5, *Pis.* 6; Cato supported *supplicatio*: Cic. *Fam.* 15.4.11.

Cato's success in arguing for the death penalty gained him immediate and increased status among the Senate, and his speech was recorded and widely read afterward. The speech was preserved because Cicero had trained a number of his clerks in a special kind of shorthand, and he had distributed several of them around the Senate House during the debate to record what was said.[52] Plutarch only summarized the content of Cato's speech, saying,

> Rising up, Cato immediately delivered his opinion in a speech full of wrath and passion, blaming Silanus for changing his mind, and accosting Caesar for overthrowing the state with feigned populism and humane speech, and for frightening the Senate in matters that he ought to fear. He said Caesar should be happy if he went away unpunished and unsuspected of the crimes that had been done, since he was clearly and hastily rescuing common enemies, and was admitting that he did not pity such an excellent and great state, which was close to falling into destruction, but he was weeping and wailing for those who ought never to have existed or been born, those who by dying would save the state from great slaughter and danger.[53]

This summary portrays the famous aggressiveness of Cato's rhetoric and the passion of his oratory, and it makes clear that he was just as interested in attacking Caesar as he was in arguing about the punishment of the conspirators. Indeed, Plutarch's text suggests that Caesar was the primary target of the speech, which was designed to implicate Caesar in the crime. Sallust, on the other hand, gives full versions of the speeches by Caesar and Cato in his history of the conspiracy, the *Bellum Catilinae*. He no doubt consulted the notes taken by Cicero's clerks when he crafted his own version of the speeches—the only version that survives—and

---

52. Plut. *Cat. Min.* 23.3.

53. Plut. *Cat. Min.* 23.1–2. Pelling ([2002] 62) discusses the details of Cato's speech as preserved by Plutarch, who refers to the Catilinarian debate in four of his biographies (those on Cicero, Caesar, Cato, and Crassus). Pelling ([1985] 311–29) has demonstrated that Plutarch tailored his presentation of the conspiracy in each biography to best develop the particular themes he wished to explore in the examination of each man's life. Pelling notes (326–7) that Plutarch "is much more interested in his moralizing, in painting his picture of the unbending political sage," and so "Cato emerges from that story as the champion of morality, with contempt for the despicable Caesar. The whole Catilinarian story is transmuted to a moral fable, for that is what the texture of the Life requires." Duff ([1999] 136) likewise observes that Plutarch's narrative here ". . . is shaped not towards a historical understanding of its causes, but towards a moral tableau, in which Cato is the hero and Caesar the villain." Taking Plutarch's moralizing program into account, however, the basic facts he presents about the Senate's debate over the Catilinarian conspirators are largely consistent with Sallust's account.

he certainly took liberties in writing them to highlight his own opinions about the natures and characters of the two speakers. Modern scholars have questioned whether this version of Cato's speech is more Catonian or more Sallustian, but the increasing consensus is that Sallust modified the speech significantly to better fit the themes he wanted to explore.[54] With this caution, the text of the speech is still very useful for understanding how Cato was viewed by his contemporaries.

Cato begins the speech by chastising the senators for taking the time to debate the punishment of the captives instead of simply punishing them, and for caring more about their wealth and possessions than about the security of their lives and freedom.[55] He complains that they are being too soft and liberal with those who mean them harm.[56] He attacks Caesar's recommendation of gentleness and mercy, complaining that it will bring the state into greater danger.[57] He characterizes Caesar's plan as foolish and perhaps seditious, and he appeals to the senators to think of their history and tradition, and rails against the moral decline he sees in the state.[58] He emphasizes the imminent destruction facing them, and says that the gods will not help them unless they help themselves.[59] He reminds them that their national hero T. Aulus Manlius Torquatus (cos. 347 and 344 BC) executed his own excellent son for disobeying military orders even though his disobedience had brought glory and advantage to his army, and he urges the senators to be no less zealous in putting to death confessed traitors who—he says—have never benefited the Republic.[60] He closes with the appeal that their imminent danger required the swift and assertive execution of the conspirators.[61] In this last part of his speech, Cato (or perhaps Sallust) exaggerates and even lies in order to push the senators into action: he claims that Catiline was at their throats, and that the captured conspirators had confessed to planning murder, arson, and other crimes. In truth, Catiline's force was far off and on the verge of being crushed by two larger state armies, and the conspirators are not recorded as having confessed

---

54. For example, see: Nelson (1950) 67, McGushin (1977) 239, Drummond (1995) 40–1, 51–9, Levene (2000) 170–91, Tannenbaum (2005) 209–23, Sklenár (1998) 205–20, Toher (2009) 226, Rosenstein (2010) 378–9, Connolly (2012) 121.

55. Sall. *Cat.* 52.2–9.

56. Sall. *Cat.* 52.10–2.

57. Sall. *Cat.* 52.13–5.

58. Sall. *Cat.* 52.16–23.

59. Sall. *Cat.* 52.24–9.

60. Sall. *Cat.* 52.30–4.

61. Sall. *Cat.* 52.35–6.

as Cato asserted.[62] As a result, Cato is presented as having a weak argument, but winning the debate by playing on the fears of the senators.[63] Whether these misrepresentations really happened or not, he is presented as galvanizing the Senate into action: he shames his audience for their departure from the ancestral customs which he represents, he presents the current debate as a dilemma between (only) two extreme positions, he avoids any discussion of compromise or a middle ground, and he employs scare tactics by presenting the state under threat of imminent destruction. These tactics succeeded in pushing the senators together into a consensus that the conspirators must be executed immediately. While much of this speech may be the work of Sallust's hand, Cato would repeatedly make use of these same rhetorical devices during his career, deftly pushing various factions of senators to come together behind certain policies.

As Sallust presents them, the contrast between Caesar's speech and Cato's speech is striking, although one must bear in mind that Sallust had supported Caesar during the civil war. Whereas Caesar is presented as urging the senators to act with calm and thoughtful rationalism—he argued that "when you assert the intellect, it prevails; if impulsiveness takes hold, it becomes master, and the mind achieves nothing"[64]—Cato's speech is reactionary and moralist in tone, urging decisive action instead of careful reflection. Both men appeal to the *mos maiorum* for support of their proposals, but whereas Caesar reminds the audience of Rome's traditional clemency in dealing with defeated enemies,[65] Cato recalled Manlius Torquatus's execution of his own son, which seems a weak and morally questionable example. While Cato insists that executing the conspirators is consistent with tradition (*more maiorum supplicium sumundum*), Caesar calls such a sentence alien to the Republic and a new type of punishment (*aliena a re publica nostra . . . genus poenae novum*).[66] Thus both men present their proposals as being consistent with tradition. Just as Cicero had claimed to understand ancestral tradition better than Cato in Murena's trial, Caesar in the Catilinarian debate argues for his own interpretation of the *mos maiorum*, which (he argued) does not allow for the execution of citizens without trial.[67] This draws an important

---

62. A point that Drummond ([1995] 75–6) establishes clearly.

63. Drummond ([1995] 77) suggests Cato won the argument because of: "senatorial susceptibility to emotional appeal and to arguments based on self-interest rather than high policy."

64. Sall. *Cat.* 51.3.

65. Sall. *Cat.* 51.4–8.

66. Sall. *Cat.* 52.36 and 51.17–8.

67. As Sklenár ([1998] 217 and 218) suggests: "if Caesar is right, then *mos maiorum* requires a policy of humane rationalism; if Cato is right, then it requires the severest possible punishment

distinction between the two positions: Caesar is arguing that the law forbidding the summary execution of citizens without trial should be obeyed, whereas Cato is trying to convince the senators to violate this law and commit an illegal act that (he argues) is for the good of the state.[68] This reveals how Cato's adherence to law, justice, and tradition could be flexible according to his own interpretation of what was good for the Republic and for his own status as a leader; as quaestor he had sought to punish Sulla's henchmen who had executed fellow citizens under the authority of the dictator, but he now argued that the right of appeal should be ignored to execute citizens who had conspired against the state. In his mind, the law needed to be set aside in order to pursue his policy for maintaining the integrity of the Senate and the state. So his performance in this case was entirely consistent with his own construal of the *mos maiorum*, but this was not necessarily the same as other men's understanding of tradition. He was not simply a conservative; he deliberately chose which values he would champion, which he would emphasize less, and which he would ignore in order to achieve his goals. Sallust illustrates this by noting that Caesar cited as support for his argument the clemency shown by Rome to the Rhodians in the Third Macedonian War—a clemency that Cato the Elder championed powerfully in a famous speech that was preserved and long remembered.[69] Thus Caesar is shown as following the example of Cato the Elder, while Cato the Younger is made to argue against his great-grandfather's example—a clear violation of the *mos maiorum*, but one that suited Cato's immediate goals. This reveals the nuance in Cato's thinking and identity, and it explains why he could absolutely refuse to deviate from the values that suited his goals (such as prosecuting Murena in a time of war), and yet make exceptions to those same values if it suited him (such as supporting the execution of citizens without a trial).

Cato's success in single-handedly changing the direction of the Senate's discussion—and changing the minds of more senior men who had already stated their support for Caesar's motion—reflects the influence he wielded. Normally such consensus formed around consular senators, who commanded the influence and authority to demand the deference of junior senators, so it was surprising that a mere tribune-elect could move senatorial opinion so effectively. To be sure, Cato's skillful and powerful oratory did much to sway the senators, but rhetorical

---

of any transgression," and "Cato's proposal harkens back to the policy of the *maiores* in war, Caesar's to their policy in peacetime."

68. Pina Polo ([2006] 95–6) makes this point well.

69. Sall. *Cat.* 51.5. Gellius (6.3.7) notes that Cato the Elder's speech on behalf of the Rhodians was published and available. See Levene (2000) 184–5.

brilliance alone cannot explain the effect his speech had on the senators, since Caesar was every bit as good an orator. Even Cicero—Rome's most famous orator—had been unable to turn the debate against Caesar despite using the consular bully pulpit to deliver his fourth Catilinarian speech, so it is unlikely that oratory alone explains Cato's success. Sallust is probably right that he manipulated the fears of the senators with false claims about Catiline's advance and the confession of the conspirators, but there were also other forces working on the senators in this debate that help explain the course of the discussion. First, Caesar's argument against capital punishment without trial probably carried an unspoken threat: senators *would* be held liable for their support of an illegal action.[70] Caesar was praetor-elect, which meant he would preside over one of Rome's courts in the coming year, and he had already made a name for himself prosecuting those who had executed fellow citizens during Sulla's dictatorship—he even dwelt on the brutality of Sulla's proscriptions in his speech, perhaps to remind the senators of the recent condemnation of Sulla's henchmen.[71] Caesar's speech may have sounded to the senators present like a threat of prosecution under a hostile judge, but Cato's powerful counterargument seems to have stiffened their resolve, and excited their fears that they may not even live to see the next year if they did not take the hardest line possible by executing Catiline's confederates. Many senators may have supported Silanus's original proposal for execution, but Caesar's speech made them waver and fear prosecution until Cato took such a strong stand. In this way, Cato made himself a rallying point for those who wished to vote for summary execution, enabling a critical mass of senators to come together.

Second, some worried that Caesar and other notable senators (especially M. Licinius Crassus; Figure 3.4) were sympathetic to Catiline and were even in league with him. Later authors report a rumor—which may or may not have been current at the time of the Catilinarian debate—that Caesar, Crassus, and Catiline had formed an earlier plot to overthrow the government in 65 BC, although that plan had been aborted at the last minute.[72] There was no evidence to support the rumor of this so-called First Catilinarian Conspiracy, and such a plot would have been contrary to the interests of all three men in 65 BC: Caesar was optimistically spending vast amounts of money as curule aedile to secure his advancement to higher offices, Catiline fully expected (at that time) to win a consulship and use it

---

70. Sall. *Cat.* 51.21–7. See Drummond (1995) 115–6.

71. Sall. *Cat.* 51.32–4.

72. Ascon. 83, Suet. *Iul.* 9.1–3. See also: Cic. *Cat.* 1.15, *Mur.* 81. For a full discussion of this conspiracy, see: Seager (1964) 338–47, Syme (1964) 89–96, Gruen (1969), McGushin (1987) 26–31, Odahl (2010) 22–5, Levick (2015) 35–40.

FIGURE 3.4. Bust of Marcus Licinius Crassus, Augustan copy of a late 1st century BC original, Louvre, Paris.
Source: Wikipedia.

to pay back his debts, and Crassus was already a *consularis* and one of the richest and most influential men in Rome, and his investments would have been seriously endangered by revolution. All three men, therefore, would have been uninterested in a disruption of the *status quo* in 65 BC, so what was the origin of this story? It may well have been a fabrication by certain senators eager to discredit Crassus and Caesar as well as Catiline, which coincides with other simultaneous efforts by Cato and Catulus to incriminate Caesar in the conspiracy (see later discussion).[73] Given Cato's central role in trying to incriminate Caesar during the Catilinarian debate, it is possible that he was involved in spreading the rumors about an earlier conspiracy, hoping they would result in the condemnation of Caesar (and perhaps Crassus) along with Catiline. Just as Cato seems to have exaggerated the immediacy of the danger posed by Catiline and his allies in order to push the Senate into voting for the death sentence, he may also have used false

---

73. Marshall ([1976] 68 and 71) makes this suggestion.

rumors about Caesar and Crassus to implicate them in the plot. Whether or not a plot had existed in 65 BC, senators at the end of 63 BC had probably heard rumors about it, and Cato would try to use the rumor to attack Caesar.

The Catilinarian conspiracy was a serious threat to the state, but Cato and several other senators also saw it as an opportunity to destroy Caesar. Before the Senate met to debate the fate of the apprehended conspirators, Catulus and C. Calpurnius Piso (cos. 67 BC) are said to have approached Cicero secretly and asked him to incriminate Caesar falsely in the conspiracy.[74] Driven by personal enmities, they used entreaties, influence, and bribes in their efforts to persuade Cicero to include Caesar's name in the evidence that had been collected against the conspirators, but the consul refused. Both of these men had personal grudges against Caesar: earlier in the year he had defeated Catulus in the election to become *pontifex maximus*, and he had accused Piso of unjustly executing an inhabitant of Transpadine Gaul when governor of that province. When Cicero refused participate in the plot, Catulus and Piso sought to inflame hostility against Caesar by spreading rumors that the witnesses had named him among the conspirators.[75] Cato is not named as part of this initial effort to influence Cicero, but he may well have been involved, since he is shortly afterward found helping Catulus to implicate Caesar falsely in the conspiracy. During the Senate's debate, Catulus and Cato worked together to oppose Caesar's speech about the Catilinarians, and Cato is said to have tried to implicate Caesar in the crime.[76] Part of his effort to incriminate Caesar is found in his speech. Responding to Caesar's suggestion that the conspirators be imprisoned in fortified towns, Cato replied:

> As if, moreover, evil and wicked men were only in the city and not throughout the whole of Italy, or as if boldness was not more capable of action where the resources for suppressing it were the smallest! Therefore this counsel is truly pointless if he [Caesar] fears danger from them, but if he alone is not afraid amid such great fear of all, then it is all the more important for me to fear for myself and for you all.[77]

Here he openly suggests that Caesar was seeking to prevent the execution of the conspirators because he was himself a part of their plot, and thus had no fear of

---

74. Sall. *Cat.* 49.1–4.

75. Sall. *Cat.* 49.4. See Stanton and Marshall (1975) 208.

76. Plutarch (*Caes.* 8.1–2, *Cic.* 21.4) is explicit that Cato tried to implicate Caesar.

77. Sall. *Cat.* 52.15–6.

whatever evil they were planning. Cato was so anxious to implicate Caesar that he took the gamble of pouncing when he saw a note being handed to Caesar. He rashly accused Caesar of receiving treasonous communications in the middle of a Senate meeting and demanded that he read the note aloud, hoping it would make him look guilty, or that he might refuse, which would also seem incriminating. This tactic famously backfired when the letter turned out to be a love letter to Caesar from Cato's own half-sister, Servilia the Elder, wife of the consul-elect Silanus.[78] While this event was certainly humorous, it highlights how desperate Cato was to destroy Caesar. Indeed, the efforts to incriminate Caesar almost succeeded: when a group of Roman knights guarding the Senate House heard these false rumors, they drew their swords and very nearly executed Caesar on the spot, and it was only Cicero's intervention that prevented the murder.[79]

What makes these attacks by Cato, Catulus, and Piso so shocking is that Caesar was—for the most part—innocent of any participation in the Catilinarian conspiracy. He certainly had acquired some knowledge about the plot, but he had rejected its goals and had assisted in the arrest of the conspirators. Cicero himself—who was willing and eager to execute the conspirators—testified in the Senate that Caesar and Crassus had each brought him information that was critical to proving the existence of the conspiracy to the skeptical senators.[80] Crassus had received anonymous letters warning of the impending attack that he had passed on to Cicero, while Caesar had probably been asked to join the conspiracy, but had decided against it because his own political future looked bright.[81] Cicero further demonstrated his confidence in Caesar and Crassus by trusting both of them to hold captured conspirators in custody.[82] Still, doubt and paranoia certainly disturbed everyone in the Senate, and suspicion about them lingered.[83] L. Tarquinius had accused Crassus of involvement, but the senators

---

78. Plut. *Cat. Min.* 24.1–2, *Brut.* 5.3–4.

79. Sall. *Cat.* 49.4, Suet. *Iul.* 14.2, Plut. *Caes.* 8.2–3.

80. Plutarch (*Cic.* 20.7) reports rumors that Cicero suspected Caesar's involvement, but was unable to prove it and so omitted his name from the accusations.

81. Suet. *Iul.* 17.2; Plut. *Crass.* 13.3, *Cic.* 15.1–2, and Dio 37.31.1. McDermott ([1949] 362) suggested that Caesar refused to get involved with the conspiracy himself, but urged an acquaintance to get involved in order to gather information.

82. Sall. *Cat.* 47.4.

83. Sall. *Cat.* 48.5–6. Twenty years later, after Caesar and Crassus were both dead, Cicero wrote in works that are now lost that he had suspected that Caesar had been a member of the conspiracy, but had kept silent, fearing Caesar's popularity with the people (Plut. *Cic.* 20.7, *Caes.* 8.4–5, *Crass.* 13.2–3, App. *BC* 2.6). Cicero may have suspected Caesar and Crassus back in 63 BC but chose to ignore their guilt in order to ensure the stability of the state, or his memories

disregarded the charge, either out of disbelief, or because they did not wish to provoke such a powerful man who was now clearly cooperating with the government.[84] Cato's accusation against Caesar, however, seems to have carried more influence, perhaps because of Cato's effective rhetoric, and perhaps because Caesar was not yet seen as a dangerous opponent, and therefore an easier target. This was demonstrated after the Senate meeting: while most of Cicero's other informants were thanked and rewarded for bringing evidence to light, and Cicero was hailed *pater patriae*, no rewards or thanks were given to Crassus and Caesar for bringing evidence to light, and Caesar was nearly killed for his efforts. Cato and others exploited this suspicion and tried to implicate Caesar in the conspiracy, which would have carried fatal consequences had they been successful.

Since Caesar was not involved in Catiline's conspiracy (or at least, there was no evidence of his involvement), these efforts to implicate him need further consideration. Cato certainly had several political reasons to dislike Caesar: he employed *popularis* tactics, he had stolen some of Cato's thunder by prosecuting Sulla's henchmen, and he was a political ally and vocal supporter of Pompey, with whom Cato had several personal and political grievances. More important, he also had compelling personal reasons for despising and even hating Caesar, who was carrying on an extramarital love affair with Cato's half-sister Servilia, causing a rumor to circulate that Caesar was really the father of Servilia's son Brutus (Cato's beloved nephew), and an even worse rumor that she was prostituting her daughter Tertia to Caesar.[85] It is also possible that Cato had resented (or had been jealous of) the fact that his uncle Mamercus had helped Caesar as a youth, protecting him from Sulla's wrath.[86] More fundamentally, he may have simply resented Caesar for his talents: Caesar was a patrician and claimed descent from Aeneas and the goddess Venus, he was very intelligent, witty, and urbane, he attracted the loyalty of important men and the love of respected women, he had the support of the Roman people and had beaten senior senators to become *pontifex maximus*. Caesar was a man of tremendous capacity, talent, and skill, and Cato may have hated him for it. For some or all of these reasons—and perhaps for reasons from their early years that we cannot recover—Cato held a deep and personal feud with Caesar that spilled over into the political arena. Feuds between families and individuals were common among the Roman aristocracy,

---

and opinions of them may have been altered by the tumultuous events of the intervening twenty years.

84. Stanton and Marshall (1975) 208.

85. Suet. *Iul.* 50.2, Plut. *Brut.* 5.2. Epstein (1987) 64–5 and 80–9.

86. Suet. *Iul.* 1.2.

and the younger members of such families were expected to pursue the enmities of their fathers.[87] If anything, feuds of this type became more intense and dangerous during the late Republic, with rivals attacking each other much more violently than had been the case in the days of the elder Cato.[88] Thus Cato was not merely mimicking his great-grandfather's feud with the Scipionic clan; he was importing the tremendous violence and hatred that had come to mark his own era in the late Republic, and was willing to take extreme steps to attack Caesar. Whether Caesar felt the same way and saw himself as being in a feud with Cato is unclear; he cannot have missed the obvious animosity, but he does not seem to have responded in kind at the time, although he would soon lash out at Catulus, whom he may have seen as the more dangerous political opponent. Cato proved a relentless opponent when Caesar was praetor (62 BC) and consul (59 BC), but otherwise Caesar was away from Rome on military commands, so he may have viewed Cato as an excessively tenacious political antagonist rather than as a personal enemy. Cato's feud with Caesar was clearly a driving force behind his actions, and highlights the role of personal animosity in Roman politics, explaining why he would try to have Caesar executed for a crime he did not commit.

At the same time, Cato's opposition to Caesar was also political. While he must have realized that Caesar was not criminally involved in the conspiracy, he probably believed that Caesar was the type of man whose ambition and egotism could bring the Republic to harm. Caesar had given many indications that he was very ambitious, and that he would use *popularis* methods in his efforts to climb the political ladder. As quaestor in 69 BC he had advertised his family's *popularis* traditions by arranging elaborate funerals for his aunt Julia (the widow of Gaius Marius) and his wife Cornelia (the daughter of Cinna), and as a part of these ceremonies he used images of Marius—the famous *popularis*—that had been banned by Sulla.[89] After his quaestorship Caesar was a vocal supporter of the *lex Gabinia* and the *lex Manilia*, *popularis* legislation that gave Pompey his two greatest commands in the face of the strong opposition by the senatorial elite.[90] As curule aedile in 65 BC Caesar had borrowed enormous sums to provide lavish public games for the people, during which he restored to public display Marius's

---

87. Syme ([1939] 157) referred to an aristocrat's participation in such a feud as "a sacred duty or an occasion of just pride." See also Epstein (1987) 64–89 and Fantham (2003) 101 for discussion.

88. Raaflaub (2003) 46–7.

89. Suet. *Iul.* 6.1, Plut. *Caes.* 5.1–5.

90. Plut. *Pomp* 25.4.

trophies (which Sulla had removed).[91] While aedile, Caesar may have been in-volved in an attempt to promulgate legislation giving Crassus a special command to annex the kingdom of Egypt (which Catulus and the *optimates* opposed), and his prosecution of Sulla's henchmen had been considered by some as an attack on the Senate's leadership (who had generally benefited from Sulla's purges), al-though he was rumored to have helped Catiline escape punishment for his role in these murders.[92] Finally, in 63 BC—only months before the debate over the Catilinarian conspirators—Caesar pulled off the remarkable coup of defeating the senior senators Q. Lutatius Catulus (cos. 78 BC) and P. Servilius Isauricus (cos. 79 BC) in the election for *pontifex maximus*.[93] Caesar had used *popularis* legislation to achieve this: when the priesthood became vacant in 63 BC, he had the plebeian tribune T. Labienus (his future legate in Gaul) promulgate a law transferring the election of priests to the popular assembly, where Caesar's popu-larity and extensive use of bribery ensured his victory.[94] This tampering with the priesthoods surely enraged many in the Senate's conservative leadership, and the fact that the junior senator Caesar (who held only aedilician rank) was chosen over two of the most respected men in the Senate would have been a deep in-sult and a violation of the principles championed by the *optimates*. Indeed, one might even wonder whether Cato's effort to implicate Caesar in the Catilinarian Conspiracy was an attempt to vacate the office of *pontifex maximus*, forcing an-other election in which Catulus would be favored. So in the eyes of Cato and other *optimates* who wanted to protect the traditional, aristocratic system of politics that privileged the current Senate leadership, Caesar was an ambitious senator who was willing to use *popularis* tactics if necessary to achieve his own personal goals. While some might have been willing to harness Caesar's ambition by finding a way to pull him into their fold and use his undeniable talents, Cato and others seem to have decided that it was safer to remove him preemptively if they could.

In Cato's eyes, Caesar had all the markings of being another, more dangerous Catiline: he had probably supported Catiline in his original campaign for the

---

91. Vell. 2.43.4, Suet. *Iul.* 10.1, Plut. *Caes.* 5.9.

92. On Egypt: Suet. *Iul.* 11.1, Plut. *Crass.* 13.1. On the prosecutions: Ascon. 90–91, Dio 37.10.2–3. See Marshall (1976) 73–4.

93. Sall. *Cat.* 49.2, Vell. 2.43.3, Suet. *Iul.* 13.1, Plut. *Caes.* 7.1–4.

94. Dio 37.37.1–2. Originally, Roman priests were selected by co-option—members of a priestly college selected men to fill vacancies in their college. In 104 BC, the tribune Cn. Domitius Ahenobarbus (cos. 96 BC) had promulgated a law giving the selection of priests over to election by seventeen tribes, but this had been reversed by Sulla in 81 BC (*MRR* 1.559 and 2.75). Labienus annulled Sulla's action, restoring the legislation of Domitius.

consulship, he was greatly in debt, his family was ancient and noble, but currently impoverished because his paternal line had not achieved the consulship for many decades.[95] Like Catiline, Caesar was in a difficult situation: if he did not reach the consulship and receive a lucrative command, his debts would crush his family, sending it into permanent obscurity. Cato could understand all of this, and saw in Caesar a very dangerous man who needed to be suppressed. Indeed, Cato and Caesar as young men had been in similarly precarious situations, but whereas Cato had chosen to climb the political ladder by associating himself closely with conservative tradition, Caesar had proven willing to use *popularis* tactics to achieve his goals. To such a person, Cato was willing to offer no leniency or consideration. In his defense of Murena, Cicero had criticized Cato's tendency to equate misdemeanors and capital crimes, to divide humans into good and bad people, and to act on his decisions without remorse. This seems to have been an accurate assessment: Cato had called for the preemptive execution of the Catilinarian conspirators, rationalizing it by arguing that those who were guilty of planning capital crimes could be treated as if they had actually committed those crimes, and should be executed in accordance with ancestral custom.[96] Such a view was sharply different from the argument Cato the Elder had put forward in his famous speech on behalf of the Rhodians, when he argued that people who had wished to commit an offense, but had not actually done so, should not be punished.[97] Yet this departure from his great-grandfather's example should not be too surprising, since his particular interpretation of the *mos maiorum* was not intended to represent his ancestor's era, or any particular era. He was engaging with—and manipulating—the broad idea of the *mos maiorum*, which allowed him to pick and choose those ideas, values, or practices that resonated with him and with his fellow Romans. In this case, he put aside his great-grandfather's clemency (for which Caesar was arguing), and instead emphasized the mercilessness of Manlius Torquatus. To Cato, therefore, believing that Caesar might one day threaten the state may have provided sufficient justification for him to act as if Caesar had already attacked the state.

The sources are clear that Cato and others tried to use the crisis caused by the Catilinarian conspiracy to do away with Caesar, but Cicero prevented them from achieving this aim. Cicero was shrewd and well informed; Caesar's early

---

95. Asconius (83) records Caesar's support for Catiline's consular campaign. See Salmon (1935) 302–16 and Odahl (2010) 22–5. On Caesar's debt, see Ferrill (1978) 169–77.

96. Sall. *Cat.* 52.36. See Drummond (1995) 75–7.

97. Cornell F88–93 (= Peter F95b–g), Gell. 6.3.36–8 and 48–51. See Canfora (2007) 58 and Cornell (2013) 143–5.

knowledge of the conspiracy suggested some level of involvement, but his action in conveying that information to Cicero demonstrated that he wanted no part of the plot. While Caesar's popularity among the citizenry may have made Cicero afraid to accuse him, it is likely that—in his eyes—Caesar's knowledge of the conspiracy did not rise to the level of a crime, and his conveyance of that knowledge to Cicero indicated sound, patriotic judgment.[98] Unlike Catulus, Piso, and Cato, who had personal reasons for hating Caesar, Cicero bore him no ill will. And unlike Cato, whose character and feud with Caesar allowed no flexibility or concession, Cicero was willing to compromise and see that there were exceptions to every rule. Although he nervously watched Caesar's rise up the *cursus honorum*, Cicero generally thought it better to tolerate and guide the ambitions of Rome's greatest men; three years later he would write that this was his intention, and that he expected that he could help Caesar become a better citizen.[99] Thus Cicero viewed him as a "man in progress" whose character and activities could be influenced for the better or worse by those around him, whereas Cato saw him as a certain and manifest enemy whose bad character was established and fixed. Despite Cicero's seniority in the Senate, however, he was a *novus homo* (a "new man" with undistinguished ancestors), so he and his political thinking were not warmly received by the great *nobiles*, who preferred Cato's better ancestry and his fiery championing of the *mos maiorum*. As a consequence, Cato brought his feud with Caesar firmly into the thinking of the *optimates*. Indeed, his personal animosity for Caesar may have shaped the way many *optimates* viewed him.

Cato failed to implicate Caesar in the plot, but his powerful speech urging the execution of the Catilinarian conspirators was otherwise a success that increased his standing in the Senate. His unique contribution was not to propose or popularize the sentence of death—Silanus, the very first speaker, had proposed this sentence, and it had been widely supported until Caesar's speech. Cicero later stated that he called for a vote on Cato's proposal not because he was the first one to call for execution of the conspirators, but because it was the most effective and best-worded proposal.[100] But as events demonstrated, Cato's speech was critical because Silanus had backed down to Caesar in the debate.[101] If Silanus had maintained his proposal for execution, Cato would merely have been one of the speakers who supported the proposal, but when Silanus changed his position

---

98. Plut. *Cic.* 20.7.

99. Cic. *Att.* 2.1.6–7 (see later discussion). See Spielvogel (1993) 111–28.

100. Cic. *Att.* 12.21.1. See discussion in Ryan (1998) 318.

101. Ryan (1998) 318.

in the face of Caesar's challenge, it was left to Cato to champion the call for execution. Despite his relatively low rank as tribune-elect, he was able to stiffen
the backbones of the senators, and to frighten, encourage, or shame them into
maintaining their original hard line.[102] There were certainly factions within the
Senate, but they tended to be organized by families and clans rather than by political platforms, and therefore alliances were normally fluid, depending upon
the topic under debate. In this debate, Cato used exhortation, shame, and fear
tactics to push those factions into clustering together for safety, drawing them
into a consensus backing the consul's intention to execute the conspirators. Cato
pushed the Senate to give Cicero what he wanted: its full support in ordering
the execution of high-ranking citizens without trial. Indeed, Cato's speech was so
instrumental to galvanizing the Senate into action that he received most of the
credit for suppressing the conspirators in Rome. Although Cicero had gathered
the evidence, driven Catiline from the city, managed everything well, and ordered the execution of the conspirators (and paid the price for it later), it was
Cato who was remembered as the hero of the hour. Two decades later, after Cato's
death, Cicero complained bitterly to his friend Atticus that M. Junius Brutus had
written an encomium praising Cato and giving him—instead of Cicero—full
credit for rousing the Senate into action against Catiline's supporters. Cicero
complained to Atticus that Brutus was seriously overstating Cato's role in the
affair, and asked him to intervene and to urge Brutus to revise his work so that
it was Cicero's diplomatic handling of the affair—rather than Cato's fiery speech
to the Senate—that was remembered as saving Rome.[103] Sallust would paint the
same picture, depicting Cato's speech as the essential catalyst that galvanized the
senators into executing the conspirators. Cicero worked tirelessly to reveal the
plot and catch the conspirators red-handed, but it was Cato who had unified the
senators behind a single course of action.

The suspicions of Caesar's involvement in the conspiracy—which Cato
and his circle had fanned into a flame—lingered into the following year, when
Novius Niger was appointed special commissioner (*iudex quaestionis*) to investigate other persons who had been implicated in Catiline's conspiracy. Two men
came forward to accuse Caesar: Q. Curius and L. Vettius, who had initially been
members of Catiline's conspiracy, but had turned informers and betrayed the plot
to Cicero.[104] Curius declared that Catiline had named Caesar as a member of the

---

102. Suetonius (*Iul.* 14.2) says Cato kept the wavering Senate in line.

103. Cic. *Att.* 12.21.1.

104. Cic. *Att.* 2.24.2, Suet. *Iul.* 17.1–2, Dio 37.41.2–4. See McDermott (1949) 351 for discussion
of Vettius.

conspiracy, and Vettius claimed he had a letter to Catiline in Caesar's handwriting. Apparently, both claims were groundless, since Cicero himself had testified that Caesar had given him advance warning of the plot. Both conspirators were ruined as a result of their false charge: Curius was forced to forfeit the bounty he had received for betraying the Catilinarians to Cicero, and Vettius forfeited the bond he had produced when making the accusation. Caesar—who was now the urban praetor—then imprisoned Vettius and even the special commissioner Niger, because he had allowed a senior magistrate to be indicted. While it is certainly possible that Curius and Vettius believed in the accusations they made (but could not prove) against Caesar, it is perhaps equally likely that they were induced to make their false accusations by some unseen paymaster. Both men were notorious: the censors had removed Curius from the Senate on account of his crimes and immorality, while Vettius seems to have made a living as an informer and false accuser—three years later he falsely accused several important senators of plotting to murder Pompey.[105] Who hired these two informants? Although no evidence survives, it does not seem a stretch of the imagination to suspect that it was one or more of the men who had previously tried to implicate Caesar in the Catilinarian conspiracy. Caesar had certainly made a number of enemies, so any number of people might have wished to see him disgraced and punished. It certainly took some daring to accuse a sitting praetor with such weak evidence, although the accusers may not have expected Cicero to come to Caesar's defense. Still, this attack suggests that powerful men had identified Caesar as an enemy to be destroyed, and Cato was clearly one of the loudest voices declaring his guilt.

Cato the Tribune

Shortly after he entered office on December 10 in 63 BC,[106] Cato introduced legislation to reduce the price of grain in Rome. Although the measure is often referred to as a *lex frumentaria*, it may have been a senatorial resolution (a *senatus consultum* or *SC*) passed by the Senate upon his motion, rather than a piece of legislation passed by the Plebeian Assembly (over which the tribunes preside).[107]

---

105. Curius: Sall. *Cat.* 23.1–2. Vettius: Cic. *Att.* 2.24.2–5, *Vat.* 24–26, *Sest.* 132, Suet. *Iul.* 20.5, Dio 38.9.2–4, Plut. *Luc.* 42.7–8. See McDermott (1949) 351–67, Allen (1950) 153–63, Meier (1961) 68–98, Seager (1965) 519–31.

106. Pelling ([2011] 173) discusses the date on which Cato entered the tribunate.

107. Rotondi ([1912] 384) was also cautious about defining this bill as a *lex Porcia frumentaria*, but Cato is generally accepted as the author. Cristofori ([2002] 148–9) identifies it as a *senatus consultum*.

Plutarch describes this legislation in his biographies of Cato and of Caesar, and in his *Precepts of Statecraft* in his *Moralia*:

> Those in Lentulus' group were executed, and in response to the allegations and charges made against him in the Senate, Caesar fell back upon the people for support, and he was stirring up many depraved and miserable parts of the citizenry and attaching them to himself. Cato was frightened and persuaded the Senate to include the poor and dispossessed mob in the grain allowance, the cost of which was twelve hundred and fifty talents, and through this benevolence and favor the threats were notably brought to an end. (*Life of Cato*)

> Wherefore Cato, fearing most of all a revolution by the poor citizens who—having hopes in Caesar—were inciting the entire multitude, persuaded the Senate to assign to them a monthly grain allowance, on account of which expense an annual seven million and five hundred thousand drachmas were added to the other government expenditures. Nevertheless, this measure clearly extinguished the great fear of the present moment, and it broke and scattered the greatest part of Caesar's power at the right time, since he was about to become praetor and would be more formidable on account of that office. (*Life of Caesar*)

> And Cato, seeing the people being thrown into great confusion by Caesar regarding the business surrounding Catiline and the people being dangerously close to rebellion against the government, persuaded the Senate to vote for grain distributions for the poor citizens, and this being done it ended the uproar and stopped the uprising.[108] (*Moralia*)

This type of proposal was a traditional *popularis* tactic because the distribution of cheap or free grain normally indebted the people to the tribune who promulgated the bill, thereby enhancing his personal power and public support. Yet Cato used this tactic in a way that was consistent with traditional conservative policy, namely by using the action to strengthen the influence of the Senate as a whole. Whereas *popularis* tactics generally ignored the Senate altogether when promulgating such legislation, Cato acted in a traditionally proper way by first bringing his proposal to the Senate for its review and approval. The preceding passages indicate that the Senate gave its approval to the measure, no doubt

---

108. Plut. *Cat. Min.* 26.1, *Caes.* 8.6–7, *Mor.* 818d. See Gruen (1974) 386, Rickman (1980) 168–71, Fehrle (1983) 98. Pelling ([2011] 171) suggests that Plutarch's chronology in this event may need adjustment.

declaring its support through a *senatus consultum*, and in the absence of any opposition from the tribunes or a citizen assembly, this would have been sufficient for the measure to be acted upon, although it is possible that Cato took the additional step of bringing it to the Plebeian Assembly for formal passage into law.[109] As Plutarch's account indicates, he promulgated this bill to strengthen the Senate and to undermine Caesar, who was clearly outraged by the treatment he had received from Cato, Catulus, and others during the debate over the Catilinarian conspirators, and who could be expected to retaliate as soon as he was in office (Caesar would indeed strike back, but not with mob violence as his enemies had feared). To undercut Caesar's famous popularity with the urban population, therefore, Cato rushed this *lex frumentaria* through the Senate—and perhaps the Plebeian Assembly—in the final weeks of December so it could be enacted before Caesar took office on January 1.

Cato's bill was a considerable expansion of the *lex Terentia Cassia* of 73 BC, which had made a defined amount of grain available at reduced prices to some of the Roman people.[110] Although it is very difficult to calculate the numbers of Roman citizens involved, he may well have doubled the number of Romans receiving public distributions of grain, making him one of the most important and generous politicians in the history of Rome's grain dole.[111] His bill made cheap grain available to many more poor and landless Romans, which was a radical shift in agrarian policy and placed a considerable burden on the state treasury—an additional 30 million sesterces each year.[112] The Senate may have been more willing to assume this expense because new wealth was expected to flow into Rome from Pompey's conquests in the East, although events would soon show that these expectations were overly optimistic. This demagogic use of *popularis* measures seems completely out of character for the staunchly conservative Cato, but Plutarch emphasizes that the *lex frumentaria* was a weapon aimed at undercutting Caesar's influence with the people, and therefore Cato and his allies looked on it as a necessary step to counter Caesar's popularity.[113] In fact, Cato's maternal grandfather

---

109. Brunt ([1971] 378–9) suggested that the measure was introduced in a *contio*, but Plutarch states only that the Senate approved the measure (see Fehrle [1983] 97–9). Pelling ([2011] 172) suggests that Cato may have taken the bill to the people because of the great expense involved in expanding the grain dole to such an extent.

110. Cic. *Verr.* 2.3.163, 2.3.175, 2.5.52, Sall. *Hist.* 3.48.19M.

111. Rickman ([1980] 170–1) makes this point well. He calculates that Cato's bill represented a much larger percentage increase of the grain dole than did Clodius's *lex frumentaria* in 58 BC.

112. Rickman ([1980] 170) gives the calculations.

113. Van der Blom (2012) 48, "the proposal in itself played upon policies expected from tribunes, it was not motivated by a wish to help the poor; but when was [*sic*] such tactics ever

M. Livius Drusus (cos. 112 BC) had done something similar as a tribune in 122 BC: to undercut the influence Gaius Gracchus was receiving from his popular legislation—which was undermining the *auctoritas* of the Senate—Drusus (in consultation with the Senate) promulgated a law proposing twelve colonies for poor citizens, which made Gracchus's proposal look small by comparison.[114] This had been done out of necessity to undermine a tribune who was challenging the Senate, but it may have served as a model for Cato to undercut Caesar's popular support while augmenting the authority of the Senate. The fact that his own ancestor had used the tactic may have given it a special value in his eyes. This was another example of Cato's selective interpretation of the *mos maiorum*; he was willing to use *popularis* measures like grain subsidies if it meant weakening Caesar, but he used them in the traditionally conservative manner of working through the Senate and acting as a corporate body, rather than as an ambitious individual.

Cato and his allies had done their best to destroy Caesar during the Catilinarian crisis, and they were right to fear reprisals. Immediately upon entering his praetorship, Caesar tried to humiliate Catulus by suggesting that he be stripped of his responsibility to restore the Temple of Jupiter Optimus Maximus. This was one of Rome's most important temples, but it had burned to the ground during civil strife in 83 BC. In 78 BC Catulus as consul had been given the responsibility of rebuilding the temple, and sixteen years later the task was nearing completion, but was not yet finished.[115] As soon as Caesar entered office—even before the new consuls had been inaugurated—he summoned Catulus before his tribunal and accused him of procrastinating and wasting time on the project, and he demanded to see the project's accounts, suggesting that Catulus had embezzled state funds.[116] Caesar suggested to the gathered crowd that Catulus should be stripped of his responsibility for the sacred temple, and that the honor of completing the restoration and dedicating it should be given to Pompey. Nor was Catulus permitted to give his defense from Caesar's tribunal as was normal, but was made to stand on the ground before Caesar like a common criminal. Caesar not only sought to humiliate Catulus; he wanted to prevent him from

---

solely aimed at helping the poor and not also the policies and careers of the politicians using such tactics?"

114. App. *BC* 1.23, Plut. *CG* 9.2.

115. Sulla started the reconstruction (Val. Max. 9.3.8, Plin. *NH* 36.45, Tac. *Hist.* 3.72), but after his retirement the Senate gave Catulus the task (Cic. *Verr.* 4.69, Gell. 2.10, Suet. *Iul.* 15.1, Lactant. *de ira dei* 22.6).

116. Cic. *Att.* 2.24.3, Suet. *Iul* 15.1, Dio 37.44.1–2.

obtaining the immense and lasting prestige that would come from being the person to dedicate the new temple once it was completed, giving the senior senator no credit for his sixteen years of work supervising the restoration project. It had been only three weeks since Catulus had tried to get Caesar executed along with the Catilinarian conspirators, and Caesar was clearly motivated by revenge, although his action also would have increased his standing in Pompey's estimation had he succeeded in transferring the dedication of the temple. Even the failed attempt might have earned him Pompey's gratitude. Catulus was saved by the timely intervention of his senatorial allies, who had left the consular inauguration and hastened to the Forum as soon as they learned of Caesar's action. This must have been an imposing crowd of leading senators, because Caesar allowed the matter to drop in the face of their united opposition. At the same time, Caesar may have been content with the humiliation he had already inflicted upon Catulus, which was lasting.[117] Cato is not mentioned by name, but there can be little doubt that he was among the first to rush to Catulus's aid.

Cato's fears about Pompey's tribune Nepos turned out to be well founded. As soon as he took office, Nepos denounced Cicero for having executed Roman citizens without trial or appeal, an execution that Cato had supported loudly.[118] Although Cicero had been hailed as *pater patriae* by his senatorial colleagues for his decisive action, the execution of citizens without trial was unpopular with a great many voters, so Nepos probably attacked Cicero in this way to build his popular support. At the start of 62 BC, the danger posed by Catiline was nearly over: his fellow conspirators in Rome had been executed, and his army in Etruria was surrounded and on the brink of destruction. There could be little doubt that Catiline and his last supporters would shortly be wiped out, but Nepos took advantage of the situation to put forward two bills: one that would recall Pompey from the East to deal with Catiline, and another that allowed Pompey to stand *in absentia* for the consulship of 61 BC and to possess military authority (*imperium*) inside Rome's sacred boundary (which was normally forbidden).[119] Both proposals were somewhat ridiculous, since Catiline's insurrection was all but extinguished, and since Sulla's *lex Cornelia* required a ten-year hiatus between repeated magistracies, meaning that Pompey was not eligible for another

---

117. Cicero (*Att.* 2.24.3) was still taking about the disgrace of Catulus a decade later.

118. Cic. *Fam.* 5.2.8, Plut. *Cic.* 23.1–3.

119. Suet. *Iul.* 16.1, Plut. *Cic.* 23.4, *Cat. Min.* 26.2, Dio 37.43.2–3. See Tatum (1999) 62–3 and Seager (2002) 72–4.

consulship until 60 BC.[120] Still, Nepos wanted to gratify his former commander by
making his return to Italy more glorious, and Pompey had a notorious penchant
for stealing the glory for conquests made by other Roman commanders—he had
taken credit for ending the slave revolt that Crassus had destroyed in 71 BC, and
he had taken over command of the Mithridatic War after Lucullus had already
pushed Mithridates out of Roman territory.[121] Whether Pompey knew about
Nepos's proposals is uncertain—he was far off in the East—but Caesar as urban
praetor seems to have supported Nepos.[122] This would have been no surprise;
Caesar had supported the legislation that gave Pompey first the piracy command
(67 BC) and then the Mithridatic War (66 BC), and he hoped Pompey would
support his bid for the consulship in two years. It is also likely that the efforts by
Cato and others to have Caesar killed along with the Catilinarian conspirators
had pushed him to seek a closer alliance with Pompey; as the Senate leadership
adopted Cato's attitude toward him, Caesar was prevented from pursuing a more
traditional career path, and was forced to more radical methods if he wanted to
build his career.

Nepos began convening boisterous public meetings (*contiones*) in which he
presented his bills to the excited crowd. When the Senate met to consider the
proposals, however, Cato was surprisingly mild. Instead of attacking Nepos with
the same kind of forceful invective that had become typical of his speeches, he
calmly gave Nepos reasonable and moderate advice, and even begged him not to
move forward with his bills.[123] This soft approach is surprising given his aggressive attacks against Caesar (another Pompey supporter), and probably reflects the
nature of factional politics in the Republic. While Cato had identified Caesar as
a dangerous threat to be crushed, Metellus Nepos belonged to a powerful, noble
family that had long been part of the conservative leadership. Cato was probably looking for a way to win over the Metelli (or at least not offend them needlessly), and so he treated Nepos as a potential political ally who was misguided
in supporting Pompey. Political factions were often transitory and changeable
in Roman politics, and they relied far more heavily on personal relationships

---

120. Livy 7.42.2, 10.13.8, App. *BC* 1.100. This requirement seems to have existed in the second
century BC, but was ignored for Gaius Marius's unprecedented five consecutive consulships.
Sulla's law, therefore, was a restatement of an older law (see Brennan [2000] 2.651).

121. See Stanton and Marshall (1975) 206–7.

122. Suet. *Iul.* 16.1, Plut. *Cic.* 23.4, *Cat. Min.* 27.1–2, Dio 37.43.1–4. Metellus Nepos was an important man from a powerful clan, so Pompey may have trusted him to act independently. If
so, it turned out to be an error.

123. Plut. *Cat. Min.* 26.3.

between individuals than on abstract political platforms or ideologies.[124] These political alliances were generally referred to as friendships (*amicitiae*) to reflect this informal structure, although the negative word faction (*factio*) could also be used.[125] Since a Roman senator could have friendships or other such relationships with many other senators, he could be a member of several different *amicitiae*, each interested in a different goal.[126] Thus Roman political factions had overlapping webs of relationships, and Cato probably hoped that he could convince Nepos and his family that they would do better aligning with him and his friends rather than with Pompey. After all, Cato's brother-in-law Lucullus was related to the Metelli, and Cato may have tried to utilize that connection.[127] He therefore sought to change Nepos's mind in a friendly way, but the latter foolishly took this soft approach as a sign of weakness, and tried to cow Cato and the senators into submission with threats that he would ignore the Senate and take his bills directly to the people. This clearly shifted Cato's assessment of Nepos; he flew into a mighty speech in which he denounced Nepos and swore that Pompey would never enter Rome with an armed force while he lived.[128] Of course, Nepos had not actually proposed that Pompey enter Rome with soldiers (Pompey would disband his army as soon as he returned to Italy), so Cato's speech reveals more about his own fears than about Pompey's intent, and provides another example of his tendency to exaggerate the danger posed by his political enemies in order to move the opinion of the senators. In the past, the Senate had generally sought safety by coming together on a policy of tolerating the ambitions of great men, but his words may have been intended to shake up that huddling of senators. Plutarch is usually complimentary toward Cato, but in the debate he says that his response to Nepos was so vitriolic that "it showed the Senate that neither man was levelheaded, nor using steady reasoning."[129] This highlights Cato's strengths and weaknesses: he had the ability to influence many in the Senate to come together on points of policy he advanced, but his unfaltering, inflexible, and aggressive advocacy for his views also disturbed senators who were accustomed to

---

124. See Syme (1939) 11 and Taylor (1949) 6–15.

125. Spielvogel (1993) 5–19.

126. Robb ([2010] 15–33) gives a good discussion of personal politics within the Roman Senate.

127. Gruen (1974) 58 n. 37.

128. Plut. *Cat. Min.* 26.4.

129. Plut. *Cat. Min.* 26.4 ἐκεῖνο τῇ βουλῇ παρέστησεν, ὡς οὐδέτερος μὲν καθέστηκεν οὐδὲ χρῆται λογισμοῖς ἀσφαλέσιν. Duff ([1999] 152) notes on this episode, "Cato's extreme virtue has important negative effects in the world of high politics."

compromising with great men. While the majority of senators sided with him, his ideas and words seem to have been troubling to many.

One can only speculate on what arguments Cato made that so disturbed the senators, but it must have struck many of them that his ideas might anger Pompey and drive the great commander to march on Rome, as he had done decades earlier as Sulla's lieutenant. The Roman Senate—and indeed, the Roman people—had a long tradition of compromise in its political system, and the Republican government of the late Republic was a product of such concessions and negotiations. Cato's approach was actually a break from this tradition, and his obvious determination to block Pompey's ambitions at all costs clearly differed from the general feeling among the senators, who seem to have worried that it was unwise and unnecessary to provoke Pompey unnecessarily. The Senate was mercurial, not only because of the overlapping nature of the political factions, but also because a large number of senators might not have a fixed opinion about a particular issue, and therefore could shift their positions as events developed. In this case, many probably felt it was in their interest to support Pompey, or at least tolerate his desire for glory, but they also admired Cato's passionate appeals to the *mos maiorum*, even if his particular interpretation of tradition ignored Rome's long history of compromise. In this dilemma, the effectiveness of the spokesmen for each side was important, but both men seem to have given a bad performance. In the end, a majority sided with Cato, but it is clear that his aggressiveness, his irascibility, and his policy of confrontation had made it difficult for many senators to agree with him.

Nepos gave up trying to move his bills through the Senate, and instead took them before the Plebeian Assembly, preparing for opposition by dispersing supporters—and even gladiators—throughout the crowd.[130] When Cato arrived in the Forum on the morning of the assembly, he saw Nepos and Caesar (who was now praetor) up on the Temple of Castor and Pollux, surrounded by a mob of supporters. Apparently, the more senior senators were not planning any resistance to Nepos's bills, but Cato and his fellow tribune Q. Minucius Thermus forced their way up onto the temple, and Cato brusquely took a seat between Nepos and Caesar, thereby preventing them from communicating privately (as a tribune, he was entitled to be among those convening the Plebeian Assembly). This confrontational style of politics had already become a hallmark of his career, and the crowd's reaction was mixed; Pompey's supporters disapproved of this arrogance, but others were impressed by his boldness and cheered. While Pompey was widely admired by the people, they also enjoyed Cato's audacious display,

---

130. Cic. *Sest.* 62, Plut. *Cat. Min.* 27.1, Dio 37.43.1–4.

which was remarkable in Roman politics. When Nepos ordered the clerk to read aloud the legislation, Cato interposed his veto, an absolute action that legally could not be overturned so long as the veto was sustained. When Nepos grabbed the document and began reading it himself, Cato snatched it away. When Nepos began reciting the legislation from memory, Cato's ally Thermus clamped his hand over Nepos's mouth.[131] In frustration, Nepos signaled his supporters, and fighting broke out in the Forum.

Caesar seems to have been unprepared for this violence and quietly disappeared from the scene. He may have underestimated Cato's tenacious obstruction, and the scale and scope of the rioting that Nepos unleashed clearly was not what Caesar had wanted. Nepos's men initially got the upper hand and forced Cato's supporters from the Forum, but Cato fought personally with his attackers and sought to maintain his veto. In the end, however, the danger to him was too great, and the consul Murena—whom Cato had prosecuted for bribery only a month before—came to his rescue and protected him from harm.[132] When Nepos tried to reconvene the assembly, however, Cato's supporters came swarming back into the Forum and put Nepos and his men to flight. Who were these supporters who flocked to Cato's side? Some were surely his friends and those who admired him, and many were probably citizens incensed at the manhandling of a plebeian tribune, whose person was supposed to be sacrosanct and inviolable. He may have collected his own partisan mob to help him oppose Nepos and Caesar, which—if true—indicates that he was willing to go much further than other *optimates* in opposing the tactics and goals of Pompey's henchmen.[133] It is perhaps likely that he gathered support by accusing Nepos (and Caesar) of ignoring a tribune's veto and trampling on the authority and sacrosanctity of his office, which were terrible violations of hallowed tradition and of the people's *libertas*. At the end of the day, the Senate met and issued some kind of resolution. It may have been a *senatus consultum ultimum* authorizing the consuls to use all necessary means to protect the state from harm, but it may have been something less drastic.[134] If the Senate passed a *senatus consultum ultimum*, it was a very assertive reaction, especially

---

131. For a discussion of Cato's use of obstruction in this case, see de Libero (1992) 39.

132. Plut. *Cat. Min.* 28.1–3.

133. Mouritsen (2001) 53 and 61.

134. It is not clear what decree the Senate issued. Suetonius (*Iul.* 16.1) says the decree suspended Caesar and Nepos from office, Plutarch (*Cat. Min.* 28.5) says the decree said the Senate would support Cato and resist Nepos's law, and only Dio (37.43.3) says the consuls were ordered to see that the state did not come to harm. See Smith (1977) 162–3, Burckhardt (1988) 155–6, and Drogula (2015) 121–5.

considering that the Senate had shown little inclination to oppose Nepos earlier. Yet Nepos's use of violence would have been an important tipping point for the senators, who were powerfully motivated by self-interest to maintain order. As Cato had already demonstrated, nothing pushed the Senate to decisive action more than the threat of violent upheaval. The *senatus consultum ultimum* would have been appropriate given the outbreak of violence in the Forum, and there can be little doubt that Cato's bold leadership helped galvanize the senators into action. Nepos, knowing himself to be the target of this decree, accused the Senate of conspiring against Pompey and quickly fled Rome to join Pompey, who was probably unaware of the debacle that had broken out in his name.

Cato won a double victory in this event, successfully beating back Nepos's legislation and humiliating Caesar as well. His assertive and even aggressive opposition to Nepos was a powerful, public challenge to Pompey's hold over the people. Pompey had been the great hero of the Roman people for a decade, during which time the rest of the Senate had done little to control his unprecedented career or to punish his efforts to roll back Sulla's legislation strengthening the Senate. By standing up to Nepos, Cato demonstrated that the Pompeians' hold on the people was perhaps not as irresistible as many believed. The Senate met to discuss the violence Nepos had incited, and (no doubt) Cato's own spirited opposition, but there is some confusion in the sources about what it decided. Suetonius records that both Nepos and Caesar were suspended or removed from office by senatorial decree (*ambo administratione rei publicae decreto patrum submoverentur*), but this cannot possibly be correct, since the Senate did not have the legal authority to invest or rescind magisterial offices (only the assemblies could do this)—Caesar, Cicero, and other senators certainly would have known this.[135] The Senate could *advise* a magistrate to resign—and such advice carried implicit threats for those who did not comply—but the Senate could not legally remove or annul a magistracy that the people had given. Plutarch wrote that the Senate was considering removing only Nepos from office, but that Cato prevented the Senate from taking this action.[136] This passage is intended to celebrate Cato's high-mindedness, but once again, the very idea of the Senate removing a plebeian tribune from office is preposterous—tribunes had been created to be independent from (and not subject to) the consuls and Senate; the magistracy of the tribunate was given and revoked by the Plebeian Assembly only. Indeed, if the Senate had the power to remove troublesome tribunes from office by a simple decree, it surely would have done this to several *popularis* tribunes dating all the way back to Tiberius

---

135. Suet. *Iul.* 16.1.

136. Plut. *Cat. Min.* 29.2.

Gracchus. Plutarch and Suetonius are certainly in error, probably because the Senate operated very differently when they lived and wrote in the Imperial Era, and so Plutarch's reference to Cato's intervention for Nepos is probably a fabrication intended to display him as exceptionally wise and fair-minded. A better explanation of the event is found in Cicero—a contemporary source—who wrote in a letter to Nepos's brother Metellus Celer that the Senate voted to "relieve" Nepos.[137] What this means is unclear, but because Cicero portrays this relief as a good thing, it probably means the Senate authorized Nepos's departure from Rome and Italy.[138] Plebeian tribunes were forbidden to leave the city and the citizens they were expected to protect during their terms in office, so Nepos's departure from Rome was probably illegal, or at least a severe violation of tradition.[139] Cicero's letter suggests that the Senate chose to interpret Nepos's improper departure as a voluntary abdication of office, and in this way declared his seat vacant, thereby relieving him of the legal peril he was in for leaving the city while a tribune. Thus Cicero may be suggesting to Celer that the Senate had helped Nepos save face by justifying his departure from Rome and Italy, which meant he would not be accused of abandoning his office. If, as Plutarch suggests, Cato objected to this, he was opposing the Senate's decision to let the matter drop, which seems in keeping with his fierce opposition and his determination to pursue even his defeated foes.

The accounts of the Senate's treatment of Caesar are also confused. Cicero and Plutarch do not mention him being removed from office, and one would think the suspension of a sitting praetor worth recording. Dio even points out that Caesar carefully avoided having a senatorial decree passed against him, as had happened to Nepos.[140] Suetonius, on the other hand, gives a different story:[141] Caesar and Nepos were suspended from office by a senatorial decree, and when Caesar ignored this decree, the Senate prepared armed men to force him out of office. When he learned of the planned violence, he voluntarily dismissed his lictors, removed his official *toga praetexta*, and retired to his house, intending to remain in permanent retirement. Then huge mobs of citizens began

---

137. Cic. *Fam.* 5.2.9, *ut senati consulto meus inimicus. . . sublevaretur.*

138. Shackleton Bailey ([1980] 122) suggests this possibility.

139. Dion. Hal. 8.87.6, Macrob. *Sat.* 1.3.8. Dio (37.43.4) emphasizes that Nepos broke the law by leaving Italy. When the civil war between Caesar and Pompey began, Pompey specifically exempted magistrates from this requirement to remain in Rome (Dio 41.6.2–3). Badian ([1996] 195–6) discusses the rare exceptions to this rule.

140. Dio 37.44.2.

141. Suet. *Iul.* 16.1–2. This story is accepted by some modern scholars (see Gelzer [1968] 57).

to gather around his house, riotously promising to compel the Senate to restore him to his office and honors. Caesar restrained the crowd and had them return home peacefully, and in response the Senate publicly thanked and praised him for his restraint and restored him to his magistracy. This dramatic story enlivens Suetonius's biography of Caesar, but it cannot be true as written. Not only is the silence in other sources suspicious (especially the silence of Cicero, a contemporary who was present in Rome), but also because—as was the case with Nepos—the Senate did not have the legal authority to remove a sitting magistrate from office. Only the assembly could have removed Caesar from his praetorship, and as Suetonius makes plain, he was much too popular for this to have happened (150 years later, when Suetonius was writing under the rule of the emperors, the appointment of curule magistrates was different). In all likelihood, therefore, this story about Caesar's retirement and subsequent recall by a chastened and fawning Senate is probably a literary invention intended to lionize Caesar. Of course, one can readily imagine that Cato and his allies tried to use the violence incited by Nepos to attack Caesar, but if the Senate had issued a *senatus consultum ultimum*, Nepos's departure from Rome seems to have relieved the crisis, and nothing further seems to have come from the event.

At some point during his tribunate Cato promulgated a second bill in cooperation with his fellow tribune L. Marius. This bill established penalties for any military commander who inaccurately reported to the Senate either the number of enemy killed in battle or the number of Roman soldiers lost, and it further required all commanders to swear to the accuracy of the numbers before the city quaestors as soon as they entered the city.[142] The purpose of this *lex* was to prevent commanders from exaggerating the number of enemies killed in hopes of winning a triumph, and therefore it was a sound piece of conservative legislation seeking to enforce the *mos maiorum*.[143] The question, of course, is why Cato thought this was particularly worthy of his time and attention. Triumph-hunting had been a preoccupation of Roman commanders for centuries, and the increasing competition for honors and offices in the late Republic had certainly made praetors and consuls more willing to exaggerate their successes if it meant the difference between entering Rome in triumph or in silence. Demanding that old-fashioned standards be upheld was certainly one of Cato's interests, as

---

142. Val. Max. 2.8.1, cf. Cic. *QF* 3.2.2.

143. There was no single set of rules and achievements a commander had to satisfy in order to qualify for a triumph. Instead, the Senate (or in rare cases, the people) reviewed the commander's accomplishments and rendered a judgment. See Beard (2007) 206–14, Lundgreen (2014) 17–32, Dart and Vervaet (2014) 53–64.

demonstrated by his own refusal as a soldier to accept military awards he felt he had not earned. Yet he probably aimed this *lex* at Caesar in particular, who as sitting praetor would soon be setting off for a provincial command in Farther Spain.[144] Since the most important wars were always assigned to consuls, the hostile tribes in Rome's two Spanish provinces were the most reliable source of triumphs for praetors like Caesar. He had shown himself to be intelligent and highly ambitious, he had proven himself to be a good soldier in his early career, and the fact that he had served as quaestor in Spain gave him the knowledge he needed to undertake extensive campaigning. It was certain that Caesar would try to win a triumph, so Cato's legislation—enacted before Caesar left Rome, so there could be no mistake—made it much more difficult for a commander to win an undeserved triumph. This was clever, because Caesar might have been able to use his popularity with the people to get the assembly to overlook any shortcomings in his request for a triumph (even if the Senate had been a stickler), but Cato's law would require him to confirm on oath that he had met the minimum requirements. This was certainly motivated by Cato's ongoing feud with Caesar, but it also reinforced his reputation as an enforcer of ancestral standards.

Cato may have also been involved in the passage of another law that placed strict controls on commanders returning to Rome. Sometime between January 63 BC and July 62 BC, a new law was passed requiring anyone wishing to stand as a candidate for office to make his *professio*—his official declaration of candidacy—*in person* before the official who would preside over the election, and presumably this had to be done at an appointed place inside the city, probably in the Forum.[145] In the past, it had been possible for a man away on military service to make his *professio in absentia*, which meant he could simultaneously hold command over an army and be a candidate for election. This posed a potential danger, because consular elections took place outside the city boundary in the Campus Martius, which meant that an unscrupulous commander could bring his army

---

144. Taylor (1949) 225 n. 35.

145. Cicero (*leg. agr.* 2.24) mentions in January 63 BC that this law did not exist previously, and it was in force by July 62 BC, when Pompey requested that the consular elections be delayed so that his lieutenant M. Pupius Piso Frugi Calpurnianus (cos. 61 BC) might have time to return to Rome and make his *professio* so that he might be a candidate (Dio 37.44.3, Plut. *Pomp.* 44.1). The law must have stipulated that the *professio* had to be made somewhere inside the *pomerium* because in 60 BC Caesar was outside the city, and yet could not make his *professio* without crossing the *pomerium* and entering the city, thereby forfeiting his *imperium* (see later discussion). See Earl (1965) 325–32, Linderski (1966) 523–6, Nicolet (1991) 240–3, Linderski (1995) 91–4.

to Rome and intimidate voters during an election.[146] By requiring candidates to make their *professiones* in person, commanders had to cross the *pomerium* and enter the city, which automatically and irreversibly terminated their military authority (*imperium*). By mid-62 BC, therefore, a man could no longer be an active military commander and a candidate for office, since he had to resign his command in order to enter Rome and declare his candidacy. This *lex* may have been intended to prevent Pompey from seeking a second consulship *in absentia* when he returned from Rome, but the law may also have been aimed at Caesar, who obviously had his eye focused on winning the consulship in the first year he was eligible (*in suo anno*), in 59 BC.[147] From the end of his praetorship in 62 BC, Caesar would have eighteen months at best to get to Spain, win a sufficient number of victories to qualify for a triumph, and return to Rome by July 60 BC to announce his candidacy for the consular elections for 59 BC. Given the shortness of this space and the greatness of his ambition, senators could reasonably expect that Caesar would seek to stand for election *in absentia* to give himself more time to extract wealth and glory from Spain. This law, therefore, may have been intended to anticipate and outlaw that request, forcing him either to cut short his command or to miss the added glory of winning a consulship *in suo anno*. This law would be one of the most important challenges to Caesar, both in 60 BC and in 51–50 BC. Whether Cato was responsible for promulgating this law on the *professio* is not known—it may even have been passed in late 63 BC before he was tribune—but he certainly would have supported it as a valuable check on the ability of ambitious commanders to use their military commands and loyal armies to win elections in Rome.

Cato's interest in carefully regulating the candidacy for the consulship is revealed by another event during his tribunate. According to Plutarch, Pompey was returning from the East to Italy that summer (62 BC), and he sent a letter to the Senate asking that the consular elections be delayed so that he could be present to assist in the campaign of his legate, M. Pupius Piso Frugi Calpurnianus.[148] The senators were willing to grant the request, but Cato opposed it vehemently and persuaded the Senate to reject it. Dio, on the other hand, says that Pompey requested that the consular elections be delayed until Piso returned to Rome,

---

146. The most famous case of this happened in 215 BC, when the presiding consul Q. Fabius Maximus used his *imperium* to threaten another candidate during the consular elections (Livy 24.7.10–9.4). See Drogula (2015) 82–3.

147. Taylor ([1949] 225 n. 35) suggests the *lex* was aimed at Pompey.

148. Plut. *Pomp.* 44.1, *Cat. Min.* 30.1–2.

and that this request was granted.[149] Piso was indeed elected consul for 61 BC, so it is likely that Plutarch simply made an error, but Pompey may have sent two different requests (one for himself that was rejected, and one for Piso that was granted), or he may have requested that the elections be delayed until he should return, but the Senate granted a delay only until Piso should return and be eligible.[150] Piso was able to return to Rome much sooner than Pompey, so it was a small concession to delay the elections for a couple of months, but waiting for Pompey—who did not return to Rome until *after* the new consuls were supposed to take office—was much too great a favor to allow.[151] Since Cato was a tribune, he could have interposed his veto and blocked any consideration of Pompey's request had he so wished, so the fact that a postponement was made for Piso indicates that Cato chose not to intervene. This raises the question of why he was willing to make any accommodation for Pompey. It is possible that he and his friends were nervous about pushing back too hard against Pompey, who was already returning to Italy with his large, experienced, and loyal army. They may also have been worried about antagonizing the urban population, which was eagerly looking forward to the return of their conquering hero. On the other hand, Cato and his allies probably did not fear having Piso as consul; he was known to be a dull and unenergetic man who was unlikely to put up much of a fight, and they were working to get M. Valerius Messalla Niger elected, who was a zealous supporter of the Senate leadership and the *optimates*, and could be counted on to oppose and neutralize Piso if he tried to advance Pompey's agenda.[152] So while Cato probably disliked allowing a special favor for Pompey's candidate, he could rest assured that it would do Pompey little good. And as events would demonstrate, he had other plans for opposing Pompey.

Cato's tribunate was certainly a success, and it increased his prominence in the Senate and especially among the *optimates*. Not only had he proven himself to be a champion of *mos maiorum*—which included upholding the central authority of

---

149. Dio 37.44.3.

150. Seager ([2002] 74 n. 93) suggests that Pompey sent different requests, while Gruen ([1974] 85 n. 9) argued that the Senate only delayed the elections until Piso returned to Rome. Hillman ([1996] 313–20) examines both proposals and supports Gruen's interpretation, arguing that Cato was willing to allow some delay, but did not want to give Pompey everything he wanted.

151. Cicero (*Att.* 1.12.4) shows that Piso was back in Rome and consul by January 1, but Pompey did not arrive until sometime between January 1 and 25.

152. Cicero (*Att.* 1.13.2) describes Piso as "doing nothing in public business, and disconnected from the *optimates*; from him you should expect no advantage to the Republic, because he does not wish to do anything, and you need fear nothing bad from him, because he dares do nothing."

the Senate, unified under traditional noble families—but also his aggressive and relentless zeal in opposing Nepos and Caesar demonstrated that he was willing to fight for his beliefs. Since Sulla's death in 78 BC, the *optimates* had offered only halfhearted resistance to the self-interested populism of Pompey and (to a lesser extent) Crassus. The decimation of senators in the Social War and Civil War had left the Senate with a fairly shallow bench of leaders, and its political unity had been fractured by Pompey and others who had sought personal advancement at the expense of the Senate's *auctoritas*. The Senate had its leaders—prestigious *nobiles* of consular rank—but these men had not been able to suppress the populist tactics used by Pompey and others. Even during the Catilinarian debate, the *consulares* who had advocated for the death penalty soon yielded to the arguments of Caesar and the *praetores*, and would not have reacquired control of the meeting had Cato not given his rousing speech calling them all to action. Amid this general weakness in the Senate's leadership, he was able to use his unusual habits and forceful rhetoric to gain prominence rapidly among the *optimates*. His self-fashioning as the guardian of tradition compensated for his junior status, and his willingness to engage in pitched political battles to defend the *nobiles'* traditional control of the Senate—and by extension, the state—made him a figurehead for the *optimates*. Speaking with the voice of ancient authority, and intimidating senators with threats of imminent disaster, Cato pushed the senators to gather around him for safety, calling for the illegal but expedient execution of citizens without trial. Without his influence, senatorial factions might have remained divided, but he successfully pushed them to come together and vote together, revealing far more influence than his status as an ex-tribune would normally merit.[153] As a result, senior *nobiles* like Catulus and Lucullus collaborated with him, and junior men looked up to him as a role model and even emulated him—as early as 61 BC, Cicero referred to a particularly excellent tribune as a *Pseudocato*, and by 59 BC M. Favonius (pr. 49 BC) had begun imitating Cato's austerity and energetic opposition to political enemies.[154] Such influence was remarkable for a man who had not yet reached the praetorship or commanded an army, and it enabled him to impart to the Senate leadership his own hostility toward Caesar. In this way, Caesar was alienated from the Senate, and was prevented from pursuing his career in a more conventional manner. To be sure, by 63 BC Caesar had given signs

---

153. Cicero (*Mur.* 58–60) remarks on the unusual *auctoritas* Cato possessed. See Fehrle (1983) 89–91.

154. Cic. *Att.* 1.14.6. Ryan ([1993] 171–3) argues that this was meant to be a positive comparison, but even if negative, it shows that Cato had become a standard of measurement for a man's excellence. See later discussion of Favonius.

of his ambition and willingness to use *popularis* tactics, but Cato's enmity would make it very difficult for him to find a traditional path forward, forcing him to look elsewhere to achieve political success. In this way, Cato's deft use of the *mos maiorum* and his tireless energy helped to strengthen and focus the *optimates*, but his mannerisms and his inability to compromise would pose obstacles in his efforts to lead.

4

Cato and the Formation of the Triumvirate

Cato versus Pompey, Crassus, and Caesar (61 to 60 BC)

The year 62 BC ended with the infamous *Bona Dea* scandal, caused when the young patrician P. Clodius Pulcher sacrilegiously entered the *Domus Publica* during the secret rites held in December by the Vestal Virgins and Rome's aristocratic women in honor of the mysterious goddess *Bona Dea*. The *Domus Publica* was Caesar's official residence as *pontifex maximus*, but he had temporarily vacated the house so his mother and his wife could take charge of the ceremony. Clodius disguised himself as a woman and sneaked into the house, perhaps to have a romantic tryst with Caesar's wife Pompeia, or perhaps just to view the secret rites.[1] Clodius was caught by Caesar's mother, and word of his impiety spread rapidly through Rome.[2] The scandal was widely talked about, and on the motion of the senator Q. Cornificius, the Senate published a *senatus consultum* referring the matter to the Vestal Virgins and the College of Pontiffs, who declared that Clodius's action constituted sacrilege, a very serious charge in Rome. The senators then passed a *senatus consultum* instructing the consuls to promulgate a bill creating a special court to investigate the crime, but one of the consuls—Pompey's man M. Pupius Piso—was friends with Clodius, and worked for the rejection of the bill.[3] In addition to the consul's influence, Clodius was making personal appeals to everyone in the Senate, as

---

1. Plut. *Caes.* 9.1–10.3.

2. The stages of this event are described in several of Cicero's letters to Atticus (1.13, 1.14, and 1.16). For further discussion of the event, see Moreau (1982) 81–129, Tatum (1999) 71–80, and Morstein-Marx (2004) 186–9.

3. Cic. *Att.* 1.13.3. See Seager (2002) 77.

(presumably) were his relatives among the *Claudii Pulcheres*, an ancient and powerful family. As a result, many senators were inclined drop their support for the bill, until Cato and the other consul, M. Valerius Messalla, rigorously championed the measure and shamed the senators for their lack of religious scruple. When it was finally time for a vote in the assembly, Piso and Clodius's other friends spoke against the bill, handed out fake ballots that only allowed for the rejection of the bill, and placed allies in locations where they could intimidate the voters. Seeing this, Cato suddenly leapt up to the speaker's platform and accosted Piso for acting contrary to the Senate's instructions, giving the consul a "remarkable thrashing."[4] He was joined by Hortensius, Favonius, and many other influential senators, and this compelled Piso to dismiss the assembly and summon a meeting of the Senate. Cato's bold championing of traditional religious piety had a powerful effect on the Senate, which voted 400 to 15 that the consuls should push the people to approve the special court. Once again, he had succeeded in using his *auctoritas* as the champion of tradition to overcome the usual fission of senatorial factions by pushing the senators to cluster together around a conservative policy.

Thus trapped, Clodius was fortunate that one of the tribunes was a friend, who vetoed the bill and maintained his veto until an alternate, more corruptible jury was selected to hear the case. During the trial Cicero exploded Clodius's alibi that he had been out of town during the festival, and Seneca says that Cato was one of the witnesses whom Cicero summoned to testify.[5] It is not clear what evidence Cato could have supplied, so Seneca might be wrong, or—more likely—Cicero summoned him as a defender of tradition to lend his considerable *auctoritas* to the prosecution, which he strongly supported. Just as Cicero had feared Cato's moral authority when defending Murena, here he hoped to use that *auctoritas* to get Clodius condemned. During the trial Clodius launched attacks against all of his accusers, and he lashed out at Cicero in particular by denigrating the vestal virgin Fabia, the sister of Cicero's wife Terentia. Cato responded aggressively to this insult against a vestal virgin, and put Clodius to shame, although the tradition that he drove him from the city is probably false.[6] Cicero believed

---

4. Cic. *Att.* 1.14.5, *commulcium mirificum* (cf. 1.13.3). On this unusual phrase, see Shackleton Bailey (1965–70) 1.310–11.

5. Cic. *Att.* 1.16.2 and Plut. *Cic.* 29.1 (cf. Sen. *Ep.* 97.3).

6. Plut. *Cat. Min.* 19.3. Keaveney ([1992] 72) suggests that Cato's rebuke of Clodius for his treatment of Fabia took place in ca. 73 BC, and that Clodius fled Rome to accompany his brother in Pompey's army. Tatum ([1999] 89) argues that Plutarch's placement of this story about Clodius's flight is wrong, and that Cato probably defended Fabia during the *Bona Dea* trials.

the evidence in the case was overwhelming, but Clodius escaped condemnation through massive bribery.[7]

Cato was outraged at Clodius's acquittal, and he turned his anger against the jury system that (in his view) had abandoned moral principle for cash. He put forward a motion for a *senatus consultum* to investigate bribery in the courts, a decree that seems to have been specifically aimed at the wealthy non-senators (equestrians and *tribuni aerarii*) who sat on the juries.[8] During his dictatorship, Sulla had limited jury membership to senators, and had established strict penalties for jurors found guilty of taking bribes.[9] When Pompey and Crassus were consuls in 70 BC, however, the praetor L. Aurelius Cotta promulgated a bill redistributing jury membership equally among Rome's three highest census groups: senators, equestrians, and *tribuni aerarii*, but there is no evidence that Sulla's anti-bribery legislation was ever revised to include those lower orders that were once again eligible to sit on juries.[10] So Sulla's harsh penalties for senatorial jurors guilty of accepting bribes remained on the books, but legally those penalties did not apply to jurors drawn from the equestrians and the *tribuni aerarii*, since these had never been added to the clauses defining the crime. This created considerable confusion for Cicero and other legal advocates, since two-thirds of jurors (the equestrians and *tribuni aerarii*) were not liable to prosecution for judicial corruption under the *lex Cornelia*.[11] Cato's bill seems to have fixed this by extending the harsh penalties for judicial bribery to include equestrians and *tribuni aerarii*, making it much easier to prosecute them. This had the predictable effect of angering and alienating these wealthy classes of citizens, who wielded considerable influence and importance in Rome. Equestrians in particular were vital to the operation of the state, since they were the thousands of wealthy citizens who chose not to pursue a political career, but whose wealth and influence were essential for the stability of the government. So Cato's legislation was morally good, but politically imprudent for one who wanted the political support of the propertied classes. Cicero in particular was exasperated by Cato and his legislation. He believed that the stability of Rome and the *auctoritas* of the Senate depended upon the political alignment and mutual support of the equestrian and senatorial orders, so he saw

---

7. Cic. *Att.* 1.16.1 (Clodius widely thought to be guilty) and 1.16.5 (massive bribery conducted by two otherwise unidentified men: Calvus and Nanneianis).

8. Cic. *Att.* 1.17.8 and 2.1.8. Taylor (1949) 130 n. 47.

9. Cic. *Verr.* 1.37, 1.47, 1.49, Vell. 2.32.3, Tac. *Ann.* 11.22.6. See Gruen (1968) 255–78, Lintott (1992) 27, Keaveney (2005) 146–7.

10. Livy *Per.* 97, Vell. 2.32.3, Plut. *Pomp.* 22.3. See Gruen (1974) 29–31, Marshall (1975) 136–52.

11. Cic. *Cluent.* 104 and 143–60, *Rab. Post.* 16–18.

the bill as a naïve move that undermined the stability of the senatorial government.[12] He did not approve of judicial bribery, but he thought Cato had handled the situation badly, and in doing so had unintentionally weakened the influence of the Senate. Cicero regretted that he had been absent from the Senate when the bill was voted upon, and he later rebuked the senators for approving legislation that undermined the stability of the government. In the end, the bill was never voted on by the people and therefore never became law (perhaps Cicero's intervention was responsible), but the damage had been done, and the equestrians were angry and alienated.[13] This episode reflects a recurring problem Cato would encounter: his own values and his self-identification as the champion of the *mos maiorum* drove him to combat all forms of bribery, but he did not realize (or did not care) that suppressing bribery and alienating the equestrians would weaken the *auctoritas* of the Senate. His *exemplum* of ancestral values was effective at uniting senatorial factions behind particular goals, but his goals were often unpopular outside of the Senate, which undercut his influence and prevented him from achieving some of his goals.

Cicero was frustrated by this alienation of the equestrian order, and he was vexed that Cato was gaining so much influence among the Senate leadership despite having risen no higher than the tribunate. Cicero was a senator of consular rank and longed to be seen as the leader among the *nobiles*, but his status as a *novus homo* weighed against him with his better-pedigreed colleagues, and his policies were too moderate for Rome's most conservative senators. These *nobiles* respected Cicero's abilities and were grateful for his frequent support of their initiatives, but he was not a true *nobilis* in their eyes. By contrast, while Cato's father's family was recently undistinguished, his family had consuls dating back well over a century and he had made connections with many noble houses. This prejudice was important to the *nobiles*, who believed that their right to govern Rome was in large part inherited—their families had led Rome for centuries, and this entitled them to their rank and prerogatives. So while Cato himself had not yet risen very high in the *cursus honorum*, the older nobility of his family carried considerable weight with the leaders of the Senate, as did his passion for the ancient traditions and his aggressive stance against those who challenged the Senate's *auctoritas*. Furthermore, Cicero and Cato offered different visions of the *mos maiorum*: Cicero wanted a broad consensus among all of the elite classes, and was willing to make concessions to strengthen that consensus, while Cato thought that authority should rest primarily with the *nobiles* in the Senate, and

12. Cic. *Att.* 1.17.8–9 and 1.18.3.

13. Cic. *Att.* 1.18.3.

so concessions should not be made because they weakened the *auctoritas* of the *nobiles*.

These different perspectives reveal the dynamic nature of senatorial politics, and emphasize how powerful the fashioning and interpretation of tradition was to the Romans. Although they were generally very conservative and believed in the importance of following the precedents and customs of their revered ancestors, there was no clear agreement about what—exactly—was and was not consistent with the *mos maiorum*. Cicero and Cato could both present themselves as following tradition, but Cato's lineage, his archaic mannerisms, and his aggressive defense of traditional senatorial prerogatives appealed to the *nobiles*. This became clear when the Senate leadership went through a major change from 61 to 60 BC: Lucullus and Hortensius seem to have more or less retired from political activity by this time, Metellus Pius had died in 63 BC, and Catulus, Silanus, and Cato's uncle Mamercus all died before May 60 BC.[14] This was a large number of *nobiles* to die (and semi-retire) within a few years, at a time when there was already a shallow bench of *consulares* to lead the Senate. Lucullus's departure was a particular loss; he more than anyone should have assumed the leadership of the *optimates* as a foremost *consularis* and *nobilis*, but he seemed to have lost his stomach for political battles. Cicero was also an obvious choice to assume the leadership, but the prejudice of the conservatives seems to have been unwilling to accept him as their leader, and so Cato gained still more influence despite his lower rank as an ex-tribune.[15] Plutarch even suggests that Lucullus retired thinking that Cato would take his place as a leader of the conservative senators.[16] Yet Cato's rapid and unusual elevation to a leadership position may have had a disrupting effect on the *optimates*, since it seems to have prevented them from coalescing around a better, more capable, and more senior leader after Catulus's death.[17] Cato would prove to be inconsistent and unpredictable as a leader, but he was such a powerful figurehead that it must have been very difficult for any other potential leader to establish himself and unify the different factions of senators.

---

14. Cic. *Att.* 1.20.3, and see list of *pontifices* in *MRR* 2.186.

15. Cicero's prominence was clear: the consuls of 61 BC recognized his *auctoritas* by calling on him second to give his opinion in debates, ahead of Catulus and Hortensius (C. Calpurnius Piso [cos. 67 BC] was called on first) (Cic. *Att.* 1.13.2). Gelzer ([1969] 45–6) remarks on the unusual position of Cato, who was counted among the highest leadership of the nobility despite never reaching the consulship.

16. Plut. *Luc.* 42.5

17. Afzelius ([1941] 183–4) suggested this point.

Caesar set out for his praetorian command in Spain at the end of 62 BC, and Pompey finally returned to Rome the following February. One of Pompey's first actions was to divorce his wife Mucia, the half-sister of his former legate Metellus Nepos, whose botched efforts as tribune in 62 BC had done more to glorify Cato than help Pompey. There was certainly a personal motive for the divorce, since Mucia was said to have carried on liaisons with other men in her husband's absence, but political calculations may have played a larger role. By divorcing Mucia he distanced himself publicly from Nepos and the riot he had started in Rome, and at the same time he freed himself to make a more useful marriage alliance (the *Metelli* clan was important and influential, but recent events had shown that other men were more prominent in the Senate). In a surprising move, Pompey straightaway asked to marry one of Cato's nieces (a daughter of Servilia and Silanus), and he further asked that another of Cato's nieces be given as a wife to Pompey's eldest son.[18] This move certainly reflects Pompey's recognition that Cato had become a major force in Roman politics. Pompey was the greatest man in Rome at the time, and many families would have been eager to ally with him, but he sought to make a double marriage alliance with Cato, even though he had shown only outward respect to him four years earlier in the East. In his biography of each man, Plutarch places Pompey's request for a marriage alliance directly after Cato's involvement in Pompey's request for a delay of the consular elections in 62 BC to accommodate his lieutenant Pupius Piso. In this context, and in light of Cato's effective resistance to Metellus Nepos (and Caesar), Pompey recognized him as an influential leader who was at the center of actions taken by conservative factions, and so he sought a marriage alliance in hopes of healing the rift between him and the *optimates*, as well as to prevent Cato (and his brother-in-law Lucullus) from opposing his future political objectives.[19] Cato recognized this, and while his nieces were reportedly eager to marry the leading man in Rome and his son, he absolutely refused because—as he said—he did not want to lose or limit his freedom to act as he thought best in politics. This rejection left Pompey in the lurch, since his divorce of Mucia had made him the enemy of her powerful brothers (Metellus Nepos and Metellus Celer), but had not secured an alliance with Cato.[20]

---

18. Plut. *Pomp.* 44.2–3, *Cat. Min.* 30.2–3.

19. Dragstedt (1969) 74, Hillman (1993) 225, Seager (2002) 76, and Tatum (2010) 197.

20. Williams and Williams ([1988] 202) argue that Pompey had been naïve to think that Cato would agree to the proposed marriage alliance.

Cato's refusal suggests that he had already decided to oppose whatever Pompey had in mind to request from the Senate.[21] As discussed earlier, he had personal as well as political reasons to dislike Pompey strongly, but he had never before been in a position to oppose him, since Pompey had been absent from Rome on military commands since 67 BC (before Cato had entered the Senate). For two decades, Pompey had angered and antagonized many in the Senate, and had used *popularis* methods to build himself up and even steal the glory of other *nobiles*, so there can be little doubt that Cato had marked him as a political enemy to be torn down and ruined. It was probably this long-smoldering desire to punish Pompey that prevented Cato from even considering the marriage proposal seriously. Plutarch saw Cato's decision to refuse the offered alliance as a key moment, since it drove Pompey into Caesar's arms, which would in turn eventually lead the two men to civil war.[22] Just as Cato had alienated Caesar from the *optimates*, he likewise worked to drive a wedge between Pompey and the Senate—at a time when Pompey was seeking to reconcile with the Senate—forcing him on the road to making his fateful alliance with Caesar.[23] Every senator must have known that Pompey would seek to build his influence through marriage, so this refusal forced him to look around for a different political ally who would not follow Cato's lead. It is understandable that Cato did not want to form an alliance or *amicitia* with Pompey, and of course he could not know that a decade later he would be working to pull Pompey away from Caesar, but his decision would have significant long-term consequences. It was not uncommon for Romans to use marriage alliances to heal rifts between men (Mark Antony's marriage to Octavian's sister Octavia in 40 BC is a classic example), so another man might have set aside his resentment and accepted Pompey's offer, but not Cato. His resolution and single-minded determination were extraordinary, as was his belief that concessions could not be made to those who acted contrary to his interpretation of tradition. Furthermore, Cato probably could not risk undermining his self-made reputation as the champion of the *mos maiorum* by accepting an alliance with a man who (in his eyes) had repeatedly ignored and transgressed tradition. As a consequence, an opportunity to draw Pompey closer to the *optimates* was lost.

---

21. Seager (2002) 76, "Cato's behavior had shown that Pompeius's worst fears of opposition from that quarter would be realized, since if Cato had not already been determined to resist Pompeius' demands when he put them to the Senate, he would have had no reason to react as he had done to his proposal."

22. Pelling ([1986] 163 n. 13) and Duff ([1999] 135) discuss Plutarch's use of this idea to shape his narrative.

23. Gelzer ([1949] 121) argues for the role of Cato's refusal in driving Pompey to align with Caesar.

Every senator knew that Pompey would want allotments of land with which to reward the soldiers who had been serving him for so many years. Such land grants for time-served soldiers were relatively new and definitely *popularis* in nature, having been instituted by Marius in 103 and 100 BC.[24] The Senate generally opposed such land grants because they were expensive, they often threatened landowners with dispossession, and they reinforced a system in which veterans owed their primary loyalty to the general who obtained the land for them. This last point was a significant concern to many senators, since veterans who received land bonuses from their generals could be expected to support his political ambitions for the rest of their lives, giving him much more influence and clientage than his senatorial colleagues. In 71 BC Pompey had successfully pressured the Senate to approve a similar bill giving land to the veterans of his Spanish campaigns, and so he expected little trouble in getting more land for the veterans of his eastern campaigns, since in 61 BC he was enjoying even higher status and influence than he had held in 71 BC.[25] In anticipation of this need for land, Pompey had sent some of his legates back to Rome to stand for the tribunate of 63 BC, and as tribunes they had brought forward an expansive bill to found colonies and purchase land at state expense for distribution to citizens, which would have included Pompey's veterans.[26] Cicero thought this bill was too expensive and would give too much power to the men appointed to purchase and allot the land, so he and his supporters defeated this bill.

The following year Pompey had sent Metellus Nepos to work for his interests as tribune in 62 BC, but thanks to Cato, nothing came of his efforts and Nepos ended up abandoning his tribunate. Pompey next had managed to get his man M. Pupius Piso elected consul for 61 BC, but he became mired down in the *Bona Dea* affair and made no headway in solving Pompey's need for land, so Pompey's position had become precarious: he had promised a great deal of land to tens of thousands of his soldiers, and his status as their patron—and as a leader in the state—demanded that he fulfill his pledge. A failure to do so would cause immeasurable damage to his standing in Rome and to his influence over the state. Pompey's agents had failed to get the job done, so Pompey hoped his presence

---

24. Auct. *Vir. Ill.* 73.1.

25. The Senate had approved a grant of land for veterans of the armies that had served under Pompey and Metellus in Spain (Dio 38.5.1, Plut. *Luc.* 34.3–4), which may have been the *lex Plotia agraria* mentioned by Cicero (*Att.* 1.18.6). Pompey's return to Rome in Feb. 61 BC: Cic. *Att.* 1.14.1.

26. This bill is the subject of Cicero's speeches on the grain law (*de lege agraria*). The tribunes T. Ampius Balbus and T. Labienus had been Pompey's legates, and it is likely that P. Servilius Rullus had been as well. See Gelzer (1968) 66–7, Leach (1978) 106–11, and Seager (2002) 81–2.

would cut through the obstacles in his path. This was a rare opportunity for those who wished to weaken him, and they seized the moment.

Since Pompey's previous efforts had failed, in July 61 BC he threw his resources into getting his legate L. Afranius elected consul for 60 BC. Like Pupius Piso, Afranius was a loyal lieutenant, but he was not a good politician, nor was he well respected by the Roman Senate, and therefore he was not a good choice for the delicate measure of arranging land for veterans.[27] Pompey spent money generously to bribe voters, and the consul Piso was even rumored to be organizing groups of agents (*divisores*) in his house to distribute bribes.[28] Cicero doubted the rumor, but Cato and his brother-in-law Domitius Ahenobarbus alleged the rumors were true and proposed two separate senatorial decrees in July: one that made it illegal for a candidate to have *divisores* in their homes, and a second allowing candidates' houses to be searched.[29] In addition, the tribune Aufidius Lurco proposed an unusual bill to punish bribery: those who promised money to voters but failed to pay were exempt from punishment, but anyone who was caught distributing bribes to voters would have to pay 3,000 *sestertii* to each tribe annually as long as he lived. Lurco received some kind of special dispensation from the *lex Aelia* and the *lex Fufia*—laws regulating the timing of the promulgation of bills—in order to bring his bill forward, which indicates that he had significant support in the Senate.[30] The similarities of these bills (especially the focus on punishing *divisores*) suggests a concerted effort by Cato, Lurco, and their allies to anticipate and prevent Pompey's use of bribery to support Afranius. Bribery in particular seems to have angered Cato, because it seriously undermined the traditional ability of the *nobiles* to control the outcome of votes through influence alone, and so it weakened the Senate's control of the state. In the absence of bribery, deferential Romans could be expected to follow the example of their social superiors, especially when senators could apply pressure on voters (especially their clients) through personal appeals and threats.[31] In Cato's eyes, therefore, bribery was not merely unjust; it was subversive because it undermined

---

27. Williams and Williams ([1988] 199) suggest that the choice of Afranius demonstrates that Pompey did not understand how the political environment of Rome had changed during his absence. Seager ([2002] 83) also remarks on Afranius's lack of talent.

28. Cic. *Att.* 1.16.12, Plut. *Cat. Min.* 30.5. Shackleton Bailey ([1965] 1.323) points out that *divisores* could be legitimate distributors of gratuities among tribes, but in this case they were clearly distributors of bribes.

29. Cic. *Att.* 1.16.12. See discussion in Gruen (1974) 233–4.

30. Cic. *Att.* 1.16.13. The nature of the exemption he received is not clear, but see Shackleton Bailey (1965) 1.323–4 and Gruen (1974) 224.

31. Yakobson (1999) 109–11.

the influence of the aristocracy, and in particular that of the *nobiles* who led the Senate. He and Ahenobarbus pushed strenuously for their bills and obtained a positive vote from the Senate, but the popular assembly refused to approve the measure. It is perhaps not surprising that the urban voters refused to pass anti-bribery laws, because they benefited from the distribution of bribes. Furthermore, Cicero and other senators probably argued against the bills in public, since they would have conflicted with the *lex Tullia* that Cicero had promulgated as consul, and because Lurco's bill in particular would have clogged up the courts with false accusations.[32] Whether the bills would have successfully checked or reduced electoral bribery cannot be known because the legislation failed, and so Pompey paid a tremendous amount of money in bribes to secure Afranius's election.[33]

Despite this success, the other consul elected for 60 BC turned out to be Q. Caecilius Metellus Celer, the half-brother of Pompey's former wife Mucia. Celer clearly took affront at Pompey's divorce of Mucia, and he was also more firmly aligned with the *optimates* than his brother Nepos had been. As a result, Celer undertook to block all actions that Afranius (or others) initiated on Pompey's behalf. The struggles began right away in January, when another of Pompey's lieutenants—the tribune L. Flavius—proposed an agrarian law that would provide the necessary land for distribution to veterans.[34] When the bill was presented to the Senate, Cicero thought it might be acceptable if the property rights of private persons were protected (evidently, the bill did not offer this protection), but a coalition led by Cato and Celer obstructed the bill and convinced much of the Senate to block it and prevent any increase in Pompey's power.[35] In the mercurial world of senatorial factions, the goals of Cato and Celer had aligned, and they proved a powerful combination. Cato once again seems to have manipulated the fear of the senators (fear of losing land, and fear of Pompey) to push them to vote together to defeat the legislation. Flavius tried to stop the obstruction by ordering Celer to be thrown in jail, but this backfired when a large number of senators continued attending on the consul in his jail

---

32. Gruen ([1974] 224) suggests Cicero's role in arguing for the rejection of the bills. Shackleton Bailey ([1965] 1.323) discusses the unpopularity of the proposal.

33. Cic. *Att.* 1.16.12–13, Plut. *Pomp.* 44.3–4, *Cat. Min.* 30.5.

34. Cic. *Att.* 1.18.6, 1.19.4, 2.1.6–8, Dio 37.50.1–4.

35. Cic. *Att.* 1.19.4, *suspicans Pompeio novam quandam potentiam quaeri*. Lucullus came out of retirement to oppose the ratification of Pompey's eastern acts (see later discussion), and he may have joined Cato and Celer in leading the opposition to the *lex agraria* as well (Dio 37.49.3–50.1).

cell.[36] Flavius tried to prevent senators from entering the prison by placing his bench across the doorway and sitting on it (tribunes were sacrosanct and therefore could not be touched), but Celer responded by ordering his supporters to smash a hole in the prison wall so they could continue to attend upon him. This debacle created such an embarrassing spectacle that Pompey told Flavius to release Celer. One can easily imagine that Cato was among the first to join his ally Celer in prison, shaming Flavius for not respecting the traditional dignity of a consul. Flavius then threatened to circumvent the Senate and take the bill directly to the people, but the senators' staunch opposition had shaken Pompey badly, and he feared that his popularity alone was not sufficient to overcome the resources that Cato, Celer, and the men around them could muster, especially since a loss would be a tremendous political defeat for him. This was a dramatic setback for Pompey, who was not accustomed to such effective opposition from the Senate. Throughout his career, he had regularly demanded and received what he wanted from the Senate, so its refusal on this occasion was new and very uncomfortable, especially considering his current glory as Rome's conqueror of the East. With Cato as their leader, the *optimates* were—for the first time—successful in blocking Pompey's tribunician legislation.

Nor was that the end of it. At the same time that Cato was working with Celer to resist Pompey's efforts to acquire land for his veterans, he was also working with other *optimates* to hold up the official ratification of Pompey's political and financial acts in the East. In the course of his command against Mithridates (66 to 62 BC), Pompey had annexed territory to the empire by forming new provinces; had made formal alliances with foreign kings; had reorganized Rome's existing eastern provinces; and had made individual settlements with countless cities and political bodies from the Black Sea to Judaea.[37] Roman commanders were entitled to make such arrangements temporarily by virtue of the military authority (*imperium*) invested in them, but when they returned to Rome and laid down their *imperium*, the legitimacy of their provincial arrangements also expired. For Pompey's extensive reorganization of the East to have permanence—and for it to be a lasting monument to his glory and achievements—it needed to be ratified by a *lex* of the Roman people, or at least by a *senatus consultum* of the Senate. In the past, commanders who brought extensive new territory under Rome's control had normally summoned a delegation of senators to advise them on the settlement of those lands, an act of consultation that facilitated the approval of those

36. Cic. *Att.* 2.1.8, Dio 37.50.1–4.

37. For discussion of Pompey's arrangements, see Magie (1950) 351–78, Seager (2002) 53–62, and Rising (2013) 196–221.

arrangements by the Senate as a whole.[38] While it is possible that Pompey simply forgot or did not know to consult with the Senate when making his arrangements in the East, it is probable that he was confident in his popularity in Rome and assumed that any requests he made of the Senate would automatically be granted (as they had been in the past).[39] Yet this turned out not to be the case, and a number of leading senators, including Cato, Lucullus, and Q. Metellus Creticus (a relation of Celer and Nepos) turned out to lead the *optimates* in blocking Pompey's requests.[40] This mobilization of important *nobiles* was perhaps not surprising—Pompey had made many enemies in the Senate during his career— but it was surprisingly effective. Lucullus had essentially retired from public life, but he emerged from his villas and fishponds to demand that the Senate review every single aspect of Pompey's eastern arrangements rather than approve them *en bloc*. This would take a tremendous amount of time, and would prevent the passage of the bill for the foreseeable future. Pompey had certainly hoped that Afranius as consul would be able to force the approval of his eastern acts through the Senate, but Cato and his circle were too effective at mustering resistance. Cicero even joked that Afranius had not realized the trouble he was getting with the consulship, and that, rather than helping Pompey, he was making the great man look bad.[41] Indeed, the *optimates* even had Crassus—Pompey's consular colleague in 70 BC and a bitter rival—in their corner working to block the approval of Pompey's eastern acts.[42] So strong was this new opposition to Pompey that Atticus cautioned Cicero against being too friendly with the besieged Pompey, since this might turn the *optimates* against him as well.[43] Pompey was stymied. He was accustomed to getting what he wanted from the Senate through intimidation or *popularis* tribunes, and he had never encountered such determined resistance, even when there had been a larger number of great *nobiles* in the years following Sulla's death. Cato was surely a prime mover of this resistance; he was successfully sowing fear among the senators and pushing them to huddle together in a conservative position to resist any diminution of the Senate's *auctoritas*.

38. See Lintott (1993) 28–9 and Drogula (2015) 268 n. 107.

39. Williams and Williams (1988) emphasize that Pompey was not a good politician.

40. Plut. *Cat. Min.* 31.1, *Luc.* 42.5, *Pomp.* 46.3, Dio 37.49.3–50.1.

41. Cic. *Att.* 1.19.4, 1.20.5.

42. App. *BC* 2.9. Ward ([1977] 204) argues that Crassus contributed to the optimate effort to block Pompey, but Marshall ([1976] 96–7) disagrees. Ferrill ([1978] 169–77) discusses Crassus as a political fixer.

43. Cic. *Att.* 2.1.6.

Pompey was not the only great man feeling new pressures from the Senate and from Cato in particular. For several months Crassus had also been encountering unprecedented trouble getting the Senate to act on business he brought before it. Indeed, his willingness to help Cato, Lucullus, and the men around them block Pompey's requests may have been in part an effort to curry favor with those who were also blocking his own interests. Crassus's problem was with provincial tax contracts. The Roman state generally outsourced the collection of provincial taxes, so groups of wealthy equestrians would form into companies (the *publicani*) and would bid for the right to collect taxes from particular areas, paying their bids in advance and then making a profit by collecting more money than they bid.[44] As the Mithridatic War came to an end, the *publicani* had submitted very large bids to secure the rights to collect taxes from the wealthy eastern cities, and from those in the rich province of Asia in particular. Yet they had failed to take into account the vast destruction that a decade of war had wrought on the finances of the region. The cities of the East had been ravaged and their economies ruined, and it became clear that the *publicani* had greatly overestimated how much tax they would be able to collect; not only would they fail to receive a profit, but they would probably be unable even to recoup their initial investments. Facing considerable losses, the *publicani* wanted to renegotiate their contracts with the Roman state, and turned to Crassus for help, since he had long been the champion of the equestrian businessmen.[45] Crassus belonged to a noble family and had achieved even greater wealth and influence as a lieutenant of Sulla, but later he had worked with Pompey (whom he disliked) to roll back several of Sulla's reforms during their joint consulship in 70 BC. While Pompey went on to seek military glory, Crassus focused on his business interests and in building up his contacts in Rome. He was censor in 65 BC and tried to use that office to advance his interests, but he was thwarted by his colleague Catulus.[46] Still, he was a very influential and well-connected senior senator, and he probably had substantial investments in the companies of the *publicani*, for which reasons they had approached him in 61 BC to be their advocate before the Senate.[47]

With Crassus's backing, the *publicani* then approached Cicero, who had always sought to build stronger connections between the senatorial and equestrian

---

44. For a discussion of the *publicani*, see Nicolet (1991) 169–77 and Kay (2014) 76–82.

45. Cic. *Att.* 1.17.9. See Marshall (1976) 97–8 and Ward (1977) 211–12.

46. Crassus tried to enfranchise inhabitants of Transpadane Gaul (Dio 37.9.3) and to annex Egypt (Suet. *Iul.* 11.1, Plut. *Crass.* 13.1, cf. Cic. *Leg. Agr.* 2.44).

47. Sall. *Cat.* 48.5, Plut. *Crass.* 7.1–4, Dio 37.56.3–5. See Stanton and Marshall (1975) 207 n. 7 and Ferrill (1978) 169–77.

orders. He was frustrated that Cato had alienated the equestrians with his judicial bribery legislation, and he was eager that the rift should not be widened by a brusque rejection of the *publicani*. Personally, he thought that the *publicani* should pay for their reckless greed, and that it was ridiculous for them to seek to have their contracts renegotiated or canceled simply because they had overestimated their potential profits. Being a realist, however, he decided that the stability of the state should be the foremost concern, which meant helping the *publicani* in order to ensure their reciprocal support for the Senate. He complained to Atticus: "it was an odious matter, a shameful demand, and an admission of foolhardiness. But there was the greatest danger that, if they received nothing from their petition, they clearly would have been alienated from the Senate."[48] So on the first day of December 61 BC, Cicero and Crassus raised the question in a Senate meeting and argued for a renegotiation of the contracts. The Senate was won over by their arguments and inclined to grant the request, until the consul-elect Metellus Celer opposed the bill. Cato also made it known that he wished to speak against the proposal, but the day ended before it was his turn to speak (although he was a leader among the *optimates*, he still ranked only as an ex-tribune, so all *consulares* and *praetores* were called upon to speak first).[49] In a letter describing the Senate meeting to Atticus, Cicero mockingly referred to Cato as their "hero" (*heros*), no doubt because he intended to oppose the proposal on moral—if impractical—grounds.

In the weeks that followed, Cato maintained his opposition to the proposal, and obstructed any attempt to allow changes to the contracts. Unlike Cicero, he either did not see or did not care that alienating the *publicani* would undermine the Senate, which depended upon the support and deference of the wealthy equestrians to maintain its *auctoritas*. On January 20 of 60 BC, Cicero wrote to Atticus and complained about Cato's singular determination in blocking the bill to help the *publicani*: "the one man who cares for the Republic, although it seems with more constancy and integrity than with sense or talent, is Cato, who is now in his third month of abusing the miserable *publicani*, whom he used to hold as his dearest friends, nor will he allow an answer to be given to them by the Senate."[50] Even years later, when Cato was dead, Cicero still looked back with frustration at this event:

---

48. Cic. *Att.* 1.17.9 (cf. *QF* 1.1.32).

49. Cic. *Att.* 1.17.9. Ryan ([1998] 319) discusses the order of precedence that kept Cato from having the opportunity to speak.

50. Cic. *Att.* 1.18.7. Dio (38.7.4) also identifies Cato as the main person blocking the renegotiation of the tax contracts.

I was often at odds with my friend Cato, who seemed to me to defend the treasury and taxes too obstinately, and to deny all things to the *publicani* and much to the allies, when we ought to be generous to them and treat them just as we are accustomed to treat our colonists, especially since the union of the orders contributes to the safety of the Republic.[51]

Cicero understood the moral objections to fulfilling the requests of the *publicani*, but he saw the bigger picture of the well-being of the state in a way that Cato did not, would not, or could not. Cato does not seem to have had enough support to defeat outright the proposal to adjust these contracts, so he resorted to filibuster tactics, giving long speeches that used up the Senate's time and prevented it from moving forward with the legislation. This was effective because the Senate's rules mandated that no *senatus consultum* could be passed after sunset, which meant a loquacious senator could keep talking until the setting of the sun ended the possibility of action.[52] This was an unusual tactic for a senator, since it prevented all progress and attempts at a compromise, much to the frustration of Cicero and Crassus. As has been stated, the history of the Republican government was full of compromises and negotiations that had contributed to the evolution of the state, so Cato's absolute obstruction of compromise was untraditional and contrary to the history of the Republic, although he no doubt imagined or presented himself as protecting the *mos maiorum* by preventing any action from being taken.

Cato again displayed his opposition to such greedy and corrupt practices later in the year (60 BC) when he supported a proposal by P. Servilius Isauricus (cos. 48 BC) that a clause be inserted into a *senatus consultum* denying official recognition of debts to Roman citizens incurred by free communities, a move that attacked wealthy moneylenders.[53] This move also aggravated Cicero, because it left many Romans who had already lent money in the lurch, including his friend Atticus. He was also surely embarrassed that Cato (a junior senator) had successfully moved the Senate to vote against his own efforts to aid the equestrians and maintain the close political alliance between the two orders. Cicero continued advocating for these goals, but Crassus was silently fuming. Cicero even complains that Crassus would not take a more vocal role in arguing for the *publicani*, especially since he was their primary supporter driving their appeal.[54] Yet Crassus was in a difficult

---

51. Cic. *Off.* 3.88.

52. Gell. 14.7.8. See de Libero (1992) 16–17.

53. Cic. *Att.* 1.19.9, 1.20.4, 2.1.10. See Shackleton Bailey (1965) 1.339 and 351 and Morrell (2017) 149–50 for discussion.

54. Cic. *Att.* 1.18.6.

position: he was probably a secret investor in the companies of the *publicani*, and his reputation and influence depended upon his ability to act as a champion for the powerful equestrian order.[55] While his embarrassment was not as public as Pompey's, Crassus was very frustrated at Cato's successful obstruction, especially since the two had worked together against Pompey.

Cato's success was remarkable. He had backed both Pompey and Crassus into corners from which they could see no escape, so that both men stood to lose *dignitas* and *auctoritas* by failing to carry out promises they had made to key constituents. Cato was a central figure in leading these attacks, and it becomes clear that he had managed to unite many senators—especially among the *optimates*—behind his efforts. Although he is often portrayed as acting alone in his filibuster speeches, he must have had significant support to continue his obstruction so effectively. Indeed, by May of that year, Cicero would lament that no one in the Senate was supporting his own moderate approach, enabling Cato's obstruction to continue.[56] This does not mean that senators were lining up to join a faction or *amicitia* with Cato, but it does suggest that many were willing to support (perhaps tacitly) his efforts to curb the power of the great men, especially since he and his allies were willing to undertake the vocal roles in the opposition. It was certainly easy to admire Cato's constant appeals to ancestral tradition, and it probably cost most senators very little to lend him their support in these debates, or at least withhold their support from Pompey and Crassus. Many senators feared or resented the power of Pompey and Crassus, but never would have dreamed of opposing them until Cato used appeals to tradition and fears of domination to push a sufficient number of them to huddle around his staunch position. This alarmed Cicero, who thought Cato's scorched earth policy—his willingness to leave the eastern provinces in legal limbo and alienate the equestrian order as a means to humble Pompey and Crassus—was reckless, and that his constant invocation of his own old-fashioned interpretation of tradition would lead the state to disaster. Cicero vented his frustration in a letter to Atticus in early June of 60 BC:

> I love our Cato as much as you do, or even more, but nevertheless, that man, possessing the finest soul and the greatest honesty, sometimes does real harm to the state. For he pronounces his judgments as if he was in the Republic of Plato rather than in the dregs of Romulus. For what is

---

55. For Crassus's investments, see Shatzman (1975) 375–8. Ferrill ([1978] 169–77) suggests that Crassus was not seriously threatened, but that his reputation would be at stake.

56. Cic. *Att.* 1.20.3.

more reasonable than that a person who takes bribes to deliver a judicial verdict should himself be taken to court? Cato proposed this and the Senate approved, and now the equestrians are at war with the Senate, but not with me, since I gave a dissenting opinion. And what is more impudent than *publicani* breaking off their contracts? Yet the expense could be undertaken for the sake of holding on to the friendship of the Equestrian Order. But Cato refused to yield, and he prevailed.[57]

Cicero here laments that Cato—for all of his patriotism and integrity—was undermining the long-term stability of the state. Instead of following Cicero's own statesmanlike approach of making concessions (even unpleasant ones) when necessary for the public good, Cato allowed no flexibility in his application of his beliefs about tradition. Cicero's famous quip that Cato did not understand—or perhaps did not care—about the political realities of his day, but instead lived as if in an idealized world such as Plato's Republic, neatly sums up Cato's unique approach to politics. Whereas Cicero spoke about the need for a strong consensus among the propertied classes, Cato pushed for a society in which the old families that championed ancient values would be preeminent.

Another sign of Cato's growing influence among the *optimates* was his second marriage. He divorced his wife Atilia sometime between 63 and 60 BC on the grounds that she had been unfaithful, and their two children appear to have remained with him in accordance with normal practice.[58] Shortly thereafter (perhaps 60/59 BC), he married Marcia, the daughter of L. Marcius Philippus (cos. 56 BC), and together they had three children.[59] Cato no doubt admired Marcia for her moral excellence, but he must have been equally drawn to her family and lineage. The *Marcii Philippi* was a very noble and ancient family that traced its ancestry back to Rome's fourth king, Ancus Marcius. Marcia's father had been praetor in 62 BC (the same year in which Cato was tribune), and her grandfather had been consul in 91 BC and censor in 86 BC. This was an impressive marriage for Cato and confirmed his rising status. Yet his marriage does not mean he had won

---

57. Cic. *Att.* 2.1.8.

58. Plut. *Cat. Min.* 24.3. See Gordon (1933) 575–6 and Fehrle (1983) 60.

59. Lucan 2.329, Plut. *Cat. Min.* 25.1, App. *BC* 2.99. The year of their marriage is uncertain. In 56 BC, Marcia is thought to have been pregnant with her third child by Cato (Lucan 2.331, Plut. *Cat. Min.* 25.5), and since Cato was in Cyprus from 58–56 BC, they were probably married no later than 60/59 BC in order to have produced the first two children. Of Cato's three children with Marcia, one was probably a boy and the other two were girls (Plut. *Cat. Min.* 52.3). On Marcia's children, see Geiger (1970) 133 and Means and Dickison (1974) 213. Tansey ([2013] 423–6) also discusses the identification of Marcia in an excerpt by Pliny the Elder.

the exclusive support of the *Marcii Philippi*; a few years later, probably in 57 BC, his new father-in-law Marcius took a new wife: Atia, the niece of Julius Caesar and the mother of Octavian (the future Emperor Augustus).[60] These marriages again highlight the complex web of alliances that often existed in the Senate, and why senators could shift their opinions easily. Marcius clearly respected Cato and wanted to be connected to him, but as Caesar's star rose dramatically after 60 BC, Marcius was also happy to connect himself to the Julian clan. Like the majority of senators, Marcius wanted to do well for himself politically, but he was not as ambitious for power as were the leading men in the state, and so (like most senators) he occupied a political space in-between the great men who drove events.[61] Most senators were connected to one or more of the great men vying for power, but they were not so committed as to risk the greatest dangers and seek the highest rewards—they shifted within their webs of alliances according to political realities and their own needs and priorities. These marriage alliances reveal the balancing act many senators had to perform, which helps to explain why Cato, Caesar, and others could acquire considerable support on some measures, but fall short in other areas, depending on how their supporters responded to particular issues.

If Cato was pleased with his successes against Pompey and Crassus, Caesar's return from Spain must have been a much-anticipated delight. Caesar arrived in June of 60 BC, and was immediately faced with a problem: he was granted the right to hold a triumph for his military victories in Spain, but apparently he could not prepare everything he wanted for the spectacle before the deadline by which candidates for the consulship needed to make the required *professio* of candidacy inside the city.[62] Commanders forfeited their *imperium* and eligibility to hold a triumph if they crossed the *pomerium* and entered the city, so Caesar was stuck: he could not have his triumph ready before he had to make his *professio*, and he could not make his *professio* without sacrificing his triumph. In the past, commanders could declare their candidacy *in absentia*, but Cato's law from 62

---

60. Vell. 2.59.2–3, Suet. *Aug.* 8.3. See Syme (1986) 403 and Southern (2014) 8–9 for discussion.

61. Southern ([2014] 10) describes Philippus very well: "Philippus was not truly interested in political advancement to the same degree as either Caesar or the leading *optimates*, and he trod a careful path between factions in Rome. . . . Philippus remained on the sidelines of the political scene, and if he was not highly distinguished, neither was he completely extinguished; he neither antagonized nor actively supported either Caesar or the *optimates*, and diplomatically remained neutral during the civil war between Pompeius and Caesar."

62. Consular elections were normally held in July, but candidates for office had to make their *professio* at least a *trinundinum* (roughly three weeks) before the date of the elections (Sall. *Cat.* 18.4). See Earl (1965) 325–32, Nicolet (1991) 241–2, and Lintott (1999a) 44–5 for discussion.

BC had forbidden this. So Caesar asked the Senate for a one-time exemption from the law so he could make his *professio in absentia*. This was a reasonable request, and the Senate had often exempted other commanders from various laws as circumstances merited.[63] Cato pounced and argued against Caesar's request, but to his chagrin, the majority of the Senate wanted to grant the exemption, which no doubt seemed routine and reasonable to them. Most senators, therefore, did not share Cato's hatred or fear of Caesar, and did not see a good reason to refuse a simple and unremarkable request that had been respectfully made. Indeed, it was exactly the kind of favor the Senate regularly granted to its members in order to foster stability and cohesion within the group—the kind of favor that might have drawn Caesar closer to the *optimates* if he had been allowed to receive it. Most senators would have understood this, and so were willing to grant the request. Given Cato's harsh and unsubstantiated attacks against Caesar in 63 BC, most probably saw his opposition to Caesar as a personal feud, which they understood, but were not inclined to support. Unwilling to relent, Cato launched into a long filibuster speech, and kept speaking until the Senate was forced to adjourn without acting on Caesar's request.[64] His move surely exasperated many senators, but he could be well pleased with this victory, since it forced Caesar to forfeit either his triumph or the special honor of winning the consulship in the first year he was eligible (*in suo anno*). A triumph was the highest military honor for which most men could aspire. Lucullus had lingered outside of Rome for three years in hopes of celebrating a triumph, so everyone surely expected Caesar to keep his triumph and delay his consular campaign one year. It was quite a shock, therefore, when Caesar did the opposite, and forfeited his triumph by crossing the *pomerium*, entering the city, and declaring his candidacy for the upcoming elections.[65]

Caesar's foes saw the boldness of this action as clear evidence of the dangerous scope of his ambition, and so they mobilized their resources to defeat him if possible, or at least constrain what he could do with the office should he win. This was a daunting challenge, because Caesar had already positioned himself well for the electoral campaign, and many of Rome's elite may not have shared Cato's urgency to defeat him, or may have calculated that opposing Caesar was

---

63. App. *BC* 2.8 emphasizes that such exemptions had been made for other commanders (see also Drogula [2015] 111–18). Balsdon ([1962] 140–1), Seager ([2002] 83), and Tatum ([2008] 38) point out that this was a reasonable request for Caesar to make.

64. Plut. *Caes.* 13.2–3, *Cat. Min.* 31.3, App. *BC* 2.8. See de Libero (1992) 17 and Ryan (1998) 130 n. 233.

65. Suet. *Iul.* 18.2, Plut. *Caes.* 13.2–3, *Cat. Min.* 31.4, Dio 37.54.3.

not worth making an enemy of him. Cato and his allies did succeed in getting the Senate to announce that the consuls of 59 BC would receive as their military commands the woodlands and paths of Italy (*silvae callesque*).[66] Such a command would offer no military glory or profit, and therefore was vastly inferior to the types of commands that were normally given to Rome's highest military commanders. This was an attempt to dissuade Caesar from standing for the consulship of 59 BC, which probably means that those opposed to him doubted their ability to prevent his election outright, and so hoped to drive him from the campaign by making the consulship itself less appealing to him. Of course, Caesar could run another year, but he would no longer be covered in the fresh glory of his victorious Spanish command, and so would not be as strong a candidate. Furthermore, Cato and his allies wanted to ensure that, if Caesar won, he would be hobbled with an opposing colleague who could block his agenda. To this end they agreed to focus their considerable resources on getting Cato's son-in-law M. Calpurnius Bibulus elected (Bibulus had married Porcia, Cato's daughter by Atilia).[67] Cato and Bibulus were close political allies and connected through marriage, and Bibulus himself seems to have disliked Caesar intensely.[68] Despite their considerable support, however, the *optimates* worried that Caesar might overwhelm them, since he was immensely popular with the people, and he could be counted on to spend lavishly on bribes to win votes. Indeed, he had even formed an electoral pact (a *coitio*) with the wealthy but little-known senator

---

66. Suet. *Iul.* 19.2. Balsdon ([1939] 181–2) and Seager ([2002] 84–5) suggested that no insult was intended in this assignment, and that the *provincia* of "woodlands and paths" was merely a placeholder. They argue that the Senate was waiting to see whether the consuls of 59 BC needed to be sent to the Gallic provinces, so to satisfy the *lex Sempronia* they assigned the consuls of 59 BC to "Italy" until the situation in Gaul became clearer. While this is possible, it seems unlikely. When word of trouble in Gaul reached Rome in March of 60 BC, the two provinces were immediately assigned to the two sitting consuls (Cic. *Att.* 1.19.2), but things seem to have quieted down by May (Cic. *Att.* 1.20.5). Although there may have been uncertainty about what would happen, the consuls of 60 BC had already been assigned to the two Gallic provinces and could have taken up their commands whenever necessary, and the fact that they remained in Rome for the rest of their terms in office indicates that neither they nor the Senate were sufficiently concerned about the danger in Gaul to dispatch new commanders and armies. It therefore seems unlikely that the Senate would have kept another two consuls (those for 59 BC) in reserve for a Gallic war by assigning them to Italy when the consuls of 60 BC had yet to leave for their Gallic commands. See Gelzer (1968) 65 n. 2.

67. Suet. *Iul.* 19.1–2. On Bibulus's marriage to Porcia, see Syme (1987) 185–98.

68. Fantham ([2003] 102) suggested that Cato frequently used Bibulus as a front for pursuing attacks against Caesar, but Cato was never one to shy away from direct confrontation, and by all accounts Bibulus was strongly attached to Cato and opposed to Caesar. Epstein ([1987] 81) points out that Cato and Bibulus both had feuds with Caesar, so the *optimates* supported Bibulus knowing he would oppose Caesar.

L. Lucceius, who could contribute a great deal of money for bribes.[69] Together Caesar and Lucceius distributed bribes on an unprecedented scale, so much that the *optimates* became alarmed and pooled their own money to pay out equally large bribes on behalf of Bibulus. Surprisingly, even Cato—the great moralist and scourge of corruption—supported this distribution of bribes, holding his nose and justifying the action as being necessary for the good of the state. He may have reasoned that this use of bribery was morally acceptable because it offset Caesar's effort to corrupt the voters; Suetonius even notes that Cato and the men around him authorized the distribution of bribes *equal* to what Caesar was offering.[70] Nevertheless, this was a serious violation of the principles that he espoused so vociferously, and it underscores once again the flexibility with which tradition could be interpreted; he could justify electoral bribery if it meant protecting his own interpretation of the Republic. It is also possible that he was willing to suspend his usual opposition to bribery because—on this occasion—it served his son-in-law, and family loyalty was certainly a core value of the *mos maiorum*. Finally, his passion to defeat Caesar may have been his top priority, overwhelming his other concerns and values.

Given the scale of the bribery, it is likely that many voters accepted bribes from both groups of campaigners, with the result that Caesar and Bibulus were elected consuls for 59 BC. Cato and his friends could be reasonably satisfied with this, since Bibulus would be able to veto Caesar's actions, and the consuls would receive the lackluster command of the woodlands and paths of Italy, which would provide no glory, wealth, or reputation to fuel Caesar's future ambitions. They had used the tools at their disposal effectively to back Caesar into a corner where his political career would slowly waste away.[71] Yet it is not entirely obvious why this group was prepared to go to such extents to stop him. Cato, of course, was driven by personal enmity, but why were the others so determined to destroy the career of a rising senator? His political support for Pompey was irksome, but many respectable senators—such as Metellus Nepos—had at one time taken up service under Pompey for their own reasons. Caesar had Marian connections and had used *popularis* tactics as a junior senator, but this was hardly unforgivable for a patrician of ancient family if he defended the Senate's *auctoritas* once he reached

---

69. Cicero (*Att.* 1.17.11) reports that Lucceius was interested in joining forces with Caesar as early as the end of 61 BC.

70. Suet. *Iul.* 19.1.

71. Gruen (1974) 89, "the friends of Cato were prepared to emasculate Caesar."

higher offices.[72] He had defeated Catulus in the election to become *pontifex max-imus*, but Catulus was now dead and gone. Caesar certainly wanted the consul-ship, a military command, wealth, and glory, but so did every single member of the Senate. And the fact that the Senate had been inclined to grant him an ex-emption from Cato's law so he could declare his *professio in absentia* demonstrates that most senators did not see him as being a threat at that time. The lengths to which Cato and his allies went to block Caesar's career are therefore unusual and even extraordinary, and a sign that Cato was having a strong influence on those around him, and was imbuing many senators with his own personal enmity to-ward Caesar. As mentioned earlier, many of the Senate's senior *nobiles* were dead or in semi-retirement by 60 BC, and many of the up-and-coming senators may have been strongly influenced by Cato's allegations about Caesar and his tyran-nical ambitions. The intensity of the opposition to Caesar—even before he had received his first command—reveals the effectiveness of Cato's influence.

In retrospect, this attack on Caesar was probably a grave error. Despite his early tendency toward *popularis* tactics, there was no good reason why Caesar could not have been co-opted by the *optimates* and brought securely into their fold. He was a patrician from a glorious—if recently undistinguished—family, and his earlier pop-ulism could have been easily overlooked and overtures made for him to continue his political career in the traditional manner. Cicero illustrates this well. He thought the moment was opportune for the *optimates* to co-opt Caesar and turn him into a pow-erful ally, and he communicated this to Atticus in June (60 BC), as Caesar returned to Rome from Spain:

> And if I make Caesar—whose winds are now indeed blowing in the right
> direction—a better man, would I truly be injuring the Republic? Indeed,
> even if no one was envious of me, and even if everyone was well disposed
> to me (as would indeed be just!), even so, the cure that heals the diseased
> parts of the Republic would be no less praiseworthy than the remedy
> that cuts away those parts. For now indeed, the Equestrian Order, which
> I once stationed on the Capitoline Hill with you as its standard-bearer
> and leader, has deserted the Senate. Our leaders, moreover, think they
> have grasped the heavens if the bearded mullets in their fishponds come
> up to their hands, but they neglect all other matters. So in your estimation,

---

72. Stanton and Marshall ([1975] 208) discuss the influence of Caesar's Marian connections on his early career.

do I not appear to benefit the state sufficiently if I bring it about that those who are able to injure the state do not wish to do so?[73]

Cicero saw in Caesar—and in Pompey—an opportunity to strengthen the Senate; by overlooking their past *popularis* activities, he thought both men could successfully be joined to the *optimates* if given the status and honor they craved.[74] In doing this, Cicero was attempting to prevent a serious rift among the senators that could undermine the *auctoritas* of the Senate. The Senate normally led the state by using the cumulative moral authority of the senators—the most respected men in the state—to influence the actions of magistrates and voters alike, but this depended upon the senators speaking with a single, unified voice that could compel the respect and deference of the Roman people. By seeking to pull Caesar (and Pompey) into a closer alliance with the leading noble clans, Cicero was attempting to maintain, and even increase, the stability, cohesion, and influence of the Senate. Many other senators probably thought the same as Cicero, and so had been inclined to grant Caesar's request to make his *professio* for the consulship in *absentia*, a favor that might have indebted him to the Senate.

Cato, on the other hand, seems to have been determined to squash Caesar's career as early and as quickly as possible, and therefore he and his allies worked hard to prevent the Senate leadership from making any concessions that might bring Caesar into their ranks. So while Cicero (and perhaps others) were willing to tolerate Caesar's ambition as a means to strengthening the Senate, Cato and his allies seem to have felt that the best way to strengthen the Senate was to crush his career early. As has already been discussed, Cato developed this intense animosity for Caesar very early, and well before Caesar's career was set on any particular path. It is possible that Cato foresaw the lengths to which Caesar would go to secure his own glory and advancement, but it is more likely that later authors such as Plutarch attributed this prophetic foresight to Cato in order to portray him as a wise sage who saw the end of the Republic coming but was unable to stop it. Instead, Cato's enmity was largely personal in nature, and derived from his feud with Caesar. As he rose into the leadership of the Senate, his feud with Caesar took on greater prominence, and personal resentment led to public consequences. In particular, his animosity prevented Caesar from aligning himself with the optimate leadership of the Senate, thereby forcing him to look

---

73. Cic. *Att.* 2.1.7.

74. Cicero (*Att.* 2.1.6) also wrote that he has been working to draw Pompey into the optimate circle.

elsewhere for political support.[75] It was a lost opportunity, since there is little reason to suspect that Caesar would have resisted co-option into the *optimates* if he had been offered the opportunity on acceptable terms. Indeed, if Cicero's attitude had prevailed, the Senate might have found a mutually beneficial way to work with Caesar, as it had found ways to work with other great men in the past, but Cato's influence seems to have prevented this possibility. It was one of several pivotal moments in which Cato and his allies directed the course of history.

After his success in the consular elections (July or August of 60 BC), Caesar had several months before entering office to survey his situation. He seems to have made an effort to help the *publicani* by speaking on their behalf in a Senate meeting, and he may have attracted some support from the senators, but Cato prevented any vote from occurring by launching into another long filibuster speech and consuming the rest of the meeting.[76] He was not intimidated by the specter of Caesar as consul-elect, and Caesar must have been worried that his entire year in office would be wasted listening to Cato's endless speeches. Just as they had done with Pompey and Crassus, Cato and his friends had backed Caesar into a corner in which he had few options: unless he found a way out, he would gain little benefit from his consulship and consular command, and his political career would probably be over. He was thus denied the option of proceeding as a regular, traditional consul if he wanted to get anything done with this office, but he did not relish the idea of depending solely on *popularis* tactics as had his uncle Marius. He therefore entered into an unusual three-way alliance or *amicitia* with Pompey and Crassus, which modern historians refer to as the First Triumvirate.[77] There is a debate over when this triumvirate officially came into being: Plutarch, Livy, and Appian placed the formation of the coalition before Caesar's election to the consulship in July of 60 BC, but Velleius and Dio suggest that it formed after the election.[78] It was most likely a gradual process, since Caesar already had connections with each man, and had counted on their support in his consular election. Crassus had been backing Caesar's career for years and was looking forward

---

75. Syme (1939) 34 and Gruen (1974) 89.

76. *Schol. Bob.* 157 and 159. See Ryan (1998) 319 and de Libero (1992) 15–16.

77. Since boards of *triumviri* were elected officials in Rome, and the group consisting of Caesar, Pompey, and Crassus was merely a political friendship, the term "triumvirate" is legally incorrect, but it will be used here for convenience. See Stanton and Marshall (1975) 205.

78. Livy *Per.* 103, Vell. 2.44.1, Plut. *Caes.* 13.1–2, *Cat. Min.* 31.2–5, *Crass.* 14.1–3, *Pomp.* 47.1–3, Dio 37.54.3–56.1, App. *BC* 2.9. Suetonius (*Iul.* 19.2) is not very clear, but seems to opt for after the election. Meyer ([1922] 59–60) and Taylor ([1949] 132) accepted Livy and Plutarch, but Stanton and Marshall ([1975] 210), Gelzer ([1968] 68), Gruen ([1974] 88–9), Ward ([1977] 215), and Seager ([2002] 83–4 and n. 71) argue persuasively for Velleius and Dio.

to the payoff of having a friendly consul in office, and Pompey had received many
good services from Caesar over the years. Although Caesar was junior in rank and
resources to Pompey and Crassus, he had proven to be very capable, and as consul
he would be in a powerful position help them get what they wanted from the
Senate. Pompey and Crassus had a long-standing animosity between them that
had prevented them from working together to achieve their respective goals, but
with Caesar as a middleman, cooperation became possible. Once again, therefore, individual priorities drove a shift in alliances, producing a new *amicitia*.

   At some point during the end of 60 or the start of 59 BC, therefore, Caesar
brought Crassus and Pompey together into a pact, and each swore not to take
any political action to which another member of the pact objected.[79] Caesar also
sounded out Cicero to see if he might be induced to join this coalition. This was a
shrewd move, since Cicero was the leading orator of the day and was a tireless politician, and although he occasionally collaborated with Cato's circle, he was not a
fully dedicated member of that group. Indeed, he was often frustrated by Cato's
policies and tactics. So in December of 60 BC, Caesar sent his friend Balbus to
sound Cicero out and ask for his help with the upcoming agrarian bill, promising that Caesar intended to be guided by Cicero and Pompey during his consulship.[80] Caesar also said (through Balbus) that he hoped to reconcile Crassus
and Pompey, news that would have pleased Cicero, who had been trying to bring
Pompey into a closer political alignment with the Senate and hoped that Crassus
with his equestrian supporters would do the same.[81] Caesar's statement of hoping
(in the future) to reconcile Pompey and Crassus may indicate that the triumvirate
had not yet been officially established in December 60 BC, but it may also be that
Caesar was not yet showing Cicero all of his cards. While long-term concealment
of the pact would have been impossible, it would have been unusually trusting
of Caesar to tell Cicero the whole truth (Cicero did—in fact—reject the proposal).[82] Caesar's solicitation of Cicero demonstrates that he was not specifically
looking at building a triumvirate, but rather was looking to build as strong a coalition as possible. As a rising senator, he wanted to gather as much support as he
could in the Senate, and since Cato was preventing him from making productive

---

79. Suet. *Iul.* 19.2.

80. Cic. *Att.* 2.3.3–4 (cf. *Prov. Cons.* 41, *Pis.* 79).

81. Cicero (*Att.* 1.20.2–3 and 2.1.6) wanted to pull Pompey away from his former *popularis* attitude.

82. Cicero's refusal of Caesar's offer: Cic. *Att.* 2.3.3–4. Gruen ([1974] 88 n. 19) provides a strong argument against those who have argued that the triumvirate was deliberately concealed from Cicero.

alliances with many of the *optimates*, he sought to build a different coalition of support, but not necessarily a long-term alliance.[83] At best, we can say the triumvirate was formed sometime between Caesar's election in July 60 BC and his promulgation of the *lex agraria* in January 59 BC.

Years later, many who wrote with the advantage of hindsight would recognize the formation of this First Triumvirate as a key turning point in the crumbling of the Republic.[84] As Cato would later quip, it was not the later enmity between Caesar and Pompey that brought down the Republic, but their friendship.[85] Of course, Cato was the single individual who was most responsible for pushing the three men together, and it is extremely unlikely that they would have united had they not been so thoroughly confounded by his opposition. The three men were natural rivals: Pompey and Crassus strongly disliked one another, and both acted against the other's interests, while Caesar was striving to eclipse both of them, and both were determined not to be eclipsed. So it is unlikely that they would have agreed to advance each other's goals unless it had been absolutely necessary for their own benefit. Such aristocrats were natural competitors, so it would have been contrary to their interests to collaborate unless they had been left no choice. Cato was the leading figure who pushed each of these men into untenable positions from which they had no escape except to cooperate with one another. He did not act alone, but he was the one person who is named as a leading player in the obstruction of each man: he worked with Metellus Celer to block legislation that would acquire land for Pompey's veterans; he cooperated with Lucullus and Crassus to block confirmation of Pompey's arrangements of the East; he worked with Metellus Celer to prevent the renegotiation of the tax contracts of the *publicani* (Crassus's clients); and he is the only figure named in the filibustering of Caesar's request to submit his *professio* for the consular elections *in absentia*. In fact, Cato must have had the support of many senators to be able to oppose the ambition of all three men so successfully, but he was clearly the central figure who led the attacks and encouraged others to join him. He had made himself a figurehead for the *optimates* by making himself the leading defender of the *mos maiorum*, but his tireless energy for political battles—at a time when the leadership of the *optimates* was becoming thin—made him a central figure and a driving force in the opposition of the great men.

---

83. Meier (1966) 280–1, Stanton and Marshall (1975) 205–6, Ferrill (1978) 169–77, Pelling (2011) 191.

84. Vell. 2.44.1, Luc. 1.84–6, Plut. *Caes.* 13.5, *Cat. Min.* 30.6, Flor. 2.13.8–17.

85. Plut. *Pomp.* 47.2–3 (cf. *Caes.* 13.5).

Caesar's Consular Legislation

Although Caesar had used some unconventional methods to climb the political ladder and win his consulship, once in office it probably suited his interests to change tactics and behave like a traditional consul, basing his authority on a united Senate, if the *optimates* would allow the *rapprochement*. That is, having achieved his goal of reaching the consulship, he could afford to follow conventional procedures, and softening the anger of his opponents would make it easier to reach his legislative goals. In his inaugural address, Caesar offered to put old conflicts behind him and focus only on the good of the state.[86] Exuding reasonableness, he sought reconciliation between himself and Bibulus, and promised that he would henceforth act only in consultation with the Senate. This was a genuine offer, and he surely hoped that his words would find a willing audience, but he was determined to achieve his goals and was prepared for opposition.

Caesar's first act as consul was to order that the business of each Senate meeting be posted publicly, enabling citizens to know what matters were under debate in the Curia.[87] He probably did this in the expectation that Cato and his allies would obstruct proposals that he brought to the senators, and he hoped that this opposition would appear mean-spirited and irrational when published for public consumption. Next he introduced his *lex agraria* to the Senate, a bill that would make public land—and whatever private land was voluntarily offered for sale—available to poor citizens as well as to Pompey's veterans.[88] Cato and the men around him had been opposing this type of legislation for three years, and Caesar apparently studied their past objections carefully and crafted his bill to make it as palatable to the aristocracy as possible.[89] Acting in strict accordance with tradition, Caesar first presented his bill to the Senate and called on the senators one by one, asking for their opinions and any suggestions for improvement they might have, promising to accept all reasonable requests for emendation or revision. This was a fine show of deference to the *auctoritas* of the Senate, and it presented Caesar as a consul who respected the *mos maiorum*. One can be certain that Cato and his allies combed through the bill with great

---

86. App. *BC* 2.10, Dio 38.1.1–2.

87. Suetonius (*Iul.* 20.1) says that Caesar established a *diurna acta*, which White ([1997] 73–84, esp. 80) has suggested must refer to the publication of notice boards rather than anything like a gazette or newspaper.

88. Cic. *Att.* 2.3.3, 2.16.2, *Fam.* 13.4.2, Vell. 2.44.4, Suet. *Iul.* 20.1, Plut. *Caes.* 14.2–3, *Cat. Min.* 31.4–32.6, *Pomp.* 47.3–48.2, App. *BC* 2.10–12, Dio 38.1.1–7. See Crawford (1989) 179–90.

89. Dio 38.2.1. Cicero (*Att.* 2.3.3) says Caesar was working on his bill as early as 60 BC. On his efforts to improve upon previous failed bills, see Gelzer (1968) 71–3.

care looking for reasons to reject it, but they were not able to identify a single objectionable clause. This placed Cato in an awkward situation, because Caesar's moderation, his deference to the Senate, his proper observance of traditional procedure, and the obvious excellence of his agrarian bill portrayed him as an utterly traditional consul, rather than the *popularis* would-be tyrant that Cato accused him of being. So the *optimates* found themselves embarrassed by the quality of the legislation and at a loss to justify their opposition.[90] Caesar was clearly—and cleverly—acting in accordance with the *mos maiorum*, showing the Senate that he was prepared to be a traditional consul, and challenging Cato's circle to find some grounds for opposition.

Despite the obvious excellence of the legislation and the proper procedure by which it was brought forward, Cato and his friends were determined to block its passage. Their motive was probably twofold: they did not want to give Pompey the victory he had been seeking for three years, and they did not want to give Caesar the credit for sponsoring a law that would be very popular with the citizenry and especially with Pompey's veterans. As Plutarch describes the situation: "Cato . . . said he did not fear the law about the land, but the reward that those indulging and enticing the people would demand in return for it."[91] When Caesar called on the senators for their opinions, Cato and his friends were unable to offer any suggestions for improvement, but they still did not speak in favor of the bill, and tried to delay its progress. Embarrassed that he could offer no explanation for his recalcitrance, Cato said only that the existing situation in the state was fine, and that no changes were necessary that year.[92] Although this does not seem like a particularly good reason to block an excellent and popular bill, it probably carried more weight and substance coming from Cato, the great defender of tradition, who could portray his position as opposing innovation in defense of the *mos maiorum*. And yet, his extreme obstructionism was again a rejection of Rome's long-standing traditions of negotiation and compromise that had typified even Cato the Elder's career.[93] In fact, Cato's determination to block Senate business seems more *popularis* than optimate. Traditionally, the Senate

---

90. Dio (38.2.2) stresses the difficult position of the *optimates*, given the obvious quality of Caesar's bill and his method of bringing it respectfully before the Senate.

91. Plut. *Cat. Min.* 31.5.

92. Dio 38.3.1–3. See Gelzer (1968) 72–3 and Seager (2002) 86–7.

93. Plutarch (*Mor.* 804c) tries to make Cato's use of the filibuster sound like a clever tactic, but as Flower ([2010b] 144–5) notes: "his politics of constant obstruction and provocation made any kind of negotiation or compromise significantly harder to achieve, and was at variance with everything that was most traditional about the republic that his great-grandfather and namesake, the famous censor, had been such a vital part of."

worked to build internal consensus, while plebeian tribunes sought to use their sacrosanctity and their veto to block actions that were harmful to the people.[94] In this debate (and in many more to come), Cato was seeking to prevent the Senate from reaching an agreement on the *lex agraria* by blocking all discussion on the matter, as if he were a *popularis* tribune interposing his veto to prevent any and all discussion, including the possibility of compromise. So while Cato claimed that his obstruction of Caesar's bill was done to prevent innovation, in reality his tactics were unconventional and even radical innovations to tradition.[95] He was trying to block senatorial consensus rather than promote it. When Caesar surprised his opponents by acting in a very regular and traditional manner, Cato was at a loss, and tried to justify his untraditional tactic of obstructionism with weak claims that he was doing it to preserve tradition.

So Cato began one of his now-familiar filibuster speeches, determined to exhaust the time remaining in the meeting and prevent any decision from being reached. He maintained his opposition to the bill throughout the month of January, employing filibuster speeches and refusing to allow the bill to be acted upon.[96] This seemed so irrational in the face of Caesar's display of reasonableness that one has to wonder whether Cato was deliberately trying to provoke Caesar, hoping he would make some misstep or even resort to violence, and thereby display the tyrannical nature that Cato claimed was there.[97] If this was the case, it worked. As Cato began yet another of his filibusters to prevent action on the bill, Caesar lost his patience and threatened to have him hauled away to prison for his obstruction. Without missing a beat, Cato willingly consented to being arrested, and to Caesar's surprise a great number of the senators left the Curia and followed him to the jail.[98] It is even possible that Cato planned this display, perhaps modeling it after Metellus Celer's behavior the previous year, when as consul he had been thrown in jail for obstructing the agrarian legislation proposed by Pompey's

---

94. Lintott (1999a) 123.

95. See Goldsworthy (2008) 140, "At Rome innovations almost invariably arrived wrapped in a cloak of tradition."

96. Dio 38.2.3–3.1. See de Libero (1992) 19 and 27–8 for Cato's continued efforts to obstruct the bill.

97. Dragstedt ([1969] 78) suggested that this was Cato's strategy, and that he wanted Caesar to drop his veneer of a conciliatory posture.

98. Sen. *Ep.* 14.13, Suet. *Iul.* 20.4, Gell. 4.10.8, Plut. *Cat. Min.* 33.1–2, Dio 38.3.2–3. Valerius Maximus (2.10.7) refers to Cato using filibuster speeches to block action on renegotiating the tax contracts for the *publicani*. Pelling ([2011] 194–5) points out that there are two stories of Cato being arrested during Caesar's consulship, and it may be that one of these is a repetition (that Cato was only arrested once).

tribune L. Flavius.[99] Cato had goaded Caesar into displaying his rashness and his willingness to force his will on others, and his allies were ready to rise and march out of the Senate House. This certainly had a chilling effect on the Senate, since it gave credence to the worst of Cato's accusations against Caesar. When Caesar accosted one of these senators accompanying Cato for leaving before the Senate had been dismissed, the man's reply—that he preferred to be in prison with Cato than in the Curia with Caesar—was a sharp rebuke for which Caesar was not prepared.[100] Cato's skillful display had the desired effect, since Caesar's unscrupulous use of force offended and frightened many in the Senate, and opened him to subsequent attacks that his consular acts were illegitimate because they had been passed through tyrannical force.[101] By pushing Caesar to act like a tyrant, Cato could justify taking almost any obstructionist action by appealing to Rome's tradition of opposing to tyranny. As a boy, he had witnessed Sulla label his political enemies as tyrants and use this accusation to justify his march on Rome and his sack of the city, demonstrating that appeals to tradition could disguise and justify almost any action.[102] He no doubt hoped that—by provoking Caesar into acting like a tyrant—he could frighten more senators away from safe tolerance and into joining his opposition. The Senate had not supported Cato's efforts to deny Caesar a praetorian triumph because it seemed motivated by a personal feud, but his successful efforts to paint Caesar as a tyrant frightened the senators and pushed them into giving their support. Caesar realized his mistake, and to prevent the situation from becoming worse, he had one of his friendly tribunes secure Cato's release before the general population was treated to the show of having the champion of the *mos maiorum* locked up in prison.

Cato's circle had won a temporary victory, but as Cicero had previously complained to Atticus, Cato's victories often came at a heavy cost to the Republic. Just as his intense opposition to bills brought by Pompey and Crassus had alienated them (and their equestrian supporters) from the Senate, so also his extreme efforts to block Caesar's initiatives left Caesar with little choice but to resort to *popularis* methods. It is possible that Caesar's display of proper traditional procedures had only been for show, but having reached the consulship and the top of the *cursus honorum*, he could afford to be magnanimous and move closer to the *optimates* if they allowed it. Cato ensured that this did not happen,

---

99. Cic. *Att.* 2.1.8 and Dio 37.50.1–2.

100. Dio 38.3.2–3. See discussion in Gelzer (1969) 72–3.

101. Plut. *Cat. Min.* 32.1.

102. App. *BC* 1.57.

probably because he believed that he could turn the Senate against Caesar. So while Cicero had seen a golden opportunity to win Caesar over to the *optimates*, Cato antagonized him and drove him away.[103] Thus repulsed, Caesar had little choice but to move forward with *popularis* methods or face political ruin.[104] He had wanted his initiatives to be approved by the Senate, and he even warned the Senate that with filibusters and inaction it was abdicating its authority over the bill to the people, but this does not seem to have had an effect.[105] Seeing no opening for progress on his *lex agraria*—despite the Senate's inability to find anything wrong with it—Caesar resolved to circumvent the Senate and take the bill directly to the popular assembly.

Caesar prepared for a showdown in the assembly by having Pompey summon all of his veterans to Rome.[106] This was to bolster the number of voters in favor of the *lex agraria*, but he also must have welcomed the intimidation that could be produced by large numbers of veterans. When Caesar presented the bill to the people and explained its contents, he asked his consular colleague Bibulus what changes or modifications he suggested.[107] Since the *optimates* still had not found any particular part of the bill to which they could reasonably object, Bibulus could only reiterate Cato's statement that the bill was an innovation to tradition, which he would neither support nor permit. Caesar must have guessed that this response would look capricious and spiteful in the eyes of the people, so he launched into a bit of political theater in which he begged and pleaded with Bibulus to change his mind and to come to the people's aid by withdrawing his opposition.[108] His supporters in the crowd (including Pompey's veterans) added their voices to the supplication, until Bibulus in his frustration stormed off, shouting, "you will not have this law this year, not even should you all want it!"[109] Just as Cato had goaded

---

103. Flower ([2010b] 145) describes Cato as having "a dangerous political stance that prevented both him and others from addressing the actual problems Rome faced and from finding solutions that could have created a more stable and less contested republic."

104. See Meier (1966) 282–5, Gruen (1974) 91–2, de Libero (1992) 72–80, Gruen (2009) 34, and Pina Polo (2011) 299.

105. Dio 38.3.3.

106. Plut. *Pomp.* 48.1 (cf. Cic. *Vat.* 5).

107. Dio 38.4.1–3.

108. This must have resembled the earlier battle over land reform in 133 BC, when Tiberius Gracchus begged his colleague Octavius to lift his veto of the *lex Sempronia* so the people could vote on the land reform bill. Octavius refused, so Tiberius had the people remove him from office by popular vote (Plut. *TG* 12.1–2). One may wonder whether Caesar had toyed with the idea of calling for a vote to try to remove Bibulus from office.

109. Dio 38.4.3.

Caesar into using force in the Senate, Caesar now pushed Bibulus into making his opposition to the bill seem baseless and petty. Although Caesar may have hoped that Bibulus would have a change of heart when confronted by the masses of citizens eager for land, he was certainly content with the answer he received, since it demonstrated to the assembly the senselessness of the opposition to the bill, and that Cato, Bibulus, and their allies were willing to go to any lengths, even to harm the people, if it meant humbling Caesar and Pompey. To underscore this point, he avoided calling on any other magistrate who might give a more rational and cogent reason for opposing the bill, and instead called upon Pompey and Crassus to state their opinions.[110] Pompey went through every point of the bill and explained its importance and reasonableness to the gathered people, and he gave his unqualified approval to the measure and asked the people—who were enthralled as they listened to Rome's great hero—to support the bill as well. Crassus then came forward and approved of Pompey's explanation of the bill, and added his support for it. This was the first official unveiling of the triumvirate, and it must have shocked Cato and most of the Senate.[111] Pompey was certainly expected to support the agrarian bill that would provide land for his veterans, but Crassus's support must have taken the wind from the *optimates'* sails, since only one year earlier he had helped Cato to block Pompey's eastern settlements. Cato's main asset was his claim to understand the *mos maiorum* better than other men, making himself an authority of what was (and was not) good and acceptable for the Republic, but the spectacle of Pompey and Crassus—two of Rome's greatest senators—coming together to support Caesar's legislation despite their known enmity for one another must have devastated public confidence in Cato's negative opinion of the bill. Cato and Bibulus had asserted that the bill was bad because it was an innovation, but Caesar, Pompey, and Crassus explained clearly why the bill was good, and their combined *auctoritas* outweighed that of Bibulus and Cato, helping the citizens—who wanted the bill—ignore the opposition and cast a positive vote. It was no longer one consul against the Senate, but rather a bloc of three immensely important senators who collectively exercised an expansive influence over the citizenry. Thus Caesar did not appear to be flouting the Senate; he was a member of one senatorial coalition arguing against another coalition. This was an enormous shift in the landscape of senatorial factions, since the union of Caesar, Pompey, and Crassus brought their respective networks of supporters into alignment, and signaled to other senators that their interests

---

110. Plut. *Pomp.* 47.4–5, *Caes.* 14.4–6, App. *BC* 2.10, Dio 38.4.4–5.5.

111. Seager ([2002] 86–7) demonstrates that the existence of the triumvirate was probably still a secret at the time of Cato's arrest in the Senate.

might be better served by supporting (or at least not opposing) the triumvirs. This first appearance of the triumvirate would have triggered a quick recalculation of the balance of influence between Cato and Caesar, and both men probably knew that the scales had suddenly dropped heavily on Caesar's side.

Despite this sudden revelation, the *optimates* continued with their plan of obstruction. Bibulus bravely maintained his opposition to Caesar's bill in the face of angry voters, and he called upon the three tribunes friendly to his cause to support him. Thinking that it would be to their benefit if they could goad Caesar into using violence to pass his legislation, Bibulus and his supporters found new and inventive ways to maintain their obstruction.[112] On each comitial day (days on which a public assembly or *comitia* could meet), Bibulus appeared before the assembly and declared that the omens for that day were unfavorable, which meant that no public business could proceed, including votes on legislation.[113] How long this went on is uncertain, but eventually Bibulus was assaulted one morning—presumably by agents of the triumvirs—while on his way to announce more unfavorable omens.[114] He and those with him were attacked and beaten, his consular *fasces* were taken and smashed, and he was forced to retreat while being pelted with manure and other hurled objects.[115] Cato was with him and was also forced to retreat, but unlike the others who ran from the attackers in a panic, he withdrew slowly from the tumult, constantly stopping to argue with those who were harassing him.[116] This was not the first time Cato had been involved in political violence—his personal bravery in facing the armed retainers of Metellus Nepos in 62 BC had been extraordinary—but this time Cato was on the losing end of the engagement. With Bibulus unable to announce adverse omens, the citizens voted and Caesar's *lex agraria* passed easily. On the following day Bibulus complained to the Senate about the treatment he had received, but no one made any kind of motion, so he returned to his house and remained there.[117] Some

---

112. App. *BC* 2.11.

113. Suet. *Iul.* 20.1, Plut. *Pomp.* 48.4, Dio 38.6.1–6. According to the *lex Aelia et Fufia* of 150 BC, a consul or tribune could order a public meeting to be disbanded if he reported seeing unfavorable omens, which indicating that the gods were opposed to whatever business was underway (Cic. *Phil.* 2.81, *Sest.* 33–4). See Sumner (1963) 337–58, Astin (1964) 421–45, Weinrib (1970) 395–425, Mitchell (1986), and de Libero (1992) 65–6.

114. The timeline of events in this year is difficult to reconstruct. See Shackleton-Bailey (1965) 406–7.

115. Cic. *Vat.* 22, Plut. *Cat. Min.* 32.2–4, *Pomp.* 48.1–2, *Caes.* 14.9, App. *BC* 2.11, Dio 38.6.1–4.

116. Plut. *Cat. Min.* 32.2.

117. Vell. 2.44.5, Suet. *Iul.* 20.1. Dio (38.6.4) says that Bibulus tried to get the Senate to annul Caesar's law (αὐτὸν λῦσαι), but this cannot be right, since the Senate did not have the authority

senators were doubtless frightened to oppose the triumvirs, but others may have simply seen the change in the political coalitions, and they went with the prevailing wind, as they had generally done in the past.

As Cato trudged off that day, he may have meditated on the incalculable odds that Pompey and Crassus would join forces with Caesar in this way. Senators like Caesar, Pompey, and (to a lesser degree) Crassus had generally adopted *popularis* measures as a way to obtain individual advantage in the face of senatorial opposition, and populism was normally a tactic that an individual used to gain personal advancement. That these three ambitious men would use *popularis* measures to work together for their mutual advantage must have been an unsettling innovation, especially since Pompey and Crassus had long been bitter rivals. One wonders if Cato understood that the effectiveness of his own tactics for opposing these men had driven them into one another's arms. Every senator must have known that Caesar, Pompey, and Crassus would individually go to considerable lengths to protect and enhance their own positions, but few would have imagined that they would agree to work together in a political alliance. Indeed, it is a sign of the effectiveness of Cato's opposition that he drove them to such unexpected and unprecedented lengths, since it is highly improbable that they would have joined forces had they not been stymied by Cato's unusual obstructionism. This was not particularly desirable—none of the three can have relished the idea of helping the other two acquire more influence and status—but only by doing so could Caesar, Pompey, and Crassus escape from the corners in which Cato had trapped them.

The formation of the triumvirate dealt a blow to Cato's influence over the Senate, and Caesar was quick to use his advantage. He had added a clause to his legislation that required all senators to take an oath within a proscribed period to uphold the new law, with dire consequences for those who refused to take the oath.[118] Since laws passed by a popular assembly were valid whether or not the senators swore to uphold them, this oath forced the opposition to choose between embarrassing themselves by taking the oath, or opening themselves to punishment should they refuse. Even worse, swearing to uphold the law would make it very difficult for Cato and his friends to claim later that the law was

---

to annul laws passed by the popular assemblies at that time. Bibulus probably wanted a *senatus consultum* asking the assembly to annul the law, or perhaps a *senatus consultum* condemning Caesar's behavior, but given the change in senatorial factions, no one was ready to risk angering the triumvirs. Afzelius ([1941] 160–1) and Gelzer ([1968] 74) suggested that Bibulus wanted the Senate to pass a *senatus consultum ultimum* to use violence against the triumvirs, but the senators refused, being afraid of Pompey's veterans.

118. Plut. *Cat. Min.* 32.3–6, Dio 38.7.1–2, App. *BC* 2.12. See Bellemore (2005) 229–31 for discussion of the penalties for those who did not take the oath.

invalid, since (Caesar could claim) their oaths had confirmed the validity of the legislation. Caesar no doubt borrowed this tactic from his great-uncle Marius, who had arranged for his tribunician ally Saturninus to add a similar oath to his *lex Appuleia* in 100 BC, and when Marius's hated rival Metellus Numidicus refused to take the oath, he was sentenced to exile.[119] Caesar put Cato and his allies in the same dilemma, confronting them with the choice of proud exile or compromising their principles to remain in Rome, an action that would have undermined Cato in particular. It was a political trap, and Cato was stuck. All of the senators took the oath promptly except Cato and Favonius, one of the young *optimates* who had taken to imitating Cato. They seemed prepared to accept exile rather than compromise their principles, but Cicero came to their rescue. Ever the realist, Cicero enabled them to save face by arguing that Rome was better served by Cato's presence than by his absence.[120] With this argument as moral justification, Cato and Favonius reluctantly took the oath on the last day before the deadline. Caesar's victory in the assembly was a dramatic reversal from the opposition he had encountered in the Senate House, and it illustrates how significant his alliance with Pompey and Crassus was in the eyes of their fellow senators. Many of those senators who had marched to prison with Cato rather than support Caesar's bill now ignored Bibulus's entreaties for action and quietly took the oath to support the bill.

Over the next few months, Caesar would promulgate several more pieces of legislation, all of which bypassed the Senate and went directly to the popular assemblies. Dio says that, after the Senate's obstruction of his *lex agraria*, Caesar did not even summon the Senate to meet on important issues.[121] In the first half of the year, Caesar arranged the passage of four major bills: the official recognition of Ptolemy XII Auletes as king of Egypt, the ratification of Pompey's eastern arrangements, the renegotiation of the tax contracts for Crassus's equestrian clients, and the addition of land in Campania to the list of land the *lex agraria* made available for distribution to poor citizens and Pompey's veterans.[122] Although the majority of the senators seem to have been cowed by the triumvirate's display of influence and power, Cato and his circle

---

119. Livy *Per.* 69, Plut. *Mar.* 29.1–8, App. *BC* 1.29–31. See Bellemore (2005) 229.

120. Plut. *Cat. Min.* 33.4–5 (cf. Dio 38.7.1–3).

121. Dio 38.4.1.

122. King Ptolemy: Cic. *Att.* 2.16.2, Dio 39.12.1; Pompey's eastern arrangements: Plut. *Pomp.* 48.2–3, Dio 38.7.4; *publicani*: Cic. *Att.* 2.16.2, *Planc.* 35, Val. Max. 2.10.7, Suet. *Iul.* 20.3, App. *BC* 2.13, Dio 38.7.4; Campania: Cic. *Att.* 2.16.1–2, 2.17.1, 2.18.2, *Phil.* 2.101, Vell. 2.44.4, Suet. *Iul* 20.3, Plut. *Cat. Min.* 33.1–2, App. *BC* 2.10, Dio 38.7.3. See Bellemore (2005) 228.

continued to resist these bills. Lucullus and Cato opposed the ratification of Pompey's settlement of the East and the renegotiation of contracts with the *publicani*, but Caesar silenced Lucullus with threats of prosecution.[123] Cato is said to have been the only one who opposed the resettlement of Campania, but Caesar had him dragged from the rostra and (again) led off to prison.[124] According to Plutarch, Cato continued to speak against the bill as he was being led away in an effort to convince others to oppose the bill, and when a large crowd of senators in a sad silence followed him to prison, Caesar had a tribune release him lest he become a martyr in the public's eyes. Given the similarity of this episode to Caesar's previous arrest of Cato, it is likely that Plutarch has duplicated the story, either as an accident or (more likely) for heroic effect to emphasize Cato's efforts to make himself a martyr for the Republic.[125] If he was not arrested (for a second time) at this meeting,[126] Caesar may have used some other method to prevent him from obstructing the bill, such as he would do later in his consulship.

Surprisingly, little opposition is recorded to the *lex Vatinia* that changed Caesar's provincial command from the woodlands and paths of Italy to Cisalpine Gaul and Illyricum with three legions for five years.[127] Not only was this was an important command, but the guarantee of a five-year tenure and an army of three legions instead of the normal two (for consuls) made this an unusual and highly desirable provincial assignment. The lack of resistance is probably explained by a boycott of official business by Cato and his friends, who hoped their absence would create some kind of obstruction, or at least would shame Caesar by their refusal to participate.[128] The triumvirate's success in pushing through legislation against opposition probably drove Cato to this new tactic, hoping a boycott would prevent Caesar from claiming legitimacy for actions passed during his consulship. So there was little resistance to the *lex Vatinia*, and when Metellus Celer—who was about to assume command of Transalpine

---

123. Suetonius (*Iul.* 20.4) says that Caesar so intimidated Lucullus that he fell on his knees and begged for Caesar's mercy, but Gruen ([1974] 92 n. 29) suggests that Lucullus was only mocking Caesar by this display. Dio (38.7.5) only mentions that Lucullus offered no further resistance to Caesar's acts.

124. Plut. *Cat. Min.* 33.1.

125. See Pelling (2002) 4 and (2011) 194 and 201.

126. Bellemore ([2005] 235–7) suggests that Cato offered little or no opposition to this bill.

127. Suet. *Iul.* 22.1, Plut. *Caes.* 14.10, *Pomp.* 48.3, Dio 38.8.5.

128. Plut. *Caes.* 14.13. See de Libero (1992) 72–3 for discussion.

Gaul—unexpectedly died in April, the Senate raised no objection to Pompey's suggestion that this province be assigned to Caesar as well, along with a fourth legion.[129] Cato alone is recorded as opposing the additional assignment of Transalpine Gaul to Caesar, and he berated the senators for allowing men to trade daughters for provinces (Pompey had recently married Caesar's daughter Julia).[130] He tried to convince them that they were setting Caesar up as a tyrant, no doubt hoping to stimulate patriotic anger and opposition, but the Senate was unwilling to move against him. It would be interesting to know the senators' response to Cato's speech; his idealism and pugnaciousness were admirable, but it must have seemed recklessly futile to provoke Caesar at that time. That no other senator resisted Pompey's proposal indicates the great influence the triumvirs exerted at this time, although such acquiescence may also have been a tactical decision: everyone knew the assembly would pass a law giving Transalpine Gaul to Caesar if asked, so the senators may have chosen to save face by making the assignment themselves. Furthermore, if the Senate made the assignment by decree (as it did), it could also withdraw the province by decree when it wished, whereas provinces assigned by a law of the people (such as Cisalpine Gaul and Illyricum) could not be withdrawn by the Senate. So the Senate may have felt it retained some authority over Caesar by giving him Transalpine Gaul, and in fact, this would prove to be a critical aspect of the later battles over Caesar's command.

Cato's response to one other piece of Caesar's legislation deserves note. As their political battles raged that year, Cato was surprised to find that he actually approved of one piece of legislation that Caesar brought forward: his *lex Julia de repetundis*, intended to suppress extortion and other crimes by Roman officials in the provinces. Rome had been struggling with this problem for over a century, and there were powerful groups interested in preventing the protection of provincials: equestrians wanted to get rich through tax collection and other contracts, and senators wanted to use their provincial commands to fill their family coffers and to make up for the increasingly high costs of a political career. Although various laws had been introduced over the years to curtail

129. Cic. *Att.* 8.3.3, Suet. *Iul.* 22.1, Dio 38.8.5. Plutarch (*Cat. Min.* 33.3), Velleius (2.44.5), and Appian (*BC* 2.13) mistakenly combine these two separate provincial assignments—one by the assembly and one by the Senate—into a single event. Metellus Celer had been assigned to Transalpine Gaul over a year earlier in March 60 BC, but he was still in Rome when he died suddenly in April 59 BC (Cic. *Cael.* 59).

130. Pompey's marriage to Julia: Cic. *Att.* 2.17.1, 8.3.3, Plut. *Caes.* 14.7, *Pomp.* 47.6. Cato berates the Senate: Plut. *Cat. Min.* 33.3.

abuses, Caesar's *lex* was a model of organization and strict enforcement, such that Cato could not object to it and Cicero praised it highly.[131] Yet this raises a question about Cato's motives: why did he fiercely resist the passage of the *lex agraria*—with which he could find no fault—but allow the *lex de repetundis* to pass unchallenged? Both were good bills, and Cato found no fault with either, and yet he fought tenaciously to block the one but not the other. It is possible that he was currently boycotting Caesar's actions when this bill came up, but it is more likely that he supported the bill because it aimed to suppress corruption, but would not benefit Caesar personally. The *lex agraria* was bad in Cato's eyes because it brought no real benefit to the state, but would increase popular support for Caesar (and Pompey and Crassus) by enabling the citizens to acquire land. The *lex de repetundis*, however, would—in Cato's opinion—bring great benefits to the state by reducing corruption, but it would not bring Caesar (or Pompey or Crassus) any great benefit, because nothing was being given away to the people. Indeed, Cato may even have hoped that Caesar would lose political support because of this bill, just as he (Cato) had lost the support of the equestrians by pushing anti-corruption legislation. Kit Morrell has gone even further, suggesting that Cato and his political ally P. Servilius Isauricus had an influence on the content of the *lex*, which included clauses protecting the rights of free communities, a reform that Cato and Servilius had proposed in the previous year.[132] Cato had promoted measures to suppress corruption in the past, so he may have supported the bill despite his loathing for its proposer, especially if it included some of his own legislative ideas. So he probably supported the bill, but he would never refer to the law by name—the *lex Julia de repetundis*—because doing so would acknowledge Caesar as the author of the law, and Cato refused to give him even that much credit.[133] He fought tenaciously to block laws that brought personal benefits to the triumvirs (even if they were also beneficial to the state), but he was willing to allow other laws to pass that he considered good for the state, so long as they did not increase the influence of Caesar, Pompey, and Crassus.

---

131. Cato: Dio 38.7.4–6, Cicero: Cic. *Sest.* 135, *Pis* 37. On the *lex*, see Oost (1956) 19–28, Brunt (1961) 90–9, Gruen (1974) 240–4, Lintott (1981) 202–7.

132. Morrell (2017) 148–51. That Servilius introduced this clause into Caesar's bill is clear (Cic. *Att.* 1.19.9). Cato's role in drafting and advancing the clause is less certain (Cic. *Att.* 2.1.10), but Morrell's argument that Cato was the driving force behind the clause is persuasive.

133. Dio 38.7.6.

Cato and His Circle in Caesar's Consulship

After the passage of the *lex agraria*, everything seemed to be going the triumvirs'
way in the first half of 59 BC. The resources they were able to muster, and their
willingness to use force to neutralize obstruction by their opponents, enabled
them to carry out their legislative program, which brought them greater status
and influence with the voters.[134] In response, Cato and his circle, having lost their
ability to obstruct legislation, adopted different techniques to work against the
triumvirs.[135] After being assaulted during his attempt to block the Campanian
legislation, Bibulus decided to remain in his house for the rest of the year, officially observing the skies for omens, which—in theory—meant that no public
business could be conducted.[136] For the remaining eight months of his consulship, Bibulus dispatched messages from his home reminding the Romans that he
was officially watching the skies for omens, and that no public business should
proceed. While he probably knew that Caesar would (and did) ignore this new
form of obstruction, Bibulus and his allies believed that it provided legal grounds
to declare all of Caesar's actions invalid.[137] Yet the legality and religious propriety
of this claim are questionable. While the *lex Aelia et Fufia* clearly established that
public business could not proceed if a consul (or tribune) declared bad omens, it
seems that the declaration (*obnuntiatio*) had to be made in person—or at least
there was the widespread expectation that the announcement should be made
in person.[138] So while Bibulus claimed that the letters he dispatched from his
house announcing adverse omens rendered all of Caesar's actions invalid, Caesar
could claim that the announcements themselves were invalid because they had
not been made in public and in person to the presiding official. Our information
on *obnuntiatio* is too scanty to tell us who was legally correct: no magistrate to
that time is known to have ignored the imposition of *obnuntiatio* as blatantly as
Caesar did, but no politician is known to have used it continually *in absentia* to

---

134. Plut. *Caes.* 14.9 points out that the political violence made opposition dangerous for Cato
and Bibulus.

135. Bellemore ([2005] 239–31) discusses Cato's cessation of active opposition to Caesar.

136. Cic. *Att.* 2.16.2, 2.19.2, *Fam.* 1.9.7, *Vat.* 16, 22, *Dom.* 39–40, *Har. Resp.* 48, Vell. 2.44.5, Suet.
Iul. 20.1, Plut. *Pomp.* 48.4, App. *BC* 2.45, Dio 37.6.5–6. The three tribunes who had supported
Bibulus reportedly did the same (Cic. *Vat.* 16). See discussions in Shackleton-Bailey (1965)
1.382, Lintott (1968) 144–6, 190–3, 213, Taylor (1949) 82–3, 133–4, Linderski (1965) 71–90,
Linderski (1986) 2165–8, Mitchell (1986) *passim*, Linderski (1995) 425–6, Meier (1995) 204–
23, Beard et al. (1998) 126–9, Tatum (1999) 126–30.

137. See de Libero (1992) 75 and 99–101 for discussion.

138. Linderski (1965) 425–8.

block all public business as Bibulus did.[139] It is probable that no one really knew whether Bibulus's use of *obnuntiatio* was valid or not; the legitimacy of Roman religious practices frequently rested upon customary practice and the vaguely defined *mos maiorum*, so no authoritative text existed to determine whether Caesar was required to observe Bibulus's written announcements.[140] Indeed, the lack of clarity on this religious question is probably what made it attractive to Bibulus, Cato, and their allies: although there was no precedent for Bibulus's use of *obnuntiatio*, there was also nothing to prevent him from claiming that his use was legitimate.[141] This gave Cato and his conservative circle some leverage in their struggle against the triumvirs, since they would claim to understand the *mos maiorum* best. On their own authority, therefore, they would loudly proclaim that all of Caesar's actions passed during Bibulus's *obnuntiatio* were void. On the other hand, by removing himself entirely from the political scene, Bibulus gave Caesar a free rein, such that some people jokingly referred to it as the consulship of Gaius Caesar and Julius Caesar.[142]

Although the triumvirs seemed to control affairs in Rome for the first half of the year, Cato and his allies eventually regained their footing mid-year and began to mount a more effective opposition. As the year went on and excitement about the *lex agraria* faded, popular enthusiasm for the triumvirs seems to have cooled. With the benefits of the popular legislation secured, some discontent (and perhaps popular regret) about the violent methods used by the triumvirs seems to have taken hold. Cicero noticed this shift in public opinion and mused on how the political wheel was turning: he placed the blame for the collapse of the Senate's influence entirely on Cato (*culpa Catonis*), whose blunders had undermined popular support for the ruling aristocracy in the first place, but he credited the shameful behavior of the triumvirs for alienating the people and turning the tide back toward the *optimates*.[143] Cato and his allies did their best to use propaganda and open letters from Bibulus to turn sentiment against Caesar. Despite having confined himself to his house, Bibulus sent out a steady

---

139. See Mitchell (1986) 173 n. 9 and Burckhardt (1988) 178–209.

140. Cicero—although an augur—could not point to any existing text that supported the interpretation that Bibulus's edicts were valid. As a result, Clodius as tribune would pass a law the next year clarifying the use of *obnuntatio* (Tatum [1999] 125–33).

141. When a *contio* was called in the following year to investigate the matter, therefore, Cicero records that a number of augurs agreed with Bibulus's interpretation, which Cicero also supported (see later discussion).

142. Suet. *Iul.* 20.2 and Dio 38.8.2.

143. Cic. *Att.* 2.9.1–2, 2.18.2.

flow of letters to the people denouncing the triumvirs and reminding everyone that Caesar's actions were invalid and contrary to the will of the gods.[144] Some of these letters hurled insults at Caesar that intrigued and delighted the crowds, including dredging up old rumors that he had engaged in a homosexual love affair with King Nicomedes of Bithynia, joking that Caesar was the queen of Bithynia, and that he had moved from desiring a king to desiring a kingdom, once again accusing Caesar of aiming at a tyranny.[145] These letters were tremendously popular, and Cicero remarked on their surprising effectiveness, comparing Bibulus to the famous Fabius Maximus who saved Rome by delaying.[146] Although Sallust would refer to Bibulus as being dull of speech, Cicero emphasizes the wit and piercing criticism of his letters, which he calls Archilochian in style, and which were eagerly read throughout Rome.[147] This was a dramatic reversal: from having manure dumped on his head to being compared to one of Rome's greatest heroes, all within a couple of months. Given their close relationship and political alliance, and the fact that Cato had also once used Archilochian poetry to attack Scipio for stealing away Aemilia, one can assume that he assisted his son-in-law in crafting and publicizing these letters as a form of resistance to Caesar.[148] Yet whereas Cato had avoided the vulgarity and crudeness that was usual of the style, Bibulus freely unleashed the full profanity of the medium.[149]

Bibulus's letters were only part of the propaganda campaign that Cato and his allies mobilized against the triumvirs. Cato had been accusing Caesar of despotic ambition for years, but Caesar's actions as consul gave new fuel to the charge of tyranny. This was an effective accusation, because it struck violently at the core Roman value of *libertas* or freedom.[150] The Romans wanted the benefits they received through *popularis* tactics, but they grew wary when they believed their *libertas* was threatened. They had a long tradition of hating tyrants and opposing the very idea of kingship, but *optimates* also made use of this tradition to justify the killing of popular leaders who sought to gain despotic power

---

144. Cic. *Att.* 2.16.2, 2.19.2, 2.20.4 and 6, 2.21.3 and 5, *Har. Resp.* 48, *Dom.* 39–40, Suet. *Iul.* 20.1, Plut. *Pomp.* 48.4, Dio 38.6.4–6.

145. Suet. *Iul.* 49.2.

146. Cic. *Att.* 2.19.2. See also Cic. *Att.* 2.19.5, 2.20.4, 2.21.4. See Collins (1955) 265–6 and Gruen (1974) 92.

147. Sall. *Epist. ad Caes.* 9.1 (*hebes lingua*), Cic. *Att.* 2.21.4.

148. Taylor (1949) 136.

149. Cowan (2015) 33–7.

150. For discussion on the power of this charge, see Syme (1939) 151–5, Hellegouarc'h (1963) 542–65, Raaflaub (2003) 48–59, Fantham (2005) 209–29, Arena (2012) *passim*, esp. 244–57.

through demagoguery.[151] Thus the potent accusation was flexible, and Cato and his allies used it to great effect, spreading rumors (true or not) of Caesar's tyrannical ambitions. These rumors began to fly across Rome and Italy, and Cicero reports anger against the triumvirs growing in towns across Italy.[152] To fan the flames of these rumors, pamphlets were published and distributed attacking the triumvirs, such as the one written by M. Terentius Varro entitled "The Three-Headed Monster."[153] These dire warnings of the impending overthrow of the Republican government sought to weaken popular support and force senators in particular to re-evaluate the situation, since they would lose the most if they ended up on the wrong side of a tyrant. Although most of the Senate seems to have initially determined that tolerating Caesar's actions was the safest course of action, Cato's efforts to brand Caesar a tyrant sought to convince them that such toleration was an unsafe position. Thus Cato and his allies worked to shift senators' thinking about how their interests were best served, which they hoped would trigger another realignment of support. As a result, new supporters joined Cato's circle, such as the young Scribonius Curio, who visited Cicero in April, saying that the young men of the aristocracy were angry and unwilling to tolerate the arrogant behavior of the triumvirs who acted like tyrants.[154] Accusations against the triumvirs spread rapidly. In July, during the *Ludi Apollinares*—the annual religious festival in honor of Apollo—a theater crowd ignored Caesar and taunted Pompey during a performance, but it received the entrance of Curio with great applause.[155] Even the equestrians whom Caesar and Crassus had helped were turning against the triumvirs, and a series of Cicero's letters reveals popular sentiment turning more forcefully against them over the summer.[156] This popular support made it increasingly difficult for the triumvirs to use violence to achieve their aims, since such actions would validate the rumors of tyranny. Indeed, when Vatinius tried to drag Bibulus from his house and arrest him, the other tribunes interceded to prevent him from carrying the action out.[157]

---

151. See Pina Polo (2006) and Hölkeskamp (2013) 15.

152. Cic. *Att.* 2.13.2, 2.21.1 (cf. 18.1–2, 19.2, 20.3).

153. App. *BC* 2.9 (Τρικάρανον). See Gelzer (1968) 63–70 and Fehrle (1983) 114–8.

154. Cic. *Att.* 2.7.3, 2.8.1.

155. Cic. *Att.* 2.19.3. The actor recited the line "by our misfortunes you are 'Great,'" making a play on words with Pompey's nickname *Magnus* ("the Great").

156. Cic. *Att.* 2.20.3, 2.21.1–2, 2.23.3.

157. Cic. *Vat.* 22, Dio 38.6.6.

This propaganda campaign against the triumvirs was particularly effective with the senatorial aristocracy, which was offended by the circumvention of the Senate and the blatant use of violence against senators and even magistrates. Cato's obstructionist tactics had driven Caesar to take his bills directly to the assembly, but this disregard for the Senate's *auctoritas* alienated Caesar from many of his fellow senators. In response, a number of them stopped attending Senate meetings whenever he did summon them for some purpose.[158] Cicero himself spent much of the year visiting country estates, and many other senators apparently did the same. According to Plutarch, Caesar once complained about how few senators answered his summons to attend meetings of the Senate, and an old senator named Considius rebuked him, saying that the senators feared the armed soldiers he employed. When Caesar asked why Considius attended if senators were really afraid, the old man simply replied that old age and the short life he had left made him fearless.[159] The absence of the senators was no empty gesture—to be disregarded by the best men in Rome was to have one's *dignitas* and *auctoritas* drawn into question, so it was a serious insult to a consul if the senators did not heed his summons. This does not mean that the entire Senate flocked to join Cato; the senators who abandoned the triumvirs went their own way, not necessarily joining Cato's group.[160] Thus the formation of the triumvirate did not polarize the Senate into two camps, but rather broke up old groups and enabled the forming of new groups that did not exist on a political line between the two poles of triumvirs and *optimates*, but rather in a three-dimensional space that allowed for a complexity of overlapping ties of friendship and cooperation. Yet this was probably good for Cato, since it gave him a larger number of senators (and factions of senators) who might support him, or at least withhold their support from Caesar, Pompey, and Crassus.

The triumvirs responded to these reversals differently. Pompey seems to have been genuinely surprised and hurt at the public disaffection. Although he relished the popularity he received for coming to the assistance of Caesar's *lex agraria* at the start of the year, Cicero's letters chart Pompey's growing discomfiture with the way public opinion had turned against him, and how the public attacks wounded him deeply.[161] Pompey was the greatest man in the state, and therefore he had the most to lose. Despite his early use of *popularis* tactics to

---

158. Cic. *Att.* 2.22.3, 2.23.3, Plut. *Caes.* 14.13. Meier ([1966] 283) believed that Cato was behind the boycott within the Senate.

159. Plut. *Caes.* 14.14–5.

160. Gruen (1974) 97 and 119. Bellemore ([2005] 238) discusses Cicero's frustration that Cato was not doing more to oppose the triumvirs.

161. Cic. *Att.* 2.13.2 (April), 2.14.1 (April), 2.16.2 (May), 2.19.2 (July), 2.21.3 (July), 2.22.6 (October).

climb the political ladder, he had in recent years been reforming his policies, and had been making extensive connections with leading senatorial families. These families were among the first to abandon Pompey when his coalition with Caesar and Crassus started appearing tyrannical, and his ego was wounded when he was jeered by the people, who had always adored him.[162] Cato's obstruction had pushed Pompey into Caesar's hands, but once his veterans had land and his eastern acts had been approved, there was no longer a pressing need for him to endure the animosity of the *optimates*. Caesar had anticipated this and strengthened their bond by arranging for Pompey to marry his daughter Julia.[163] Cicero indicates that the wedding occurred in late April or early May—early enough that it bonded Pompey closely to Caesar before they felt the full weight of the attacks by the *optimates*.[164] Yet given the haste of the wedding, Caesar may already have been concerned about Pompey's loyalty: Julia was only days away from marrying a Servilius Caepio when Caesar broke that engagement to give her to Pompey.[165] To compensate Caepio, Pompey gave his own daughter Pompeia to be Caepio's bride, breaking her engagement with Faustus Cornelius Sulla, the son of the dictator Sulla and the ward of Lucullus. That Pompey would break a marriage alliance with Sulla's son (a *nobilis* and staunch conservative) to further secure his alliance with Caesar was a potent statement that he saw Caesar as critical to his political success at this time, although there can be no doubt that Julia's character and charms were powerful inducements.[166] Pompey seems to have partially retreated into private life for some period to enjoy his new marriage, which must have lessened the effect of the negative propaganda for a while.

Caesar himself married the daughter of Calpurnius Piso, whom he would help get elected to the consulship for the following year, thus ensuring that his

---

162. See Gruen (1974) 95.

163. Suet. *Iul.* 21.1, Plut. *Pomp.* 47.6, *Caes.* 14.7–8, Dio 38.9.1. The sources suggest that Caesar arranged the marriage to secure Pompey's loyalty to their alliance.

164. Cic. *Att.* 2.17.1.

165. Plut. *Pomp.* 47.6. The identity of this Servilius Caepio is unknown, but he is described as Caesar's loyal ally, and helped Caesar to suppress Bibulus. He may have been a relative of Caesar's lover Servilia (Cato's half-sister), but his political activity on Caesar's behalf makes it unlikely that he was Servilia's son Brutus, who had been adopted by his mother's brother and therefore was often referred to as Q. Servilius Brutus (see Syme [1939] 34 n. 7 and Seager [2002] 80 n. 1). Leach ([*Pompey*] 126) identifies him as the Caepio identified by Florus (1.41.9–10) as being one of Pompey's legates during his piracy campaign.

166. Pompey doted on his new wife (Plut. *Pomp.* 48.5, 53.1–4). Caepio seems to have died before his marriage to Pompeia, and she ultimately ended up marrying Faustus Sulla.

successor in the consulship would be an ally.[167] Cato objected vehemently to these
marriage alliances, complaining that "it was unbearable that political supremacy
was being traded for weddings, and that—through women—men were handing
over provinces and armies and powers to one another in turn."[168] He was not
opposed to the use of marriages to form political alliances, but to the unprecedented scale and power of the alliance the triumvirs forged by these unions, which
enabled a handful of men to control the state.[169] Cato again raised the specter of
tyranny before the eyes of his fellow senators, declaring that these marriages were
more than mere aristocratic unions—they were dynastic marriages that would
direct the affairs of state. Few people could have missed the significance of a marriage alliance between Caesar and Pompey, but there was little Cato could do
except watch the solidification of the triumvirate.

A strange event happened during the summer of 59 BC that reveals the
growing tensions between the triumvirs and the *optimates*. In July or early August,
L. Vettius—the informer who three years earlier had accused Caesar of com-
plicity in the Catilinarian conspiracy—revealed to the Senate that he was part of
a plot to murder Pompey and perhaps Caesar. Our sources give conflicting details
about the incident, making it difficult to interpret. Dio and Appian give similar
descriptions of the event. Dio writes that Cicero and Lucullus were working with
Vettius to murder Caesar and Pompey, but Vettius was exposed and arrested.[170]
When questioned by the Senate, he confessed and named Cicero and Lucullus,
but he also named Bibulus falsely, having been prompted to do so by Caesar and
Pompey. Since Bibulus could prove his innocence on the grounds that he had
previously warned Pompey about the plot, the Senate doubted Vettius's entire
confession and ordered him imprisoned. Vettius repeated this confession in a
public *contio*, naming the same three men as conspirators, and was returned to
prison, where he was later found dead. Appian's version is similar: Vettius ran
into the Forum with a dagger and announced that he had been sent by Bibulus,
Cicero, and Cato to kill Caesar and Pompey.[171] Caesar used the confession to
arouse the anger of the people, and Vettius was thrown into prison and was
killed there that night. In both versions, the *optimates* initiated a plot to murder
Caesar and Pompey, but it unraveled, and the conspirators were lucky to escape

---

167. Suet. *Iul.* 21.1, Plut. *Caes.* 14.8, *Cat. Min.* 33.4, Dio 38.9.1.

168. Plut. *Caes.* 14.8. See Pelling (2011) 199.

169. See Steel (2009) 117.

170. Dio 38.9.1–4.

171. App. *BC* 2.12.

condemnation. In this account, several *optimates* sought to murder the triumvirs in cold blood.

Cicero, however, gives a very different description of what happened. A contemporary source, he writes that Vettius had promised Caesar that he would get Curio (Cato's young supporter) falsely accused of a crime, so he befriended the young man and initiated a discussion about murdering Pompey.[172] Cicero suspected that Vettius's plan had been to get himself discovered carrying concealed weapons, and in exchange for immunity would confess to a plot and implicate Curio. But Curio ruined this plan by immediately telling his father about Vettius's suggestion, and the elder Curio told Pompey, who brought the entire matter before the Senate. When questioned, Vettius testified that the younger Curio was the leader of a group of young aristocrats who were plotting to kill Pompey. Vettius provided a list of names, and claimed that he had received a dagger for the murder from Bibulus's secretary. His story utterly collapsed under scrutiny, in particular because one of the so-called conspirators was in Macedonia, and also because Bibulus himself had apparently heard the rumors of a plot earlier, and had written Pompey to make him aware of the details. The Senate ordered Vettius imprisoned, but the next day Caesar took him from prison to the rostra and instructed him to tell the people what he knew. Vettius repeated what he had told the Senate, but with slightly different details: he added to the list of conspirators Lucullus and Domitius Ahenobarbus (Cato's brother-in-law), and he now hinted that Cicero was encouraging the conspiracy, but he omitted any mention of Brutus (the son of Servilia—Caesar's lover and Cato's half-sister), whom he had previously named before the Senate.[173] Vettius was put back in prison, but Vatinius brought him back to the rostra to add further names to his list of accused conspirators, all of them opponents of the triumvirate.[174] Vettius was returned to prison, but the next day was found dead, having been strangled during the night.[175] Suetonius gives a briefer version of the same story: Caesar bribed Vettius to falsely accuse certain men of trying to murder Pompey, but when Vettius proved ineffective at convincing the people, Caesar had him poisoned in prison.[176] Thus Cicero and Suetonius report a botched plot, initiated by Caesar or to please Caesar, in which several *optimates* were to be falsely implicated in a

---

172. Cic. *Att.* 2.24.2–4. On Vettius in this incident, see Shackleton Bailey (1965) 1.399.

173. Cic. *Att.* 2.24.2–4, *Flacc.* 96, and Plut. *Luc.* 42.7–8.

174. Cic. *Vat.* 26.

175. Cic. *Vat.* 26.

176. Suet. *Iul.* 20.5.

conspiracy to murder Pompey. This version would suggest that Caesar wanted to make his new son-in-law frightened of their political opponents to prevent any reconciliation, revealing continuing concern that Pompey's loyalty to the triumvirate might be wavering. It is also possible from Cicero's telling that Caesar originally had nothing to do with Vettius or the plot, but he subsequently pressured Vettius to recant his accusation against Brutus.[177] This version seems more likely than the version given by Dio and Appian. Cicero already knew that Pompey was having reservations about his alliance with Caesar and Crassus, and was trying to pull Pompey away from them, which makes it unlikely that he was simultaneously plotting to kill Pompey and the others.[178] Caesar was most likely behind the Vettius affair, attempting to frighten Pompey and prevent Cicero and the *optimates* from tampering with Pompey's loyalty.[179] Furthermore, the triumvirs had recently been hissed at during gladiatorial games, and Pompey was mocked by an actor in the *ludi Apollinares*, and these embarrassments may have driven them to arrange the Vettius affair as a piece of propaganda to make their opponents look bad.[180]

If Cicero's version of the event is therefore to be accepted, which places Caesar behind Vettius's actions, it is curious that Cato is not among the *optimates* accused of plotting against Pompey. McDermott suggested that it was too dangerous for the triumvirs to have Cato's name included among the accused, but this does not seem likely.[181] Whether he was personally implicated or not, Cato was sure to involve himself and defend his allies, so omitting his name would not have kept him out of the affair. Perhaps the triumvirs thought that no one would believe that Rome's paragon of ancient virtue would involve himself in a murder plot, or perhaps Caesar feared that it would be too easy to trace the plot back to him if Cato, his long-standing political nemesis, was named as a conspirator. Finally, if Caesar's main concern was to prevent Cicero and the *optimates* from making overtures toward Pompey, then perhaps he felt no need to name Cato, since Cato appeared far too obstinate and uncompromising to ever soften his opinion of Pompey. Whatever the reason,

---

177. Gruen (1974) 96 suggests this possibility.

178. Allen (1950). Cicero (*Att.* 2.23.2) notes Pompey's unhappiness with his situation in the triumvirate, and (*Phil.* 2.23–4) discusses his efforts to pull Pompey over to the side of the *optimates*.

179. McDermott ([1949] 362) suggested that the triumvirs organized the Vettius affair in an effort to counteract the shift of popular opinion against them over the summer.

180. Cic. *Att.* 2.19.3, Val. Max. 6.2.9.

181. McDermott (1949) 365.

the mysterious Vettius affair hints at the complexity of personal politics at the time, and how alliances were malleable and could shift. Cato's activities had forced the triumvirs to unite their respective resources, Cicero was trying to pry Pompey away from the triumviral faction, and Caesar was trying to make him afraid of their opponents.

Crassus provides a different example of this world of senatorial factions.[182] He does not seem to have been deeply concerned by the swing of popular support away from the triumvirate, and he probably even enjoyed watching Pompey's distress. Unlike Pompey, whose entire career after Sulla had been dependent upon *popularis* politics, and therefore upon the goodwill of the people, Crassus seems to have moved away from *popularis* activities following his consulship, and to have focused instead on building influence among the senatorial and equestrian orders. This does not mean that he was embraced by the leading senators, who remained suspicious of his activities and goals, but his influence was more conventional, and therefore not as dependent upon popular sentiment. Whereas Pompey seems to have truly loved being adored by the masses, and was wounded when he was no longer the people's darling, Crassus seems to have been more aristocratic in his outlook, and was less concerned about popular opinion. Crassus was also securely tied to Caesar through debt: he had invested vast sums to finance Caesar's climb up the *cursus honorum*, and he needed to recover those loans, and profit by having a consul indebted to him.[183] For this reason, Crassus had a powerful motivation to continue backing Caesar even after the tax contracts for the *publicani* had been renegotiated. So while it took a marriage to the charming Julia—and perhaps a fabricated assassination plot—to keep Pompey loyal, Caesar knew he could count on Crassus's support, at least until Crassus had gotten all he wanted from him.

Caesar was the junior member of the triumvirate and had the most to gain from the alliance, so he was strongly motivated to fight all obstacles in his path. Crassus and Pompey were rich men of consular status with significant fame and clientage, and even if Cato's circle had succeeded in blocking their goals and thereby diminishing their *dignitas* and influence, they would always be important senators. Caesar, on the other hand, still needed to make his wealth and reputation, and therefore was willing to push back against any opposition. As already seen, he had ordered Cato to be arrested and hauled from the Curia for obstructing the *lex agraria*; he had allowed (perhaps even instructed) his

---

182. Marshall ([1976] 113–27) and Ward ([1977] 262–6) describe in detail Crassus's activities between Caesar's consulship and the meeting at Luca.

183. See Adcock (1966) 41–7, Marshall (1976) 82–4, Ward (1977) 169–70, 209, 213–4.

supporters to assault Bibulus, Cato, and their tribunes physically; and he had used force to keep Cato and others away from the final vote on the agrarian legislation. Caesar did not stop there. When theatergoers—both common folk and equestrians—gave him a cold shoulder, but enthusiastically applauded Curio, he threatened to punish them by repealing the *lex Roscia* (which reserved special theater seats for equestrians) and Cato's *lex frumentaria* (which subsidized grain for citizens).[184] This was a serious threat to revoke important privileges, but it was also cunning in that it threatened to revoke Cato's most popular piece of legislation. Furthermore, when Cicero also became an outspoken critic of the triumvirs in April, Caesar responded robustly. He had been well disposed toward Cicero initially, and had sought a friendly way to win him over, even offering him a special commission (a *libera legatio*) to act as an official envoy to Egypt, which would enable him to tour that fabled land in style. Although tempted, Cicero was very concerned that Cato and others would accuse him of having been bribed by Caesar if he accepted the commission, a sign that Cato was already pushing a "with us or against us" platform in his opposition to the triumvirs.[185] When Cicero began to show more resistance to the triumvirs, Caesar determined to force him out of Rome, thereby removing his influential criticism. He did this by enabling P. Clodius Pulcher—Cicero's greatest enemy—to be adopted into a plebeian family so he would be eligible to stand in the tribunician elections for 58 BC.[186] Clodius hated Cicero for his testimony in the *Bona Dea* trial, and Caesar surely knew that he would use the considerable powers of the tribunate to attack Cicero. Clodius had been ineligible for that office because he was a patrician, but Caesar (as consul and *pontifex maximus*) and Pompey (as augur) arranged for his official adoption into a plebeian family, and there could be little doubt that he would win the office and use it to attack Cicero.[187] Confronted by this threat, Cicero left Rome for a while to visit his country estates. Caesar once again tried to find an honorable position for Cicero away from Rome, offering him a place on a grain commission or on Caesar's staff in his Gallic command, and even offering him a *libera legatio* to fulfill a vow (which would allow Cicero to travel at

184. Cic. *Att.* 2.19.3.

185. Cic. *Att.* 2.4.2, 2.5.1. A *libera legatio* enabled a person on official business to travel at state expense, so Caesar was essentially offering Cicero a free trip to visit Egypt. See Shackleton Bailey (1965) 1.359 and Spielvogel (1993) 58–9.

186. Cic. *Dom.* 41, *Sest.* 16, Suet. *Iul.* 20.4, App. *BC* 2.14, Dio 38.12.1–2, 39.11.2.

187. Tatum ([1999] 96–111, esp. 104) gives a detailed explanation of Clodius's efforts to become a plebeian in order to stand for election to the tribunate.

state expense to many pleasant places).[188] Cicero rejected all of these offers, but kept his distance from Rome for a while, staying in touch with friends by letter.

In July, Bibulus published an edict moving the consular elections from that month to October 18.[189] No reason is given for this action, but it is likely that he and Cato were aware of the shift in public opinion that was taking place, and hoped that a delay would further strengthen opposition to the triumvirs and bring about the election of consuls for the next year who could work to undo Caesar's actions. They may also have hoped that Caesar would leave for his province, and so not be in Rome to influence the voting directly. Why Caesar did not simply ignore this edict as he did the rest of Bibulus's edicts is unclear, although the supervision of the elections at this time was determined by *sortitio* (a drawing of lots) among the consuls, and Bibulus had probably obtained this prerogative when entering office.[190] Whatever the reason, it was an effective tool that angered and inconvenienced Caesar, who wanted to get his preferred successors elected before his popular support dropped much more. He even tried to whip the people into a frenzied mob that would drag Bibulus from his house and force him to allow earlier elections, but Cicero noted that the people had become unwilling to take such steps for him.[191] By the end of July, Cicero was anticipating that Caesar and his allies would lash out at the citizenry in retribution for the public insults they had received. He wrote to Atticus:

> For we have experienced the rage and immoderate behavior of these men, who—being furious with Cato—have destroyed everything. But they seem to be using so gentle a poison that we seem to be able to die without suffering. Yet now I fear that they will blaze in fury at the hissing of the mob, at the remarks of the respectable, and at the tumult throughout Italy.[192]

Once again, Cicero identifies Cato as the key figure who drove the triumvirs together, unleashing their willingness to overthrow the traditional senatorial

---

188. Grain commission: Cic. *Att.* 2.18.3, *Prov. Cons.* 41–2. *Legatus* on Caesar's staff: Cic. *Att.* 2.18.3, 2.19.5, *Prov. Cons.* 41–2. *Libera legatio*: Cic. *Att.* 2.18.3, *Prov. Cons.* 41–2. Plutarch (*Cic.* 30.4) suggests that Clodius tricked Cicero into remaining in Rome in order to keep him vulnerable.

189. Cic. *Att.* 2.20.6.

190. Taylor (1968) 171.

191. Cic. *Att.* 2.21.5.

192. Cic. *Att.* 2.21.1.

government. Cicero was clearly worried about how far the triumvirs might go
to suppress those who opposed them, but Cato and his allies continued their opposition, sensing that the changing mood in Rome gave them an opportunity.
In the end, Bibulus's seclusion in his house meant that Caesar presided over the
elections on October 18, and he was indeed able to get two of his supporters
elected consul: his new father-in-law, L. Calpurnius Piso, and Pompey's trusted
lieutenant A. Gabinius.

While the triumvirs had lost popularity with the people and senatorial elite,
they still commanded tremendous resources and had loyal supporters, both
among the commons and in the Senate. Thanks to their assistance in securing
his adoption into a plebeian family, P. Clodius had won election to the plebeian tribunate, and he would gain influence rapidly in the next year (58 BC) by
promulgating popular legislation, including distributions of free grain to the citizenry that significantly expanded—and so drove from memory—Cato's own *lex
frumentaria*.[193] And when Gaius Cato (perhaps a relation of Cato the Younger)
applied to prosecute Gabinius for electoral bribery (*ambitus*) before he took office, he was unable to get a hearing before the praetors, no doubt because Pompey
was protecting his former lieutenant.[194] Gaius Cato tried to whip the people into
a frenzy over this abuse of power, accusing Pompey of acting like a dictator despite
holding no office (a *privatus dictator*). This effort to brand Pompey as a tyrant and
an abuser of traditional *libertas* may have resonated in the ears of the bystanders,
but Pompey's men attacked Gaius Cato and beat him severely. Yet the appeals
to *libertas* and the accusations of tyranny were effective, forcing the triumvirs to
use their combined might to enact their aims. As the year came to a close, Caesar
exited the city, taking up his military authority (*imperium*), which conferred absolute immunity from prosecution, while Pompey and Crassus settled in for what
they hoped would be a period of enhanced importance and influence in the city.

Subsequent Attacks on Caesar in Early 58 BC

While the triumvirs had ensured that their allies won both consulships for 58 BC,
their opponents succeeded in getting their members into several lower offices,
and they would quickly begin their attacks, making Caesar's consular legislation
their prime target. Cato, Bibulus, and their allies had taken several shrewd steps in
the previous year to establish a basis from which to call into question the validity
of Caesar's legislation, and they hoped to exploit these opportunities to overturn

---

193. On Clodius's legislation, see *MRR* 2.195–6 and Tatum (1999) 114–49.

194. Cic. *QF* 1.2.15.

everything the triumvirs had achieved. The staunch *optimates* L. Domitius Ahenobarbus (Cato's brother-in-law) and C. Memmius had both won election to the praetorship, and they began pushing the Senate to discuss the legitimacy of Caesar's legislation as soon as they were in office, no doubt claiming that it was invalid because it had been passed through violence and during Bibulus's declaration of *obnuntiatio*. The legal attacks against Caesar seem to have increased substantially in 58 BC, no doubt because he had previously used the consulship to block legal actions by his opponents, but now Cato and his allies were better able to launch their attacks.[195] Suetonius suggests that they brought their complaint before the Senate in the final days of Caesar's consulship, and even held some kind of hearing before the senators at that time, but this seems unlikely given the distortions and problems with his chronology.[196] Cicero indicates only that Domitius and Memmius as praetors attacked Caesar's legislation in 58 BC, working to get it declared invalid and annulled.[197] While they surely deployed their best arguments, the triumvirs had left a secure situation behind them: both consuls and many lower magistrates were friendly to them, and Pompey and Crassus were both still in Rome and able to exert their influence. Caesar was personally immune from prosecution once he had taken up his *imperium* and military command at the end of 59 BC, but he remained near Rome for two months to prepare his army for Gaul and to keep an eye on the evolving situation.[198] Cato and his allies were clearly a threat that needed to be watched.

---

195. Bellemore (2005) 241 (cf. Pelling [2011] 198).

196. Suetonius (*Iul.* 23.1 and *Nero* 2.2) wrongly describes Domitius and Memmius as praetors in the same year that Caesar was consul, and therefore he believes that Domitius summoned Caesar to a hearing before the Senate, but when the Senate failed to take any action after three days, Caesar exited the city and took up his *imperium* and military command, thus obtaining legal immunity. Since Domitius was only a praetor-elect in 59 BC, he could not have summoned a sitting consul to a hearing before the Senate, so it must be either that Caesar—confident in his influence and resources—allowed Cato's allies to attack his legislation in the Senate, or Domitius and Memmius held their fruitless debate in the following year (58 BC). Gelzer ([1968] 97) did not seem to note the discrepancy in Suetonius's chronology, but Billows ([2008] 128) and Ramsey ([2009] 37) suggest the trial took place in 58 BC and inside Rome, which does not work, because Caesar would have forfeited his *imperium* had he crossed the *pomerium* and entered the city for a meeting in 58 BC. Taylor ([1949] 137) suggests that the Senate's discussion was held in 58 BC and that Caesar attended, which is possible if the Senate met outside the *pomerium*, thereby allowing Caesar to attend without forfeiting his *imperium*. On the relationship of *imperium* and the *pomerium*, see Drogula (2015) 8–45.

197. Cic. *Sest.* 40.

198. Caesar only left Rome in March when developments in Gaul required his presence (Caes. *BG* 1.7).

As praetor, Memmius next tried to prosecute Vatinius for the actions he had taken as tribune in the previous year, sending him a public notice to appear in his court in thirty days. This not only threatened Vatinius, but also Caesar himself, since his possession of his Gallic command depended upon the legitimacy of the *lex Vatinia* that had given him Cisalpine Gaul and Illyricum for five years. The nature of Memmius's accusation is not clear, but it seems that he tried to prosecute Vatinius for using improper legislative procedures in violation of the *lex Licinia Junia* of 62 BC.[199] Caesar had anticipated an attack on Vatinius by appointing him a legate (high-ranking lieutenant) in his Gallic command, thereby protecting him from prosecution under the *lex Memmia*, which forbade the prosecution of officials away from Rome on public business.[200] Indeed, Vatinius was already outside of Rome and helping Caesar prepare his campaign when the prosecution began. He could have simply ignored the prosecution entirely under the aegis of his immunity, but he surprised his opponents by voluntarily entering the city to answer the charges. Why he did this is not recorded, but there were certainly two contributing factors. First, Vatinius may have been relying on a new law that he had successfully promulgated the previous year, which gave prosecutors and defendants greater prerogatives in rejecting jurors.[201] He may have hoped that this and the influence of the triumvirs would assure him a favorable jury, or perhaps even scuttle the trial altogether by making the constitution of a jury too difficult. Second, he probably wanted to stand in the next year (57 BC) for the aedileship for 56 BC, and therefore he wished to deal with any litigation right away while Caesar was still near enough to employ his full influence in Vatinius's defense.[202] With these reasons in mind, Vatinius appeared willingly before Memmius's tribunal, but when Memmius tried to appoint a court president (*quaesitor*) by lot and would not allow Vatinius to challenge this appointment as was permitted by the *lex Vatinia*, Vatinius decried this violation of the law and appealed to the tribune Clodius for help.[203] It is not clear what means Clodius used to stop the trial, but it was clearly a violent disruption of the proceedings. Cicero was shocked both that Vatinius would appeal to a tribune in this manner, and that Clodius—who was understood to be Caesar's man at the time—would resort to

---

199. Cic. *Vat.* 33–4, *Sest.* 135. See Bauman (1967) 93–104, Gruen (1971) 65–7.

200. Vatinius as Caesar's legate (Cic. *Vat.* 34); *lex Memmia* (Val. Max. 3.7.9).

201. Bauman (1967) 103. On this law, see also Gelzer (1968) 93 n. 1, Gruen (1974) 243, and Williamson (2005) 378–9.

202. Badian (1974) 154–8 and Tatum (1999] 140–1.

203. Tatum ([1999] 140–1) is surely correct that Vatinius had previously met with Clodius to ensure his support would be available when needed. See also Badian (1974) 155–6.

such violence in the courtroom.[204] With this dispersal of the court proceedings, Vatinius left the city to rejoin Caesar, and the *optimates* had another defeat.

While Caesar did not respond personally to these attacks, he probably had a hand in the violent response that Clodius was launching against key *optimates*. Immediately upon entering office, Clodius had promulgated popular legislation to gain the support of the people, and his willingness to use mob violence to obstruct trials and other public meetings was rapidly becoming apparent.[205] In late February or early March he promulgated a *lex Clodia de capite civis Romani*, which reaffirmed the citizen's right of appeal and outlawed anyone who had executed a Roman citizen without trial.[206] The threat against Cicero was obvious, and when he returned from his country estate to the city, Clodius began attacking him relentlessly in public meetings. Cicero received considerable sympathy and support from the equestrians and from some in the Senate, but neither Cato nor the consuls nor the triumvirs came to his assistance.[207] He had expected help from Pompey in particular, whom he had long supported, but Cicero's previous criticisms of the triumvirs probably rendered him untrustworthy in their eyes, and they saw Clodius as a more promising ally. Caesar's offer of a commission in his army was still on the table, and would have provided Cicero with a safe haven for up to five years, but this option did not appeal to him because it would have removed him from politics for a long period, and he probably hoped that Clodius's attacks would not last beyond his year as tribune. Lucullus advised Cicero to stay and fight, and Dio says that Cicero actually did consider resorting to armed violence to defend himself against Clodius's mob, but Cato and Hortensius prevented him from taking this step, fearing that it would trigger a civil war.[208] So, bereft of allies, Cicero left Rome on March 18/19, and Clodius had his exile confirmed in law on March 20.[209]

Cato's failure to support Cicero is difficult to understand. It is possible that Clodius prevented him from coming to Cicero's aid by offering him a special command to Cyprus (see later discussion), effectively purchasing his neutrality

---

204. Cic. *Vat.* 33–4.

205. Tatum ([1999] 114–213) gives a complete analysis of Clodius's tribunate and subsequent career.

206. Cic. *Att.* 3.15.5, *Sest.* 53–4, *Pis.* 16, 30, Livy *Per.* 103, Vell. 2.45.1, Plut. *Cic.* 30.5, App. *BC* 2.15, Dio 38.14.4.

207. Cic. *Att.* 3.15.6, *Sest.* 25–6, 41–2, *Pis.* 77, Plut. *Cic.* 31.1–4, Dio 38.16.2–6. Tatum (1999) 153–5.

208. Plut. *Cic.* 31.5, Dio 38.17.4. Lintott ([1999b] 60) discusses Cicero's contemplation of violence.

209. Cic. *Sest.* 53–4. For the date, see Kaster (2006) 396.

with the prestigious and potentially lucrative commission.[210] On the other hand, there are good grounds for doubting that Cato actually wanted this special commission, and the sequence of events is problematic, since Clodius may not have proposed Cato for the special Cyprian command until after Cicero had already gone into exile.[211] If this latter point is correct, then either Cato was involved in a secret deal to barter Cicero's life for a prestigious command, or he had another reason for not coming to Cicero's defense. The second possibility seems more likely. Given his previous willingness to confront political opponents vigorously and even aggressively when necessary, his passivity in the face of Cicero's exile should probably be understood as a lack of commitment to his defense. He did not see Cicero as a close political ally, and they held very different views on how the triumvirs should be handled. Cicero later complained that the *optimates* had failed to support him out of jealousy, although he had good words for Cato, whom he did not think had betrayed him or acted inconsistently.[212] He had never been a member of Cato's inner circle, and although their political views had occasionally aligned in the past, they generally espoused different policies and moved in different factions. Cicero blamed Pompey for promising and then withholding his support against Clodius, but he thought Cato had at least acted consistently in not rushing to his aid. Yet it is odd that Cato did little to help a fellow senator who was being attacked by an agent of the triumvirs, so he may have been satisfied to see Cicero—and his moderate approach to politics—run out of town. At the same time, there was probably very little that Cato and his friends could have done given the uniqueness of Clodius's activities. Cato had been willing to push, shove, and even fight in order to be heard during public meetings, but the organized gang violence that Clodius was using to disrupt meetings and attack opponents was different. Although some *optimates* would eventually approve the reciprocal use of violence to oppose Clodius's mobs, in 58 BC Cato's concern that it would escalate into civil war says much about his character. He was willing to fight with might and main to champion his beliefs, but he wanted to avoid civil war at all costs, including the cost of Cicero.

---

210. Rundell (1979) 315–6, Tatum (1999) 155–6.

211. Kaster ([2006] 395–7) provides a timeline for these events.

212. Cic. *Att.* 3.15.2. See comments by Spielvogel (1993) 68–71.

5

Cato's Cyprian Mission and Its Aftermath

Cato's Mission to Cyprus

Cato was no doubt frustrated that Caesar had achieved all of his primary goals during his consulship, including having his consular command changed from the woodlands of Italy to Transalpine Gaul, together with Cisalpine Gaul and Illyricum, for five years with four legions. This was a formidable command on the doorstep of Italy, which surely worried his political enemies. Caesar had proven his exceptional military talents in his Spanish command, so there could be little doubt that he would seek to extract as much status-enhancing prestige, glory, and wealth as possible from his Gallic command. The size and duration of the command must have been another source of concern, since it put too much power in one man's hands, and thereby denied a share of the glory and profits to other senators.[1] And because the command had been created for Caesar by *popularis* tribunician legislation, the Senate was denied its usual supervisory role over military commands.[2] The length of the command was also surely frustrating for Cato and his allies, because they were eager to prosecute Caesar in the courts for his behavior as consul. Caesar would be immune to prosecution as long as he retained his military authority (*imperium*), so his enemies would have to focus their efforts instead on rolling back his legislation, including the *lex Vatinia* that

---

1. The *optimates* had strongly opposed the *lex Gabinia* that gave Pompey a command against Mediterranean largely on the grounds that such an expansive command should not be entrusted to a single individual (Cic. *leg. Man.* 52, Vell. 2.32.1, Plut. *Pomp.* 25.3–7, Dio 36.35.1–36.3). See Seager (2002) 44.

2. See Drogula (2015) 131–42 on the extent and limits of senatorial control of Roman military commands.

had given him his command. Cato's circle would also use his absence to work on pulling apart the triumvirate, in particular by trying to draw the disgruntled Pompey away from the alliance.

In late February or early March in 58 BC, Clodius promulgated a bill ordering the annexation of the island of Cyprus, which meant deposing its ruler, King Ptolemy (the brother of King Ptolemy XII Auletes of Egypt), and confiscating the island's wealth. The Romans were able to claim Cyprus in this way because Ptolemy's father—King Ptolemy XI Alexander II of Egypt—had apparently bequeathed his kingdom (which included Cyprus) to Rome when he died in 80 BC.[3] The Romans had not acted on this claim at the time, so Egypt had fallen to Ptolemy Auletes while his brother assumed rule over Cyprus, although their right to rule remained an open question in Rome's eyes. In 59 BC Ptolemy Auletes paid the triumvirs a massive bribe to secure official Roman recognition of his kingship, but Ptolemy of Cyprus received no such recognition, and the decision to annex his island kingdom may have been taken during Caesar's consulship.[4] Clodius also had personal motives for promulgating the bill: he wanted the wealth of Cyprus to fund his popular legislation, and he had a personal grudge against Ptolemy of Cyprus, who (Clodius thought) had not done enough to help him when he had been captured by pirates as a young man.[5] He therefore proposed legislation deposing Ptolemy and confiscating the wealth of Cyprus, and no doubt expected that the consul Gabinius (Pompey's man) would receive the assignment, since he was to take up a command in nearby Cilicia.[6] When Gabinius decided he would rather hold the province of Syria, however, Clodius had the opportunity to propose a different commissioner for Cyprus. This was certainly a desirable appointment, since the chosen official would have ample opportunity to help himself to the treasury of an eastern monarch. It may have surprised many, therefore, when Clodius promulgated a bill in late March or April appointing Cato to the commission with the title *pro quaestore pro praetore*,[7] with the additional task of arranging the restoration of exiles to Byzantium.

---

3. Cic. *Leg. agr.* 1.1, 2.41–4, *Reg. Alex.* 3 and 5 = *Schol. Bob.* 92. The existence of this will is debated, since the evidence from Cicero suggests that nobody actually saw it, but Harris ([1985] 155–6) and Green ([1993] 554) suggest that it was probably genuine.

4. Cic. *Att.* 2.16.2, *Rab. Post.* 4–6, Suet. *Iul.* 54.3, Dio 39.12.1.

5. Strabo 14.6.6, Dio 38.30.5, App. *BC* 2.23.

6. Cic. *Dom.* 20–21, 52–3, *Sest.* 57, Livy *Per.* 104, Vell. 2.45.4–5, Plut. *Cat. Min.* 34.2–3, Dio 38.30.5. See Oost (1955) 98–112, Balsdon (1962) 134–6, Badian (1965) 110–8, Rundell (1979) 315–17, Fehrle (1983) 136–55, Tatum (1999) 155–6, and Morrell (2017) 116–22 for further discussion.

7. On Cato's title, see Vell. 2.45.4 (*quaestor cum iure praetorio*), Auct. *Vir. Ill.* 80.2 (*quaestor*).

There are two views explaining why Clodius—who seemed to be Caesar's man—chose to assign this highly desirable and potentially lucrative commission to Cato. The traditional view is that the whole thing was a ploy to get Cato out of Rome and away from Roman politics for a while: Clodius and the triumvirs saw Cato as a threat to their plans, so they arranged to get him out of Rome by sending him to Cyprus on state business.[8] Cicero and Plutarch believed that this was the reason for Cato's appointment, and Cicero would later claim that Caesar had congratulated Clodius on the clever political maneuver.[9] Indeed, he later declared of the commission: "thus the despised Marcus Cato—as if as a favor—is relegated to Cyprus."[10] Furthermore, by including a high-status command for Cato in his tribunician legislation, Clodius made it difficult for him to turn around later and attack the legitimacy of that legislation. Clodius's adoption into a plebeian *gens*, and therefore his eligibility to be a plebeian tribune, depended upon the legitimacy of Caesar's acts as consul (because Caesar, in spite of Bibulus's declaration of *obnuntiatio*, had summoned the *comitia curiata* that approved the adoption),[11] so Clodius may have calculated that Cato would be made more docile and less likely to attack Caesar's acts if he had benefited from them. Cicero supported this interpretation, stating later in a public meeting that Clodius had given Cato the special commission specifically to prevent him from speaking against other such extraordinary commands (which he had always opposed) in the future.[12]

Other historians have suggested that Clodius might have intended to honor Cato with the assignment, and saw it as an opportunity to forge a political friendship with him through the bestowal of an important and desirable commission.[13] This is possible, but it is hard to imagine that Cato would willingly commit himself to Clodius, who was seen as Caesar's man, when he had previously refused a marriage alliance with Pompey because he wanted to maintain his independence.

---

8. For example, see Fehrle (1983) 142–5.

9. Cic. *Dom.* 22, *Sest.* 60, Plut. *Cat. Min.* 34.1–4, *Cic.* 34. Plutarch (*Cat. Min.* 34.2) thought Clodius's plans to have Cicero exiled were the main force behind sending Cato to Cyprus, and Dio (38.30.5) merely says Clodius wanted Cato gone so he could more easily advance his plans.

10. Cic. *Dom.* 65.

11. Tatum ([1999] 104 and [2010] 201) indicates that Caesar summoned the curiate assembly in his capacity as consul, whereas Williamson ([2005] 381) suggests that he did this as *pontifex maximus*. Sumi ([2005] 183) also thinks it likely that Caesar convened the curiate assembly as *pontifex maximus*, but points out that our sources do not make this clear.

12. Cic. *Dom.* 22 and *Sest.* 60.

13. Rundell (1979) 315–6 and Tatum (1999) 155–6.

It seems unlikely, therefore, that Cato deliberately sacrificed Cicero in order to obtain the Cyprian commission, and Cicero's statements that Clodius wanted to remove Cato seem more convincing. Still, the two positions are not irreconcilable: Clodius may have primarily acted to get Cato out of town, but the special command was certainly desirable, and there are many reasons why Cato would have accepted and even been glad for it. In the first place, this legislation conferred upon him the rank and regalia of a praetor, even though he had not yet reached the praetorship.[14] The title *pro quaestore pro praetore* meant he was being sent out as one who had held the quaestorship (*pro quaestore*), but that he was sent "in place of a praetor" (*pro praetore*) and so was given the honors and trappings of a praetor. This was very desirable, because praetorian rank conferred the coveted curule regalia, including lictors bearing *fasces* and the right to use an ivory chair in emulation of Rome's ancient kings, all of which permanently enhanced a man's *dignitas*. It is also possible that Cato was to receive a grant of *imperium*—absolute military authority—as part of his commission, but this is less clear. *Imperium* was used to command Roman citizens in battle, but Cato did not have an army or a military force beyond a small bodyguard, and he certainly did not need *imperium* to enforce his will on non-Roman provincials.[15] Like all aristocrats, Cato sought high magistracies and the distinguishing honors they conferred, so the offer of praetorian rank before he had actually reached the praetorship would have been very welcome. He may have also believed that no one else should be trusted with the assignment. There was great wealth in Cyprus, and he may have worried that—if he refused the commission—it would go to someone who would plunder these riches, such as an ally of the triumvirs. Furthermore, the temptations offered by the wealth of Cyprus would give Cato another opportunity to demonstrate his old-fashioned integrity. Just as he had earned fame as a quaestor through his immaculate care for Rome's finances, so he could use the Cyprus mission to bolster his reputation for incorruptibility and authentic Roman virtue.

Yet there were also reasons why Cato might have hesitated to accept the commission. As previously stated, he had always been opposed to extraordinary

---

14. Tatum (1999) 155–6, Marin (2009) 123–6.

15. Cicero (*Dom.* 20) says that Cato could have waged war—apparently by himself and without an army—if Ptolemy had resisted, but Velleius (2.45.4) says Cato had only the *ius praetorium*, a term that usually refers to the legal activity of praetors (see Schiller [1978] 422–7). Plutarch (*Pomp.* 48.6) says only that Cato was given the pretense of a command (προφάσει στρατηγίας), while Florus (1.44.1) and Dio (39.22.4) indicate that Cato did not use military force on Cyprus. Clodius's bill was called the *lex Clodia de imperio Catonis*, but *imperium* here need only mean "power" in the most abstract sense (see Drogula [2015] 87–9).

commands, which were usually made for the benefit of great men, and as Cicero said, accepting this commission would undermine Cato's credibility in opposing such commands in the future. Furthermore, the entire object of the mission was morally dubious: Cicero would later complain that King Ptolemy of Cyprus had been a friend of the Roman Empire, and that deposing him without just cause, merely to acquire his treasury, was a very sordid business.[16] Cato may well have considered the entire expedition to be immoral, and he probably feared that accepting it would diminish his reputation for justice. Cato also surely knew that the commission was intended to get him out of Rome, and he may not have wanted to gratify his enemies by removing himself from the political fray. On the other hand, he may have calculated that he could accomplish little against the triumvirs in the near future: the two consuls in 58 BC were friends of the triumvirs and could be counted on to hinder or block attacks by the *optimates*, and the *lex Vatinia* had given Caesar five years in his Gallic command, which meant five years of legal immunity from prosecution. He may also have found it difficult to refuse the assignment, which had been given to him by a law of the people, which made the commission as much a public duty as an honor. Many citizens who voted to give Cato the command probably thought they were showing respect and conveying honor upon him, so his refusal of that honor might have offended them and undermined his standing.[17] Thus trapped, he may have decided that he could accept the Cyprian commission and reap its rewards, and then to return to Rome in plenty of time to attack Caesar before his five-year command ended.

There are two different accounts about Cato's reaction to his appointment. Cicero in a public speech praised Cato for accepting the commission for the good of the state, saying that—although the annexation was immoral—Cato had recognized he was the best person for this particular task, and he could not refuse a law duly passed by the citizenry.[18] Plutarch, on the other hand, says that Cato initially refused to undertake this mission, so Clodius had the people pass a law forcing him to go, adding "if you do not take it as a favor, you will sail in distress."[19] Plutarch adds that Clodius further insulted Cato by refusing to equip his enterprise properly, assigning him only two clerks, one described as a thief, and the other as a client of Clodius. It is difficult to choose between these two accounts; both seek to praise Cato's service to the state, and perhaps apologize for

---

16. Cic. *Sest.* 57–63 and *Dom.* 20–1.

17. Gelzer ([1968] 100) points out, "he was now in a difficult position; if he refused to go, he would have been sharply attacked for insulting the majesty of the Roman people."

18. Cic. *Sest.* 60–1.

19. Plut. *Cat. Min.* 34.3 (εἰ μὴ χάριν ἔχεις, ἀνιώμενος πλεύσῃ).

his involvement in an immoral scheme cooked up by Clodius. It seems unlikely that Cato could have been coerced into undertaking a commission to which he was utterly opposed, so he probably did not mind being absent from Rome while Caesar's agents controlled the city, especially if it offered the opportunity to enhance his own reputation further to aid his future election to higher offices. He also knew he would not be gone from Rome too long: he received the task in February of 58 BC, but a few months later the Senate announced that Cyprus would be linked with Cilicia as a consular province for one of the consuls of 57 BC, which meant that Cato would be succeeded by early 56 BC at the latest (as was indeed the case).[20] Knowing that he would be gone less than two years, he accepted the assignment.

Cato spent one or two months preparing for his trip, leaving Rome a short time after Cicero went into exile (March 18/19).[21] Among his entourage, he brought his nephew Brutus (the son of his half-sister Servilia), who was now twenty-six or twenty-seven.[22] Instead of sailing straight to Cyprus, he paused his journey on Rhodes, sending ahead his friend Canidius to present Rome's intentions to King Ptolemy on Cyprus.[23] The decision to go to Rhodes was part precaution, part logistics, and part preference: precaution because Cato did not know how Ptolemy was going to react to the news (he seems to have briefly contemplated some kind of rash action); logistics because (as events would show) he planned to complete the restoration of exiles to Byzantium before starting the longer business of liquidating the Cyprian treasury; and preference because Rhodes was a famously pleasant island for Rome's elite, and visiting such places was one of the attractions of serving on such commissions.[24] While on Rhodes he received a visit from King Ptolemy Auletes of Egypt, who had been expelled by his own people and was en route to Rome to seek help in reclaiming his throne.[25] Cato advised

---

20. Cicero (*Fam.* 1.7.4) writes that P. Cornelius Lentulus Spinther (cos. 57 BC) was in Cilicia in the summer of 56 BC and that he controlled Cyprus as well. Since the *lex Sempronia* required consular commands to be assigned before the elections, which in 58 BC were held by July (Cic. *Att.* 3.13.1, 3.14.1), Cyprus must have been assigned as part of a consular province within a few months of Cato's departure from Rome.

21. Cato was still in Rome when Cicero decided to go into self-exile in March of that year (Cic. *Att.* 3.15.2, Plut. *Cat. Min.* 35.1, Dio 38.17.4).

22. Plut. *Brut.* 3.1.

23. Plut. *Cat. Min.* 35.1–2 and *Brut.* 3.1.

24. Ptolemy seems to have considered sinking his treasure in the ocean, but changed his mind (Val. Max 9.4.ex.1, Dio 39.22.2–3), although Appian (*BC* 2.23) suggests he did dispose of his treasure in this way. See Fehrle (1983) 150.

25. Plut. *Cat. Min.* 35.2–5.

Ptolemy against seeking help from Rome, warning that corrupt politicians (certainly a reference to the triumvirs) would demand ever-greater amounts of money for promises of their support. Instead, he suggested that Ptolemy return to Egypt and reconcile with his people. He even offered to accompany the king and assist in the reconciliation if possible. Ptolemy did not heed this advice. In the previous year he had paid the triumvirs a tremendous sum to recognize his rule over Egypt, so he dismissed Cato's words and proceeded to Rome, expecting a return on his investment. He would linger in Rome for three years waiting for his restoration.

Canidius arrived at Cyprus and presented Rome's decision to King Ptolemy. Cato clearly shared Cicero's feelings that deposing a friendly king without just cause was unseemly, and he sought to soften the blow by offering to make Ptolemy a priest at the rich and important sanctuary of Aphrodite on Paphos.[26] This was a prestigious and respected position that would ensure Ptolemy a life of wealth, comfort, and honor, but instead the king committed suicide rather than suffer the indignity of losing his throne. With the king out of the picture, Cato instructed Canidius to begin collecting and cataloging the royal treasures while he himself went on to Byzantium to settle the business of the exiles there. To help Canidius and to keep an eye on him, Cato sent his nephew Brutus to Cyprus as well, summoning him from Pamphylia, where he was recovering from a serious illness. According to Plutarch, Brutus disliked being dispatched in this manner, because he thought Cato was wrongly insulting Canidius by sending the young Brutus to be an overseer for the older man, and because Brutus had little interest in the painstaking accounting that would be necessary to tabulate the king's possessions.[27] In spite of his resentment, however, Brutus did as his uncle instructed. And because the restoration of exiles to Byzantium seems to have taken little of Cato's time or effort, he was soon on Cyprus himself, where he enthusiastically threw himself into the liquidation of the royal possessions, converting all property into cash for shipment back to Rome. The king of Cyprus had been very wealthy, and the great number and value of his possessions seem to have made Cato suspicious. Rather than rely on local auctioneers to dispose of the goods, Cato undertook every aspect of the cataloging and appraisals himself. He scrutinized the value of each piece and spoke with each prospective buyer to encourage them to bid on items and drive up the prices.[28] Cato had been celebrated for his conscientious work as quaestor, and he seems to have brought the same energy and meticulousness to his Cyprian mission.

---

26. Plut. *Cat. Min.* 35.1–2.

27. Plut. *Brut.* 3.2–3.

28. Plut. *Cat. Min.* 36.2.

While his diligence and industry were remarkable, he once again seems to have alienated those around him with his punctiliousness. In his determination to extract as much money as possible out of the king's estate, he became suspicious of his friends as well as of his assistants, criers, and buyers. His friends came to feel that Cato did not trust them, and they were offended by his behavior toward them.[29] In particular, he seems to have neglected his old friend Munatius Rufus, who had come all the way from Rome to offer his assistance. Plutarch consulted Munatius's own account of this event, so there is little reason to doubt this story of Cato's insufferable treatment of his friends.[30] He failed to offer any welcome, hospitality, or entertainment when his dear friend arrived from Rome, and he further insulted Munatius by ignoring his friend's arrival at his house, instead continuing a discussion of finances with Canidius. When Munatius complained of this treatment, Cato faulted his friend's excessive affection. Munatius then refused to attend on him when asked, and in response Cato threatened to force Munatius to pay a security to guarantee his good behavior. In response to this threat, Munatius quit the island and returned to Rome, and the two men were only eventually reconciled through the interventions of Cato's wife Marcia. Such treatment of a friend who had traveled from Rome is surprising, but it underscores the general view that Cato was difficult, even as an ally and friend.

When the liquidation of the royal possessions of Cyprus was complete and the proceeds totaled up, Cato had raised the impressive sum of nearly 7,000 talents. To make sure this treasure returned to Rome safely, he had special chests made, which he tied together and to which he attached a long rope with a large piece of cork at the end, which would float in case of shipwreck to show the location of the sunken treasure and facilitate in its recovery.[31] Florus mistakenly believed this sum was larger than any that had been previously brought to Rome in triumph, but he was in error: Pompey had brought back nearly 12,500 talents from his conquests in the East, although he admittedly had a much larger area to pillage.[32] Cato's haul from Cyprus was certainly impressive, but some well-informed senators may have wondered why it was not bigger. Diodorus visited Egypt in the early 50s and estimated the king's *annual revenue*—not total assets—to be around 6,000 talents a year (Strabo would say 12,500/year), Ptolemy Auletes had paid the triumvirs a bribe of 6,000 talents in 59 BC, and in 56 BC he would

29. Plut. *Cat. Min.* 36.2–3.

30. Plut. *Cat. Min.* 36.3–37.5.

31. Plut. *Cat. Min.* 37.1.

32. Flor. 1.44.5. On Pompey: see Oost (1955) 104.

allegedly pay Gabinius a bribe of 10,000 talents to restore him to the Egyptian throne.[33] Egypt was certainly larger and much wealthier than Cyprus, but one may wonder whether the total value of the Cyprian monarchy—including lands, buildings, possessions, slaves, and cash—was really only slightly higher than the annual income of the king of Egypt. This discrepancy is often overlooked, perhaps because the ramification seems so strange: Cato may have embezzled some money, or may have allowed his friend Canidius or his nephew Brutus to embezzle money.[34] While this may seem impossible for Rome's paragon of virtue, some curious facts make it plausible. First, Cato was reportedly very distressed that both copies of his account books were destroyed on the journey home: one was lost at sea when a boat capsized, and the other was consumed by a fire that accidentally ignited Cato's tent.[35] While this might be ascribed to bad luck, it was made particularly serious because Cato had failed to obey the law requiring that Roman officials leave one copy of their accounts in the province they were leaving, and forward another copy to the treasury of Rome.[36] He certainly knew of his responsibility to leave a copy in Cyprus, since it was set down in the *lex Julia de repetundis*, the law that Cato had favored in 59 BC. Such neglect is odd, since Cato was famous for following every law, even those that he disliked.[37] Perhaps he ignored the law because he was a special commissioner rather than a provincial governor, but even that would be a splitting of hairs that was unusual for Cato. Furthermore, he had the foresight to bring the royal stewards of Cyprus with him to Rome—which was a strange precaution for one not expecting to lose his account books—and they testified to his honesty, although the veracity of their testimony is open to question, since Cato subsequently rewarded at least one of them with his freedom.[38] Rudolf Fehrle attempted to defend Cato by suggesting that he must have left an official copy of his account books in Cyprus, but this reading does not seem likely given the clarity of the evidence.[39] Indeed, the whole episode of the lost books would hardly have been worth remembering if another

---

33. Diod. 17.52.6, Strabo 17.1.13. Bribes: Cic. *Rab. Post.* 19–22 and 34–5, Suet. *Iul.* 54.3, Dio 39.12.1, 39.55.1.

34. Oost ([1955] 105–7) made this point, but it has been widely ignored, although Dragstedt ([1969] 80) also notes, "Cato may even have had private reasons for wishing the records lost—a maneuver of which he would not have been incapable."

35. Plut. *Cat. Min.* 38.2–3, Dio 39.23.3.

36. Cic. *Att.* 6.7.2, *Fam.* 5.20.2.

37. Cic. *Sest.* 61, Dio 38.7.6 (Cato follows laws even if he disapproves of them).

38. Plut. *Cat. Min.* 39.3.

39. Fehrle (1983) 153–5.

copy was secure in Cyprus and could be obtained. Cato's distress—not to mention Clodius's later effort to embarrass Cato for the loss of his accounts—make little sense unless the records were beyond recovery. So the surprising neglect of the law regarding the preservation of accounts, the disappearance of the only two copies of the accounts, and Cato's foresight in bringing persons who could attest to the contents of those lost accounts are certainly suspicious, especially given the extreme care Cato took in making sure the wealth transported on his ships could be recovered even if the ships sank.

Is it possible that the scrupulous Cato embezzled money? It seems impossible if one thinks of him as a paragon of Stoic virtue, but if one understands Cato instead as his own caricature of a traditional Roman, then his willingness to enrich himself modestly through embezzlement does not seem particularly surprising. After all, Cato had approved the use of bribery in the consular campaigns against Caesar in 60 BC, and he was planning to stand for election to the praetorship upon his return to Rome, so he may have taken some personal profits to provide options for his campaign. Cato was honest, but in the current political environment it would be difficult for a senator of only average means to reach the consulship, even with the connections he had. Furthermore, a discreet amount of self-enrichment by provincial commanders had long been considered normal and acceptable among the Roman elite—it was one of the reasons men sought high office and commands—so Cato would still receive high praise for honesty so long as his profiteering was restrained and within normal limits. Furthermore, he would not have been stealing money from provincials who might complain to Rome's extortion court, but merely keeping for himself certain items from a dead king's treasury, and the fact that Cato cataloged, appraised, and auctioned all the items himself gave him ample opportunity to keep certain items aside for himself. From this perspective, it may even be that Cato's unusual efforts to run up the prices in his auctions was done to cover over his own discreet embezzlement—the large scale of his haul could have disguised his taking of profits. Indeed, Cato was known to have kept at least some items from the Cyprian treasury: Pliny mentions that he kept for himself a bronze statue of the Stoic philosopher Zeno, although he insists that it was the subject—and not the value or artistic quality of the statue—that made it important to him.[40]

It is also possible that one or more people on Cato's staff seized the opportunity to profit from the confiscated treasures, such as his nephew Brutus, who had a reputation as an unscrupulous moneylender. Brutus certainly used his contacts on Cyprus and his influence in the Senate to arrange a large and technically illegal

---

40. Plin. *NH* 34.92.

loan to the Cyprian city of Salamis at the grossly usurious interest rate of forty-eight percent. Although such a high rate of interest might have been appropriate for high-risk loans, Salamis should have been considered a safe financial bet, and Brutus surely understood this.[41] Years later, when Cicero was the governor of nearby Cilicia, he would complain in several letters how Brutus was pestering him for help in collecting the vast sums of money owed him on account of these loans.[42] It would seem, therefore, that Brutus had used the opportunity of his uncle's commission to make extortionate loans to at least one city on Cyprus, and we also learn that by 51 BC King Deiotaurus of Galatia owed Brutus a great deal of money as well.[43] Cato may have been ignorant of his nephew's actions (Cicero did not think Cato would have approved),[44] but that seems out of line with what we know about Cato's meticulousness and attention to fiscal details. It may be that Cato simply turned a blind eye to his nephew's activities. He had exempted his brother-in-law Silanus from prosecution for bribery in 63/2 BC, and he had supported the use of bribery by his brother-in-law Bibulus in 60 BC, so Cato's interpretation of ancestral custom may have allowed him to make exceptions to his famous morality for family members, especially the son of his half-sister, and the adopted son of his beloved half-brother Caepio. Plutarch notes that it was Brutus who was primarily responsible for shipping most of the Cyprian treasure back to Rome on his uncle's behalf, which created opportunities for discreet profiteering.[45] It is only the later lionization of Cato as a Stoic hero that makes it difficult to believe that he would have indulged in some modest profiteering from this command, or at least allowed his nephew to do so.

Cato's homecoming to Rome in 56 BC was a fantastic spectacle, as his fleet of ships worked its way up the Tiber to the city.[46] According to Plutarch, when

---

41. Oost (1955) 107–9 and Shatzman (1975) 372.

42. Cic. *Att.* 5.21.10–12, 6.2.7, 6.3.5.

43. Cic. *Att.* 5.18.4. Eilers ([2002] 42 and 260) points out that Cato became the patron of King Ariobarzanes of Cappadocia (or his father) during this trip, illustrating the extent of Cato's influence while on Cyprus, and thus the range of opportunities open to Brutus in lending money.

44. Cic. *Att.* 6.2.8.

45. Plut. *Brut.* 3.4. Brutus may have been descended through his mother from the Q. Servilius Caepio who was consul in 106 BC. This Caepio famously captured a massive hoard of treasure from the Volcae Tectosages, and when this treasure mysteriously disappeared while in transit back to Rome, Caepio was believed to have purloined it (Strabo 4.1.13, Gell. 3.9.7). One can only wonder if family legends about the missing treasure went through Brutus's mind as he transported the Cyprian hoard back to Rome.

46. The date of his return in 56 BC is not recorded, but given the dangers of sailing in winter months, he likely returned to Rome in the spring or early summer.

word of his arrival spread, the Senate and people flocked to the banks of the river to watch the procession. They were treated to the grand sight of Cato floating up the river and into Rome aboard a royal *hexeris*—a massive warship powered by hundreds of rowers divided into six banks of oars—which was even larger than the *quinqueremes* that the Romans used as their primary battleships. An assortment of other ships rounded out his flotilla. The consuls and praetors, along with the Senate, formed themselves into a welcoming committee on the bank of the Tiber, but Cato reportedly sailed right past them and anchored his ships further upriver, probably at Rome's naval docks.[47] His dismissal of this formal welcome surely gave offense to his fellow aristocrats—Velleius wrote that it was almost insolent.[48] He did not even spare those closest to him: one of the consuls who formed the welcome party, only to be ignored and passed by, was his new father-in-law, L. Marcius Philippus. Cato was usually more careful about protecting the *auctoritas* of the Senate, so his slighting of that body probably served a purpose. By docking further upriver he essentially celebrated a naval parade through the heart of the city—and in particular past the bustling Forum—as he escorted the wealth of Cyprus to Rome. Not only did this give Cato the opportunity to show off the success of his mission, but to most viewers his aquatic procession through Rome with his spoils in tow must have been reminiscent of a victorious general's triumph.[49] In fact, his arrival was probably designed to copy the famous naval spectacle made in 167 BC by L. Aemilius Paullus, the conqueror of Macedonia. In that event, Aemilius Paullus had sailed into Rome on the captured Macedonian royal galley, which he had adorned with the spoils of war.[50] This had been a famous and memorable event—the royal flagship was long kept on display near Rome's naval docks—and Cato no doubt wanted his audience to equate his own naval spectacle to Aemilius Paullus's great victory celebration, yet another deft use of tradition. Once docked, Cato arranged a second procession—this time by land— as he had the treasure removed from his ships and carried through the Forum on its way to the treasury.[51] He also brought back a large number of Cyprian slaves, who must have marched in his procession, much like captives would have been paraded in the triumph of a victorious commander.[52] He went so far as to speak

47. Plut. *Cat. Min.* 39.1–3, Vell. 2.45.5.

48. Vell. 2.45.5 *insolentia paene*.

49. Val. Max. 8.15.10, Plut. *Cat. Min.* 39.1, Dio 39.23.1.

50. Polyb. 36.5.9, Livy 45.35.3 and 45.42.12.

51. Plut. *Cat. Min.* 39.3.

52. Dio 39.22.4–23.2.

of his success as a conquest by claiming (wrongly) that his financial contribution to the city was greater than Pompey's had been.[53] Like all Romans, Cato was determined to squeeze as much status-enhancing glory as possible from his mission to Cyprus, even if that meant dressing up his financial mission in a military cloak.

Despite his slight of the senators who tried to welcome him, Cato's friends were ready to celebrate his accomplishments. The Senate met in a special session to welcome him back to Rome, and with loud praises it voted extraordinary honors for him. The sources had differing accounts of what these honors were: Plutarch and Dio thought that Cato was to receive an extraordinary praetorship and the right to watch games wearing a *toga praetexta*, whereas Valerius Maximus wrote that his candidacy was to be accepted *extra ordinem* at the praetorian elections.[54] The first two cannot be right: it is not possible that the Senate was offering just to *give* Cato a praetorship, because election to the praetorship was the sole prerogative of the Centuriate Assembly. Rather, the Senate probably offered him the right to wear praetorian regalia (*ornamenta*) even though he had not yet been praetor, and it may have offered him a special dispensation to stand for the praetorship of 55 BC even though the date had passed for candidates to make their *professio*.[55] The first of these offers was probably done to resolve a problem: Cato had been assigned to Cyprus *pro quaestore pro praetore*, and therefore had been entitled to wear praetorian *ornamenta* outside of Rome. When he re-entered the city, however, his right to wear praetorian *ornamenta* may have been questionable, since he had not yet actually held the praetorship. Valerius Maximus says that Cato rejected these special offers, believing such privileges inappropriate.[56] It may also be the case that he did not think he needed special exemptions—he stood for election to the praetorship of 55 BC, indicating that his *professio* was made in a timely manner, and he may have believed that the rejection of offered praetorian *ornamenta* would bring him more glory than actually possessing them (as had happened when he rejected military honors as a youth). Instead of honors, he only asked that the Senate grant freedom to Ptolemy's steward, but this only happened after the slave had sworn to Cato's honest accounting of the Cyprian treasure.

The glory that Cato received from his special commission seems to have irked Clodius, who wanted to appropriate some of Cato's accomplishment for himself

---

53. Plut. *Cat. Min.* 45.2 (cf. Dio 39.22.4).

54. Val. Max. 4.1.14, Plut. *Cat. Min.* 39.3, Dio 39.23.1.

55. Brennan (2000) 428–30.

56. Val. Max. 4.1.14.

and knock him down a peg or two. Cato had brought back from Cyprus a number of slaves that had belonged to the royal house, and they became the property of the Roman state and therefore public slaves. Since he had been responsible for the legislation that gave Cato the Cyprian commission, Clodius proposed that these new slaves be named *Clodiani* in his honor.[57] Cato's supporters in the Senate naturally opposed this, going so far as to suggest that the slaves should be named *Porciani*. Cato declined this honor, so the slaves were simply called *Cyprii*. In revenge for this defeat, Clodius (who was now aedile) attacked Cato in the courts, demanding to see the missing account books recording his handling of the Cyprian treasury.[58] This was tantamount to accusing Cato of embezzlement, which was a direct attack on his famous integrity. Perhaps Cato had tried to hide the fact that the records were missing, but it is more likely that Clodius wished to draw attention to their absence and thus to Cato's inability to prove his fastidious and honest accounting. Furthermore, Clodius spread a rumor that Cato had urged the consuls (one of them his father-in-law) to offer him a praetorship *extra ordinem*, just so he could turn the offer down;[59] that is, Clodius tried to draw into question Cato's honesty and famous austerity by suggesting he actively sought honors just to reject them. Those attacks achieved little, except to annoy Cato and his supporters.

Cato defied expectations with his Cyprian mission. Clodius and others had viewed the mission as a lucrative but morally compromising enterprise; the commissioner would become rich by helping himself to the king's treasury, but would receive little glory (since no conquest was involved) and would be tainted by the unjust deposition of an allied king. Few could have anticipated that Cato would achieve glory and fame from this fiscal assignment. As he had done with his quaestorship, he found status-enhancing glory even in routine financial endeavors by using them to advertise his old-fashioned virtues and his dedication to the *mos maiorum*. Cato was fully aware that the Cyprian mission had increased his *dignitas*, and that he needed to defend the integrity and legitimacy of this expedition against challenges. This occasionally became uncomfortable, because it also meant defending some of Clodius's actions, which had probably been Clodius's purpose when assigning the command to Cato. For example, when Cicero— now recalled from exile—renewed his attacks against the legitimacy of Clodius's tribunate, Cato had to step forward and defend Clodius. Cicero argued before the Senate that his tribunate—and therefore all of his legislation—was invalid

---

57. Dio 39.23.2–3. See Tatum (1999) 221.

58. Dio 39.23.3–4.

59. Dio 39.23.4.

because his adoption into a plebeian *gens* had been improperly conducted.[60] Many *optimates* would have supported this accusation, since it would annul all of Clodius's *popularis* acts, but Cato was forced to argue that his adoption and tribunate had indeed been legitimate. According to Plutarch:

> But Cato opposed Cicero while he was speaking, and at last rising, he said that he believed nothing healthy or useful had come from the whole of Clodius' time in office, but if someone annulled all the things Clodius did while tribune, then all of his own work on Cyprus would also be annulled and the expedition itself would not have been legal, since the magistrate conducting the vote for the mission had been illegal. . . .[61]

Cato goes on to argue that Clodius's adoption and election to the tribunate had been legal, and therefore his office should not be retroactively invalidated, but rather his acts should be reviewed individually. If Plutarch is right, then Cato was acting out of self-interest because he was more concerned to maintain the legitimacy of his own Cyprian command than to investigate the legitimacy of Clodius's magistracy. Everything he had done on Cyprus—including deposing an allied king—depended upon Clodius's legislation, and the glory and honors he had received would be tarnished if the command itself was rendered unlawful.[62] It was not unusual in the shifting world of Roman politics for a senator to change a position or alliance in order to prioritize his own (or his family's) interests, but this must have been particularly awkward and uncomfortable for Cato. Not only had Clodius's sacrilege in entering the *Bona Dea* rituals deeply offended him, but he had tried to steal some of his glory by having the Cyprian slaves renamed *Clodiani*, and he was currently embarrassing Cato by demanding to see the lost account books. Yet to protect his own accomplishments on Cyprus, Cato was forced to defend an odious man and prevent the annulment of his tribunate. This understandably enraged Cicero, who felt betrayed and refused to speak to Cato for a long time.[63]

As Cato surveyed the political situation in Rome after his long absence, he found that much had changed, and not for the better. The leadership of the *nobiles* had been further thinned sometime in 57 or 56 BC by the death of

---

60. Plut. *Cat. Min.* 40.1–2, *Cic.* 34.2, Dio 39.22.1.

61. Plut. *Cat. Min.* 40.2.

62. Fehrle ([1983] 159–63) develops this point. See also Mitchell (1991) 190–2 and Tatum (1999) 219–21.

63. Plut. *Cat. Min.* 40.2 and *Cic.* 34.3. See Epstein (1987) 39.

Lucullus, who had named Cato the guardian for his young son.[64] Another source of concern for the *optimates* was Clodius, who had become more unpredictable and was using street gangs to incite violence and disrupt public events. After Cicero's and Cato's departures from Rome in 58 BC, Clodius had surprised people by turning against Pompey, assaulting him in the streets and inciting public outcry and mockery against him in the theater. It became difficult for Pompey to move about in the city, so he withdrew from public life and began pushing for Cicero's recall. With the help of the consuls and some of the tribunes of 57 BC, Cicero's exile was canceled and he was recalled to the city, arriving in September to rejoicing crowds that now lamented how he had been treated. Cicero was extremely grateful to Pompey for his (belated) efforts, and two days after his return, he proposed a law giving Pompey a special commission to supervise the grain supply for the city. This assignment was needed to deal with the serious and recurring grain shortages, but the scope of this commission was vast, comprising most every source of grain in the Roman world. Pompey had shown a talent for organizing such expansive operations when he suppressed piracy throughout the Mediterranean, but it was also a great honor and a very powerful position. The law passed, and Pompey was given all the resources he asked for, including *imperium*, men, ships, equipment, and complete authority over the grain supply throughout the Roman world.[65] Many in the Senate were frustrated at this expansion of Pompey's authority. Cato's imitator and ally M. Favonius seems to have taken the lead in fighting the proposal, but he was unsuccessful in blocking the popular bill. In addition to proposing the grain commission for Pompey, Cicero also proposed an exceptionally long, fifteen-day *supplicatio* to celebrate Caesar's tremendous victories in Gaul.[66] In return for these efforts, Pompey announced that Cicero was his first choice of lieutenant for the grain command, and Caesar gave Cicero cheap or interest-free loans, and a few years later would support his petition for a triumph.[67] In spite of these actions, however, it is not accurate to say that Cicero had changed sides and joined the triumvirs. Pompey (for his own reasons) had come to his aid and had proved decisive in getting Cicero recalled to Rome, and Caesar too was offering assistance, and so he felt a strong obligation

---

64. Varro *RR* 3.2.17.

65. Cic. *Att.* 4.1.6–7. Seager ([2002] 107–9) discusses Pompey's assignment on the grain supply.

66. Pompey's commission: Cic. *Att.* 4.1.7. Caesar's *supplicatio*: Caes. *BG* 2.35, Cic. *Pis.* 59, Plut. *Caes.* 21.1, Dio 39.5.1.

67. Pompey: Cic. *Att.* 4.1.7. Caesar's support for Cicero's triumph: Cic. *Att.* 7.1.7. Caesar's loan: Cic. *Att.* 5.1.2, 5.4.3, 5.5.2, 7.3.11. Shatzman ([1975] 416–7) argued that Caesar's loan of HS 800,000 to Cicero was probably made in 54 BC, and the interest rate was less than 1%.

to return these favors as best he could, within the bounds of his conscience. But this does not mean that Cicero had joined their faction, but rather that he and his circle of friends had temporarily grown closer to the triumvirs on account of their services to him. He still held the fundamental position that the triumvirate was bad for Rome, but he thought it was wiser to handle the great men carefully and tolerate their ambitions (especially Pompey's) in order to make their triumvirate unnecessary.[68] Like most senators, Cicero's web of political connections could easily overlap as situations changed: he still felt a strong ideological connection with many *optimates*, but he also was grateful for the assistance he had received from the triumvirate.

One of the stranger events of Cato's life occurred shortly after his return from Cyprus (in 56 BC). With his successful Cyprian commission bolstering his reputation, Cato was increasingly admired and recognized as a leader among the *optimates*. At this time, his friend Q. Hortensius (cos. 69 BC)—a senior *nobilis* and optimate—expressed a desire to be more closely related to Cato. It is possible that they were already connected, since Hortensius's daughter may have been the widow of Cato's deceased half-brother Caepio.[69] Wishing to strengthen their connection, Hortensius proposed marrying Cato's daughter Porcia, who was already married to Bibulus and had borne him two sons.[70] Hortensius argued that Porcia had given Bibulus enough children, and that it was not right for a beautiful and young woman to stop having children altogether or to give Bibulus more children than he wanted. Hortensius added that the joining of so many good men into one family would be good for the state, and he promised that— if Bibulus truly loved Porcia—he would return Porcia to Bibulus after she had borne Hortensius a child. Cato rejected these arguments and refused to take his daughter from her husband, so Hortensius changed plans and asked permission to marry Cato's own wife Marcia, since she was young enough to give Hortensius children, and she had already given enough children to Cato. Although Marcia was currently pregnant, Cato agreed to speak with her father about Hortensius's request, and when Marcius gave his approval, he divorced Marcia and returned her to her father, who together with Cato gave her to Hortensius.

Two themes seem to be at work in this love triangle. First is the obvious goal of forming political alliances through marriage and children. Hortensius was

---

68. From the formation of the triumvirate in 59 BC, Cicero had hoped (*Att.* 2.7.3) to split the triumvirs apart.

69. The identification depends upon *ILS* 9460. See Hallet (2014) 57–9.

70. Luc. 2.332–3, Strabo 11.9.1, Plut. *Cat. Min.* 25.2–5, Quint. *Inst.* 3.5.11, 10.5.13. Fehrle (1983) 201–2.

already a senior senator and a leading figure among the *nobiles*, but he was estranged from his only son, although they were eventually reconciled.[71] Elderly and effectively childless, he wanted to acquire an heir who would continue and enhance his family's legacy. His first choice of Porcia, therefore, indicates that he saw Cato as a lasting figure in Roman politics, whose grandchildren would possess especially high political clout. When Cato refused to give him Porcia, Hortensius then sought Marcia, who brought the advantage of having a sitting consul as her father, and whose children would be half-brothers or half-sisters to the children she had borne Cato. Such political calculations are to be expected among Rome's aristocracy, but this was an extreme case, including Cato's decision to surrender a pregnant wife. The second factor in this story is the theme of Stoic detachment. Plutarch was writing years later, when Cato was widely viewed as a Stoic sage, and he pointedly emphasized that, although Cato was happy with Marcia (who was carrying his child), he was willing to hand her over to Hortensius as an example of his Stoic detachment and apathy.[72] Thus Plutarch provided Stoic explanations for these actions because he believed that Cato was a great Stoic; his interpretation of the episode came from this assumption about his motives. Yet this was probably a mistake. As will be discussed in the epilogue, Cato's reputation as a Stoic philosopher was greatly exaggerated after his death, and there were other stories at the time explaining his treatment of Marcia: Caesar suggested that Cato was fishing for Hortensius's wealth, while Strabo says that he gave Marcia to Hortensius in accordance with an ancient custom of the Romans.[73] Strabo's explanation is usually ignored because there is no other example in Republican history of a Roman handing over his wife in this manner, but in Cato's case, the reality of the custom may not have been as important as its antique appearance. After all, Cato had discovered his bizarre clothing style by looking at some old statues on the Capitoline Hill, and as a military tribune he marched on foot instead of riding a horse probably in observance of a long-defunct custom regarding dictators. So his handing over of Marcia may not have been motivated by Stoicism or wealth, but—as Strabo says—by his own ideas about ancient Roman culture and his desire to project an image of extreme adherence to the *mos maiorum*.[74] In that case, handing over Marcia did not need to follow a real (even archaic) custom, since

---

71. Val. Max. 5.9.2.

72. See Gordon (1933) 574–8, Münzer (1999) 313–8, Fraschetti (2001) 5–7, Cornell (2013) 3.467–8, Hallet (2014) 57–9.

73. Plut. *Cat. Min.* 52.4, Strabo 11.9.1 (κατὰ παλαιὸν Ῥωμαίων ἔθος).

74. Cantarella ([2002] 269–82) argued that the transferral of Marcia may not have been so strange in ancient Rome, since the production of children was a civic virtue.

Cato used the flexibility of tradition to create his own amalgam of practices that he believed (or wanted to believe) were authentic. So while other people thought it very strange that he handed over Marcia, in Cato's mind it may have been another outstanding example of his own unique dedication to tradition.

Ravenna, Luca, and the Triumvirate

The triumvirs had many reasons to be concerned in 56 BC. For three years they had managed to hold off their opponents and retain their preeminence in Rome, but their alliance was under heavy stress. Cato and the men around him maintained steady opposition, and their attacks seem to have increased pressure on the triumvirs. While Caesar was gaining wealth and fame in Gaul, Pompey's reputation and standing had been seriously bruised by repeated blows from the *optimates* on one side, and from Clodius on the other.[75] At the same time, some of the *optimates* were trying to pull Pompey over to their side and thus break up the alliance. So Pompey was becoming jealous and resentful at the rapid growth of Caesar's fame, and was being tempted by Cicero's overtures to move away from his fellow triumvirs. The account of Pompey's jealousy is probably exaggerated, but he may have supported the attack on Caesar's *lex Campana* made by the tribune P. Rutilius Lupus, who—immediately upon entering office in December of 57 BC—attempted to prevent Caesar's veterans from having access to this land.[76] Experiencing more costs than benefits in the alliance, Pompey's natural inclination to challenge Caesar's influence was growing. This was motivated by competitive self-interest, but would have been very appealing to many *optimates*. Pompey's original alliance with Caesar had been a temporary solution to present problems rather than a long-term partnership, so their positions vis-à-vis one other were changeable. At the same time, Pompey surely knew that many *optimates* were interested in him simply because they hoped to pull him away from Caesar and Crassus, and that—once the triumvirate was broken—they would no longer continue to lavish attention on him.[77] That is, when the threat of Caesar (in particular) was gone, the *optimates* would have little interest in tolerating Pompey's preeminence—he knew as well as any the shifting nature of senatorial factions. So he resented Caesar's success and wanted to limit it, but at the same time he needed his alliance with Caesar in order to increase his own importance and value in the eyes of the *optimates*. As for Crassus, little is known

75. Cic. *QF* 2.3.2, 2.5.4, Plut. *Pomp.* 48.7, Dio 39.19.1–2, 39.25.1–4.

76. Dio 39.25.1–26.1. See Lazenby (1959) 68.

77. Seager (2002) 109.

about his feelings at the time, but he and Pompey were old enemies, and in the absence of Caesar's mediation they seem to have reverted to working against one another: Pompey complained to Cicero that Crassus was secretly funding both Gaius Cato (perhaps a relative of M. Cato) and Clodius, Pompey's chief tormentors.[78] Pompey and Crassus still had strong individual connections to Caesar—Pompey was devoted to Julia, and Crassus had financial interests in Caesar's success—but these elder members of the triumvirate may have felt that their alliance had run its course, in which case Pompey was probably the most inclined to seek better ties with the *optimates*.

Caesar, on the other hand, wanted his command in Gaul extended by an additional five years, and to achieve this he would need the support of his alienated allies. The following year (55 BC) would be critical, because in that year the Senate would decide what would happen with Caesar's command when the *lex Vatinia* expired. With this in mind, Cato's brother-in-law Domitius Ahenobarbus had declared his candidacy for election to the consulship of 55 BC, and was determined to have Caesar recalled to Rome and prosecuted at the end of his command. This was an imposing challenge, since Domitius wielded immense influence, and his ancestral *dignitas* was such that Cicero referred to him as having been designated a consul from birth.[79] Domitius had strong connections with Gaul, which his ancestors had helped conquer and settle, so as consul he would have a very strong claim to replace Caesar in command of Transalpine Gaul.[80] In anticipation of this sequence of events, the plebeian tribune L. Antistius seems to have initiated a prosecution against Caesar and his unnamed quaestor in this year, but this came to nothing because Caesar was still protected by his immunity as a commander (the fate of the unnamed quaestor is not recorded, but this silence must mean the prosecution failed).[81] As a final threat, Cato was eligible to stand for the praetorship, and if successful, he would be in charge of one of Rome's courts in 55 BC. Cato announced his candidacy, no doubt hoping that he would preside over Caesar's trial and finally get to see his personal enemy destroyed in his court. Given this range of threats, Caesar needed to secure his alliance if he wanted to receive an extension of his command and legal immunity.

---

78. Cic. *QF* 2.3.4.

79. Cic. *Att.* 4.8a.2.

80. Syme (1939) 44 n. 4.

81. Suetonius (*Iul.* 23.1–2) is clumsy with the chronology of this event. His description suggests that Antistius attempted to prosecute Caesar in 58 BC (so Gruen [1971] 62–4), but Badian ([1974] 147–8) has argued persuasively that it belongs in 56 BC. Ramsey ([2009] 41) concurs with Badian.

Since Pompey's allegiance to the triumvirate was fading, Caesar first arranged to meet with Crassus in Ravenna early in 56 BC, close to Rome but still in Caesar's province of Cisalpine Gaul.[82] The relationship between these two men had always been based on money, so Caesar probably had little difficulty confirming Crassus's continued support in exchange for something profitable—either for Caesar's support in helping Crassus win election to the consulship of 55 BC, or perhaps for his help in getting Crassus assigned to restore Ptolemy Auletes to the throne of Egypt (which would offer many opportunities for business and profit).[83] Caesar also arranged to meet with Clodius's older brother Ap. Claudius Pulcher (cos. 54 BC) and with Metellus Nepos (cos. 57 BC), inviting both men to Ravenna or perhaps to Luca.[84] These men were politically aligned with each other (they were cousins), and they were key to affirming Pompey's support. Appius and Nepos were staunch supporters of their relative Clodius (Appius had been one of only three senators to vote against Cicero's recall), and their families ranked very high among the aristocracy—Appius had married Lucullus's sister, and Nepos's family (the *Caecilii Metelli*) included many famous consuls. Both men were traveling to military commands when they paused their journeys to discuss their futures with Caesar, who had a talent for understanding how to use his resources to obtain the support of his fellow senators. Appius was the head of his noble and influential family, but he probably lacked sufficient resources to guarantee consulships for himself and his brothers, although his younger brother Gaius was currently praetor. He therefore came to an arrangement with Caesar: the *Claudii Pulchri* would become supporters of the triumvirate, Appius's daughter would marry one of Pompey's sons, and Appius would receive the full backing of the triumvirate in his campaign for the consulship of 54 BC.[85] Nepos was probably won over by similar promises of support, but his death a short time later obscured the consequences of his meeting with Caesar. Appius and Nepos were valuable allies in their own right, but Caesar was also interested in their influence over Clodius, who was Pompey's single greatest tormentor. Caesar calculated that Pompey would rededicate himself to the triumvirate if it meant bringing an end to Clodius's relentless attacks.

Caesar's successful negotiations with Appius provide another valuable look into the shifting world of senatorial factions. Appius was from an old

---

82. Cic. *Fam.* 1.9.9. See Jackson (1978) 175–7.

83. Marshall ([1976] 126–8) explores Crassus's motives.

84. Cic. *QF* 2.5.4, Plut. *Caes.* 21.5, App. *BC* 2.17.

85. See Tatum (1999) 214–5 for discussion of their agreement.

patrician family that normally would have been considered very conservative and a strong supporter of the traditional political order, but he and his brother Gaius supported their brother Clodius's feud against Cicero, which vexed the *optimates* who opposed Clodius's unconventional behavior and political tactics. In this way, their political alignments had shifted to support their family over the other *optimates*. Appius's meeting with Caesar yielded a similar shift. Appius had looked over his situation and realized that, in the current political climate, his interests (and his family's) were best served by aligning with Caesar and the triumvirate. He was forty-one years old when he met with Caesar, which meant he was eligible to stand for a consulship in the next year, but the odds of a victory were slim; not only were the triumvirs sure to throw their considerable resources behind two candidates, but also the *optimates* were putting up the *nobilis* Domitius Ahenobarbus and probably other candidates as well. Appius's support of his brother Clodius had alienated him from many *optimates*, so he was unlikely to win in that election, and his odds would not improve with time. Faced with this reality and the need to protect and enhance his family's status, wealth, and influence, Appius shifted his support (and that of his political allies) to the triumvirs, knowing that it would virtually guarantee him a consulship. This was not a permanent change of factional alliance, but a temporary shift that enabled both sides to achieve their immediate goals, which was a recurring problem for Cato: he and many of his allies had a deep, personal animosity toward Caesar, but the majority of senators were like Appius and allowed their loyalties to shift in reaction to changing events. They tolerated and even aided Cato's obstruction of the great men's priorities in 60 BC, but had withdrawn their support in the face of the power and influence of the triumvirate in 59 BC, only to become more sympathetic toward Cato's circle when Caesar's behavior appeared tyrannical. So while Cato and his friends were working to turn senatorial factions against Caesar with claims of his tyrannical aspirations, the triumvirs (Caesar in particular) were trying to use their resources to win over important connections like the *Claudii Pulchri*.

Once Caesar had secured the support of Crassus, Appius, and (probably) Nepos, he turned his full attention to winning over Pompey. The two men met at Luca while Pompey was en route to Sardinia on business relating to his grain commission, and they succeeded in patching up their differences and renewing their cooperation in the triumvirate.[86] The price of Pompey's support is not clear,

86. Cic. *Fam.* 1.9.8, Suet. *Iul.* 24.1, Plut. *Caes.* 21.5, *Pomp.* 51.3–4, *Cat. Min.* 41.1, *Crass.* 14.5–6. Jackson ([1978] 175–7) suggested that Crassus was not present at Luca. For general discussion of the meeting at Luca, see: Gruen (1969), Luibheid (1970) 88–94, Hayne (1974) 217–20, Ward (1978), Marshall (1978), Ward (1980).

but facing a united Caesar and Crassus, and waning popular support in Rome, he probably could not demand too much. More important: Caesar's new influence over Clodius would have been tantalizing, and Caesar probably made the irresistible offer of bringing an end to Clodius's harassment.[87] This alone would have been worth a great deal to Pompey, whose status and ability to move about in Rome were suffering badly from Clodius's persistent attacks. Indeed, once Pompey had agreed to renew his support for the triumvirate and for an extension of Caesar's Gallic command, Clodius ceased his harassment and would even be found publicly expressing his friendship with Pompey by the end of the year.[88]

Cicero also moved closer to the triumvirs after the meeting at Luca, but for different reasons. In exchange for his support of Cicero's recall from exile, Caesar seems to have expected assurances that Cicero would not attack the triumvirate, and after Luca, Caesar began calling upon Cicero to fulfill his debt.[89] This put Cicero in a difficult position: he did not like the way the triumvirs dominated the Republic, but he also had little respect for the actions of many *optimates*, who had wounded him personally through their neglect. He seems to have vacillated when contemplating whether the triumvirs or Cato's circle posed the greater threat to the state, but finally decided to give the expected support to the triumvirs.[90] He justified his decision to himself and others by saying that the triumvirs deserved their high rank and status because of the many services they had rendered to the state, but he was also pleased that his decision to support Pompey and Caesar would be a dagger in the heart of the *optimates* who had neglected him.[91] Nevertheless, he would still strive for the middle course that characterized his approach to politics, and despite giving assistance to the triumvirs, he would continue to be galled by their use of force in politics, but he did not believe that Cato's circle offered a much more compelling approach to politics. As had been the case with Appius, Cicero's movement toward the triumvirs demonstrates the complexity and fluctuation of senatorial factions, and highlights the difficulty of

---

87. In addition to Appius's fraternal urging, Clodius was probably convinced to support the triumvirs with a promise of a special commission (Cic. *QF* 2.8.2). See Lazenby (1959) 67–76.

88. See Seager (2002) 120. Tatum ([1999] 320 n. 7) argues that Seager follows Cicero too closely when he says that Clodius was obviously insincere about his new friendship with Pompey.

89. Cic. *Att.* 9.2a.1, *Pis.* 79, *Fam.* 1.9.9 and 12.

90. Cic. *Att.* 4.5.2, 7.1.2–3, *Fam.* 1.8.3, 1.9.4–22. Cicero not happy being aligned with triumvirs: Cic. *Att.* 4.6.1–2, *Fam.* 1.8.3–4, 7.1.4.

91. Cicero's defense of the triumvirate: Cic. *Fam.* 1.9.4–22, *Planc.* 91–4, *Balb.* 60–1; his satisfaction at confounding the *optimates*: Cic. *Att.* 4.5.1, *Balb.* 61.

Cato's situation, since he and his allies simply could not match the rewards that the triumvirs were able to offer senators for their support.

With the strength of the triumvirate thus confirmed and reinforced by the additions of Cicero and Appius, the *optimates* were once again confronted by the full force these powerful men could wield. Not only did all attempts to remove Caesar from his Gallic command fail, but efforts to undo his agrarian legislation on Campanian land also collapsed, and Cicero helped overcome obstruction of a bill providing funds for Caesar's Gallic command.[92] Cato's ally and emulator Favonius tried valiantly to block Cicero's proposal, and even tried to raise a public outcry among the people over the approval of money and supplies for Caesar, but senators and common folk alike seem to have ignored him because (as Plutarch says) they were in awe of Pompey and Crassus, and wanted to please Caesar in hopes of his favors.[93] Cato returned from Cyprus amid this resurgence of the triumvirate, and his satisfaction with his glorious entry into the city must have been tempered by the realization that the triumvirate's grip on Rome was little different than it had been two years earlier. Cato intended to stand in that year's elections for the praetorship, but his greatest hope was that his brother-in-law L. Domitius Ahenobarbus would succeed in the upcoming consular elections. Domitius was an outspoken opponent of Caesar: as *aedile* in 61 BC he had supported Cato's legislation against electoral bribery (which was aimed at Pompey and his lieutenant Afranius), and as praetor in 58 BC he had launched the first major attack against Caesar's consular legislation.[94] A member of an ancient and noble family, Domitius was a leader in Cato's circle, and had been one of those falsely accused of plotting against Pompey's life in 59 BC. Now, as a candidate for the consulship, he was loudly promising to strip Caesar of his Gallic command and to force him back to Rome to answer for his actions in court.[95] This may have been bluster, since it was not within his power to abrogate Caesar's *imperium* or remove him from Cisalpine Gaul and Illyricum, but it probably illustrates his expectation of the influence that a sitting consul could exercise on the Senate. He may have believed that an energetic and determined consul could push a majority of senators to take a stance opposing Caesar, enabling them to strip Caesar of

---

92. Gallic provinces: Cic. *Fam.* 1.7.10, *Balb.* 61; Campania: Cic. *QF* 2.7.2; additional funds and support: Cic. *Fam.* 1.7.10, *Prov. cons.* 28, *Balb.* 61, Suet. *Iul.* 24.2, Plut. *Caes.* 21.6.

93. Plut. *Caes.* 21.9.

94. Aedile: Cic. *Att.* 1.16.12; praetor: Suet. *Iul.* 23.1–2, *Nero* 22.2. See Fehrle (1983) 108 and Carlsen (2006) 55–7.

95. Suet. *Iul.* 24.1, Plut. *Cat. Min.* 41.3.

Transalpine Gaul and the legions assigned to it, which would have been a mortal blow to Caesar's further ambitions in his command.

Caesar responded to the threat of Domitius's candidacy by urging his friend Crassus to stand for the consulship as well. This decision was made at Luca or shortly afterward, and it would position Crassus to veto any of Domitius's actions as consul. Crassus would have found a second consulship desirable in itself, but he also must have hoped to increase his official authority vis-à-vis his triumviral colleagues, both of whom already possessed *imperium* and a prestigious command or commission. It is unclear, however, whether Caesar had encouraged Pompey to seek the consulship as well. Pompey did not need the consulship, since he already had *imperium* as part of his far-reaching grain commission, and his agreement in Luca would relieve him of Clodius's harassment. Indeed, Caesar may not have wanted Pompey to hold another consulship, since it would elevate his status further and make it harder for Caesar to achieve preeminence. It may be, therefore, that Caesar did not want Pompey to stand for the consulship of 55 BC, but Pompey unilaterally decided upon this course of action. Caesar had not promised his support for Pompey's campaign at Luca, but he could hardly withhold it if he wanted Pompey's support for an extension of his Gallic command. As it happened, the decision that both Pompey and Crassus would stand for the consulship seems to have been made very late; when they attempted to make their *professiones* of candidacy for election, the consul Cn. Lentulus Marcellinus—a political opponent of the triumvirs—prevented them on the grounds that the appointed deadline for such declarations had already passed.[96] This delay in making their *professiones* seems strange if they had made the decision at Luca back in April to stand for election, so Pompey may have decided on his own to seek the consulship both to gain an advantage over Caesar and to prevent his rival Crassus from having too much of an advantage over him.[97] If true, this highlights the underlying tensions that remained between Pompey and Caesar, but in the end the inner workings of Pompey's mind cannot be recovered here.

---

96. Dio 39.27.3. Plutarch (*Pomp.* 51.5–6, *Crass.* 15.1–2) and Dio (39.30.1–2) claimed that there was a period after Luca during which the intention of Pompey and Crassus to stand for the consulship was not known. It is not clear whether Pompey's possession of *imperium* contributed to his inability to make his *professio* in Rome (as had been Caesar's problem in 60 BC). Since his curatorship of the grain supply was different from a military command, it may be that he was entitled (like a consul) to lay down his *imperium* when entering the city, and then take it up again when leaving, or he may have simply forfeited his *imperium* because he intended to win the consulship, and therefore would have received a new grant of *imperium*.

97. Lazenby (1959) 67–76. He suggests that the revolt of the Veneti may have been a sufficient setback for Caesar that Pompey contemplated seeking the consulship in order to take over Caesar's command himself if Caesar faltered.

Barred from standing in the regular elections, the triumvirs decided to scuttle the whole election process in that year (56 BC), thereby requiring special elections to be held in 55 BC, in which Pompey and Crassus would be eligible to stand. To achieve this, they looked to their new supporter Appius Claudius, whose brother Clodius had great influence over the tribune Gaius Cato. So Gaius Cato now threw his support behind the triumvirs, and used his office's powers of intervention to block all efforts to hold regular elections. The *optimates* did all they could to thwart the plans of the triumvirs, but Gaius Cato sustained his tribunician obstruction, and was supported by Clodius's use of gang violence.[98] The plan succeeded, and when Marcellinus left office at the end of the year having failed to bring about the election of successors, an extraordinary magistrate called an *interrex* was appointed to hold a special consular election.[99] Since these special elections were being held in winter, Caesar was able to send many of his soldiers back to Rome to cast votes for their commander's allies.[100] Given the resources of the triumvirs and their willingness to use violence to intimidate rivals, most other candidates were frightened out of the race, but Cato refused to allow his brother-in-law Domitius to drop out, and the two of them campaigned tenaciously. Plutarch—an admirer of Cato—portrays Domitius as rather cowardly in this contest, and sustained only by the remarkable bravery and determination of Cato, but this is probably an exaggeration, since Domitius would prove very determined in later years.[101] When elections were finally held in January of 55 BC, the meeting quickly devolved into violence. Both sides tried to seize the Campus Martius in order to control the casting of ballots, and in the ensuing violence Cato was wounded in the arm and was forced to flee together with Domitius and their supporters.[102] With all other candidates thus driven away, and with the triumvirs having distributed bribes throughout the city, Crassus and Pompey were elected consuls.[103]

Cato and the men around him were outraged by this blatant use of violence and intimidation in the consular elections, and most seem to have retreated and retrenched. There was little for the *optimates* to hope for with Pompey and Crassus as consuls, but some of them may have contemplated whether the

---

98. Livy *Per.* 105, Dio 39.27.3–29.3.

99. Dio 39.27.3, 39.31.1. See Staveley (1954) 203–4.

100. Plut. *Crass.* 14.6.

101. Plut. *Cat. Min.* 41.2–5, *Crass.* 15.2–4.

102. Plut. *Pomp.* 52.1–2, *Crass.* 15.2–5, *Cat. Min.* 41.5, Dio 39.31.1–2.

103. Plut. *Pomp.* 52.1–2, *Cat. Min.* 42.1.

triumvirate's reliance on violence to win the election indicated a weakening of their support among the voters—Domitius had not been beaten in the election, but rather had been prevented from competing.[104] Still, the triumvirs had seized both consulships, so any hope of recalling Caesar faded for the year. Cato would have been personally dismayed, because his campaign for the praetorship would now be conducted under the auspices of Pompey and Crassus, who took office immediately, but nevertheless he refused to abandon his campaign. Having gone so far to keep Domitius out of the consulship, the new consuls would surely stop at nothing to deny Cato the praetorship. Even more galling to Cato, the triumvirs were backing Vatinius—Caesar's hated tribune—for the praetorship, and they employed large-scale bribery to secure his election, and even sought to win votes by throwing gladiatorial games during his campaign, which was in blatant violation of the *lex Tullia de ambitu*.[105] In spite of these illegal efforts, Cato's popularity and influence were impressive, as was the support he must have received from the senators and common voters alike. Even Cicero, who had decided to lend his support to the triumvirs for the moment, campaigned for Cato and not for Vatinius (whom he loathed), showing that his current support of the triumvirs did not involve a complete rejection of his previous beliefs.[106] Despite the strength of the triumvirs, popular respect for Cato was very high, and the first century to vote in the election (the *centuria praerogativa*) cast its ballot for him.[107] It was widely believed that the vote of the *centuria praerogativa* accurately predicted the outcome of entire elections, and therefore its vote was particularly influential. Pompey was the presiding magistrate, and he did not want to risk allowing the voting to continue, so he interrupted the election by claiming to have heard thunder, despite the clear sky. Voting was suspended on account of this declaration of an ill omen, allowing Pompey and Crassus time to distribute even more bribes and to remove those voters known to support Cato. When the assembly was reconvened and the voting restarted, Vatinius was elected praetor and Cato was not.

While the triumvirs must have taken pleasure in his electoral defeat, Cato maintained his opposition to them without flagging. During the interval before the praetors-elect took office, Cato and his allies intended to prosecute Vatinius for bribery (*ambitus*) in hopes of preventing him from ever taking office, but

---

104. Gruen ([1974] 147) points out that it was the increasing threats to the triumvirate that drove Pompey and Crassus to such extensive use of violence in these elections.

105. *Lex Tullia de ambitu* (63 BC): Cic. *Sest.* 133, *Vat.* 37.

106. Cic. *Fam.* 1.9.19.

107. Plut. *Cat. Min.* 42.3–5, *Pomp.* 52.2. See Fehrle (1983) 166–74.

Pompey's ally Afranius anticipated them by moving a decree in the Senate that
no inquiry or accusations should be made against the praetors-elect.[108] This
was clearly improper, and Cato protested loudly and demanded that the inauguration of the praetors-elect be delayed for sixty days to allow time for prosecution.[109] Pompey and Crassus as consuls squashed Cato's proposal, asserting
that the delay in holding the elections (which they had caused) made it essential
that the praetors-elect take office immediately. In a letter to his brother, Cicero
emphasized that Pompey and Crassus did this specifically to repudiate Cato,
and to make a display of their power.[110] All in all, the elections for 55 BC had
been a rout for Cato's circle, but mainly because the blatant use of violence had
prevented a fair competition. Indeed, the willingness of the triumvirs to go so
far and rely so heavily on violence and bribery may indicate their awareness that
the voters were inclined to support the *optimates*, as the strong support for Cato
suggests. At the same time, Cicero observed in February that the triumvirs were
able to control everything because certain persons had alienated Pompey and the
equestrians from the Senate—a clear statement that Cato's policies had brought
the *optimates* to their current state.[111]

Not one to quit, Cato is said to have addressed his supporters following his
electoral loss, urging them to persist in resisting Crassus and Pompey. He continued working to turn public opinion against the triumvirs, making himself into
a martyr for the Republic by accepting and even seeking abuse from his political
enemies. When the tribune Trebonius promulgated a bill giving Crassus the province of Syria and Pompey the two Spanish provinces, each for a five-year term, the
optimates put up strong resistance. At least two of the new tribunes—C. Ateius
Capito and P. Aquillius Gallus—were politically opposed to the triumvirs and
fought to veto the bill, but violent opposition prevented them from maintaining
their obstruction.[112] Undeterred, Cato and Favonius dared to speak publicly
against the bill in spite of the obvious danger. While they were certainly motivated
to oppose any initiative that favored the triumvirs, Ateius and Cato argued
strongly that Crassus's eastern campaign was immoral because there was no just
cause for war with Parthia.[113] Their accusation was probably correct, although

---

108. Cic. *QF.* 2.8.3, and Plut. *Cat. Min.* 42.2 (who misreports the legislation).

109. Plut. *Cat. Min.* 42.3.

110. Cic. *QF* 2.8.3.

111. Cic. *Fam.* 1.8.4.

112. Plut. *Cat. Min.* 43.1–4, Dio 39.33.3.

113. Plut. *Crass.* 16.3 (cf. Cic. *Fin.* 3.75).

how important it was to most Romans is questionable—it does not seem to have increased opposition to the bill, although it was useful propaganda for attacking the triumvirs. At the public assembly, Favonius wasted the hour he was given to speak by protesting about the shortness of his time, but Cato—having been given two hours to speak—consumed his full time denouncing the general affairs of the state. Dio remarked that this was not without purpose, since his strategy was to give the appearance of having more to say when his time ended, so Trebonius appeared to be acting unjustly by cutting him off from speaking further.[114] When Cato refused to stop speaking at the end of his allotted time, Trebonius ordered him to be removed from the speaker's platform, and when Cato still would not stop calling for the citizens' attention, Trebonius ordered his attendants to arrest Cato and take him to jail.[115] As Cato had hoped, the voters were unwilling to see such a respected senator treated in this way, and a large crowd left the Forum and accompanied Cato to the prison. Once again, Cato had successfully goaded the triumvirs and their supporters into resorting to naked violence, which jarred the Roman electorate and gave substance to the charge that the triumvirate was aiming at tyranny.[116] Thus outflanked, Trebonius ordered that Cato be released, but the violence and intimidation continued, and Plutarch even records that the senator L. Annalius was struck in the face by Crassus and was driven from the Forum for speaking against the bill.[117]

Cato's tactic of displaying himself as a victim and the triumvirs as tyrants was effective, so the triumvirs responded by planning to keep Cato and his friends away from the Forum during the next meeting of the assembly. Anticipating this, the tribune P. Aquillius Gallus tried to ensure his access to the Forum by spending the night before the assembly meeting in the Senate House, from which he could emerge directly into the Forum in the morning to interpose his veto on discussion of the *lex Trebonia*. Unfortunately for him, Trebonius and his allies occupied the Forum that night, took control of its entrances, and locked the doors of the Senate House, thereby trapping Gallus and his supporters inside the building.[118] In addition, mobs forcibly prevented Cato, Favonius, and their allies from entering the Forum when they arrived in the morning. They struggled to get into the assembly, and even climbed onto one another's shoulders to shout

114. Dio 39.34.1–4.

115. Cic. *Att.* 4.9.1, Livy *Per.* 105, Vell. 2.46.2, Plut. *Pomp.* 52, *Crass.* 15.4–5, *Cat. Min.* 43.1–2.

116. See Gruen (1974) 443.

117. Plut. *Comp. Nic. and Crass.* 2.2.

118. Dio 39.35.3.

out to the voters, going so far as to announce obstructing omens such as thunder and lightning in an effort to stop the meeting.[119] It is perhaps surprising that a conservative moralist like Cato would falsify religious omens for political ends, but Pompey had done this, too, and Cato no doubt believed that his actions were beneficial to the state. Trebonius sent attendants to drive away Cato and his allies, wounding and even killing some who resisted. The bill passed, but some of Cato's circle continued to resist, bringing their bloodied comrades before the people in an effort to stir up hostility against the triumvirs, and tribunes in Cato's circle did their best to hinder the recruitment of soldiers for the provincial commands and to agitate for annulment of the legislation.[120] This was a powerful display of the tyrannical actions of the triumvirs, but the outcry against the violations of tradition were insufficient to match the force used by the triumvirs. Still, the accusations of tyranny and despotism were loudly repeated and began to spread.

Pompey and Crassus immediately brought forward a bill extending Caesar's command in Gaul for a further five years. Cato once again led the opposition, but instead of his usual combative obstructionism, he earnestly warned Pompey against his continued support for Caesar.[121] As Plutarch records these admonitions:

> ... Cato no longer spoke to the people, but turning towards Pompey himself, he called him to witness and foretold how even now he did not realize that he was hanging Caesar around his own neck, and that, by the time he began to feel the weight and be overwhelmed by it, he would no longer be able to remove the burden nor to endure bearing it, and so it would fall upon the city as well as on him, at which time he would remember the counselling of Cato, and how it was profitable to Pompey's own affairs no less than to the public good and to justice. Pompey heard these things many times, but having faith in his own good luck and power, he was negligent and dismissed them in his ignorance that Caesar would change.[122]

---

119. Plut. *Cat. Min.* 43.3–4, Dio 39.35.4–5. See discussions in Fehrle (1983) 172, de Libero (1992) 62, and van der Blom (2012) 51–2.

120. Dio 39.36.1–2, 39.39.3–4.

121. Pelling ([2002] 91–2) points out that Plutarch gives greater attention to the *lex Trebonia* and the *lex Licinia Pompeia* in his biography of Cato than he does in other biographies, no doubt wishing to spend more time praising Cato as a hero of the Republic.

122. Plut. *Cat. Min.* 43.5–6.

This passage is curious because—if it is accurate—it seems to reveal a shifting strategy against the triumvirs. Rather than attacking them altogether, as he had been doing unsuccessfully for several years, Cato was attempting to drive a wedge between them, playing on Pompey's ambitions and fears in an effort to make him afraid of Caesar. This was the same strategy that Cicero had been trying to pursue for several years, and he also warned Pompey that he was digging his own grave by extending Caesar's command in Gaul.[123] It is possible, therefore, that Cato began to see the advantages of Cicero's approach. This should not be taken as an indication that he was considering an alliance with Pompey, since he remained opposed to Pompey in most of the important political events of their day.[124] Rather, the inability of the *optimates* to suppress the triumvirate as a whole may have convinced him that a new strategy was needed, or at least a wider range of tactics. At the moment, however, Cato failed to persuade Pompey, and the *lex Licinia Pompeia* easily passed, giving Caesar his wished-for extension of command.[125]

The triumvirs had acquired their respective goals by the end of April (55 BC): Caesar's command was renewed, Crassus had received the province in Syria and expected to reap glory and wealth by attacking Parthia, and Pompey had acquired the two Spanish provinces but would remain at Rome and govern them through legates.[126] With these goals achieved, the triumvirs probably felt a great deal of satisfaction, since they would all possess *imperium*, a command, and legal immunity from prosecution for five years. Having achieved these victories, Pompey and Crassus seem to have done little that was controversial for the remainder of their consulships, but their successes had come at a significant cost. Their blatant use of bribery and violence caused a backlash of public opinion against them, and gave credence to Cato's accusation that the triumvirs were tyrants trampling Rome's ancient traditions. Cato was an expert at using (and manipulating) tradition for political ends, and his persistent warnings that the triumvirs were laying the groundwork for a tyranny that would destroy Roman *libertas* began to bear fruit. In the summer elections, the Romans gave their votes to candidates known to oppose the triumvirate, electing Domitius Ahenobarbus to the consulship and Cato to the praetorship of 54 BC. Cato drew the presidency

---

123. Cic. *Phil.* 2.23–4. See discussion in Seager (2002) 124.

124. See Gruen (1974) 153–4.

125. Vell. 2.46.2, Plut. *Crass.* 15.5, *Cat. Min.* 43.5–6, *Pomp.* 52.3, *Caes.* 21.5, Suet. *Iul.* 24.1, App. *BC* 2.18, Dio 39.33.3–4 (Dio wrongly says the extension was for a three-year period).

126. The *lex Trebonia* was passed by April 27, but Pompey and Crassus had not yet drawn lots for the two provinces (Cic. *Att.* 4.9.1); Crassus was planning an (unsanctioned) war against the Parthians (Plut. *Crass.* 16.3).

of the extortion court as his praetorian assignment, which must have pleased him very much, since he would preside over trials of men accused of corruption in the provinces. It is possible that the triumvirs—secure in their military commands and with legal immunity from prosecution—did not attempt to block their political opponents, or it may have been that the popular support for these respected *nobiles* had grown too strong to suppress at the time, but they did make sure that their new ally Appius Claudius was also elected to the consulship.

Their success in the summer elections certainly cheered Cato's circle, and they continued to oppose the triumvirate by bringing charges against several of its supporters during the rest of the year.[127] They even used citizen complaints about military recruitment for the triumvirs' Syrian and Spanish commands to argue (unsuccessfully) for the annulment of these provincial assignments.[128] More spectacular was the opposition to Crassus's departure for Syria. Several in Cato's circle argued that the campaign was immoral because the Parthians had given no justification for war, and the tribune C. Ateius Capito went so far as to announce false omens in his attempt to manufacture a religious reason to keep Crassus from leaving the city.[129] On the day that Crassus and his army were departing for Syria, Ateius gathered a mob of supporters and physically blocked Crassus's path, calling down dire curses that seemed to doom the expedition. Only the intervention of Pompey and the other tribunes enabled Crassus to take up his command. This was a serious abuse of customary religious practices, and Ateius was later blamed when Crassus's army was wiped out at Carrhae in 53 BC. How far Cato participated in these efforts to block Crassus's departure is unclear, but the calling down of curses on a Roman army was probably too extreme for him. Crassus was destroyed along with his army at Carrhae, and in 50 BC Appius Claudius (as censor) ejected Capito from the Senate for declaring false omens.[130]

Valerius Maximus tells one final story about Cato's activities in 55 BC that deserves attention. The festival of the Floralia began on April 28 each year to honor to goddess Flora, and by the late Republic these games were infamous for being licentious and racy—prostitutes were common performers.[131] The plebeian aedile supervising the festival was C. Messius, the same man who as tribune in 57

---

127. For example, they prosecuted L. Balbus: Cic. *Balb. passim* (acquitted), Caninius Gallus: Cic. *Fam.* 7.1.4, Val. Max. 4.2.6 (perhaps condemned); and L. Libo: Val. Max 6.2.8. See Gruen (1974) 312–3 for discussion.

128. Dio 39.39.1–3.

129. Cic. *Div.* 1.29–30, Vell. 2.46.3, Plut. *Crass.* 16. 3–6, Dio 39.39.5–7.

130. Cic. *Div.* 1.29.

131. Val. Max. 2.10.8, Sen. *Ep.* 97.8. See Culham (2004) 144.

BC had proposed extraordinary powers for Pompey's special grain commission and had pushed for Cicero's recall from exile. Despite the normally obscene nature of the performances, Cato decided to attend in the company of his friend and emulator Favonius. Apparently, at a point in the performance when the audience normally called out for the actress to be stripped naked, they declined to do so out of respect for Cato's presence. When Favonius mentioned this to him, Cato rose and left the theater, lest the people should be denied their entertainment on his account. According to Valerius, the audience recalled Cato to the theater and ordered that the actress remain clothed, showing deference to his more austere morals. This story—whether true or not—is similar to others that portray the Roman people responding positively to Cato's ascetic lifestyle and his self-representation of the *mos maiorum*, but one does wonder what he was doing at games famous for indecency. Perhaps he wished to make a demonstration of his moral *auctoritas* in this powerful way, or perhaps he intended to embarrass Messius, who was a supporter of the triumvirate and would be prosecuted by the *optimates* in the next year. While Cato had not been able to prevail against the combined resources of the triumvirs, incidents like this demonstrate the powerful influence he had over the Roman people. At the same time, he must have realized that many of those people who displayed such respect for his embodiment of tradition in the theater had taken money from the triumvirs to vote for Vatinius (and not Cato) in the praetorian elections the previous year. Cato's *exemplum* was effective at moving people to support him, but this support could be more emotional than pragmatic, and it often failed to translate into real political support. Such stories of popular respect for Cato's moral authority, therefore, clash with the reality that the voters often did not back his policies, revealing considerable complexity in how the people received and internalized appeals to tradition.

6

Shifting Alliances

Prosecutions of 54 BC and Cato's Praetorship

Despite the successes of the triumvirs in 55 BC—or perhaps because of those successes—the *optimates* did well in the elections for 54 BC. L. Domitius Ahenobarbus finally won his consulship, and Cato was elected praetor and drew as his judicial assignment the supervision of the extortion court (*quaestio de repetundis*). Both were determined to use their offices to attack the triumvirs and their supporters, and a flurry of prosecutions was initiated in the first half of the year. Other scholars have given full and detailed discussions of these trials, so a brief overview is sufficient to illustrate the tenacious determination of Cato and his circle to attack those connected to the triumvirs.[1] Gaius Cato (abbreviated: C. Cato) was a particular target of the *optimates*, no doubt because he had joined the triumvirs and along with Clodius had obstructed elections in 56 BC, thus enabling the candidacy of Pompey and Crassus. He was first prosecuted and acquitted in May or June for violating the *lex Junia Licinia* (a law of 62 BC that required promulgated laws to be published and recorded in the treasury at least three days before any vote on them was taken), and then he was prosecuted under the *lex Aelia* and the *lex Fufia* (second-century BC laws that prohibited the passage of laws during the days in which elections were being held), but he had a strong defense and was again acquitted.[2] In a related case, M. Nonius Sufenas—who as

---

1. Gruen (1974) 314–37 and Alexander (1990) 137–49.

2. Cic. *Att.* 4.15.4 and 16.5, Sen. *Contr.* 7.4.7, Ascon. 18. The exact content of the *lex Aelia* and the *lex Fufia* is not known, but they seem to have forbidden legislation being passed too close to elections. See Bleicken (1955) 57–8, Sumner (1963) 338–58, Astin (1964) 421–55, and Marshall (1985) 97–8. The prosecutor in the first case is unknown, but in the second case it was a fairly young Asinius Pollio, who was outmatched by C. Cato's defenders, C. Licinius Calvus and M. Aemilius Scaurus (friends of the triumvirs), and was physically threatened by ruffians loyal of C. Cato.

tribune in the previous year had aided C. Cato's delay of the elections—was also charged with bribery and disrupting elections, and was also acquitted.[3] Cato's circle also prosecuted C. Messius, who as tribune in 57 BC had proposed extraordinary powers for Pompey's grain commission.[4] The consul Appius tried to protect Messius by arranging a commission for him in Caesar's army, but the praetor P. Servilius Isauricus (husband to one of Cato's nieces) pressured Messius to return, so the triumvirs urged Cicero to defend Messius. The result of the trial is not known, but he may well have been acquitted.[5]

Cicero was also called upon to defend M. Aemilius Scaurus against a charge of extortion (*de repetundis*) stemming from his command in Sardinia.[6] This was dangerous, because Cato was presiding over the extortion court, and not only was he a scourge of criminal offenses, but he also enjoyed close personal ties with the prosecutor, P. Valerius Triarius.[7] According to Asconius, however, Scaurus was pleasantly surprised to find that Cato maintained his sense of justice (his *aequitas*), and did not allow personal feelings to influence his execution of his duties.[8] Of course, Scaurus had many supporters in the courtroom, who were remarkable for their importance as well as for their diversity of political views: he had six advocates (a very high number) including Cicero, Hortensius, Clodius, M. Marcellus, M. Calidius, and M. Messala Niger, while nine *consulares* testified on his behalf, included Pompey, Metellus Nepos, and Servilius Isauricus.[9] This case reveals the complexity of Scaurus's political network, which connected with a surprising range of senators, making even Cicero and Clodius temporary allies in his defense. All of this senatorial support may have urged Cato to maintain a strict neutrality in the case, but Kit Morrell has offered the intriguing suggestion that he was eager to secure a condemnation, and so he aided the prosecutor by making the trial as quick and efficient as possible, in the hope that Scaurus would be found guilty early enough to hinder or prevent him from standing in the

---

3. Cic. *Att.* 4.15.4. For the identity of this man, see Gruen (1974) 315 n. 24.

4. Cic. *Att.* 4.15.9, *QF* 3.2.3.

5. So suggests Gruen ([1974] 316), noting that Messius was still in Italy in 49 BC (Cic. *Att.* 8.11d.2).

6. Cic. *Scaur. passim*, *Att.* 4.17.4. For discussion, see Courtney (1961) 151–6, Bucher (1995) 396–421, Morrell (2014) 678–80.

7. Ascon. 18–19, Val. Max. 3.6.7.

8. Ascon. 20. See Linderski (1985) 90.

9. Ascon. 20, 28.

consular elections of that year.[10] For example, she argues that Cato overlooked certain irregularities in the prosecution, such as Triarius's failure to visit Sardinia to gather evidence, and his introduction of only a single witness. If true, this would mean Cato was bending laws to condemn his enemies, but he tried to do it as quietly as possible.[11] While he certainly wanted Scaurus condemned—both as a way to strike at the triumvirs, and because of his personal connections to the prosecutor—he no doubt felt it essential for his reputation as champion of the *mos maiorum* to behave in strictest observance of the law, as he had done when quaestor in the treasury. Whether Cato was neutral or pushed for conviction, Scaurus was acquitted by a margin of 70 to 8.[12]

In addition to defending Scaurus, Cicero was galled when the triumvirs pressured him to defend Vatinius against a charge of bribery (*ambitus*) arising from his campaign for the praetorship two years earlier.[13] Cicero disliked Vatinius and had previously attacked his tribunician legislation, but defending him became part of the price Cicero paid for the support he had received from the triumvirs, and so he acted against his own political convictions and used his skills to help secure Vatinius's acquittal. Erich Gruen also identifies three more (likely) supporters of the triumvirate who were prosecuted by Cato's circle for a range of charges, but none of these is known to have been condemned.[14] This flurry of prosecutions against supporters of the triumvirs demonstrates that Cato and his allies had lost none of their determination and energy, but it also shows that the triumvirs were still capable of defending their allies, in large part because the complex network of connections among senators meant that the litigants could not be reduced to stark choices between two political parties or ideologies. Cato must have been outraged by Cicero's role in defending these men; the two of them had rarely seen eye to eye on how to best serve the state, but Cicero's successes in the courts must have seemed to Cato as a betrayal of the *optimates*.

Another source of frustration to Cato was surely that—as president of the extortion court—only one of these cases (Scaurus) came before his tribunal, and

---

10. Morrell (2014) 669–81 and (2017) 168–72.

11. Morrell (2014) 678–9, "Cato's conduct during Scaurus' trial seems to have made him some enemies . . . possibly Cato was thought to be abusing his office as praetor to pursue his anti-bribery agenda."

12. Ascon. 28.

13. Cic. *QF* 2.16.3, *Fam.* 1.9.19, Val. Max. 4.2.4.

14. Gruen (1974) 317–8. He identifies M. Livius Drusus Claudianus (Cic. *Att.* 4.15.9, 4.17.5, *QF* 2.16.3), Cn. Plancus (Cic. *Planc. passim*) and A. Plotius (Cic. *Planc.* 54). Plotius may not have been prosecuted, but merely accused.

that case had resulted in acquittal. This changed in September when Gabinius returned to Rome from his provincial command in Syria. Cato and the men around him despised Gabinius not only for being a high-profile lieutenant of Pompey, but also for his tribunician and consular legislation, for his poor administration of his province, and most especially for his illegal invasion of Egypt (in 55 BC) to restore Ptolemy Auletes to the throne, in return for which Ptolemy reportedly paid Gabinius 10,000 talents.[15] Tainted by so many accusations, the Senate had taken the remarkable step of refusing to approve a *supplicatio* proposed for his military victories, and Gabinius slunk back into Rome by night to avoid conflicts with political foes, although he was verbally assaulted when he next attended a Senate meeting.[16] Once back in Rome, several senators applied to bring suits against Gabinius for treason (*maiestas*), extortion (*repetundae*), and bribery (*ambitus*).[17] He arrived in Rome on September 27, and by October 10 Cato was hearing from two different sets of prosecutors who wanted to charge Gabinius with extortion.[18] At first the consul Appius tried to delay any case from coming to court by manipulating the comitial days, but in the end he surprised Cicero by joining in the attack against Gabinius.[19] It is possible that Appius wanted to distance himself from the triumvirate now that he had gotten the consulship he had wanted from it, or he may have switched sides because he had been caught in a scandal earlier in the year regarding his *imperium* (see later discussion), and he wanted to build up his support among the most influential *nobiles*. Appius's pivot is consistent with the normal tendency of senators to adjust their alliances as their priorities changed. Cicero provides another example: despite great pressure from the triumvirs to defend Gabinius, he simply could not bring himself to do it, although—to stay on Pompey's good side—he refrained from undertaking the prosecution himself (but he did testify for the prosecution in the *maiestas* trial).[20] Cicero owed the triumvirs a great deal, and he had been willing to bend his principles to repay that debt, but defending Gabinius would have been a

---

15. Gabinius mistreated the *publicani* in his province: Cic. *Prov. Cons.* 10–11, *Pis.* 41, 48; invaded Egypt without proper authority: Cic. *Rab. Post.* 19–21, *Pis.* 48–50, Strabo 17.1.11, Livy *Per.* 105, Plut. *Ant.* 3.2–6, App. *BC* 2.24, Dio 39.55.1–6, 42.2.4.

16. Cic. *QF* 2.7.1, 3.1.24, 3.2.2, *Phil.* 14.24, Dio 39.62.1.

17. For a full discussion of these cases, see Gruen (1974) 322–31, Fantham (1975) 425–43, Crawford (1984) 188–97.

18. Cic. *QF* 3.1.24, 3.2.1, Dio 39.62.2–63.5.

19. Comital days: Dio 39.60.2–4; Cicero's surprise: Cic. *QF* 3.2.3, Appius attacks Gabinius: Cic. *QF* 3.2.3, Dio 39.60.3. See discussion in Tatum (1999) 233–4.

20. Cic. *QF* 3.4.2–3. See Gruen (1974) 324–5.

bridge too far for him. The trial for *maiestas* was held first, and Gabinius was narrowly acquitted, much to Cicero's outrage.[21] It is likely that Pompey exerted his full influence to secure his man's acquittal, although Cicero blamed the poor performance of the prosecutor, who had made a very bad case.[22] Erich Gruen also points out that optimate propaganda about the lawlessness of the triumvirs had paradoxically contributed to Gabinius's acquittal because the jurors were afraid that Pompey would resort to violence and have himself declared a dictator if his man were condemned.[23] So Cato and his allies had successfully planted fears of tyranny in the minds of the citizenry, but the response to this use of propaganda was not quite what they expected, since, in this case at least, it may have contributed to a willingness to yield to the triumvirs.

In a letter to his brother, Cicero adds an interesting detail about the conclusion of this trial. He writes: "Regarding the jury, two *praetorii* sat on it, Domitius Calvinus, who openly cast a vote for acquittal so that all might see, and Cato, who ran away from the gathering after the votes had been counted and was the first to report the result to Pompey."[24] The identity of this Cato is debated. Some scholars have ruled out M. Cato, suggesting that—as praetor in charge of the extortion court—he should not have been a juror on the treason court, and so Cicero may be referring to C. Cato or to an otherwise-unknown Cato.[25] On the other hand, it is not known for certain that the praetor in charge of one court could not be a juror in another court, and so M. Cato may well have been the juror in question.[26] Given the limits of our knowledge (and the lack of other Catos), the latter possibility seems very plausible, and it portrays a typically combative Cato, who was furious at Gabinius's acquittal—caused by a deficient prosecutor—and so rushed to confront Pompey and decry his protection of a clearly guilty man. Cato no

---

21. Cic. *Att.* 4.18.1, 4.19.1, *QF* 3.4.1, Dio 39.55.4–5, 39.62.2–3.

22. Cic. *Att.* 4.18.1, *QF* 3.4.1.

23. Gruen (1974) 323–4. He cites Cic. *Att.* 4.18.3 and *QF* 3.4.1.

24. Cic. *QF* 3.4.1.

25. Linderski (1971) 281–9, Gruen (1974) 326 n. 75. Linderski suggested that the delayed elections for 55 BC enabled C. Cato to move straight from a tribunate to a praetorship, and so he was an ex-praetor in 54 BC, but Gruen points out that in 59 BC Cicero (*QF* 1.2.15) described C. Cato as an *adulescens*, and therefore he may not have been old enough to be praetor in 54 BC (a minimum age of thirty-nine years old was required for the praetorship), so Gruen suggests the passage may need emendation.

26. Brennan ([2000] 417) argues this position, and suggests that M. Cato's rush to bring the news to Pompey may have been to "deflate the mood of Gabinius' foremost adherent by also predicting that man's imminent condemnation in his own extortion court, where the process had already started." See also Seager (2002) 129.

doubt threatened that he would prevent any corruption of the jury in his court when Gabinius was prosecuted for *repetundae*.

The triumvirs did everything they could to defend Gabinius when he appeared before Cato's tribunal for extortion. Although Cicero had refused to defend him in his *maiestas* trial, Pompey was fearful about Gabinius's prospects in Cato's court, and so applied tremendous pressure on Cicero, coercing him to undertake the defense.[27] Furthermore, Caesar sent letters advocating for Gabinius, and Pompey himself spoke on his former lieutenant's behalf.[28] Gabinius also had substantial resources of his own to add to his defense—the wealth he had accumulated in the East surely enabled him to distribute bribes, and it was probably his relationship with King Ptolemy of Egypt that resulted in an embassy arriving from Alexandria to speak on Gabinius's behalf in his trial.[29] Yet the jury convicted Gabinius in spite of these exertions, and when he was unable to pay the assessed fine of 10,000 talents (the same amount he reportedly received from Ptolemy), he was forced to go into exile.[30] Pompey's manipulation of the judicial system to secure the acquittal of Gabinius on the *maiestas* charge had likely led to a surge of resentment against the triumvirs, which contributed to his condemnation in his extortion trial.[31] Accusations of *repetundae* were easier to prove than *maiestas*, and there seems to have been little doubt that Gabinius had received money from Ptolemy, but it cannot escape notice that Gabinius was the only triumviral supporter known to have been condemned during this year of many prosecutions, and that this happened in Cato's court. Cato may have been able to use his own immense *auctoritas* to prevent or deflect some of Pompey's efforts to influence to jurors, and his own example as a model of Roman tradition and severity may have made the jurors ashamed to acquit the obviously guilty man.

That Cato was not entirely fair or neutral as the president of the extortion court is also suggested by the prosecution of C. Rabirius Postumus later that year. When Gabinius had been unable to pay the fine imposed on him and so went into exile, his political foes used a clause in the *lex Julia de Repetundis* to seek payment from others who may have received from Gabinius some part of Ptolemy's 10,000-talent bribe.[32] Rabirius was one of their chief targets. He was an equestrian and a financial agent connected to Gabinius, as well as to Caesar

---

27. Cic. *QF* 3.1.15–16, 3.4.2–3, 3.5.5, *Fam.* 1.8.2–3, *Rab. Post.* 19, 32–3, Val. Max. 4.2.4, Dio 39.63.2–5.

28. Dio 39.63.4–5.

29. Cic. *Rab. Post.* 31–3.

30. Cic. *Rab. Post.* 8, 38, App. *BC* 2.24, Dio 39.55.5–6, 39.63.1–5.

31. Gruen (1974) 328.

32. Cic. *Rab. Post.* 8.

and Pompey, so attacking him was an effective way to strike at the triumvirs. As an equestrian, it seems that Rabirius was not—strictly speaking—liable for prosecution before the extortion court, but Cato as the presiding magistrate overlooked this fact and allowed Rabirius to be charged with a host of crimes, including receiving money from Gabinius and even aiding in Gabinius's restoration of Ptolemy to the throne of Egypt. Cicero was once again pressed into service by the triumvirs, and he spent much of his defense speech protesting against the irregularities of the case and the ways in which the law was being twisted to allow the prosecution of his client. In particular, he argued that Rabirius was not liable to the extortion law as an equestrian, that no evidence existed showing that Rabirius had ever received money from Gabinius, and that Rabirius's name had not even been mentioned in the trial of Gabinius.[33] These arguments seem to have been valid, and reveal how Cato had allowed the prosecution tremendous liberties in making their accusations. Cicero's arguments carried the day, however, and Rabirius was acquitted. Cato's behavior in this case, and in particular the way in which he seems to have allowed the manipulation of the law by the prosecution, has led some to suspect that he was actually behind the prosecution, or at least ideologically aligned with its intent.[34] Kit Morrell has also suggested that Cato was attempting to use his position as praetor to enact anti-bribery reforms that he had thus far failed to advance through the Senate.[35] This is probably correct, and it reveals Cato's determination to advance his own ideals, even if that meant bending the laws to aid the prosecution of Rabirius.

The condemnation of Gabinius was certainly the high point of Cato's praetorship, but on the whole he does not seem to have made a particularly good impression in this magistracy. When Cato took office and began holding court from his tribunal, he shocked his fellow citizens by continuing his eccentric style of dress. Senior magistracies were meant to inspire the deepest respect and deference from citizens, which was visually reinforced by the use of curule regalia descended from Rome's early monarchy—the *toga praetexta*, the *fasces*, and the curule chair. Yet the dignity and stateliness of the curule symbols were marred by Cato's continued refusal to wear a tunic under his toga or sandals on his feet. The appearance of the majestic symbols of office on a man with no footwear or underwear was jarring and even ridiculous.[36]

---

33. Cic. *Rab. Post.* 8–19.

34. See discussion in Siani-Davies (2001) 67–74, Morrell (2017) 171–6.

35. Morrell (2017) 174.

36. Ascon. 29 and Val. Max. 3.6.7.

While this strange style of dress had gained him useful attention earlier in his career, the Romans found it inappropriate in a high magistrate. As Plutarch described Cato's style of dress: "although governing well, he did not seem to deliver so much dignity or greatness to the magistracy, as much as he diminished and dishonored it, repeatedly going up to the tribunal barefoot and without a tunic, and in this way judging the capital cases of distinguished men."[37] In this way Cato gave offense to many because his style of dress seemed inappropriate to the gravity of the courtroom. Indeed, some litigants and jurors probably felt they were being mocked by having the president of the court dress in such an outlandish manner. There is also a tradition that Cato presided over his court while intoxicated, but Plutarch dismisses this outright as a false rumor (perhaps spread later by Caesar), although he does note elsewhere that he drank very generously.[38] The negative reaction that Romans had toward Cato's attire as praetor illustrates the limitations to the appeal of his extreme self-representation of Roman conservatism. While the Romans could admire his archaic interpretation of the *mos maiorum* as a senator or even as a quaestor, they wanted their senior magistrates to manifest their own understanding of the might and majesty of curule office. As Plutarch observed, "the popular opinion of Cato was greater than his power; he was admired more than he was powerful."[39] The Romans respected and even cherished their earliest and most austere traditions, but they wanted their praetors and consuls to represent the current splendor of Rome. So the deference Romans felt toward his *exemplum* was limited by the incongruity of his display with the contemporary glory of Rome.

In addition to presiding over the extortion court, Cato continued to push for reforms to reduce the corruption that seemed pervasive in Roman politics. While praetor, for example, he seems to have convinced the Senate to pass a *senatus consultum* intended to suppress electoral bribery. The decree required the successful candidates in elections to submit their fiscal records to a special court before they could take office, even if no charge of bribery had been made against them.[40] Cicero referred to Cato's effort to move the bill forward as a "silent process," but the bill was not confirmed into law, and so the effort ultimately collapsed

---

37. Plut. *Cat. Min.* 44.1.

38. Plut. *Cat. Min.* 6.1 and 44.1.

39. Plut. *Crass.* 7.7. Plutarch repeats this sentiment in his *Life of Phocion* (3.1–2), where he points out that Cato's display of antique values was admired but not adopted by his peers.

40. Cic. *QF* 2.16.2, *Att.* 4.17.3, Plut. *Cat. Min.* 44.2–4. See discussions in Fehrle (1983) 190 n. 157 and Morrell (2014) 670–2.

and was discarded.[41] One reason for its failure was a serious illness that struck Cato at this time (September/October), which prevented him from advocating for the proposal, although his friends certainly tried to push the decree forward in his absence.[42] Another explanation for the failure is the widespread unpopularity of the bill among the people. While tradition-minded senators generally looked on electoral bribery as a terrible corruption that was ruining the state because it reduced their ability to guide public affairs through influence alone, the citizens on the whole profited from the large annual disbursements of cash by wealthy senators, and they no doubt wanted those payments to continue. Indeed, the vast expenditures by candidates in recent elections was probably an important part of the urban economy, and the people reacted violently against Cato as the sponsor of this resolution: they assaulted him on his tribunal and pelted him with hurled objects, and it was only with tremendous bravery and perseverance that he was able to calm the mob.[43] Once again, Cato had found the limit of his ability to influence the people with moral authority alone. He later rebuked his fellow senators sharply for not coming to his aid during the tumult, and he surely reminded them of how often he had risked his own life and limb to support many of them against angry mobs. So his efforts seem to have backfired because his decree would have created an economic loss for a significant percentage of the Roman citizenry. Finally, the bill would also have been a disruption and a source of concern to the candidates: they were surely nervous about the new scrutiny of accounts, but they were also afraid that they would lose the election if they abstained from bribery and their rivals did not. Thus candidates were afraid to obey the *senatus consultum* because it might cost them the election, but the increased supervision of their campaigns increased their chances of being caught. So the *senatus consultum* increased fear without improving the electoral process. In all of these ways, Cato's attempt at reform seems idealistic, but not well suited to contemporary politics.

Despite this bad beginning, Cato's bill did have some positive effect. During the election for tribunes that summer, the candidates did not trust their rivals to follow the Senate's edict against bribery, but rather than ignore it, they made Cato their private monitor and judge, and gave him the authority to determine

---

41. Cic. *Att.* 4.17.3 (*tacitum iudicium*). See Shackleton Bailey (1965) 2.215, and Morrell (2014) 669–73 and (2017) 171–2 for discussion.

42. Cic. *Att.* 4.17.4.

43. Plut. *Cat. Min.* 44.3.

whether any of them were guilty of bribing voters.[44] The candidates put forward monetary pledges for their good behavior, and after observing the election Cato determined that one of them had violated the terms of their agreement and ordered his pledge forfeit, although the others forgave the penalty on the grounds that the humiliation suffered by the perpetrator was punishment enough. Cicero remarked that this was a great success for Cato, and that this voluntary agreement among candidates was a better display of honesty than any behavior compelled by legislation.[45] While Cicero was full of praise for this action, Plutarch suggests that some blamed Cato for making himself the sole authority in the state, taking for himself the prerogatives of the Senate, the courts, and the magistrates.[46] Curiously, this was the same type of charge that Cato usually threw at the triumvirs (Caesar in particular), suggesting that some were using Cato's rhetoric about tyranny and *libertas* against him. It is perhaps likely that agents of the triumvirs were paying Cato back by portraying him and his friends as the real tyrants who were trying to dominate the people. Such was the flexibility of appeals to tradition that both sides could accuse the other of trying to subvert the freedom of the people.

Although the triumvirs were immune to prosecution as long as they retained their *imperium*, Cato continued to look for opportunities to attack them directly. Therefore, when Caesar reported his destruction of two entire tribes (the Usipetes and the Tencteri, in 55 BC), Cato pounced. This was a controversial victory, because Caesar seems to have mistreated enemy messengers and attacked during a truce, but the scale of his success was enormous: he reported that he had killed 430,000 Germans (including women and children), which is certainly inflated, although Plutarch's estimation of 300,000 may be close.[47] The Roman people were jubilant at such a slaughter of their ancient foes and were calling for sacrifices and celebrations, but Cato alone expressed anger at the victory. He considered Caesar's actions to be a gross violation of "international law" (*ius gentium*), an impiety that could bring the wrath of the gods down upon the Roman people.[48] Cato therefore urged that Caesar be handed over to the survivors of the massacre in atonement for the crime, and he suggested that Rome perform

---

44. Cic. *Att.* 4.15.7–8, *QF* 2.15.4, Plut. *Cat. Min.* 44.5–8. See Jehne (1995) 57 n. 33 and Yakobson (1999) 145.

45. Cic. *Att.* 4.15.7–8.

46. Plut. *Cat. Min.* 44.5.

47. Caes. *BG* 4.15, Plut. *Caes.* 22.1–7, *Cat. Min.* 51.1, App. *Gall.* 1.4 and 18, Dio 39.47.1–53.2. See discussion in Fehrle (1983) 176–8 and Pelling (2011) 252–3.

48. Morrell ([2015] 73–93) discusses Cato's argument that Caesar had committed a violation of Roman *fides*.

propitiatory sacrifices to avert the anger of the gods.[49] The Romans do not seem
to have given much consideration to his suggestion, and they probably thought it
an outrageous and inappropriate response to such a victory.[50] Cato's proposal was
over the top, and Caesar was sufficiently angered that he wrote a letter to be read
in the Senate, in which he attacked Cato and denounced his behavior. Cato used
the opportunity to criticize Caesar once again, and claimed that the entire Gallic
campaign was merely a prelude to Caesar's plans to take over the state. How seriously the audience took this charge is not known, but Cato's fiery oratory was so
effective that Caesar's friends regretted that his letter had given Cato the opening
to launch such an attack.

In prosecuting the allies of the triumvirs, Cato and his circle do not seem
to have differentiated between Pompey and Caesar—both men found their
supporters under attack. The death of Julia in childbirth in August/September
of 54 BC, however, marked an important shift in the relationship between Caesar
and Pompey, and laid the groundwork for a new strategy against them.[51] Caesar
recognized that his daughter's death severed an important unifying bond between him and Pompey, so he hastened to find a way to re-establish that bond
and keep his hold over Pompey. Caesar offered his grandniece Octavia to
Pompey as a bride, and suggested further that he take Pompey's daughter in marriage to create a double bond.[52] To fulfill these offers would have required several divorces: Octavia was married to C. Claudius Marcellus (cos. 50 BC), Caesar
was married to Calpurnia (the daughter of L. Calpurnius Piso [cos. 58]), and
Pompey's daughter was either betrothed or married to Faustus Sulla. That Caesar
would go to such lengths and risk alienating influential aristocrats demonstrates
how important this marriage alliance was to him. Yet Pompey refused the offer,
choosing instead to keep his options open. This refusal, as well as Pompey's later
decision to look elsewhere for a new wife, has often been taken by ancient and
modern authors as a decisive break in the triumvirate that started them down the
road toward civil war, but this view is mistaken. There was no demonstrable rupture between Pompey and Caesar at this time, and their alliance would remain

---

49. Plut. *Cat. Min.* 51.2, *Caes.* 22.3–4, *Comp. Nic. Crass.* 4.3, App. *Gall.* 18, Suet. *Iul.* 24.3. Pelling
([2002] 92) notes that Plutarch places Cato's motion to hand Caesar over to the Gauls much
later in his biography of Cato, connecting it with Cato's other attacks on Caesar's Gallic command right before the outbreak of the civil war. See also Morrell (2015) 73–93.

50. Fantham ([2003] 101) described Cato's proposal as grandstanding: "exciting listening, but
unlikely to lead to any action." Morrell ([2015] 82–3) discusses Cato's anti-imperialist ideas.

51. Cic. *QF* 3.1.17, Liv. *Per.* 106, Vell. 2.47.2, Suet. *Iul.* 26.1, Plut. *Pomp.* 53.3–5, *Caes.* 23.5–7, App.
BC 2.19, Flor. 2.13.13, Dio 39.64.1. See Seager (2002) 130.

52. Suet. *Iul* 27.1.

strong for several years as they continued to support one another in politics.[53] Yet Julia's passing changed the nature of their relationship in an important way: as Caesar's beloved daughter and Pompey's beloved wife, Julia had strengthened their alliance when it was under strain, particularly in the years following 59 BC when Caesar was accruing the benefits of military command while Pompey was enduring the verbal and physical attacks from their enemies and the odium of the masses in Rome. By all accounts, Pompey had been deeply devoted to Julia, and had even been criticized for paying more attention to her than he did to public affairs. There is little evidence that Caesar and Pompey were genuine friends, but for love of his wife, Pompey had been willing to endure much to maintain good relations with her father; this changed when she died. Without Julia linking the two men in a familial bond, the alliance between Caesar and Pompey rested solely on mutual benefits, and therefore it would more easily shift, weaken, and dissolve when one of them no longer felt the distribution of those benefits was fair or attractive.

Although Julia's death would eventually become an advantage to Caesar's enemies, in the short run their botched response to her passing backfired seriously. It was Pompey's intention to bury Julia privately in a tomb at his estate at Alba, but the Roman people—because of their respect for the dead woman, and to gratify Caesar and Pompey—took up her ashes and interred them with great ceremony in a tomb in the Campus Martius.[54] This type of public burial was a rare and great honor given by the state, and one that traditionally required the approval of the Senate, so the consul Domitius and some like-minded tribunes attempted to prevent the interment on the grounds that it had not been officially sanctioned. The people were outraged at this display of disrespect for the cherished Julia, and they refused to acknowledge the prohibitions of the consul. Why risk the anger of the mob to prevent the public burial of a young woman? In the eyes of the *optimates*, this public burial for Julia was loaded with political significance. It was a remarkable honor given—without sanction or even input from the Senate—to the daughter of a man whom Cato claimed was a tyrant and a despot. He had castigated her wedding to Pompey as something that threatened the state. Sulla had received a public funeral in the Campus Martius at state expense by decree of the Senate, so Julia's funeral (although lacking the decree) was

---

53. Gruen ([1974] 449–60) gives references to ancient and modern authors who saw Julia's death as a breaking point between the two men, but argues rightly that their alliance did not rupture at this time, saying (450): "Julia's death involved sore bereavement for both father and husband, but did not make the political reasons for continued collaboration any less cogent."

54. Livy *Per.* 106, Plut. *Pomp* 53.4–5, *Caes.* 23.7, Dio 39.64.1.

an extraordinary honor on the level of that given to the dictator Sulla.[55] Julia represented the union of Caesar and Pompey, and the people's eagerness to honor her with a public burial in the Campus Martius must have felt like a great insult to the *optimates*, who considered themselves to be the traditional and rightful rulers of the state. To Cato and his allies, it must also have seemed that the people were sanctioning the tyranny of the triumvirate by giving Julia an almost-royal funeral. So they tried to prevent the burial from happening, which may have played into the narrative that they (rather than the triumvirs) were acting tyrannically by trying to subvert the will of the people.

In spite of Cato's efforts as praetor to suppress corruption, the candidates for the consular elections were spending so much money on bribing the voters that by mid-July the interest rates in Rome had doubled from four to eight percent.[56] Competition for office had reached such a peak that candidates were willing to risk being caught bribing the voters, or perhaps they just ignored the *senatus consultum* against bribery since it was merely a resolution and not a law. The corruption was so bad that the Senate debated the problem for several days, and decided to delay the elections until September, although by December the elections still had not been held.[57] Bribery seems to have become so common, and so expected by the voters, that men running for high office felt compelled to pay out bribes on a large scale, even if they would have refused to do so under different circumstances. Such men would have preferred to win elections through traditional aristocratic methods—relying on influence, reputation, and connections—but in the current circumstances they were forced to at least match their rivals' use of bribery if they wished to win a consular election. This boded ill for senators with small resources and strong morals, such as Cato.

The ability of Cato's circle to attack the triumvirs effectively was further undercut in the autumn when the sitting consuls Domitius (Cato's brother-in-law) and Appius (Caesar's wavering ally) were caught in a tremendous scandal. For reasons that are not clear, they had failed to receive a *lex curiata* when entering office, which meant they were not entitled to take up *imperium* and a provincial command at the end of their magistracy.[58] Such a failure seems too great to be a mere accident, so it is possible that their efforts to obtain a *lex curiata* had been blocked in some manner, perhaps by an unrecorded tribunician veto or by the

---

55. See Flower (1996) 123–4 and Sumi (2005) 41–6.

56. Cic. *Att.* 4.15.7, *QF* 2.15.4.

57. Cic. *QF* 2.16.3, 3.7.3.

58. Cic. *Att.* 4.17.2, *Fam.* 1.9.25, *QF* 3.2.3. See my full discussion of this episode in Drogula (2015) 107–9.

urban violence that was being unleashed by Clodius and his rival Milo. However it happened, Domitius and Appius were afraid that they would be disqualified from holding military commands (and the opportunities for glory and wealth that came from command), so in the summer of 54 BC they entered into a secret pact with C. Memmius (a supporter of the triumvirate) and C. Domitius Calvinus (an opponent of the triumvirs), who were standing for election to the consulship of 53 BC.[59] A deal was struck: Domitius and Appius as sitting consuls would throw their full weight behind the candidacy of Memmius and Calvinus who, in exchange, would secure three augurs to swear falsely that a *lex curiata* had indeed been passed for Domitius and Appius, and (once elected) would promulgate a *senatus consultum* giving Domitius and Appius choice provinces. The fluid nature of political alliances enabled this surprising combination of *optimates* and supporters of the triumvirate, all—including Cato's brother-in-law—acting solely for their own interests and not for any political platform. Apparently, the terms of this secret pact were even recorded in writing, including a proviso that, if Memmius and Calvinus failed to hold up their side of the bargain, they would pay the consuls four million *sesterces*.[60] Yet Memmius betrayed his fellow conspirators and delivered the written text of this pact to the Senate, exploding the entire scheme. As a result of this disclosure, all four candidates were disgraced and charged with *ambitus*, which would make it nearly impossible to hold elections that year, since both consuls stood implicated in serious crimes.[61]

Memmius's decision to reveal the pact to the Senate needs explanation, because he seems to have done himself considerable damage for no obvious benefit. It seems likely that Pompey advised Memmius to become a whistle-blower and reveal the scheme to the Senate, apparently ignoring Caesar's wishes to the contrary. Cicero described the affair to Atticus in a letter dating to October 1:

> This pact, since it is said to have been made not in words, but with the names and records of many men set down in the written accounts, was on Pompey's advice handed over by Memmius with the names erased. This leaves Appius the same as before; there is no loss at all for him. But as for the other consul, I dare say he is ruined and plainly undone. On the other hand, with the pact ruptured contrary to Calvinus' wishes, Memmius has

59. See Tatum (1999) 231–3 and Carlsen (2006) 59–60 for discussion of these men's alliances.

60. Cic. *Att.* 4.17.2.

61. Cicero (*Att.* 4.17.2–4, *QF* 3.3.2) records the tribune Q. Mucius Scaevola as making continual use of *obnuntiatio* to delay elections from being held in order to influence the outcome.

grown stale, most especially now, since we understand that Memmius' declaration has displeased Caesar greatly.[62]

Caesar was no doubt angry because Appius was a valuable ally who was now damaged, but why did Pompey urge Memmius to betray the plot? Perhaps Pompey felt that he personally gained nothing from the triumvirate's alliance with Appius, and that only Caesar's interests would be harmed if Appius was disgraced and alienated. On the other hand, Cicero makes it clear that Appius was not particularly harmed by the exposure—a man in an alliance with the triumvirs could handle scandal—so perhaps Domitius was Pompey's true target. As Cato's brother-in-law and a champion of the *mos maiorum* and conservative values, the publicity of his participation in this plot to rig the consular elections and to induce augurs to swear falsely to the existence of a nonexistent *lex curiata* was a collapse that left him "ruined and plainly undone," which would benefit the triumvirs. Domitius and Memmius appear to have been the only casualties of this incident: Domitius bowed to circumstances and accepted that his right to a provincial command was lost, and Memmius apparently progressed no further in politics. Calvinus, on the other hand, actually won election to the consulship of 53 BC, and Appius used a questionable legal justification to claim the right to a provincial command even without a *lex curiata*, and so at the end of his consulship he took up his previously allotted command in Cilicia.[63] So Domitius was the biggest loser of this episode, and his disgrace—and the disgrace of those connected to him—was significant. When the Senate discussed the matter, very few were willing to speak freely, and even Cato excused himself from attending the Senate on account of illness.[64] Given Cato's famous ascetic toughness and passion for engaging in political battles, one cannot help but wonder if he felt tainted—or at least exposed—by the disgrace of his closest ally and brother-in-law, and stayed away from the Senate meeting to avoid having to speak about Domitius's criminal act.

At the revelation of this secret plot, the Senate delayed elections until an inquiry could be held, but disputes arose about how this should proceed, and tribunes began interposing vetoes. By October 1, the Senate decreed that elections should be held quickly, but obstructions continued through tribunician vetoes

---

62. Cic. *Att.* 4.17.2–3. See Shackleton Bailey (1965) 2.214–5 and Tatum (1999) 232–3 for discussion.

63. For a discussion of Appius's legal justification, see Drogula (2015) 108.

64. Cic. *Att.* 4.17.4.

and by declarations of bad omens, so no elections could be held.[65] Amid this chaos, rumors began to circulate that Pompey should be called upon to take over the city as dictator, and many (including Cicero) wondered if Pompey was the originator of those rumors.[66] These rumors frightened Cato and the *optimates*, who had long claimed that the triumvirs were aiming at a tyranny. Rome's last dictator had been Sulla, who used the office to slaughter his political enemies, so Cato and the men around him were determined not to allow Pompey (or any political opponent) to be appointed dictator and wield tyrannical power. Still, Pompey felt that the instability in the city worked to his advantage, so he made no move to calm the situation or quell the talk about appointing him dictator.[67]

There was one event at the end of 54 BC in which Cato and Caesar seem to have been unintentionally aligned: the prevention of a triumph to C. Pomptinus, who had been praetor in 63 BC and had held the province of Transalpine Gaul from 62 to 58 BC. While in command he had suppressed a significant uprising of the Allobroges in 62 and 61 BC, and had expected to be replaced by Metellus Celer (cos. 60 BC), but Celer never arrived (he delayed in Rome and then died unexpectedly in 59 BC), so the Senate kept Pomptinus in Transalpine Gaul until the province was handed over to Caesar in 58 BC.[68] During Caesar's consulship in 59 BC the Senate voted a *supplicatio* for Pomptinus's victories, which was a little late (the victories were won in 62 and 61 BC), but the Senate's action was probably an attempt to insult Caesar, since the *supplicatio* implied that Transalpine Gaul had been pacified, and therefore did not need a consular commander. For this reason Vatinius as tribune tried his best to block the *supplicatio* and he refused to recognize it, but in the end the celebration took place.[69] Pomptinus returned to Rome sometime in 58 BC and made a request for a triumph, but for five years his request had been obstructed, and during that time he had remained lingering outside the *pomerium* in hopes that a political shift would enable him to triumph. Caesar's supporters were certainly among those blocking Pomptinus's request, because a Gallic triumph by Pomptinus would undermine the significance of Caesar's accomplishments and steal his glory. In what must have been a surprising coincidence, Cato joined with the Caesarians in obstructing Pomptinus's request, albeit for a different reason. There had been some error or irregularity

65. Cic. *Att.* 4.17.3, Dio 40.45.1.

66. The rumors started as early as June (Cic. *QF* 2.14.5) and grew through the remainder of the year (Cic. *QF* 3.4.1, 3.6.4–6, 3.7.3, Plut. *Pomp.* 54.2–3, App. *BC* 2.31).

67. Plut. *Pomp.* 54.1–2.

68. See Brennan (2000) 577–80.

69. Cic. *Vat.* 30–31.

in the way Pomptinus had acquired his *lex curiata* back in 63 BC, so Cato and others claimed that he did not properly possess *imperium*, meaning his command had been invalid and he had no right to triumph.[70] Cato's opposition is perhaps surprising, because giving Pomptinus a triumph over Transalpine Gaul in 54 BC would have deflated Caesar's accomplishments in the eyes of the Roman people, a thing Cato must certainly have wanted. But blocking Pomptinus's triumph took priority, even over embarrassing Caesar, because of the way the issue had developed. The situation erupted in the autumn of 54 BC when the praetor Ser. Sulpicius Galba held a secret, and most likely illegal, pre-dawn meeting of select senators to push through Pomptinus's request for a triumph. Cato was outraged at the manipulation of senatorial procedures, and swore to block Pomptinus at the gates of Rome. Cicero thought this threat would evaporate into thin air like other of Cato's boasts (*id ego puto ut multa eiusdem ad nihil recasurum*), a comment that reveals what many of Cato's fellow senators must have thought about his frequent bombast.[71] On the day of the triumph, however, Cato as praetor, along with P. Servilius Isauricus and the tribune Q. Mucius Scaevola, did all they could to block the triumph, but they were overwhelmed when the consul Appius Claudius gave Pomptinus his full backing and support.[72] Appius certainly acted out of self-interest: like Pomptinus, he had failed to receive a proper *lex curiata*, and so—if Pomptinus celebrated a triumph in spite of the irregularities regarding his *imperium*—Appius would have a precedent upon which to base his own claims for a future triumph. Nevertheless, Cato and his supporters disrupted the celebration and even caused physical violence and bloodshed in their efforts to obstruct the triumphal procession.

As 54 BC came to a close, there was little to cheer Cato and his circle. Although they could be pleased with the conviction and exile of Gabinius, their other numerous efforts to prosecute supporters of the triumvirate had failed, showing the extensive influence and deep pockets of Caesar and Pompey in particular. Domitius's consulship had also been a disappointment; not only had he failed in his electoral promise to recall and prosecute Caesar, but also his involvement in a scandal had tarnished his reputation and made a mockery of Cato's campaign against corruption. Cato himself had been able to accomplish little with his praetorship beyond the prosecution of Gabinius, and his heavy-handed efforts to reduce bribery and corruption met with only limited success but cost him significantly in public opinion. The Romans respected Cato's *exemplum*, but few

---

70. Cic. *Att.* 4.18.4.

71. Cic. *Att.* 4.18.4.

72. Cic. *Att.* 4.18.4, *QF* 3.4.6.

were willing to go as far as he was to resurrect ancient customs and austerity. This had not been as obvious when he was a junior senator, and his meticulous honesty as a quaestor in the treasury and as proquaestor in Cyprus had served popular interests and had drawn admiration. As praetor, however, his appearance as a judge did not suit the Romans' opinion of what a senior magistrate should be, and his legislative attempts to end corrupt practices fell flat and even backfired on him.[73] The people obviously admired his speeches against electoral and judicial corruption, but they were not willing to give up the extra income they received through bribery. This may have been because (as Plutarch notes) Cato was less eloquent when speaking to the people than to the Senate, but it is also likely that the people simply did not want to live as he did.[74] So Cato faced a serious problem: his extreme devotion to the *mos maiorum* had made him a major figure among the leaders of the *optimates*, but the Romans as a whole do not seem to have been willing to follow his example.

Shifting Alliances (53–52 BC)

Since no elections had been held in the previous year, 53 BC began without consuls or praetors, a situation that, incredibly, continued until July. Dio attributes this failure to elect consuls primarily to the activities of the tribunes, who used declarations of unfavorable omens to block the appointments of *interreges* (short-term officials created to hold elections when no consuls were available), and who otherwise prevented magisterial elections from being held.[75] These delays are presented as continuing efforts to pressure the state into appointing Pompey as dictator, but it is also possible that tribunes who supported the triumvirs were trying to prevent or delay consular elections in which *optimates* may have been favored. In the midst of this turmoil, the tribunes C. Lucilius Hirrus and M. Coelius Vinicianus advised the people to call for Pompey to be made a dictator, most likely in a *contio* (a public meeting in which magistrates gave speeches on various proposals).[76] Cato immediately unleashed a verbal barrage against the tribunes, loading them with such abuse that Plutarch says they nearly lost their office. There can be little doubt that Cato accused Pompey of seeking a tyranny,

---

73. Plut. *Phoc.* 3.1–4 emphasizes that Cato's *exemplum* was outdated for his society.

74. Plut. *Phoc.* 3.1, cf. Quint. *Inst.* 11.1.36. As van der Blom notes ([2012] 42), "he could silence the crowd through this oratory and *auctoritas*, but he was never adored by the people: his effect on the people was more one of awe and fear than of fondness and affection."

75. Dio 40.45.1–5.

76. Cic. *Fam.* 8.4.3, Plut. *Pomp.* 54.2.

an accusation for which he had long been laying the groundwork. Pompey was not present, because his position as proconsul with *imperium* meant he had to remain outside the *pomerium*, but his friends were there and defended Pompey vigorously, insisting that he had no interest in the office.[77] At this, Cato deftly pivoted and began praising Pompey for his civic-minded position, and urged him to devote himself to the law and traditional government. Pompey may have been testing the waters by allowing his supporters to suggest that he be made dictator, but Cato's staunch resistance blocked the possibility, and yet his praise opened a door for Pompey to draw closer to the *optimates*.

This event seems to have created a momentary period of stability in which elections could be held, and the *optimates* C. Domitius Calvinus and M. Valerius Messalla Rufus were elected consuls. They and other curule magistrates entered office immediately, but they were able to accomplish little because of continued violence in the city. Their one recorded legislative act was to propose a senatorial resolution that magistrates should observe a five-year hiatus between leaving office and taking up a provincial command.[78] This was a solid piece of conservative legislation intended to reduce corruption and electoral bribery. The long delay between magistracy and command would eliminate the ability of sitting consuls to influence their own provincial assignments, and it would delay the financial payoff of holding the consulship, making it much harder and more expensive for consular candidates to borrow money for electoral bribery. In recent years many consular candidates had financed their campaigns with borrowed money on the expectation that those loans could be quickly repaid from the profits of provincial command, but this proposed reform would require them to carry those debts (and accruing interest) for five years, and the uncertainty about what provinces they would ultimately obtain—and how profitable those provinces would be—might make lenders more hesitant to lend money.[79] This would have pleased the *optimates* greatly, because in reducing the role of money in elections, traditional aristocratic ways of controlling elections through influence and connections would have become more effective. Kit Morrell has recently argued that Cato was the driving force behind this proposal, because it complemented other anti-corruption measures he had tried (and would try) to advance, and because he

---

77. Plut. *Pomp.* 54.2.

78. Dio 40.46.2.

79. Caesar is perhaps the most famous example of massive borrowing to fund his consular campaign, but the phenomenon was widespread: in the current campaigns for the consulship of 52 BC, Milo was said to have borrowed far more than he could have repaid from his own resources (Plin. *NH* 36.104, *Schol. Bob.* 169). See Fredericksen (1966) 128–41.

had close ties to the consul Valerius Messalla, one of the proposers.[80] Morrell's argument is good, and it shows once again how active Cato was as a political operator within the Senate. Once again, however, his effort failed. The Senate seems to have issued a decree supporting the consuls' measure, but the resolution was not confirmed in law, no doubt because it was unpopular among the voters (who would lose income from bribes) and among younger aristocrats (since it delayed their opportunities for command). Yet this episode reveals how Cato and his allies were constantly working to move the Senate to act upon their policies.

Despite the chaos that marked the year—especially the first half when there were no consuls or praetors—Cato continued his assaults on the triumvirs undaunted. If Cato's praise of Pompey in the previous year had indicated his openness to pulling Pompey over to the *optimates*, his continued attacks on the triumvirate showed that he was not prepared to compromise much to make this happen. That winter (54/53 BC) Caesar had decided to increase the size of his army to face an expected rebellion, and he wrote to Pompey requesting the loan of a legion, a loan that Pompey made without hesitation.[81] Cato railed against this loan in the Senate, denouncing Caesar and Pompey for making private military arrangements that were properly the prerogative of the Senate. Plutarch reports his address to the Senate:

> And even now [Pompey] has furnished Caesar in Gaul with a legion of six thousand soldiers, an army that Caesar did not request from you [the Senate], nor did Pompey give it in consultation with you, but such great forces, weapons, and horses are now the favors and exchanged gifts of private citizens. Pompey is called an *imperator* and a general, but he has given his armies and provinces to other men, and he himself has encamped by the city, stirring up factions in the campaigns for office and creating confusion, and with these activities—which do not deceive us—he is wooing from this anarchy a monarchy for himself.[82]

Cato's point was that the Senate traditionally determined what provinces and military resources commanders received. If Caesar needed more resources for his campaign, he should have sent his request to the Senate. Similarly, it was not Pompey's prerogative to lend a legion that the Senate had given to him for use

---

80. Morrell (2017) 200–3.

81. Caes. *BG* 6.1, Plut. *Caes.* 25.1, *Cat. Min.* 45.3, and *Pomp.* 52.3 (Plutarch gives the wrong time for this loan in his biographies of Caesar and Pompey).

82. Plut. *Cat. Min.* 45.3–4.

in Spain. Caesar and Pompey had not broken any laws through this transaction, but they had circumvented the Senate in a way that was sure to give offense to the status-conscious senators. This was perhaps not a serious offense—Pompey's loan of a legion did no harm, and even served Rome well by aiding Caesar's army—but Cato could reasonably describe this as an act of tyranny since Caesar and Pompey were acting as sole rulers of Rome's foreign policy, and were among themselves determining the allocation and placement of Rome's legions. In this way, Cato continued working to make the public afraid of the triumvirs by once again raising the specter of tyranny.

Word of Crassus's defeat and death reached Rome shortly before or after the July election of Calvinus and Rufus to the consulship. Eager for glory and wealth, and foolishly disregarding the advice of those who meant him well, Crassus had marched his army right into the hands of the Parthian cavalry on June 9, and he had been destroyed along with his army in the day-long Battle of Carrhae.[83] Fortunately, the Parthians were not inclined to follow up on their victory with an invasion of Roman Syria, but it was a tremendous loss for Roman honor and prestige. Plutarch marked Crassus's death as an event that made civil war between Caesar and Pompey inevitable, but there was no notable change in their relationship at the time, nor any indication of alienation from one another.[84] Indeed, for the past eighteen months Crassus had been far off in the East and hardly involved in politics, so his death should have caused little immediate change in the relationship between Caesar and Pompey. Even so, his death was an important change in the political chessboard, because it decreased the stability of the triumvirate and increased the possibility that a rift could form—or could be created—between Caesar and Pompey. The combination of three men had always ensured that no one of them could obtain a preponderance of power over the other two, which (along with their mutual interests and marriage alliances) had ensured stability and prevented conflict. Crassus's death left Caesar and Pompey to wonder where the balance of power lay between them, and because neither seemed inclined to replace Crassus with a new triumvir, it became possible for one of them to gain decisive superiority over the other.

Only one month after entering office, the consuls of 53 BC had to begin organizing elections for the next year, but the process was complicated hopelessly by widespread political violence and bribery. Gang violence continued to be a particular problem. Following his tribunate in 58 BC, P. Clodius Pulcher had

---

83. Livy *Per.* 106, Vell. 2.46.4, Plut. *Pomp.* 53.6, *Caes.* 28.1, *Crass.* 21.1–31.7, App. *BC* 2.18, Dio 40.27.2. See Marshall (1976) 139–61 for a discussion of Crassus's Parthian campaign.

84. Plut. *Caes.* 28.1–2 and *Pomp.* 53.6 (cf. Luc. 1.99–101 and Flor. 2.13.13). Gruen (1974) 453–60.

remained a potent force in Rome by using street gangs to disrupt public business, to break up votes on legislation he opposed, and to harass politicians, including Pompey (the pact at Luca had offered only a temporary reprieve). Since Rome had no police force to maintain order, Pompey and his allies had resorted to sponsoring gangs of their own, and their most successful agent was T. Annius Milo, whose gangs openly battled Clodius's gangs in the streets.[85] This violence continued intermittently for several years, but Milo's opposition to Clodius had been very welcome to the *optimates,* not least because it had enabled the recall of Cicero. When Milo stood in the elections for the consulship of 52 BC, therefore, he had strong backing from the senatorial elite, including from Cato.[86] His rivals in the election were Q. Caecilius Metellus Pius Scipio Nasica and P. Plautius Hypsaeus. Scipio enjoyed the most distinguished lineage of the group, but he was not closely allied with Cato's circle, perhaps because Cato still resented their rivalry over Aemilia many years earlier. Pompey, however, chose to support his old lieutenant Plautius rather than Milo, and so the unusual situation developed in which Pompey and Clodius were united in their opposition of Milo's candidacy, albeit for different reasons.[87] Thus the violence in Rome intensified as Clodius's gangs increased their harassment of Milo and his supporters (including Cicero and Cato), while Pompey did little to intervene. Battles between armed gangs of rival candidates became common, and it once again proved impossible to hold elections before the end of the year.

Amid this chaos Pompey chose a new wife: Cornelia, the daughter of Scipio Nasica (who was still a candidate for the consulship) and the widow of P. Licinius Crassus, who had died serving in his father's army at Carrhae. As noted earlier, following the death of Julia, Caesar had sought to re-establish a formal marriage bond with Pompey by offering him the hand of his grandniece Octavia, but Pompey seems to have politely declined the offer.[88] When Pompey's marriage to Cornelia occurred is not certain: it may have taken place near the end of 53 BC, or at the start of 52 BC.[89] It is tempting to see this event as a break between Pompey and Caesar, but this is probably an overstatement (as was the impact of the deaths of Julia and Crassus). Scipio was a scion of two illustrious families,

---

85. Cic. *Att.* 4.3.3, *Mil.* 38–43, *Sest.* 85–7, Ascon. 30–31, Dio 40.48.1–3. See Tatum (1999) 170–85, 201–5.

86. Cic. *Fam.* 2.6.3, *Mil.* 25, 34, Ascon. 31. Cicero and Hortentius were also backing Milo, and probably M. Marcellus (cos. 51) as well (he helped defend Milo in court the next year).

87. Ascon. 31, *Schol. Bob.* 112.

88. Suet. *Iul.* 27.1.

89. Plut. *Pomp.* 55.1, Dio 40.51.3.

the *Cornelii Scipiones* (by birth) and the *Caecilii Metelli* (by adoption), and he
certainly held traditionally aristocratic views on how the Republic should be
run. Yet Scipio was not a member of Cato's circle, and the two actually had a
long-standing feud dating to their competition for the hand of Aemilia in marriage, so Pompey's new connection with Scipio did not signify a connection with
Cato, or a break from Caesar.[90] Rather, Pompey was attempting to broaden his
network of supporters (which still included Caesar), and an alliance with Scipio
seemed very desirable: not only was he an influential figure in the Senate, but
he was also a strong candidate in the upcoming consular elections. Furthermore,
Cornelia was the widow of Crassus's son (P. Licinius Crassus), so Pompey may
have hoped the union would draw some of Crassus's supporters to him, including
Crassus's surviving son, who was a proquaestor in Caesar's army. So he probably chose Cornelia to broaden his network of political alliances, rather than to
switch his primary alliance. In this light, his marriage is simply another example
of how fluid senatorial alliances could be. It certainly was not to Caesar's advantage, although it did not necessarily do him harm. Since the formation of the
triumvirate, Caesar had been the primary beneficiary of Pompey's extensive influence and resources, and fear of the combined power of Caesar and Crassus
had prevented Pompey from breaking away from them. From 59 to 53 BC, the
hostility between Pompey and Crassus had made Caesar the linchpin of their
alliance—he had been able to rely on the support of both Pompey and Crassus,
although the two of them had not always been able to rely upon each other. Thus
Caesar had been at the center of the triumvirate, even though he was originally
the least powerful member. Crassus's death and Pompey's new marriage significantly changed this political equation, since Caesar was no longer in the middle
of a three-man alliance, but on one side of a two-man alliance. By choosing to
forge a new political connection with Scipio rather than reinforcing his bond
with Caesar, Pompey broadened his network of political allies, thereby balancing
his dependence upon Caesar by acquiring new and powerful friends. This was a
shrewd move, since Pompey hoped to benefit from alliances with both Caesar
and Scipio, although those two would be unlikely to collaborate directly with
each other. So Pompey's new marriage did not draw him closer to Cato, although
it did weaken his dependence upon Caesar.

Since no consuls had been elected before the end of 53 BC, an *interrex* should
have been appointed to oversee elections in January, but the tribune T. Munatius
Plancus vetoed this appointment, leaving no supervising magistrate at all for

---

90. Scipio and Cato were related by marriage, since Scipio had married Cato's cousin Aemilia,
the daughter of his uncle Mamercus, but Cato is known to have been on bad terms with Scipio.
See Gruen (1974) 454.

the start of 52 BC.[91] It seems that Plancus did this at the behest of Pompey, who had decided that chaos would work in his favor. Asconius suggests that Pompey thought Milo would win the elections if they were held immediately under an *interrex*—Cato and Cicero were both backing Milo—so Pompey sought to delay the process to benefit his preferred candidates. So the year 52 BC began without consuls or an *interrex* to hold elections. Then, on January 18, Milo and his men killed Clodius in a brawl on the Appian Way.[92] The public uproar over this killing spread rapidly through the city, unleashing waves of destruction and violence. The Senate House was burned to the ground as a funeral pyre for Clodius, and the flames spread to the adjacent Basilica Porcia and destroyed it, thereby erasing Cato's family monument from the Forum (it would not be rebuilt).[93] Plancus and two other tribunes were in large part responsible for whipping the people into this frenzy, and public opinion turned sharply against Milo.[94] Amid this groundswell it became possible to appoint M. Aemilius Lepidus (cos. 46 and 42 BC) *interrex*, and the other two candidates for the consulship (Scipio and Hypsaeus) urged Lepidus to hold the elections immediately, since they hoped the angry citizens would not vote for Milo.[95] When Lepidus refused to do this for procedural reasons, mobs of Clodian supporters laid siege to his house in an effort to compel him to act, while others seized consular *fasces* and carried them to Scipio and Hypsaeus.[96] When the two men refused to accept the *fasces* in such a manner, popular outcry called for Pompey to assume control of the city. Not long afterward, the Senate met and passed its final decree (the *senatus consultum ultimum*) instructing the *interrex*, the tribunes, and Pompey to take all necessary steps to protect the state, but this seems to have accomplished little since the rivals for the consulship began attacking each other in court.[97] Pompey sensed that the chaos was working to his advantage, so he deliberately delayed taking any action, giving time for the people to increase their demand that he be appointed dictator.

---

91. Ascon. 31.

92. For a full narrative and discussion of this event, see Tatum (1999) 214–40.

93. Ascon. 33.

94. Ascon. 32–4, App. *BC* 2.21, Dio 40.49.1–2.

95. Ascon. 33, 43, Dio 40.49.5. The choice of Lepidus as *interrex* is unusual, since he had not yet held the praetorship or consulship, although Broughton (*MRR* 2.228) assumes that he must have been curule aedile in 53 BC in order to qualify to be *interrex* the next year.

96. Ascon. 33, 43. Lepidus had refused because—as the first *interrex* appointed—there was some question about the legitimacy of his *auspicia*.

97. Cic. *Mil.* 70, Ascon. 34, Dio 40.49.5–50.1.

Cato and those around him probably guessed Pompey's intent and were alarmed at the prospect. Large mobs of citizens were calling for Pompey to be made dictator, while others demanded that Caesar be recalled and named consul together with Pompey.[98] Neither of these possibilities was attractive to the *optimates*, so in what must have been a carefully choreographed plan, they brought forward a different suggestion. In the next Senate meeting, Bibulus surprised many by putting forward a motion that Pompey should be named consul but without a colleague.[99] Plutarch gives different presentations of Cato's role in this proposal. In his biographies of Pompey and of Cato, he writes that Cato surprised everyone by supporting Bibulus's motion. In the biography of Pompey he writes that Cato "would not have proposed the motion, but he was persuaded to recommend the motion as proposed by another, preferring all types of government rather than anarchy, and thinking there was no one better than Pompey to be in charge during such political confusion," while Plutarch says in the biography of Cato "he stood and—with no one expecting it—he commended the proposal and counselled that any government was better than anarchy, and moreover he expected that Pompey would best deal with the present affairs of state and guard the entrusted city."[100] This shows Cato as being reluctant to approve the proposal, or at least as presenting himself as being reluctant (or perhaps Plutarch wanted him to appear reluctant). In his biography of Caesar, however, Plutarch portrays Cato as supporting the proposal in order to prevent Pompey from being appointed dictator, saying, "Cato's circle persuaded the Senate to appoint Pompey sole consul, so that—being appeased with a more customary type of monarchy—he would not require that he become dictator."[101] Appian even states that Cato himself made the proposal that Pompey be made sole consul, and Bibulus is not mentioned.[102] On balance, it seems most likely that Bibulus—who as an ex-consul would have spoken early in the meeting—made the proposal, but Cato clearly supported the motion, and was probably involved in its conception and articulation.[103] Indeed, it is hard to believe that Bibulus would have made the proposal had he not been certain of Cato's active support. The proposal

---

98. Ascon. 35, App. *BC* 2.23, Dio 40.50.3.

99. Ascon. 36, Plut. *Cat. Min.* 47.3, *Pomp.* 54.4–6, Suet. *Iul.* 26.1, Dio 40.50.4.

100. Plut. *Pomp.* 54.4, *Cat. Min.* 47.3. Ramsey ([2016] 298–308) gives a recent analysis of these different accounts of Bibulus's motion.

101. Plut. *Caes.* 28.7. See Pelling (2011) 280–1.

102. App. *BC* 2.23.

103. Ryan (1998) 264–5.

must have been surprising given Bibulus's long-standing enmity toward Caesar and Pompey, but Cato's support for the bill must have been thoroughly shocking to those not forewarned of the plan. The idea of a sole consul was a complete violation of the *mos maiorum*—which provided the dictatorship as a means of responding to urban upheaval—so Cato's rejection of the traditional dictator in favor of an unheard-of sole consul must have been jarring to his audience, since it was an innovation that was contrary to traditional practice. Why would the champion of the *mos maiorum* reject the traditional response to crisis in favor of a radical innovation? Dio suggests that there was a fear among the senators that the people would vote Caesar into office *in absentia* if a regular election were held, but this is probably overstated. John Ramsey has argued that Bibulus's proposal was the result of a deal forged between the *optimates* and Clodius's faction: the latter would end their obstruction of elections in order to restore regular government, and the *optimates* would recommend the election of Pompey as sole consul, thereby leaving Milo vulnerable to prosecution for Clodius's death.[104] This argument is ingenious, but it is difficult to imagine that Cicero and Cato—both of whom supported Milo to the bitter end—would have tolerated this betrayal of Milo merely to bring about the cessation of electoral disruptions.[105] It is true that both men made political compromises when needed, but it is difficult to imagine them sacrificing Milo to help Pompey.

It is perhaps more likely that Cato and his circle realized that sooner or later the people would circumvent the Senate and vote Pompey extraordinary powers to take over the government and suppress the urban violence, and Cato was afraid of what Pompey might do with the unrestricted power of the dictatorship.[106] While a sole consulship was unheard-of, it would be an office of lesser authority and power than the dictatorship, and by authorizing Pompey to hold the consulship without a colleague, the Senate retained significant authority to advise and direct him in the use of his office. In Plutarch's words,

> Cato recognized that the affairs of the state should be handed over to Pompey as a voluntary favor from the Senate rather than from the utmost necessity, and that using the most restrained of illegal measures as a treatment for the restoration of the most important matters, they should

---

104. Ramsey (2016) 308–18.

105. Cicero (*Fam.* 15.4.12) later wrote to Cato about how they tried to save Milo together (cf. Ascon. 53–4).

106. See discussion in Gruen (1974) 153–4, 339–40, Fehrle (1983) 210, Brennan (1989) 79–85, Seager (2002) 134–5.

themselves arrange for a monarchy to be employed rather than watch civil discord bring it to pass.[107]

These words indicate that Cato was very reluctant to entrust Pompey with such authority, but that the situation in Rome had become dire enough that some form of monarchy was inevitable, if even just to calm the situation down, and so he preferred the sole consulship because it conferred the least amount of authority in one man.[108] Although this was not the traditional way that Rome's ancestors had dealt with upheavals in the city, it has already been seen that Cato lived and promoted his own particular interpretation of the *mos maiorum*, some elements of which flowed from his own personal beliefs rather than from actual custom. To Cato, an unconstitutional sole consulship was preferable to the traditional dictatorship because it better maintained the *auctoritas* of the Senate, and his rendering of ancestral custom was sufficiently flexible in this case for him to support the lesser of two evils.

Although the suggestion was a radical departure from tradition, Cato's call for a sole consul rather than a dictator was intelligent and shrewd. In the first place, it gave the initiative for resolving the turmoil to the Senate, which was preferable to whatever the popular assembly might do under the influence of an ambitious tribune. And although as sole consul Pompey would be free from collegial obstruction, his authority was still limited by the law. Whereas a dictator could impose martial law and use the unrestrained power of *imperium* inside the *pomerium*, a consul required the approval of the state to employ the military force of *imperium* in the city, his actions were subject to the tribunician veto, and he could be prosecuted for abuses of the law.[109] Furthermore, by giving Pompey one half of a dual office, Cato and the Senate left open the possibility that he could be pressured into appointing or electing a colleague as soon as he had suppressed the violence within the city (which he in fact did). Most important, Cato and his allies must have known that Pompey would be deeply flattered when they offered him a third consulship, especially since it involved giving him an extraordinary exemption from the required ten-year hiatus between repeated consulships.[110]

---

107. Plut. *Cat. Min.* 47.2.

108. Pelling ([2011] 278) discusses Cato's idea that a one-man rule was needed to cure the ills of the state.

109. See Drogula (2015) 46–130, esp. 117–25 for discussion and references.

110. The Genucian plebiscite of 342 BC was thought to have required retiring magistrates to observe a ten-year period before holding the same office again, but this was frequently ignored. The ten-year hiatus before repetition of office was more firmly imposed in the second century BC and was reiterated by Sulla in 81 BC. See: Cic. *Leg.* 3.3.9, Caes. *BC* 1.32, App. *BC* 1.100, and

Cicero had long believed that Pompey could be made into a valuable asset for the Senate if his ambitions and his desire for recognition could be appeased in a way that was acceptable to the Senate, so by flattering him with the great honor of a sole consulship, the *optimates* may have hoped to win him over, thereby driving a wedge between him and Caesar.[111] Cato must have been annoyed by the need to promote Pompey in this way, but he was surely soothed by the knowledge that doing so would undermine Caesar's position. Although the deaths of Julia and Crassus had not dissolved the alliance between the two surviving triumvirs, Cato and his allies must have been calculating whether these events could be used for their own advantage. Pompey's marriage connection with Scipio had indicated that alliances were evolving, and the *optimates* may well have used the necessity of naming Pompey sole consul as leverage in their efforts to use him for their own goals.

After Pompey was named sole consul in late February by the *interrex* Ser. Sulpicius Rufus, he asked Cato to be his counselor and associate in running Rome.[112] Cato declined the request, saying his sole interest was the well-being of the republic, so while he would happily share his personal opinions with Pompey in private when asked, he declared that in public he would always speak as he thought best for the state. On the surface, this story seems designed to celebrate Cato's famous integrity, but there is no reason to doubt that Pompey—confident in his *auctoritas* and secure his third consulship—made some kind of overture toward Cato, who clearly held considerable influence over the *optimates*.[113] In all likelihood, Pompey wanted to sound him out and see what his support of Pompey's sole consulship meant. He cannot have hoped that he was suddenly in his good graces, and his offer to make Cato a counselor and associate was probably meant to flatter him more than offer him a real place in the government.[114]

Brennan (2000) 65–7 and 651. On the efforts of the *optimates* to flatter Pompey, see Fehrle (1983) 210.

111. See Taylor (1949) 148–52, Gelzer (1968) 151–2, and Morrell (2018) 165–80.

112. Plut. *Cat. Min.* 48.1–2, cf. *Pomp.* 54.5–6. See Seager (2002) 134.

113. Such overtures may have been a normal way to sound out potential allies: Caesar had made an approach to Cicero when forming the triumvirate in 60 BC, and after crossing the Rubicon and invading Italy in 49 BC, Caesar wrote Cicero asking for his advice, influence, status, and help (Cic. *Att.* 9.6a.1).

114. Marin ([2009] 141) suggests that Pompey may have been offering to give Cato an official role as some kind of legate or even co-consul, but both of these seem highly unlikely; consuls did not use *legati* in the city, and it would have been much too risky to offer Cato a consulship at this time. At most, Pompey may have been asking Cato to be on his consular *concilium*, which was not generally considered an official position.

Cato's response seems to recognize this: he emphasizes that any conversation between them about state policy would be strictly private and non-binding, and
that in public he would say whatever he thought best for the state, and would
not feel constrained to agree with Pompey or support his initiatives. Although
Velleius Paterculus believed that Pompey's sole consulship indicated his reconciliation with the *optimates*, there is not much evidence that Cato felt any particular
closeness to Pompey afterward.[115] Whatever Pompey's intent, Cato made it clear
that he had no interest in a personal alliance at that time.

As sole consul, Pompey took quick action to restore order in Rome. He
brought soldiers into the city and seems to have used brutal methods in keeping
the peace. There is evidence that he allowed his soldiers to kill unruly citizens,
and Appian suggests that some fled to Caesar for protection.[116] He delivered
proposals to the Senate regarding new legislation to reduce political violence and
bribery, and he maintained the peace in the city during several high-profile trials,
including the trial of Milo in early April.[117] Cicero did his best to defend Milo
in court, but Pompey was determined to see Milo condemned, and his soldiers
intimidated Milo's supporters and made an effective defense impossible.[118] Cato
was a juror in the trial, and Cicero refers to him often in his speech, portraying
him as a supporter of Milo's cause in the hope that this might influence other
jurors.[119] Cato's allies Domitius and Favonius were both *quaesitores* in the case
(important officials who helped direct trials), and this prominent placement
of Cato, Domitius, and Favonius has led Kit Morrell to argue that Pompey was
collaborating with them in bringing Milo to trial, an arrangement that may
have been agreed upon as a consequence of their support in having Pompey appointed sole consul.[120] If this argument is correct, it highlights that Cato's support of Pompey was not entirely altruistic or disinterested; he expected to benefit
from Pompey's sole consulship. And yet, when the jurors cast their secret ballots,

---

115. Vell. 2.47.3, Gruen (1974) 153–4, Fehrle (1983) 210–11.

116. App. *BC* 2.24 and Dio 40.53.3. The letter to Caesar ascribed to Sallust (Sall. *Ad Caes. sen.*
4.2) probably goes too far in saying that Cato and Domitius arranged for the murder of forty
senators during this time.

117. For a discussion of these measures, see Seager (2002) 135–51.

118. Cic. *Mil.* 1–3, 67–8, Ascon. 40–1. Seager (2002) 133–7 discusses the trial and Pompey's
changed attitude toward Milo.

119. Cic. *Mil.* 16, 26, 44, and 58, and Ascon. 53–4. Alexander ([1990] 151) includes Cato and
Favonius among the witnesses in the trial, but Morrell (2018) 165–80 suggests that this is incorrect, and that Cicero was merely stating things that had been said to Cato and Favonius.

120. Morrell (2017) 205–9.

Velleius says that Cato ostentatiously made it clear that he was voting for acquittal, but this obvious attempt to influence the other jurors was unsuccessful because a majority had already cast their ballots.[121] If true, this would mean that he was not interested in working with Pompey to see Milo condemned. Asconius states that Cato had voted for acquittal because he believed that Clodius's death was good for the state, but Asconius also notes that he may have voted for condemnation, because the exile of Milo may also have been good for the state.[122] This position—that all who acted contrary to the good of the state should be condemned—seems typical of Cato, and it paints a picture of him as being willing to justify the destruction of anyone who threatened his own interpretation of the *mos maiorum*. The evidence is unclear, but the tactic of brazenly showing his ballot for acquittal to the jurors in an effort to sway their vote seems very much like Cato, and he is said to have supported Milo in earlier hearings before the Senate, so it is likely that he voted for acquittal. Although they had once been allies, Pompey had turned against Milo and had made no effort to help him, so he was condemned and went into exile.

Further evidence that Pompey was not yet aligned with Cato is found in his support of the "law of the ten tribunes," which was passed in the face of Cato's vocal and determined opposition. This law began as a proposal by the tribunes that Caesar should be recalled to Rome in order to serve as Pompey's co-consul for the remainder of 52 BC, but Caesar had further Gallic conquests in mind, so he persuaded the ten tribunes instead to promulgate a law permitting him to stand for election to the consulship *in absentia* once his command in Gaul ended.[123] Caesar had good reasons to want this special privilege. In the first place, it was a great public honor that distinguished him and marked him out as uniquely honored by the Roman people. Second, he wanted to prevent Cato from repeating his successful tactic of 60 BC, when Caesar had been forced to choose between his triumph and his eligibility to stand in the consular elections. Caesar had been willing to sacrifice his praetorian triumph in order to reach the consulship of 59 BC, but he surely expected his consular triumph over Gaul and Britain to exceed all previous victory celebrations in glory and magnificence, and so being allowed to make his *professio in absentia* would ensure that Cato did not rob him of another triumph. Third, he knew full well that his enemies intended

---

121. Vell. 2.47.4–5. See Woodman (1983) 76.

122. Ascon. 53–4.

123. Caes. *BC* 1.32, Cic. *Att.* 7.1.4, 7.3.4, 8.3.3, *Fam.* 6.6.5, *Phil.* 2.24, Livy *Per.* 107 and 108, Suet. *Iul.* 26.1, Flor. 2.13.16, App. *BC* 2.25, Dio 40.56.2–3. See Pelling (2011) 287 and Ramsey (2016) 298–324 for discussion and references.

to prosecute him in the courts as soon as he returned to Rome—Cato and his friends had been promising this for many years[124]—so he wanted to avoid any step that would require him to lay down his *imperium* and revert to being a private citizen and therefore liable to prosecution. If he were elected to the consulship *in absentia*, Caesar could imitate his great-uncle Marius, who had celebrated a triumph and had been inaugurated consul on the same day in 104 BC, thus stepping directly from the role of *imperium*-bearing commander to sitting consul. If Caesar managed to do the same, he would retain his legal immunity uninterrupted, moving from proconsulship to consulship, and then to another proconsulship and a new provincial command. All senators surely understood Caesar's intent, and while Pompey was happy to help his ally by supporting the bill, Cato opposed it with all his might.[125] In spite of this opposition, however, the "law of the ten tribunes" passed. Nothing could have been more frustrating to Cato and his circle, who had been waiting years to prosecute Caesar only to see their best opportunity slipping from their grasp. Cato and Ahenobarbus had sworn to prosecute Caesar as soon as possible for his actions as consul and as proconsul, but it now seemed they would have to wait many more years for the opportunity, and Caesar would probably be an even more powerful adversary by the time they had the chance.

Pompey promulgated two laws while sole consul that require brief attention. First, he took the previously mentioned senatorial decree requiring a five-year hiatus between holding a magistracy and a provincial command, and moved it through the assembly to become a law.[126] This was a major reform to Rome's system of provincial administration because it prevented men from stepping directly from their magistracy to their command, thereby delaying for five years the profits one might acquire from a provincial governorship. This would make electoral bribery much more difficult, since loans (taken out for cash to pay bribes) would have to be carried for years. D. R. Shackleton Bailey first suggested that Cato may have been behind this bill, but Kit Morrell has now examined this idea at length and has argued not only that Cato assisted Pompey in drafting the legislation, but that it was part of his larger effort to reform how Rome governed its provinces.[127] In Morrell's view, Cato's philosophic principles led him to be deeply

---

124. Suet. *Iul.* 30.3.

125. Pompey's support: Cic. *Att.* 7.3.4–5, 8.3.3, Flor. 2.13.16; Cato's opposition: Caes. *BC* 1.32, Plut. *Pomp.* 56.3.

126. Dio 40.56.1. See discussion in Marshall (1972) 887–921, Seager (2002) 138–9, Steel (2012) 83–93, and Morrell (2017) 214–34.

127. Shackleton Bailey (1965–70) 3.246, Morrell (2017) 214–34.

concerned about the way Rome governed its empire. This is possible, but it is equally likely that his concern for Rome's provincials came from the fundamental Roman value of *fides*, which was a traditional value that had long required earlier generations of Romans to keep faith with their friends and allies—it had even driven the Romans to establish Rome's first extortion court in 149 BC to protect provincials from rapacious governors.[128] But it is indeed likely that Cato worked with Pompey on this legislation, both to reduce corruption and to snare Caesar. Every senator must have known that Caesar intended to seek a second consulship and a second military campaign, and that he would remain immune to prosecution if he achieved this, so Cato and his allies may have pushed for legislation to force Caesar to become a private citizen again for five years in-between his next consulship and command. Creating a period when Caesar would be vulnerable to prosecution was a primary goal for Cato and the men around him, and they must have been delighted that Pompey was willing to work with them on a bill that would bring this about. Whether Pompey intended his bill to put Caesar in jeopardy, or whether he assumed Caesar would use *popularis* tactics to bypass any law the *optimates* put in his way, is not clear. Of greater importance to him must have been the approval he received from the *optimates* for his support of this bill; even if he did not intend to break with Caesar, gaining the good opinion of Rome's *nobiles* would have been very desirable.

Pompey's second law at this time raises even more questions. It required that all candidates for office had to deliver their *professio* in Rome in person, which was a restatement of the similar law that Cato had promulgated as tribune a decade earlier, and may reveal the growing influence he and the *optimates* were gaining over Pompey.[129] Caesar had already received a vote of the people permitting him to stand for the consulship *in absentia*, and the effect of Pompey's law on that previous law is not clear. Some could argue that the new law superseded—and so essentially annulled—the previous law, whereas others might insist that the "law of the ten tribunes" remained valid because it was a special privilege given to Caesar by the people exempting him from observing a particular legal principle.[130] The special privilege given to Caesar was exactly that—a unique, one-time authorization for Caesar to stand for the consulship *in absentia*—so one could easily

---

128. Hellegouarc'h (1963) 23–35, 275–9.

129. Suet. *Iul.* 28.3, Dio 40.56.1.

130. See Balsdon ([1962] 141), who argued that Pompey's *lex* cannot have overturned the "law of the ten tribunes." *Contra*: Seager ([2002] 139 n. 45), who believes the added codicil and the complaints of Caesar's friends demonstrate that Pompey did indeed intend to revoke the privilege given Caesar by the "law of the ten tribunes."

argue that this privilege remained intact regardless of changes made to the usual process of declaring candidacy for office. Of course, most Romans, and even most senators, were not legal experts, so there may have been no clear understanding of the impact of Pompey's law on Caesar's special privilege to stand for election *in absentia*. The diverse interpretations were immediately apparent: although some interpreted this law as an attack against Caesar, Pompey insisted that it was not, and to prove his assertion he independently inserted a new clause into the engraved *lex* stipulating that Caesar was exempt from its terms.[131] And yet, this codicil was added after the law had already been passed and inscribed on a bronze tablet, which means it was not legally a part of the law; it was little more than a graffito carved onto a published law. Pompey may have believed that his *lex Pompeia* had not canceled the privilege given to Caesar by the "law of the ten tribunes," so the last-minute addition to his own law was merely a symbolic gesture that acknowledged that Caesar's special exemption remained intact.[132] On the other hand, he may have meant this last-minute addition as a double-message, showing the Senate that he still supported Caesar, but also showing Caesar that he (Pompey) had the power to protect or destroy him.[133] To be sure, true legal experts such as Cicero and Cato could not have been duped into thinking that Pompey's addition to the text of the law was legally binding.[134] Yet, since it was unclear whether the *lex Pompeia* had overturned the "law of the ten tribunes," Pompey's codicil confirming Caesar's exemption did not *need* to be legal; it was merely a message that Pompey recognized Caesar's right to stand for election *in absentia*. While some of Caesar's friends seem to have criticized Pompey for attacking Caesar with this law, these complaints were probably an overabundance of caution; if the *lex Pompeia* really had been a threat to Caesar, then surely one of the tribunes who had just promulgated the "law of the ten tribunes" would have objected or interposed his veto.

If Cato had indeed contributed to the drafting of Pompey's two new laws, then we would very much like to know his reaction to Pompey's added codicil exempting Caesar. While he surely approved the anti-corruption elements of these laws, he must have also valued them as ways to strike at Caesar, since both laws would make him vulnerable to prosecution: one when he laid down his *imperium* to make his *professio* for the consulship, and the other before he took up

---

131. Cic. *Att.* 8.3.3, Suet. *Iul* 28.2–3, Dio 40.56.2–3.

132. Gruen (1974) 457–60, Mitchell (1991) 237 n. 18.

133. Seager (2002) 138–9.

134. Shackleton Bailey ([1965–70] 4.329) notes that Cicero's reference to Pompey's codicil suggests doubt in its validity.

his next military command. It must have been a terrible shock for him, there-fore, when Pompey insisted that the second law did not apply to Caesar, and that there would be no opportunity to prosecute Caesar before his next consulship. If Pompey was being honest, and had never intended the bill to annul Caesar's privilege, then it would seem likely that Cato or other *optimates* had misled him about their full purpose in supporting it. More likely, however, Pompey had un-derstood the bill's potential to provide a legal basis for claiming that Caesar's priv-ilege was void, but he was unprepared for the outcry by Caesar's supporters, and so added the codicil to avoid an irreversible break with Caesar. Either way, Cato must have been deeply annoyed at Pompey's reaction.

Pompey's legislation was similar to his new marriage alliance: they did not ac-tually harm Caesar directly, but they appealed to senators not already allied with the two surviving triumvirs. By promulgating legislation that he knew would be attractive to the more conservative senators, Pompey indicated his willingness to move closer to the *optimates*. He emphasized this by arranging in July or August to have his new father-in-law, Metellus Scipio, elected as his co-consul for the remainder of the year, advertising his growing web of political connections.[135] Scipio was under indictment for bribery at the time, so Pompey manipulated the jury and intimidated the prosecutor into dropping the case.[136] Cato is said to have rebuked Pompey sharply for abusing the law, and for overlooking the crimes of friends and relatives (like Scipio), but to those who knew him, this accusation must have seemed hypocritical given Cato's own tendency to turn a blind eye to the misdeeds of his own relations.[137] What Cato and his circle thought about Pompey's appointment of Scipio is not recorded, but they were probably relieved and even pleasantly surprised by how well Pompey had performed as sole consul, and by his selection of a conservative, tradition-minded senator (albeit not one from Cato's circle) to be his co-consul. While he had not broken with Caesar, Pompey had unmistakably shifted closer to the *optimates* by reaching out to other senators and seeking a wider network of allies, which reduced Caesar's share of Pompey's loyalty and support, and reduced Pompey's dependence on Caesar. Cato's relentless attacks in 61–60 BC had prevented Pompey from making this kind of shift toward the *optimates* at that time, but by 52 BC Cato and his friends seem to have become willing to accommodate Pompey if it meant an opportunity to humble Caesar.

---

135. App. *BC* 2.25, Dio 40.51.2–3.

136. Plut. *Pomp.* 55.4.

137. Plut. *Cat. Min.* 48.3–4.

Three further events in 52 BC help to illuminate Cato's character and behavior at the time: his role as a juror in the trial of Plancus, his actions in helping his ally and admirer M. Favonius organize his aedilician games, and his campaign for the consulship of 51 BC. First, Cicero prosecuted T. Munatius Plancus (tr. pl. 52 BC) in a new court for trials involving accusations of violence (*quaestio de vi*), which had been established by legislation promulgated by Pompey earlier in the year to deal with Milo's trial.[138] The law establishing the court (the *lex Pompeia de vi*) had forbidden the delivery of panegyrics on behalf of defendants, but Pompey violated his own law by composing a panegyric on Plancus's behalf to be read in court.[139] Cato was a juror in the trial, and he was outraged by this violation of the law. When the designated person began reading out Pompey's laudation of Plancus, Cato first covered his own ears in an ostentatious fashion in protest to the illegal panegyric, and then leapt up and forcibly tried to stop Pompey's testimony from being delivered. Just as he had started physical brawls on the Rostra to stop legislation he deemed improper from being read aloud, so he was quick as a juror to move from vocal opposition to physical confrontation. Cato was ejected from the jury, although Plancus was still condemned and went into exile in spite of Pompey's panegyric. This episode drove Plutarch to remark, "Cato was an impractical and hard-to-attack factor for defendants, who did not wish to allow him as a juror in their trials, but neither did they dare refuse him."[140] Furthermore, this event portrays Cato as someone who tended to over-react: the *lex Pompeia de vi* had only been established a few months earlier, but he defended its terms as if it had been something handed down by the founders of the Republic. Two generations later, Valerius Maximus commented that it would have been outrageous arrogance for anyone else to act like this in the courtroom, but he excused Cato on the grounds that he was driven by his unique confidence.[141] Perhaps he was just cantankerous and thought every aspect of every law ought to be obeyed, or he may have been particularly annoyed that he had been instrumental in getting Pompey elected sole consul, only to see him blatantly flout the law in order to protect a lieutenant. On the other hand, it may be that Cato's outrageous behavior had an influence on the other jurors, who did vote to condemn Plancus.

138. Cic. *Fam.* 7.2.2–3. See Brennen (2000) 328–9 for discussion.

139. Plut. *Cat. Min.* 48.4–5, *Pomp.* 55.5, Val. Max. 6.2.5, Dio 40.55.2.

140. Plut. *Cat. Min.* 48.5.

141. Val. Max. 6.2.5.

Second, M. Favonius (pr. 49 BC)[142] was Cato's greatest admirer and emulator: he and Cato had been the very last to take the mandated oath to support Caesar's agrarian legislation back in 59 BC (Favonius refused to take the oath until Cato did), and they had been the only two senators to speak publicly against the *lex Trebonia* in 55 BC, being lucky to escape with their lives from the angry mob that supported the triumvirs. Favonius took Cato as his role model, and imitated his nature, behavior, and values.[143] Indeed, Cato's own famously confrontational behavior is visible in Plutarch's description of Favonius: "very emotional and greatly excited in responding to arguments, which fixed on him like unmixed wine—not gentle or soft, but like a frenzied madness."[144] One can only wonder whether Favonius acted this way naturally, or whether he was simply mimicking Cato's own behavior. Whichever the case, Cato took a particular interest in supporting his protégé's career: when Favonius was a candidate for election to the aedileship of 52 BC, Cato paid close attention and observed the casting of votes carefully enough to notice irregularities in the ballots as they were being cast.[145] He urged the tribunes to intervene and put a stop to the fraudulent balloting, with the result that Favonius was successful in the election. One can only wonder how Cato (a private citizen at the time) was able to observe enough of the ballots to notice the irregularities—he must have forced himself among the voters in such a way as to see a number of the ballots—but his intervention secured his protégé's electoral victory.

Furthermore, Plutarch says that Cato took over responsibility for some of the official duties expected of Favonius, which must mean that Favonius followed Cato's advice in the performance of his official duties as aedile. In particular, Cato apparently arranged and executed the aedilician games, giving unusually simple and old-fashioned prizes that were far less valuable than the gold crowns and other lavish prizes normally handed out at the games. Whereas Caesar as aedile had thrown games of unprecedented opulence and tremendous cost, Cato—acting for Favonius—deliberately did the opposite, giving simple and inexpensive prizes in a happy and sportive mood, conveying a message to the Romans that attention and care to the details of the games were more important than costly

---

142. Ryan ([1994] 542–4) discusses the dispute on whether Favonius actually reached the praetorship.

143. Plut. *Cat. Min.* 32.6 and 46.1, *Caes.* 21.8, 41.3, *Pomp.* 60.4, *Brut.* 12.3, 34.4–5, Val. Max. 2.10.8, Suet. *Aug.* 13.2, Dio 38.7.1.

144. Plut. *Cat. Min.* 46.1.

145. Plut. *Cat. Min.* 46.2. Linderski ([1972] 181–200) points out that Favonius may have been aedile in 53 or 52 BC.

extravaganzas.[146] The public reception of this spectacle was mixed: while some in the audience were said to have respected Cato for the simplicity of the prizes he provided, many other Romans just laughed.[147]

Third, three men are known to have campaigned for the consulship of 51 BC: Cato, Ser. Sulpicius Rufus, and M. Claudius Marcellus. According to Dio, Cato claimed to be seeking the consulship for selfless reasons only: he felt summoned to office in order to defend the state from Caesar and Pompey.[148] This is the same magnanimous and heroic type of justification that Cato had publicly given for seeking the tribunate years earlier—that the public interest, rather than private ambition, called him to office. There can be no doubt that he felt that the Republic needed him to suppress the two remaining triumvirs, but his disavowal of personal interest seems hollow. Every Roman senator dreamed of reaching the consulship, and it was to be expected that every senator with potential and resources would try to rise as far as possible up the *cursus honorum*. For this reason, no senator should have felt the need to offer an explanation for seeking the consulship—it was the normal and logical objective of any member of the senatorial order. The consulship sat on top of the *cursus honorum*, the "race of honors," so seeking a consulship was a competition for honor and status that should have needed no explanation. Therefore Cato's claim of disinterest and his justification for why he wanted the office were significant deviations from prevailing Roman aristocratic norms if he made them, but they probably reflect a later idealization of his legacy. Stoics such as Cicero eagerly and unabashedly sought the consulship, so the idea that Cato would only seek the consulship if summoned to it is overly romantic. If he did indeed profess disinterest in the office, it is more likely that he did so wishing to be compared to legendary heroes such as Cincinnatus (cos. suff. 460 BC), who was summoned from his plow to assume the dictatorship and save Rome from disaster. Creating this type of comparison would have been a deft manipulation of tradition, and would have a much stronger influence on the tradition-loving Roman voters than presenting himself as a disinterested Greek philosopher.

Cato was said to have been pleased with his two rivals: he and Sulpicius had collaborated on legislation and prosecutions in the past, and Marcellus was a known enemy of the triumvirate. True to his values, Cato refused to offer bribes or make standard campaign promises, and he persuaded the Senate to issue a decree forbidding candidates from using third parties in their campaigning—all

---

146. Plut. *Cat. Min.* 46.5.

147. Plut. *Cat. Min.* 46.3.

148. Dio 40.58.1–2. See Fehrle (1983) 214.

candidates had to campaign in person.[149] This was an effort to dismantle the elaborate networks of campaign agents that had become common in elections, and it also attempted to suppress bribery, since money was often distributed by agents of the candidates. Equally important, it was in keeping with Cato's vision of Rome's past when (he thought) candidates were elected based upon their families, their personal reputations, and their networks of clients and political allies.[150] On the other hand, the decree also leveled the playing field for Cato: he could not distribute bribes without destroying his carefully constructed reputation for old-fashioned virtue, so he used the decree to make it harder for his rivals to gain an advantage over him through bribery;[151] that is, since he did not want to use bribery, he tried to prevent his opponents from benefiting from that advantage. While this decree suited Cato's aims, the people were predictably incensed with it, not only because it deprived them of the bribe money normally paid by candidates and their agents, but also because it denied them the satisfying attention they were accustomed to receive from each candidate's network of supporters, who fanned out each year to solicit the people earnestly for their votes.[152] As Plutarch described the situation, "Yet Cato alienated the people even more not merely by taking their pay, but also by taking away their ability to give favors, and so he made the people both needy and without honor."[153] Still, the effectiveness of the Senate's decree was limited at best, since it was impossible for Cato or his rivals to prevent their respective networks of supporters from instructing their dependents upon how to vote.[154] As part of his campaign, Cato promised to recall and prosecute Caesar, but this does not seem to have interested the voters at that time, who passed over him and instead gave their votes to his two rivals.[155] After this loss, Cato made a good show of indifference: instead of slinking off, he took his usual exercise in the Campus Martius, and then walked

149. Plut. *Cat. Min.* 49.2–4, Dio 40.58.1–3.

150. Gruen ([1974] 156) says that Cato employed his candidacy "as a showcase for proper electioneering. He ostentatiously scorned stratagems and pandering to the populace."

151. Plut. *Cat. Min.* 49.4, "and in this activity, he was not himself persuasive in canvassing for votes on his own behalf, because in his disposition he wished to maintain the dignity of his life more than to gain in addition the dignity of the consulship by appealing for votes, and he did not allow his friends to perform these actions by which the mob is won over and flattered."

152. Yakobson (1999) 107, 216–7.

153. Plut. *Cat. Min.* 49.3–4.

154. Yakobson (1999) 107.

155. Gruen ([1974] 156) suggested, "the campaign seems to have been designed to win admiration rather than votes." See also Fehrle (1983) 214 and Duff (1999) 153–4.

around the Forum for hours, as usual wearing only his toga (no tunic or foot-wear).[156] Yet this apathy may have been forced: when Cicero faulted Cato for not making a better effort to win over the voters through simple friendly discourse, he responded rather bitterly that he would not seek office again if it meant changing his behavior.[157] There can be no doubt that Cato had very much wanted both the honor of the consulship and the opportunity to use the office against Caesar and Pompey, so this show of indifference is probably the product of later authors who wanted to portray Cato as the ideal Stoic philosopher.[158] Indeed, Caesar later wrote that Cato's defeat in the election greatly enflamed his hostility and enmity toward him, and while Caesar was not a neutral witness, one must assume that Cato resented the fact that he had been passed over by the voters, and that the people had refused to honor him as they had Caesar.[159]

While Cato made a fine display of conducting an old-fashioned, simple con-sular campaign, his allies were surely chagrined that he had not done more to win the election. Cato had supported the use of electoral bribery to get Bibulus elected to the consulship in 59 BC, but he refused to use bribery in his own elec-tion, and he even angered the voters by trying to suppress the use of bribery by others. Although Cato was publicly lauded for his outstanding morals, this praise did not translate into votes among the people, and his austere morality even seems to have turned some voters against him. He had advanced rapidly during the early stages of his career, and the people had been happy to elect him to lower offices, but the competition for the consulship was much more intense, and the people were accustomed to profit from those elections, so Cato's *exemplum* was not enough to outweigh that expectation.[160] Cicero blamed him for failing to act in ways that would win him the consulship, saying the state desperately needed him in that office, but Cato had been unwilling (or perhaps unable) to put aside

---

156. Sen. *Ep.* 104.33, Plut. *Cat. Min.* 50.1.

157. Plut. *Cat. Min.* 50.2–3 (cf. Dio 40.58.3–4).

158. Morrell (2017) 209, "The notion we find in the sources that Cato was indifferent to the office or to his failure at the polls must be rejected. Such sentiments look like face-saving or products of the 'Stoic martyr' tradition."

159. Caes. *BC* 1.4.

160. Van der Blom ([2012] 54 and 56) suggested: "by acting in the exact opposite way of ex-pectation, Cato failed to connect with the people" and "Cato's strong brand in the Senate secured him high status and influence there, but although he was well known to the public, his brand did not translate easily into popular favour or successive magistracies." Duff ([1999] 148–9) takes this even further, arguing that Plutarch "forewarns the reader to be alert to ways in which Cato does not conform to the positive paradigm we might expect from one of Plutarch's protagonists. He will become a man to praise, but not to imitate." See also Yakobson (1999) 222.

his own vision of the *mos maiorum* to do what was necessary to win an election. Having built his reputation as a champion of tradition and law, he could not easily adopt the contemporary practices that were needed to win a consulship. So the aspects of Cato that the *optimates* found most appealing were the very things that seem to have limited his broader appeal. Whether he recognized this is unclear, but he did not stand a second time for the consulship.

7

Collapse

The Overture: 51 BC

Although Pompey resisted breaking entirely from Caesar in 52 BC, the *optimates* would keep trying to drive a wedge between the two men. A unified Pompey and Caesar could still muster the necessary resources to dominate the Republic—especially since Caesar had acquired considerable resources and influence from his Gallic campaigns—but the goals of the two men were becoming incompatible. They had originally formed their alliance in 60 BC simply to get around Cato's obstruction and achieve their immediate goals, but by 51 BC Caesar and Pompey both wanted to be preeminent in Rome. Caesar no doubt believed that it was his "turn" to build up his status and prestige as high as he was able, and that Pompey—having already risen to the pinnacle of Roman society many years earlier—should allow Caesar to seize what opportunities he could and be content to remain in their mutually beneficial alliance. Pompey, on the other hand, was increasingly convinced that Caesar's rise meant his own diminution, and he refused to yield the preeminence he had enjoyed for nearly two decades. Cato and the men around him certainly fostered Pompey's famous paranoia, urging him to distrust and even to fear Caesar. For his part, Pompey must have realized that the *optimates* were trying to separate him from Caesar, and he certainly could calculate the advantages and disadvantages that each alliance offered him. So he tried to maintain an intermediate position between Caesar and the *optimates*, drawing political strength from both sides and making both sides dependent upon him. Whereas Caesar had benefited immensely by acting as the mediator between Pompey and Crassus in their triumvirate, Pompey now wanted to use this middle position between Caesar and the *optimates* to enhance his own position. He probably would have preferred to maintain this arrangement, which was very beneficial for him, but he was unable to control the *optimates* in the same way that Caesar had managed his fellow triumvirs. Cato and his allies would not allow Pompey to remain in his middle position, but would force him to pick a side by driving Caesar to war.

As the *optimates* increasingly worked to pull Pompey over to their side, the role of Cato becomes more difficult to track. While there can be no doubt that he was very active behind the scenes—influencing and even driving the actions of his political allies—he faded from prominence as Caesar's primary political opponent as Pompey increasingly adopted Cato's view that Caesar must be suppressed.[1] At the same time, the Senate was not organized into distinct political parties, so those opposed to Caesar had never been firmly united into a single faction with a single leader.[2] Cato had his own circle of political allies, and he continued to work with other senators and groups of senators to align senatorial factions against Caesar, but he was not the single driving force at the center of all opposition to Caesar. In the early stages of their careers, Cato had pursued a personal feud with Caesar, and the men who joined him also had personal motives for attacking Caesar (such as Catulus, who had lost the election to *pontifex maximus* to him). Yet the effectiveness of Cato's attacks, his strong influence among the depleted leadership of the *optimates*, and his deft use of the language of traditional values such as *libertas* and hatred of tyranny all enabled him to alienate many senators from Caesar, and Caesar from them, driving him to more radical actions such as the formation of the triumvirate. So by 51 BC, many senators were attacking Caesar for political motives, fearing—rightly or wrongly—that he was indeed aiming at tyranny, the accusation that Cato had leveled at Caesar for years. This accusation not only played on traditional Roman hatred of monarchs, but it also aimed to make the senators afraid for their own status and privileges, because—if he did indeed acquire sole power—the senators would lose their traditional places as the leaders of the state. Whether or not Caesar entertained ideas of making himself a monarch, Cato convinced many senators that it was so, pushing them to abandon their usual tolerance for great men, and to cluster together to oppose Caesar. In all of this, Cato was a great success, but as the fear of Caesar grew among the senators, and as Cato's allies increasingly stepped into leadership roles in the Senate, Cato himself became less important in driving the opposition to Caesar. This turned out very badly for Rome, because the men who assumed the leading roles in opposing Caesar did not share Cato's deep loyalty to the state, and they were willing to go to any length to destroy Caesar, even if that meant a civil war.

---

1. Dragstedt (1969) 84–5.

2. See Gruen (1974) 95–102 and Botermann (1989) 62–85, esp. 84.

When M. Claudius Marcellus entered the consulship in January 51 BC, he made good on his earlier boasting and began attacking Caesar with great enthusiasm. Marcellus was ardently opposed to Caesar, and while it is not clear whether he was close to Cato or a member of his circle, he was determined to force Caesar back to Rome as a private citizen, thereby making him vulnerable to prosecution.[3] Yet this was easier promised than done. As discussed earlier, Caesar's possession of Cisalpine Gaul and Illyricum had been guaranteed for five years by the *lex Vatinia*, and had been extended by the *lex Licinia Pompeia* for another five years. When each of these two periods of command started and ended is not clear, so modern scholars cannot agree on when—exactly—Caesar's legal possession of Cisalpine Gaul and Illyricum ended.[4] In all likelihood, the *leges* giving and extending Caesar's command probably had not identified specific start and end dates for Caesar's possession of Cisalpine Gaul and Illyricum, so there was no specific date by which Caesar had to vacate his provinces. Roman practices had always allowed considerable flexibility in the handover of a province from one commander to his successor, since the timing of a successor's arrival could be difficult to coordinate.[5] Further complicating the issue, the laws giving and renewing Caesar's command stipulated that he was to hold it for five years, but probably did not identify start and end dates. The absence of a precise date enabled Caesar's enemies to push for an earlier turnover (perhaps identifying the passage of the *lex Vatinia* in mid-59 BC as the start of his command), whereas Caesar and his allies could justify his claims for more time in command of his provinces by asserting that his command had not begun until he had arrived in Gaul in 58 BC. Caesar's possession of Transalpine Gaul, however, had been given to him by a *senatus consultum*, and therefore could be canceled or transferred to another commander

---

3. Marcellus had sided with the *optimates* in defending Milo in 52 BC (Ascon. 34, 40), and he may be the Marcellus who served as quaestor with Cato and whom Plutarch (*Cat. Min.* 18.3–4) describes as Cato's friend from childhood, but Gruen ([1974] 156 n. 146) notes that Cato is associated with Sulpicius only in the consular campaign for 51 BC (Plut. *Cat. Min* 49.2). It would be strange for Cato to neglect the consular campaign of a boyhood friend. Epstein ([1987] 85) points out that Marcellus's animosity toward Caesar suggests that they were personal enemies as well as political enemies.

4. The debate is commonly referred to as the *Rechtsfrage*. For summaries of this debate, see Adcock (1932) 14–26, Balsdon (1939) 57–73, Jameson (1970a) 638–60, Girardet (2000a) 679–710, Seager (2002) 191–3, Morstein-Marx (2007) 159–78, Pelling (2011) 281–93.

5. In the late Republic, commanders were not supposed to leave their provinces until authorized to do so by the state (Cic. *Pis.* 50), and once a successor did arrive, the retiring commander was required to leave the province within thirty days (Cic. *Fam.* 3.6.3). On the other hand, when Cicero arrived to assume command of Cilicia, he was annoyed to find that his predecessor—Appius Claudius—remained in the province for several more months, continuing to act as governor despite Cicero's arrival (Cic. *Att.* 5.16.4).

when the Senate wished, although such action could be blocked by a tribunician veto, and Caesar was usually careful to have at least a couple of allies holding the tribunate. And even if the Senate could remove Transalpine Gaul from Caesar's authority, this would not force him back to Rome until the expiration of his other provinces. Furthermore, the "law of the ten tribunes" had authorized him to stand for the consulship *in absentia*, which meant he did not have to give up his legal immunity in order to run for the consulship, and he could step directly from his proconsulship to a second consulship, and from there to another multi-year proconsulship, while remaining immune to prosecution the entire time. Pompey had openly supported this special privilege for Caesar, and had inserted a codicil into his *lex Pompeia* exempting him from its provisions. Caesar had arranged things very well, to the frustration of Marcellus, Cato, and their allies.

For the *optimates*, therefore, the main question was how to circumvent the terms of the *lex Licinia Pompeia*, which in 55 BC had renewed Caesar's command of Cisalpine Gaul and Illyricum for five years. Their first effort was clever but ineffective: when news of Caesar's great victory over Vercingetorix at Alesia reached Rome early in 51 BC, Marcellus seized upon the news to argue that he had completed his Gallic campaign and therefore should return to Rome immediately, which (he claimed) would mean that Caesar's authorization to stand for the consulship *in absentia* would be unnecessary and therefore void.[6] In doing this, he was making a very specific argument about the nature of Caesar's command. In the Republic, the Latin term *provincia* could be defined in two different ways: as a task to be completed (such as a war against Mithridates or pirates), or as a territorial possession under continual Roman administration (such as Cisalpine Gaul, Asia, or Africa).[7] The distinction between these two types of *provincia* was not always clear, so Marcellus and his supporters exploited this ambiguity by asserting that Caesar's command was a task, and so could (and had been) completed by his victory at Alesia and his subjugation of the Gauls. If this interpretation was upheld, it would mean that Caesar's great victory had completed his provincial assignment, and therefore that the assignment itself was over and so ceased to exist. This would require Caesar to return to Rome immediately, just as generations of Roman commanders had returned to Rome once their assigned enemies had been vanquished. This was a clever argument, but it was not convincing. The actual wording of the *lex Vatinia* is lost, but most Romans seem to have understood that Caesar was holding provincial territories, which were ongoing assignments (Transalpine Gaul had been a Roman possession for at least fifty years), and so the

---

6. Suet. *Iul.* 28.2. See Gelzer (1968) 172–3, Gruen (1974) 461–2, Seager (2002) 140.

7. Drogula (2015) 232–94.

stipulation in the *lex Vatinia* and in the *lex Licinia Pompeia* that he should retain those provinces for five-year periods seemed perfectly clear.[8] Marcellus's colleague Sulpicius Rufus and several tribunes resisted this effort to recall Caesar, and on March 1 Pompey also announced his own opposition to Marcellus's efforts.[9] As the spring turned into summer, Pompey continued to block the effort to remove Caesar from his provinces. At first, discussion of Marcellus's proposal seems to have been delayed until June 1, but that date came and went without any action being taken.[10] Pompey's inaction was probably done to help Caesar, but it also left the door open to the *optimates*, since Pompey did not declare himself against any discussion of Caesar's command.

Despite Marcellus's bold promises to recall Caesar, therefore, the majority of senators were unwilling to take this step; they would not anger one great commander unless they were sure of the support of the other. As Cato had frequently demonstrated, it was much easier to obstruct a bill than to push one through the Senate, so there was little Marcellus could do in the face of such opposition, and this seems to have contributed to rumors that Marcellus was slow and inefficient.[11] Stuck in this corner and wanting to lash out against Caesar in some way, Marcellus introduced a senatorial resolution in April declaring that Caesar's establishment of a Roman colony (Novum Comum) in Cisalpine Gaul had been illegal.[12] The bill was vetoed in spite of having moderate support from the Senate, but nevertheless, Marcellus gave a powerful display of his disregard for Caesar's authority by staging a public flogging in which a leading citizen of Novum Comum was brutally whipped—a type of punishment that could not be inflicted on Roman citizens, and thus a cruel statement that Marcellus did not view Caesar's grant of citizenship to the man as valid. Cicero was outraged

---

8. Transalpine Gaul was probably organized as a province as early as 120 BC, but did not start receiving regular governors until the Cimbric War (see Ebel [1976] 76–8 and Woolf [2000] 35–7). Cisalpine Gaul had been a Roman province since the third century BC, but Illyricum—where Caesar spent the least time—would not be fully organized as a province until the Augustan Era.

9. Suet. *Iul.* 29.1, Dio 40.59.1–3. Seager ([2002] 140) suggests that Pompey opposed such disregard for laws that he himself had promulgated (the *lex Licinia Pompeia*) and supported (the "law of the ten tribunes").

10. Cic. *Fam.* 8.1.2, 8.2.2. Caesar (*BG* 8.53) suggests that—at some point—Marcellus succeeded in getting a vote on his proposal, and the Senate overwhelmingly opposed his motion.

11. Later in the year Caelius would refer to Marcellus as *tardus et parum efficax* (Cic. *Fam.* 8.10.3).

12. Cic. *Att.* 5.2.3, 5.11.2, Plut. *Caes.* 29.2, App. *BC* 2.26. Although provincial commanders did not have the right to grant citizenship on their own authority, Caesar claimed to have been given this right by the *lex Vatinia* (Suet. *Iul.* 28.3).

by the action, not only because it was appalling and shameful, but also because it was probably illegal: the inhabitants of Transpadane Gaul probably held Latin rights (*ius Latini*), which meant that their magistrates received Roman citizenship and so could not legally be flogged.[13] Since Marcellus's victim was a leading citizen, he was probably an ex-magistrate and thus already a Roman citizen.[14] Cicero's outrage not only draws the legality of Marcellus's action into question, but also forces one to wonder why the consul would take such a controversial step, since it offended Pompey as well as Caesar, and does not seem to have accomplished anything.[15] It may have been an act of frustration and cruelty, but the *optimates* probably feared that Caesar's bestowal of Roman citizenship to inhabitants in Cisalpine Gaul would increase his *clientela* and political influence considerably, but thrashing a citizen of Novum Comum would not undo Caesar's action. Indeed, all it would do was insult and anger Caesar, which may have been the purpose of the display. Cato and his allies had successfully goaded Caesar into reckless displays of force in the past, and it is likely that the whipping of the Transpadane citizen was intended to provoke him to some rash step.

Marcellus continued pushing his plan to recall Caesar throughout the summer, but he was unable to get enough senators to attend a Senate meeting on the subject.[16] He came to the Senate meeting on September 1 armed with a number of resolutions, but he found very little support for his anti-Caesar rhetoric. His first suggestion seems to have been to replace Caesar in his provinces effective on March 1 of the next year (50 BC), no doubt thinking that he would be able to accomplish little in the remaining winter months of his command.[17] In doing this he was conceding to Sulpicius and Pompey that Caesar could not legally be replaced before that time, but he wanted him stripped of his command on the first date legally possible. Still, Pompey, Sulpicius, and Pompey's father-in-law Scipio thought this resolution was too confrontational and insulted Caesar unnecessarily. Pompey expressed the opinion that the Senate should take no action, and his new father-in-law Metellus Scipio proposed putting off any discussion about Caesar's provinces until the meeting on March 1 of the next year (50 BC).[18] What this choice of date meant is unclear: Pompey clearly refused to break

---

13. Shackleton Bailey (1965–70) 3.207. See also Taylor (1960) 125–6 and Gruen (1974) 461 n. 43.

14. Suet. *Iul.* 28.3, App. *BC* 2.26.

15. Cicero (*Att.* 5.11.2) refers to Pompey's anger at the event.

16. Cic. *Fam.* 8.2.2, *Fam.* 8.5.3.

17. Cic. *Att.* 8.3.3 (cf. 8.5.3), Dio 40.59.1.

18. Cic. *Fam.* 8.8.4 and 9, 8.9.2 and 5, Dio 40.59.3.

with Caesar before that time, but he also left open the possibility that he would
consider recalling Caesar to Rome sooner than Caesar wanted to return. This
latter point was not lost on the senators, some of whom wondered if Pompey
was preparing to move against Caesar in the spring.[19] Sulpicius (a legal scholar)
supported the proposal by Pompey and Metellus Scipio, and to Marcellus's chagrin, the majority of senators agreed. What Cato thought of these proceedings
is not known, but Marcellus's efforts to bring Caesar back to Rome for prosecution certainly mirror Cato's own feelings. The majority of senators, however, were
clearly taking their lead from Pompey, no doubt because they did not want to
provoke a civil war or other disturbance that would harm their interests.

By the end of September, Pompey's position became clearer. The Senate met
on September 29, and a resolution was brought forward requiring the consuls
of the next year (50 BC) to make the question of consular provinces the only
item on the agenda for the Senate's meeting on March 1.[20] Cato's brother-in-law
Domitius Ahenobarbus and Pompey's father-in-law Metellus Scipio were among
the drafters of the resolution, which was approved on the motion of the consul
Marcellus. Given Domitius's close relationship and previous collaboration with
his brother-in-law, it is probable that Cato had some influence on the resolution.
Yet everyone involved surely knew that the resolution in itself could not force
Caesar out of his command. Caesar was adept at using tribunes to veto unfavorable legislation, and there was always the fear that he would resort to violence
and civil war to achieve his aims.[21] So the true weight of the resolution rested on
Pompey's willingness to help the Senate enforce it. According to Caelius Rufus,
Pompey had signaled to the *optimates* and to the Senate as a whole that he was
open to curtailing Caesar's ambition, but he was not ready to withdraw his support entirely from his ally. Caelius writes:

> Furthermore, those comments from Cn. Pompey have been noticed,
> which have brought the greatest confidence to people, since he said that
> he was not able lawfully to make a decision about Caesar's provinces be-
> fore the Kalends of March (March 1st), but that he would not hesitate

---

19. Cic. *Fam.* 8.9.5. See discussion in Seager (2002) 141–2.

20. Cic. *Fam.* 8.8.5–6.

21. The drafters of the resolution tried to prevent Caesar from using tribunes or military force
with additional decrees (Cic. *Fam.* 8.8.5–8): one forbidding the use of the veto in the discussion of provinces, a second forcing Caesar to send home all soldiers who had completed their
terms of service, and a third requiring that all other provinces for the next year be assigned
to praetors, which would leave the Senate no choice but to assign Caesar's provinces to the
consuls. All three of these were vetoed by Caesar's tribunes.

after the Kalends. When he was asked what would happen if some persons interposed vetoes at that time, he said that it made no difference whether C. Caesar would himself disobey the mandates of the Senate, or whether he would arrange for someone who would not permit the Senate to pronounce its decision. And someone else asked, "What if he wishes to be consul and to keep his army?" But Pompey very calmly replied, "What if my son wishes to swing a cudgel at me?" With such words he has made men think that he is having trouble with Caesar.[22]

These lines suggest that Pompey had come to the conclusion that March 1, 50 BC, was a proper and fair date to construe as the end of Caesar's command—the date after which he could be removed from command legally or "without injustice" (*sine iniuria*).[23] This was certainly a plausible interpretation of the *lex Licinia Pompeia*, albeit the one least friendly to Caesar. Pompey's statement equating a tribunician veto with Caesar's disobedience of the Senate was more ominous, because tribunician vetoes were legal, and their absolute ability to block senatorial decrees should have been unquestioned. Pompey may have been suggesting that he would treat Caesar's tribunes as enemies of the state, but he more likely meant this as a general statement of support for the *optimates*. Pompey's portrayal of Caesar as his son was meant to express both protection and superiority; so long as he obeyed Pompey as a dutiful son should, Pompey would protect him as a *pater* or patron.[24] This demonstrates that Pompey was attempting to walk a line between Caesar and the *optimates*, since his longed-for preeminence in Rome required that both sides be dependent on him.

By the end of 51 BC, therefore, Pompey had further adjusted his position vis-à-vis Caesar. Their alliance was still intact, but the growing support he felt from the *optimates* gave him the confidence to assert his superiority by making it clear that Caesar would not get everything he wanted. Caelius told Cicero that Pompey seemed to have left open two different possibilities for Caesar: stay

---

22. Cic. *Fam.* 8.8.9.

23. In this calculation, the year 55 BC (the year of the *lex Licinia Pompeia*) was counted as the first year of the extension of Caesar's command, which means the first year of Caesar's five-year extension of his command overlapped with the last year of the five-year-command given him in 59 BC. See previous citations for modern scholarship.

24. Seager (2002) 143, "this reply puts his position in a nutshell. He saw himself as a father, Caesar as his son. In that there was a message, for the *optimates* and for Caesar. The *optimates* could rest assured that Pompeius would act to keep Caesar in his place, subordinate as a son should be to his father, but they were also being warned that he was still not prepared to abandon Caesar, that a bond still existed between them as close as that between a father and his son."

in his command and forgo running for the consulship as soon as he was eligible, or give up his military command and try to win a second consulship.[25] Both of these scenarios would protect Caesar from prosecution in the courts, although they would prevent Caesar from standing for the consulship with an army at his back (as Pompey and Crassus had done in 71 BC). Thus Pompey was working to protect his own preeminence, but he did not please either side by this measure: Caesar was surely frustrated that his plans were being upset by Pompey, while the *optimates* must have been angry that Pompey was not doing more to weaken Caesar. Pompey had sought a middle position, and became caught in a tug-of-war between Caesar and the *optimates*, since both sides needed his full support.[26] Cicero suggests that Pompey may have wanted to escape these forces by leaving Italy and assuming direct command over his provinces in Spain, but was persuaded that his presence was necessary for the well-being of the Republic.[27] On the other hand, Pompey may have only floated the idea of leaving for Spain as a threat to terrify the *optimates*, forcing them to cling more tightly to him as their only buttress against Caesar.[28] Still, Pompey was in a precarious but powerful position, since the death of Crassus had left him as the linchpin between Caesar and the *optimates*. He would wield immense influence if he could find a way to control both sides and keep them dependent upon him, but such a balancing act would prove impossible.

Although Cato appears less prominently in the events of 51 BC, he nevertheless continued to be active in Senate debates and in the shaping of policy. Following the defeat and death of Crassus in 53 BC, the Parthians had begun making incursions into Roman Syria. Crassus's quaestor, C. Cassius Longinus (the future assassin of Caesar), had survived the disaster at Carrhae and had repelled the subsequent incursions into Syria, but new commanders were needed, and the Senate had a limited pool of ex-consuls who (in accordance with the new *lex Pompeia*) had been out of office for at least five years, and so were eligible to take up provinces under the terms of the new law.[29] Bibulus was assigned to Syria, and Cicero very reluctantly accepted the command of Cilicia.[30] Cato was

25. Cic. *Fam.* 8.8.9.

26. See comments by Raaflaub (1974a) 45–6.

27. Cic. *Att.* 5.11.3, *Fam.* 3.8.10.

28. Seager (2002) 141.

29. Joseph *AJ* 14.119 and *BJ* 180–181, and Dio 40.28.1–29.3.

30. Cicero (*Fam.* 3.2.1) wrote that he had no interest in being sent to Cilicia. For a discussion of these eastern commands, see Magie (1950) 388–404.

instrumental in shaping the instructions that Cicero (and perhaps Bibulus) received, convincing the Senate to instruct Cicero to prioritize the safety of King Ariobarzanes of Cappadocia, which was strategically sound advice to help block the Parthian advance, and he also put Cicero in touch with some reliable agents in Ariobarzanes's court.[31] Of course, Cato probably knew more about the East than most senators—he had traveled there as a young man, and counted King Deiotarus of Galatia among his clients—but his understanding of the region and his role in advising the Senate reveal the broad scope of his activity in state matters. Perhaps for this reason, when Cicero arrived in Cilicia and learned that the Parthians were mustering a large army on the Euphrates and threatening Rome's interests, he took special care to write Cato a letter informing him of the situation.[32] Cicero did not send an official dispatch to the Senate, thinking that Bibulus—as the commander in Syria—would be sending a much more detailed report to the senators, but he nevertheless wanted Cato to be particularly informed, perhaps to earn his gratitude for the effort, or perhaps because he recognized Cato's interest in the region. This brief episode illustrates the extent to which Cato kept informed about foreign affairs, and his wider influence on the shaping of Rome's foreign policies.[33] While it is impossible to gauge how much the average Roman senator knew about distant parts of the Mediterranean world, it is clear that Cato was very attentive to how Rome ran its empire, and that his knowledge was recognized by his fellow senators.

The Showdown of 50 and 49 BC

As the new year (50 BC) began, Caesar certainly understood that his alliance with Pompey was shifting, and that he could not count on the full support of his former son-in-law, although there had not yet been a real break between the two. The Senate was expected to discuss the disposition of the Gallic provinces on March 1, and Pompey had given little indication that he would fight to enable Caesar to retain his command much beyond that date. Caesar would later tell his soldiers that Pompey had been corrupted by their political enemies, and he may well have believed it, since—after a decade of resisting attacks from Cato and the *optimates*—Pompey now seemed to be moving closer to them. Caesar therefore took steps to acquire new allies as well, using the considerable wealth he had acquired in Gaul to reduce his dependence on Pompey. One of the new consuls was

---

31. Cic. *Fam.* 15.4.5–6.

32. Cic. *Fam.* 15.3.1–2.

33. On this, see the recent discussion by Morrell (2017) 183–93.

C. Claudius Marcellus, who was the cousin of the retiring consul M. Marcellus, and was equally hostile toward Caesar. The other new consul was L. Aemilius Lepidus Paullus, whose political support Caesar was able to purchase with a bribe so large that it enabled Paullus to refurbish the Basilica Aemilia, originally built by his ancestor M. Aemilius Lepidus (cos. 187, 175 BC) in 179 BC.[34] Even more surprising, Caesar succeeded in winning over C. Scribonius Curio, who was plebeian tribune in 50 BC and had previously been a vocal supporter of Cato and opponent of Caesar.[35] Curio's motives for switching sides and backing Caesar are debated. Alliances in the Senate had always been fluid, and senators could be expected to shift their support to suit their own changing priorities, but Curio was an important up-and-coming senator embraced by the *optimates*, so his shift of allegiance was particularly surprising. He himself claimed that he abandoned the *optimates* because they refused to insert an intercalary month into the calendar to provide him with enough days to get his desired legislation passed, but some senators believed that Caesar had paid him a massive bribe. Cicero disregarded rumors of such a bribe, saying that Curio was naturally volatile and had become angry with the *optimates*.[36] This may be true, or it may reflect Cicero's own frustration with the policies that Cato and his circle often employed, since Curio was not the first senator to find Caesar's friendship more rewarding than that of the *optimates*. Much of Caesar's success had depended upon his ability to win over men like Curio, Appius Claudius, and even (for a while) Cicero—men who felt they had not received appropriate recognition and status among the *optimates*, and so were willing to make other alliances to advance (or protect) their political careers. Whichever the reason, Curio would be one of Caesar's most effective spokesmen in the coming political battles.

On March 1 in 50 BC, the consuls convened the Senate and raised the question of Caesar's Gallic command. The consul C. Marcellus proposed reassigning Caesar's provinces to other commanders, but his colleague Paullus refused to support him.[37] The opinions of the first senators to speak are not recorded, but since Pompey had indicated his willingness to see Caesar recalled to Rome after

---

34. Cic. *Att.* 6.3.4, Plut. *Pomp.* 58.1–2, *Caes.* 29.3, Suet. *Iul.* 29.1, App. *BC* 2.26. On C. Marcellus's hostility towards Caesar, see Epstein (1987) 85.

35. Cic. *Fam.* 8.6.5, Livy *Per.* 109, Vell. 2.48.3–4, Luc. 4.819–20, App. *BC* 2.26–7, Dio 40.60.2–62.2.

36. Cic. *Fam.* 2.7.2, 2.13.3. See Lacey (1961) 318–19. Raaflaub ([1974a] 49 n. 181) and Gruen ([1974] 481–2) both point out that Curio was also working to enhance his own position and influence in Rome.

37. App. *BC* 2.27, Suet. *Iul.* 29.1.

March 1, it is likely that many agreed with C. Marcellus. Then Curio derailed the discussion. When it came time for him to speak, Curio supported the proposal, but he suggested further that Pompey should similarly be succeeded in his Spanish provinces, so that Caesar and Pompey would both be disarmed.[38] This was surely an unwelcome surprise, because the proposal painted Pompey not as the champion of the Republic, but as part of the problem facing the Republic. It was a very clever proposal, because it offered a peaceful de-escalation of tensions, which Curio probably calculated would be more attractive to most senators than the rhetoric of inflexible confrontation coming from his opponents. Caesar and Curio probably guessed that Pompey would refuse to lay down his legions and provinces, which would make him appear to be the one standing in the way of peace. They also must have calculated that—in the case that Pompey did agree—Caesar's tremendous popularity, new wealth, and *popularis* tactics would ensure that he won the second consulship he wanted. It was a powerful move, and Curio's proposal sounded so reasonable and in keeping with the *mos maiorum* that it must have taken Pompey and the *optimates* completely by surprise. Up to that point, the *optimates* had presented themselves as acting to save the traditional Republican government from the tyrannical ambitions of Caesar, but Curio's proposal outmaneuvered them by making Caesar seem the most moderate and the most dedicated to the Republic. He appeared as one asking only for equality and fair treatment, not for advantage. This was surely aimed at the majority of senators who were primarily interested in peace and stability, and who would therefore be inclined to compromise, especially since Caesar could present his claims as reasonable and in accord with tradition. This put Pompey and the *optimates* in a tight corner, since they had to justify rejecting such a reasonable suggestion for averting civil war.

More subtly, Curio's proposal was a clear statement that Caesar considered himself to be Pompey's equal, an implication that must have been highly irksome to the great man. Whereas Pompey had suggested that he enjoyed a paternalistic superiority over Caesar—a relationship that gave higher status to Pompey without shaming Caesar—Curio's proposal was a clear statement that Caesar would accept nothing less than an equal relationship.[39] This no doubt played into Pompey's fears of being eclipsed by his younger colleague. As a young man, Pompey himself had boasted to the dictator Sulla that people worshipped the rising sun, not the setting sun, which was a taunt that the people at the time

---

38. Caes. *BG* 8.52 (see Raaflaub [1974a] 302–3), Livy *Per.* 109, Plut. *Pomp* 58.3–4, *Caes.* 30.1–2, *Cat. Min.* 51.5, App. *BC* 2.27, Dio 40.62.3.

39. See Seager (2002) 144 for discussion.

admired the rising hero (Pompey) more than a great man who had passed his acme (Sulla).[40] Now Pompey was the old hero resting on his laurels while Caesar's fame swelled, and he must have felt himself falling under the younger man's shadow. Lucan captured this conflict of personalities well when he observed that Caesar could not tolerate a superior, nor Pompey an equal.[41] Furthermore, Pompey's improving status among the *optimates* depended upon his ability to control Caesar, but if he laid down his command in the name of peace, he would no longer be a bulwark against Caesar, and therefore he would no longer be so valuable to the *optimates*.[42] So Curio's proposal, although very moderate and fair in appearance, actually threatened to remove Pompey entirely as a political opponent to Caesar. Previously, Pompey seems to have been willing to help Caesar so long as he recognized and accepted Pompey's preeminence, but Curio's proposal rejected this, and attempted instead to diminish Pompey's standing and influence. So while Curio's proposal was highly effective in derailing the March 1 discussion in the Senate, it probably pushed Pompey closer to the *optimates*, since his standing with them required that Caesar be seen as a threat to them.

Curio's proposal received a mixed reaction. Pompey's supporters were opposed to the motion, claiming it was unfair to remove Pompey from his Spanish command before the appointed time, but the Roman people cheered for Curio's proposal and treated him like a hero for suggesting a way to avoid civil war.[43] One can presume that a great number of senators supported this proposal for stability and a de-escalation of tensions. Cato is presented as reacting differently to Curio's proposal. According to Plutarch, Cato rose in the Senate and shouted out, "now those things which I warned you about have come: that man is acting with open violence, using the power which he acquired by deceiving and tricking the state!"[44] This may be a fabrication by later authors, but if Cato actually said anything like this, it was a very skewed interpretation of Curio's proposal, which says a great deal about Cato's own thoughts. The Senate had not yet sent Caesar any official instructions regarding laying down his command, and Curio had

---

40. Plut. *Pomp.* 14.3.

41. Luc. 1.125–6.

42. Tatum ([2010] 206–7) pointed out that Curio's proposal must have pushed Pompey even closer to the *optimates*: the *optimates* were only flattering Pompey to use him as a military asset against Caesar, so if Pompey laid down his army, he would no longer be an important ally to them.

43. Plut. *Caes.* 30.2, App. *BC* 2.27. Pompey's Spanish command had been extended in 52 BC: Plut. *Caes.* 28.8, App. *BC* 2.24.

44. Plut. *Cat. Min.* 51.5.

proposed only that Caesar and Pompey both lay down their commands, so Cato's conclusion that Caesar was aiming at tyranny seems premature at best, and must reflect his own fears and rhetoric more than reality. Indeed, one might have expected Cato to be pleased with Curio's offer, since it would weaken the positions of both great men by bringing them to Rome without their armies. But in his eyes, Curio's proposal was proof that Caesar was aiming at nothing less than monarchy. Yet the majority of Romans did not see it that way, and Plutarch goes on to say that Cato's influence was limited to a number of senators, while the people as a whole favored Caesar and paid little heed to Cato's dire warnings. Perhaps many saw this outburst simply as the product of personal hatred and decades of feuding, rather than a fair description of what was happening. In that case, they did not support Cato because they saw him as pursuing a personal vendetta against Caesar, rather than giving an honest consultation of what was best for the state. So the majority of senators at that time were not influenced by Cato's assessment of the situation, but determined that Curio's proposal offered safety and better security.

While Cato raged at Curio's proposal, Pompey seems to have recovered and retrenched. Either in that same Senate meeting or in another one not long after, Pompey suggested that Caesar should keep his command until November 13.[45] This would give Caesar another full campaign season in Gaul, allow him to stand for the consulship *in absentia*, and require that he lay down his army only six weeks before entering his second consulship. These were considerable concessions, and may reflect Pompey's discomfort at Curio's proposal and its potential to make him look like the cause of civil war in the eyes of the citizens. Yet this offer still implied that Pompey was the greater man, and that Caesar would owe his political survival to Pompey's good graces.[46] His insistence that Caesar lay down his command six weeks before taking up the consulship suggests that he wanted Caesar at his mercy, but this does not necessarily mean that he wanted or intended to harm him in any way. To maintain his new standing with the *optimates*, he needed to present himself as the necessary shield between them and Caesar. What Cato and the *optimates* thought about this is not recorded, but according to a letter from Cicero's friend Caelius, in April the majority in the Senate supported Pompey's deadline, probably because they hoped it would be

---

45. Cic. *Fam.* 8.11.3. Seager ([2002] 144 n. 85) points out that the sequence of Curio's offer and Pompey's counter-offer cannot be positively determined, but that Curio's proposal probably came first (cf. Raaflaub [1974a] 306). The choice of November 13 is not explained, and Seager may be correct that it was a random date.

46. Seager (2002) 144–5.

a workable compromise that avoided violence.[47] In that letter, Caelius makes it clear that the political situation was on a knife's edge and could easily be pushed to extremities: "mark my words, if they use all means to suppress Curio, Caesar will come to his tribune's rescue. If, as seems probable, they are afraid to do that, Caesar will stay as long as he pleases."[48] Caelius cannot be the only one who recognized the precariousness of the situation, so those supporting Pompey's new deadline were probably hoping for a workable solution that would appease both commanders. Yet Caelius clearly understood that imposing a deadline on Caesar was a form of attack, and for that reason Curio vetoed the offer outright.[49] Cato's ally M. Marcellus tried to convince the Senate that they should negotiate with the tribunes, which meant opening discussions with other members of the college of tribunes to see if they could pressure Curio into lifting his veto, but the Senate rejected this, no doubt fearing (as Caelius did) that Caesar would respond violently if his tribunes were pressured or abused.[50] Everyone knew that the situation was tense, and that the first side to use force would give legitimacy to the use of violence by their opponents. Yet delays favored Caesar, because they kept him in his command and brought him closer to the consular elections. If nothing happened and existing laws were honored, Caesar would achieve his goals, while Cato and the *optimates* would miss their opportunity to strike at him. Although a small number of senators were eager to push the Senate to action, the majority would have been happy to satisfy both Pompey and Caesar if a solution could be found.

The conflict dragged on over the summer, and the delay must have been very frustrating to the anti-Caesarians, since each day brought Caesar closer to bringing his soldiers home and to standing in the consular election. Curio continued to veto any discussion of replacing Caesar, and kept lobbying for his proposal that Caesar and Pompey should both lay down their commands.[51] During a prolonged illness over the summer, Pompey wrote the Senate offering to accept Curio's proposal, stating that he was prepared to lay down his command and was certain Caesar would do the same.[52] Curio accepted and asked Pompey to step down first as a sign of good faith, but Pompey refused, and the matter dissolved

---

47. Cic. *Fam.* 8.11.3.

48. Cic. *Fam.* 8.11.3.

49. Cic. *Fam.* 8.13.2.

50. Cic. *Fam.* 8.13.2.

51. App. *BC* 2.27–9.

52. App. *BC* 2.28.

into recriminations. Pompey's offer may have been a ploy to undercut Curio's own proposal, but it is also possible that during his illness—and his time away from politics and from the influence of the *optimates*—Pompey had relented from his need to keep Caesar beneath him, or perhaps he had been persuaded by more moderate senators (such as Cicero) that compromise was better than civil war.[53] Pompey's motive cannot be recovered, but his offer to give up his command, and then his refusal to do so, may well have been the consequence of the intense pressure he felt from Caesar's supporters on the one hand, and the *optimates* on the other.

Another example of the growing tensions between Caesar and Pompey resulted from the prospect of a new war with Parthia. Back in 51 BC many senators had started thinking that Pompey or even Caesar might be sent to wage war against the Parthians in vengeance for Crassus's defeat, a campaign that would separate and distract the two men from their personal competition.[54] As 50 BC progressed and the impasse of Curio's veto seemed secure, discussion of sending one of Rome's great men to the East increased. As early as February, Cicero in Cilicia had already received a letter from Pompey announcing his intention to come East and take up a war against Parthia.[55] In anticipation of this possibility—or perhaps simply as a pretext for weakening Caesar—the Senate decided to ask Caesar and Pompey each to send one of their legions to Rome in preparation for the Syrian expedition.[56] Pompey shrewdly named as his contribution the legion he had lent to Caesar back in 53 BC, forcing him to reduce the size of his current army by two legions instead of one. There was nothing improper or wrong with this: the legion was Pompey's to command (even if he had lent it to Caesar), and he could reasonably claim that he could not further weaken his army by giving away a second legion. Given the current situation, however, few would have missed that this was a clever maneuver to weaken Caesar's army without diminishing Pompey's forces. Caesar could not refuse, since to do so would undermine his claim of legitimacy and reinforce Cato's propaganda of tyranny. When these two legions arrived in Italy (where they would be detained), their officers—one of whom was Appius Claudius, the nephew of the Appius Claudius who had been consul in 54 BC— for some reason reported falsely that morale in Caesar's army was exceptionally

---

53. See comments by Seager (2002) 146.

54. Cic. *Fam.* 8.10.2. On this see Raaflaub (1974a) 45.

55. Cic. *Att.* 6.1.3 and 14, cf. *Fam.* 8.14.4.

56. Caes. *BG* 8.54, *BC* 1.2, 1.4, 1.9, Plut. *Pomp.* 56.3, *Caes.* 29.4, App. *BC* 2.29, Dio 40.65.2–66.1.

low, and that Pompey would have little trouble defeating Caesar in war.[57] This
false report was a serious disservice to Pompey, because it made him overcon-
fident and diminished his ability to assess his military position accurately. One
can only speculate on why these officers gave false reports, but in all likelihood,
they were attempting to curry favor with Pompey and advance the goals of the
optimates. The consequence was to make Pompey much more willing to contemplate going to war with Caesar, thereby nudging him away from his previous inclination to consider peace terms. This may have been the intended purpose of
the false rumors, but if so, it would have fatal consequences.

Cicero's letters from Cilicia throughout 50 BC illustrate his deep disapproval
of how this struggle between Caesar and Pompey was being handled. Whereas
opinion-makers among the *optimates* such as Cato and his allies were pushing for
confrontation, Cicero had always advocated a more tolerant approach to dealing
with the ambitions of great men. Despite being in Cilicia, Cicero had a good understanding of the characters and ambitions of the remaining triumvirs: he had
long been a supporter of Pompey, and he had recently received many favors from
Caesar, including his support for the *supplicatio* proposed in honor of Cicero's
victories in Cilicia, a loan of 800,000 *sesterces* at very low interest, and a high position for Cicero's brother in the Gallic campaign.[58] Despite these many favors,
however, Cicero knew he would have to side with Pompey and the *optimates* if
the conflict deteriorated.[59] Still, he recognized that the scope and destruction of
such a conflict would be devastating to the Republic, and therefore he thought
the best choice was to avoid war at all costs, a policy that the majority in the
Senate probably favored, since very few of them would have seen any advantage
in a civil war.[60] On the other hand, Cicero also recognized that many *optimates*
were eager for war if it meant destroying Caesar, and therefore he did not blame
Caesar alone when hostilities finally started.[61] Different groups within the Senate
had different interests, and Cicero was very frustrated that his absence prevented
him from throwing himself fully into the business of swaying opinions.

---

57. Plut. *Pomp.* 57.4, *Caes.* 29.5–6, App. *BC* 2.30. See Gelzer ([1968] 186), who points out that
Caesar's *legatus pro praetore* T. Labienus was already negotiating with *optimates* in anticipation
of abandoning Caesar.

58. Friendship to Caesar: Cic. *Att.* 7.1.2–7, 7.2.7, 7.3.11, *Fam.* 1.9.6–21, 7.17.2; loan of 800,000 *sesterces*: Cic. *Att.* 5.1.2, 5.4.3, 5.5.2, 5.6.2; Quintus made a legate: Cic. *QF* 2.14.1, 2.16.4, *Fam.* 1.9.21.

59. Cic. *Att.* 7.3.3–5, 7.6.2, 7.7.7, 7.9.4.

60. Cic. *Att.* 7.5.4, 7.7.7, 8.11d.6, *Fam.* 2.15.3, *Marc.* 14, *Phil.* 2.24.

61. Cic. *Att.* 7.5.4, *Fam.* 16.11.2, 16.12.2.

A letter from Cicero to Atticus, written on February 20 of 50 BC, offers a curious comment about Cato. He begins the letter by complaining at length about the corrupt practices of certain Romans in the East, and in particular about Cato's nephew Brutus, whose loans to Cypriot Salamis at dramatically high rates of interest shocked Cicero, as did Brutus's insistence that Cicero use his military authority to collect on those loans.[62] Cicero refused to bring financial ruin upon the Salaminians just to help Brutus collect on his loans, but decided against asking Cato to intercede.[63] He knew that Cato would disapprove of his nephew's extreme usury, but probably doubted that he would do anything about it, since Cato had already proven that he possessed the aristocratic trait of overlooking the misdeeds of family. After discussing some other matters in his letter, Cicero makes a curious statement about how eastern provincial governors have been behaving:

> You hear correctly that Thermus and Silius are being praised, for indeed they are carrying out their responsibilities with integrity. You may add M. Nonius, Bibulus, and me also if you wish. Yet I wish Scrofa had someplace where he was able to do more, for it is a noble business. The others strengthen[64] the *politeuma* of Cato.[65]

Cicero's use of the Greek word *politeuma* here is usually taken to signify a "policy," but there is some debate regarding exactly what he meant by "Cato's policy." D. R. Shackleton Bailey identified the men named in this passage as the governors of Rome's eastern provinces, and so suggested that Cato's policy was "the policy of protecting the provincials from governmental rapine," and he thought that Cicero might have been thinking about Pompey's recent law imposing a five-year hiatus between holding office and a provincial command.[66] Albert Dragstedt suggested instead that Cato wanted to "transcend metropolitan centralism and to incorporate provincials into a Stoic cosmopolis."[67] Rudolf Fehrle, on the other hand, thought Cicero was referring to Cato's earlier governance of Cyprus, while

62. Cic. *Att.* 6.1.3–7.

63. Cic. *Att.* 6.1.7–8.

64. The MSS have the word *infirmant* (weaken) here, but given the context of the passage, Shackleton Bailey has suggested emending the word to *firmant* (strengthen), which seems correct.

65. Cic. *Att.* 6.1.13. Cicero uses the Greek word πολίτευμα ("policy").

66. Shackleton Bailey (1965–70) 3.246.

67. Dragstedt (1969) 94.

Catherine Steel suggested that the phrase referred to a broader concept of legal and moral government.[68] Most recently, Kit Morrell has examined Cicero's statement and has suggested that it refers "in particular to the policy of ethnical government associated with the *lex Pompeia*, the law which sent Cicero, Bibulus, Thermus, and the others to provinces in 51. . . ."[69] She suggests that Cato had been working systematically to change the way his fellow senators understood provincial administration, and that his ideas had swayed several important men, including Pompey, Bibulus, and Cicero. This idea is very difficult to document, but it is consistent with the rest of Cato's career as a member of the Senate: although he never reached the consulship, he was a persistent and compelling influence on his colleagues, and time after time he played a decisive role in pushing groups of senators into taking one position or another. Precisely what Cicero meant by "Cato's *politeuma*" may not be able to be recovered, but it is clear that Cato had succeeded in advancing certain ideas about how provincial command should be exercised, such that Cicero could use this phrase without confusion to his friend Atticus.

Cicero's letters from Cilicia also show his growing aggravation with Cato. On October 13 of 51 BC, Cicero and his lieutenant C. Pomptinus (pr. 63 BC) had led their army to a modest but significant military victory against hostile tribes in the Amanus mountain range that separated Cilicia from Syria, and the soldiers had acclaimed Cicero *imperator*.[70] Cicero hoped to receive the honor of a triumph for this victory, and to pave the way for this he wrote the Senate and requested a *supplicatio*—an official thanksgiving to the gods for his accomplishment. The quintessential politician, he also wrote several important senators seeking their support on the motion for the *supplicatio*, including Cato and the two incoming consuls of 50 BC.[71] The letters to the two consuls were fairly brief, but Cicero wrote to Cato at great length, recounting his actions in Cilicia leading up to the battle, and then narrating the battle itself in detail. Cicero clearly understood that Cato could be a powerful advocate or opponent, and that he would want a full understanding of the merits of Cicero's accomplishment before lending his support, especially since he had promulgated legislation to prevent unearned triumphs. So Cicero called upon Cato to support his request out of respect for

---

68. Fehrle (1983) 144–5, Steel (2001) 204–5.

69. Morrell ([2017] 237) examines in detail the activity of the governors Cicero mentions.

70. Cic. *Att.* 5.20.3, *Fam.* 15.10.1, Plut. *Cic.* 36.6.

71. Cic. *Fam.* 15.10.1–2 (to C. Marcellus), 15.13.1–3 (to L. Paullus), and 15.4.1–14 (to Cato). See Wistrand (1979) 10–22 for general discussion of these letters.

their mutual friendship, which was a powerful social obligation in Roman culture.[72] For these reasons, Cicero was surprised and angry to learn that Cato was one of only a handful of senators to speak in opposition to the *supplicatio*. The Senate as a whole supported Cicero and overwhelmingly approved the proposed thanksgiving, but Cato, his emulator Favonius, and a certain Hirrus (who held some serious grudge against Cicero) all spoke against it.[73] Caelius wrote to Cicero about the debate in the Senate, and he urged Cicero to see the opposition of these three men in a favorable light, because Cato limited himself to speaking against the *supplicatio* but did not obstruct the vote, while Hirrus and Favonius merely agreed with Cato and did not seek to prevent the passage of the proposal.[74] Cicero was hardly cheered to hear that Cato had offered only limited opposition to the proposed recognition of his accomplishments.

Cato wrote to Cicero in late April or early May explaining his opposition to the *supplicatio*, and because it is probably the only surviving document in Cato's own voice, it is worth presenting here in full:

> M. Cato sends greetings to M. Cicero *Imperator*.
>
> I freely rejoice—as the Republic and our friendship urge me to do—that your bravery, integrity, and attentiveness, which have already been recognized in your great deeds in the city, are applied with equal diligence to military affairs away from home. Therefore I have done what I was able to do in accordance with my judgment: in my speech and vote I praised that, thanks to your integrity and determination, the province was defended, the kingdom of Ariobarzanes and indeed the king himself were saved, and the goodwill of our allies was restored to its zeal for Roman rule.
>
> Regarding the decree for a *supplicatio*, I am delighted if you prefer that—rather than give you the credit—we thank the immortal gods for the favor given to the Republic, which did not at all happen by chance, but by your own excellent conduct and moderation.
>
> But if you are thinking that a *supplicatio* is a preliminary vote for a triumph, and for that reason you prefer that chance receive the credit rather

---

72. Wistrand ([1979] 17) points out: "a negative answer from Cato would amount to a violation of the laws of friendship."

73. Hirrus's grudge (*iratus*): Cic. *Att.* 7.1.7. See Ryan (1994a) and (1994b) 543 on the question of Favonius speaking in this meeting of the Senate. Wistrand ([1979] 41–9) gives an analysis of the Senate's discussion.

74. Cic. *Fam.* 8.11.2.

than yourself: a triumph does not always follow a *supplicatio*. Much more glorious than a triumph is for the Senate to judge that a province has been retained and preserved more by the gentleness and integrity of its commander than by the force of soldiers and the benevolence of the gods, which is the opinion I gave in my speech in the Senate.

Therefore, contrary to my customary practice, I have written this to you at great length, so that (as I greatly wish) you will appreciate that I am taking pains to persuade you that I wanted what I judged to be most honorable to your dignity, and I rejoice that what you had preferred has happened.

Farewell and hold me dear, and maintain in your chosen path your seriousness and diligence for our allies and the Republic.[75]

Although Cato expresses friendly feelings here, his letter is rather cold and impersonal, and lacks the warmth and personal connection that Cicero generally expresses in his own letters.[76] Cato and Cicero were on fairly good terms when this letter was written, so the aloof tone in Cato's letter is awkward, and leads one to suspect that he frequently spoke to his peers in such a brusque and moralizing manner. Furthermore, Cato's argument here is rather ridiculous: Cicero should be pleased that he argued against the *supplicatio*, because the denial of the thanksgiving would have meant Cicero—rather than the gods—received the credit for the military victory; that is, receiving no thanksgiving at all would have contributed more to Cicero's glory than a public ceremony thanking the gods for their role in bringing about Cicero's victory. This type of argumentation seems forced, as if Cato were using his own unconventional logic in an attempt to justify a bad action; he attempts to claim the moral high ground for denying Cicero the favor he had sought. To make matters worse, while congratulating Cicero on receiving the *supplicatio* from the Senate, Cato puts him on notice that triumphs do not necessarily follow *supplicationes*, a clear attempt to deflate Cicero in his moment of glory. His argument is once again awkward, suggesting that it was more glorious for governor to keep his province peaceful and quiet than to win a war. This was a considerable contortion of Roman tradition, which had always attributed its highest honors to military conquest.[77] Cato's opposition to the

---

75. Cic. *Fam.* 15.5.1–3.

76. Compare with Cicero's own letter to Cato (*Fam.* 15.4.1–16).

77. Stockton (1971) 238, "Cato's letter is a remarkable amalgam of pomposity, insensitivity, and downright rudeness, and its style awkward and insincere." *Contra*: Wistrand ([1979] 31–4) and Fehrle ([1983] 230), who interpret the letter as being friendly and complimentary toward Cicero.

supplicatio, his half-hearted praise, and his warning that a triumph would not be forthcoming were unnecessary insults to a friendly senior senator, and so they require a little more consideration.

Cato's refusal to support a *supplicatio* for Cicero's victory seems strange, since there was no obvious motive for opposing the measure. If there was something truly unacceptable or inappropriate about the proposal, why did Cato make so little effort to oppose it, especially since he was famous for opposing and obstructing votes on all kinds of public matters? If the matter of the *supplicatio* was of little importance, why bother to oppose it in the first place, when it would only exasperate or even antagonize Cicero and his supporters at a time when Cato was seeking support to isolate Caesar? Perhaps Cato was simply making a display of his own very conservative interpretation of the *mos maiorum*; he voted against Cicero's *supplicatio* because the victory in Cilicia did not meet his old-fashioned standards for the honor (and in fact, Cicero's victory was not particularly amazing).[78] On the other hand, he may have had an entirely different reason for trying to diminish Cicero's accomplishment: he may have been trying to build up the deeds of his son-in-law Bibulus, who held command of Syria at the same time that Cicero was in Cilicia. Cicero wrote to Atticus detailing Bibulus's inadequacies as a governor, and one can easily imagine that Bibulus similarly wrote letters to Cato disparaging Cicero's performance and minimizing his military accomplishment in Cilicia.[79] Indeed, in a letter to another friend, Cicero even alleges that Bibulus was claiming credit for several of Cicero's successes, and was hiding his own failings by blaming them on Cicero.[80] Thus Cato may have been deceived about the significance of Cicero's conquest, or he may have been properly informed but chose to assist in minimizing Cicero's accomplishment in order to enhance the fame and glory of his son-in-law Bibulus. Cato had previously been willing to bend his principles to serve his family, so he may have sought to diminish Cicero's victory in order to make Bibulus's performance in Syria appear better by comparison.[81] This became clear soon enough: while he had opposed a *supplicatio* for Cicero, Cato proposed and strongly advocated for a twenty-day *supplicatio* for Bibulus's reportedly minor victories in the East. The length of this *supplicatio* was enormous, no doubt to match the twenty-day *supplicatio* that had been given to Caesar in 55 BC. Cicero was outraged at this

---

78. See Afzelius (1941) 126–8 and Wistrand (1979) 31.

79. Cic. *Att.* 6.1.14–15, 6.5.3, 6.8.5.

80. Cic. *Fam.* 2.17.6–7.

81. Stockton (1971) 239, "when his own intimates were concerned [Cato] forgot the high-minded sentiments of his letter to Cicero, his contempt for empty honours."

and insisted that Bibulus had falsified the victories for which he requested the *supplicatio*, but with Cato's support the *supplicatio* was approved.[82] Cicero vented his anger to his friend Atticus:

> Cato has been shamefully horrible towards me. He gave me a testimonial that I did not seek for integrity, justice, moderation, and reliability, but he denied me the thing I actually requested. And so Caesar, in his letter congratulating me and promising me everything in whatever way, is in an uproar at Cato's terribly ungrateful injury towards me. But this very same Cato supports giving twenty days to Bibulus! Forgive me, but I cannot and will not bear these things.[83]

Cicero had endured Cato's opposition to his *supplicatio* with an even temper (no doubt because the thanksgiving had still been approved, despite Cato's objection), but he clearly saw hypocrisy and betrayal in Cato's subsequent advocacy for Bibulus. He also saw snobbery and pomposity in Cato's actions: "when Cato bestowed honors upon Bibulus, he declared that the only people he does not envy are those for whom little or nothing is able to be added to their prestige."[84] Cicero's bitterness may have been increased yet further by the recognition that Cato was breaking (or at least seriously bending) his own law regarding triumphs: as tribune in 62 BC he had promulgated a law establishing higher standards for the granting of triumphs (Caesar had been his target at the time), but now that his own son-in-law Bibulus was requesting a triumph for a mediocre or nonexistent victory, Cato ignored his own law and advocated loudly that the minor accomplishment should receive Rome's highest honor. Although such reversals were surely common when Roman senators defended the interests of their family and friends, Cicero thought it unworthy of Cato's self-fashioned reputation for high morality and adherence to traditional values. There was no philosophic principle here; only traditional Roman prioritization of the family.

Despite his anger, Cicero's reply to Cato was statesmanlike and skillful. He opened by taking the philosophical high ground, and asserted that the praise and good opinion of a noble man like Cato were more valuable to him than any triumph: "Indeed I consider that there is nothing that I have not attained

---

82. Cic. *Att.* 7.2.6–7.

83. Cic. *Att.* 7.2.7. Taylor ([1949] 169) points out that Cato betrayed his own moral arguments here, saying that he "proved that he was not the figure of perfection his admirers made him out to be."

84. Cic. *Att.* 7.3.5.

from the congratulations in your letter or from the testimony of your speech before the Senate, and it was most wonderful and gratifying to me that you freely rendered to friendship what you would have plainly rendered to the truth."[85] At the same time, Cicero pointed out that there was only one Cato in Rome, and that the rest of the Roman people did not follow the same high-minded principles: "And if not all, but only many in our state were Catos—it is amazing that one has appeared!—what triumphal chariot or laurel should I compare with your commendation?" Sidestepping the warning that a triumph was not guaranteed, and the implication that a wise man should serve the state without seeking glory, Cicero responded that—while he did not covet the honor of a triumph—he would not spurn it if offered by the Senate.[86] He closed with his hope that Cato would be true to his word: Cato had said he respected him and was glad that Cicero had received what he wanted (the *supplicatio*), and so Cicero asked him to continue holding this same favorable view should the Senate decide to give him a triumph for his Cilician victory.[87] Cicero no longer seemed concerned about the vote on the *supplicatio* or Cato's attempt to justify his action, but was eager to commit him to his own fine words of praise. Despite Cicero's careful response, one can sense his frustration in dealing with Cato.

Cato did one other thing in 50 BC that surprised and intrigued much of Rome's aristocracy. Hortensius, the great orator and senior statesman, died at the end of the summer, and there was great curiosity about how his will would dispose of his extensive property.[88] This was intriguing not only because Hortensius was very rich, but also because he was still married to Marcia, whom Cato had famously (or infamously) divorced and handed over to Hortensius. Hortensius left all of his property to Marcia in his will, and shortly thereafter the newly rich widow returned to Cato's house. Plutarch indicates that he remarried Marcia, whereas Lucan suggests that he took her into his home without a formal remarriage.[89] Appian does not indicate whether or not Cato remarried her, but said that the entire event gave the appearance that he had merely lent Marcia to Hortensius.[90] His original decision to give Marcia to Hortensius had appeared strange and

85. Cic. *Fam.* 15.6.1. See Wistrand (1979) 35–40 for discussion of Cicero's reply.

86. Cic. *Fam.* 15.6.2.

87. On this, see Steel (2013) 212–13.

88. Cicero (*Att.* 6.6.2) mentions that Hortensius was dying at the start of August, and by November (*Att.* 7.2.7) he was asking Atticus about the contents of Hortensius's will.

89. Plut. *Cat. Min.* 52.3–4, Luc. 2.326–91.

90. App. *BC* 2.99.

perhaps inappropriate to the Romans, but his decision to take her back again—
along with Hortensius's estate—seemed almost conspiratorial. Several years
later, Caesar would scold Cato for this behavior and for trafficking in marriages,
writing: "What man who wanted his wife would hand her over, and what man
who had not wanted his wife would take her straight back again, if it was not the
case that the woman was prepared as bait for Hortensius from the beginning,
and Cato gave him use of the woman while young, in order that he might take
her back again when she was rich."[91] It seems undeniable that Cato acquired great
wealth by lending his wife to Hortensius, but Plutarch denies that he could have
been swayed by love of money, and suggests instead that he took Marcia back to
care for his house and children, because he was soon to leave Rome on account
of the coming civil war.[92] This may well be accurate. Although Cato was certainly
pleased to acquire such wealth, his financial situation was already comfortable
thanks to several inheritances he had received, and he needed someone to look
after his children during the rapidly approaching war, and Marcia was the best
choice.[93] So while Plutarch has no doubt overstated Cato's apathy to wealth in
order to make him appear more Stoic, there is no reason to assume that he took
Marcia back solely to gain Hortensius's wealth.

Throughout the autumn Cato's circle was very active in advocating that the
Senate throw its full weight into supporting Pompey against Caesar. Although
many of Cato's allies were eager for war, and wanted to confront and destroy
Caesar on the battlefield, Cato probably expected that he would back down
when confronted forcefully by Pompey and the Senate. As later events would
show, Cato detested the idea of civil war—even to destroy Caesar—and so his
efforts were primarily focused on building a powerful coalition that could overwhelm Caesar and force him to admit defeat without actually resorting to war.
To this end, he and his closest supporters took a very hard line against granting
Caesar any further concessions or privileges, and they argued that confrontation was inevitable and that every senator needed to pick a side.[94] They may even
have employed false rumors to push senators into action. As early as October,
Cicero mentions ominous reports of Caesar repositioning his legions, and while

---

91. Plut. *Cat. Min.* 52.4.

92. Plut. *Cat. Min.* 52.5.

93. In addition to the inheritance he received from his father, Cato received an inheritance from
Lucullus (Macrob. 3.15.6), another worth 100 talents from a cousin (probably the M. Cato, son
of the consul of 118 BC, who died at Narbo) (Plut. *Cat. Min.* 6.4), and a third from his half-
brother Caepio (Plut. *Cat. Min.* 11.4). See Shatzman (1975) 393–4.

94. Cic. *Att.* 7.6.2, 7.9.3.

these rumors turned out to be baseless, they agitated senators and common cit-izens alike, and fed Cato's propaganda that Caesar was seeking a tyranny.[95] The source of this particular rumor is unknown, but less than two months later Cato's friends were openly spreading false rumors to frighten the people into supporting their push for war (see later discussion), so it is possible that misinforming the people about Caesar's activities was part of their strategy to push their senatorial colleagues to oppose him.

The November 13 date that Pompey had suggested as a deadline for Caesar to lay down his provinces came and went, but Caesar still held his command. On December 1 the consul C. Marcellus once again asked the Senate what it wanted done with the Gallic provinces. Curio continued to advocate for his pro-posal that Caesar and Pompey should both lay down their commands, believing that most senators did not hold the hard-line position that Caesar had to be backed forcefully into a corner, but were eager for peace and were willing to treat Caesar more gently. The small number of senators who were fiercely opposed to Caesar, however, would not accept Curio's proposal, because it would remove their strongest threat against Caesar (Pompey's army), and they probably did not believe—or want to believe—that Caesar would return to Rome peacefully. Marcellus therefore adopted a new tactic and divided Curio's proposal into two parts: he first asked the senators whether Caesar should lay down his forces (the majority approved), and then he asked them whether Pompey should lay down his army (the majority disapproved).[96] Curio erred seriously in not vetoing these proposals, and he may have been duped into allowing the division of the bill.[97] It was a critical error, because it gave Marcellus and the *optimates* what they had long wanted: a clear senatorial opinion that Caesar alone should lay down his command. Where did this consensus come from? On one level, it reflects the fact that Caesar's command was, and always had been, the point of contention; his legitimate period of command was coming to an end, and it was appropriate for him to return to Rome and allow his provinces to be assigned to others. Pompey's command was not truly a problem, because he had obtained an extension of authority in 52 BC that Caesar had not received, and so it was not appropriate to ask him to resign his command. Curio's motion had presented the political problem as tension between the two great men, and many in the Senate prob-ably thought that Pompey should lay down his command early simply to satisfy Caesar and avoid civil war. By dividing the question, however, Marcellus asked

---

95. Cic. *Att.* 6.8.2, 6.9.5.

96. Plut. *Caes.* 30.4–6, *Pomp.* 58.4–5, App. *BC* 2.30.

97. Botermann (1989) 74.

the senators to weigh Pompey's command solely on its own merits, and they had trouble justifying why he should be removed from command early. Added to this, the rumors of Caesar's intention to march on Rome no doubt terrified senators and planted the idea that civil war was already inevitable, in which case most preferred to side with Pompey. So many of the senators who supported Curio's proposal instructing both Caesar and Pompey to resign their commands were unwilling to vote for the second of Marcellus's proposals, that Pompey should lay down his command. Given the choice, they preferred that Caesar alone step down, but to keep the peace they were willing to demand that both men resign.

Curio quickly realized his mistake. Before Marcellus and his supporters could use the divided vote to their advantage, he called for a vote on his motion that both commanders should resign their commands, and the senators voted overwhelmingly in favor of the proposal: 370 senators approved, and only 22 senators disapproved.[98] This seems like a dramatic change, and Curio may have threatened the Senate with civil war if they tried to deprive Caesar of his command while allowing Pompey to keep his army and provinces.[99] If so, he capitalized on the Senate's traditional willingness to compromise with its most powerful members, as well as on their fear about Caesar's intentions. At the same time, there had always been considerable support for Curio's motion, because most senators (and common citizens) simply wanted to avoid civil war, and disarming both great men surely seemed a sensible way to accomplish this. These votes reveal three opinions held by the majority of senators: (1) Caesar needed to lay down his command; (2) Pompey did not need to lay down his command; but (3) Pompey *should* lay down his command in order to ensure peace and avoid civil war. This was a powerful and clear statement that the vast majority of senators did not think direct confrontation was the best strategy for dealing with Caesar, and that compromise should be sought. A small number of *optimates* were opposed to compromise, but the Senate as a whole was not.

Was Cato one of the twenty-two senators who voted against the disarmament of both men? No source records how he voted, but given his tremendous and relentless efforts to destroy Caesar over the years, one must assume that he voted against the proposal. On the other hand, Helga Botermann has suggested that Seneca's letters show that Cato actually supported Curio's motion, voting that

---

98. Caes. *BG* 8.52, Plut. *Caes.* 30.4–6, *Pomp.* 58.4–5, App. *BC* 2.30. Syme ([1939] 22) pointed out that the twenty-two senators who opposed Curio's motion were not a unified faction or gang, but a group of like-minded senators.

99. Botermann (1989) 74–5.

Caesar and Pompey should both disarm.[100] The strongest evidence is Seneca's statement:

> Finally, during that crisis of the Republic, when Caesar was on one side supported by ten extremely warlike legions and by so many contingents of foreign peoples, and when Pompey was on the other side, prepared to go alone against everything, and when some people were leaning towards Caesar and still others towards Pompey, Cato alone made another group, a party for the Republic. If you were willing to grasp in your mind an image of that time, you would see on one side the plebs and the whole multitude of the people excited for revolution, while on the other side were the *optimates* and the equestrian order, whoever was conscientious and excellent in the state. In the middle only two were left: the Republic and Cato.... Indeed he condemns both sides, and he disarms them both. He delivers this opinion to both, saying: "if Caesar prevails, I will die, and if Pompey, I will live in exile."[101]

This evidence is certainly problematic. Not only was Seneca living in an era when Cato's reputation had been transformed and recast as a great Stoic philosopher, but also the event as Seneca describes it is patently wrong in several ways.[102] The Republic was not divided between the elites and the proletariat, since Caesar and Pompey each had their share of supporters from both groups. More to the point, the image of Cato standing in the middle of a divided Republic is quite wrong; Cato either voted with the vast majority of senators who wanted both Caesar and Pompey to disarm, or else he voted with the small minority who pushed for war. So Seneca's description seems more revisionist fiction than fact. On balance, Cato must have been among the small minority voting against Curio's proposal, but his purpose was to pile pressure on Caesar. As later events would show, Cato was horrified by the civil war and lamented the carnage it caused, so it is difficult to believe that he intended or wanted the war that ultimately broke out. Rather, Cato's goal was certainly to bring a majority of the Senate into a consensus against Caesar, hoping that this would pressure him to lay down his command and return to Rome. This was the purpose of Marcellus's tactic of dividing Curio's proposal into two questions, which did indeed generate at least the appearance of a decisive

---

100. Botermann (1989) 62–85.

101. Sen. *Ep.* 104.30–32.

102. Botermann ([1989] 80) notes that is it very difficult to distinguish the real Cato from the mythic Cato. Regarding the recasting of Cato's memory, see later discussion.

senatorial consensus that Caesar should disarm while Pompey kept his command. Cato no doubt expected that Caesar would back down when confronted by this unified vote by the Senate. Curio's quick action in bringing about the 370-to-22 vote spoiled the opportunity, but Cato may not have known what some of his fellow *optimates* would do next.

Despite the overwhelming vote and the clear assertion of the Senate's will, the twenty-two hard-liners would not permit the vote to stand. The consul Marcellus immediately dismissed the Senate before this vote could be ratified and formalized as a *senatus consultum*, and in this way the minority was able to scuttle the vote of the majority.[103] In spite of the consul's action, Curio stepped outside the Curia and announced the result of the vote to those citizens who were assembled to hear the news, and they rejoiced to hear that the Senate had overwhelmingly supported a compromise that would avert civil war. Meanwhile, Marcellus was incensed at what he perceived to be the fear and weakness of the senators, and told them that he would take all necessary steps to protect the Republic even if they would not.[104] Leaving the Senate without further discussion, he is said to have falsely reported to the people that Caesar was marching on Rome with his army, and using this lie as a pretense he and his supporters hastened to Pompey and—placing a sword in his hand—they asked him to take command of all forces in Italy to defend Rome from Caesar.[105] The legality of this request is questionable; although Pompey was a legitimate military commander with *imperium*, it was the prerogative of the Senate or the people—but not the consuls—to assign military commands.[106] The evidence is clear that Marcellus took this step on his own and without consultation with the Senate, so his action was definitely improper and possibly illegal.[107] Curio recognized this and demanded that the consuls issue a decree that citizens need not obey calls for conscription issued by Pompey, but they refused.[108] Pompey accepted the task with a show of reluctance, and shortly afterward he left Rome to take command

---

103. Caes. *BG* 8.52, App. *BC* 2.30. See Fehrle (1983) 236–7.

104. Botermann ([1989] 62–85) argues that this happened at the next meeting of the Senate, and that the sources have conflated two Senate meetings into one. Pelling ([2011] 306) also gives a full discussion of variations in the sources.

105. Caes. *BG* 8.55, Plut. *Pomp.* 58.6–59.2, App. *BC* 2.31, Dio 40.64.4 and 40.66.1.

106. On this question, see Raaflaub (1974a) 33–55.

107. Botermann ([1989] 70, 76–7) gives a full discussion of the evidence showing that Marcellus acted on his own authority.

108. App. *BC* 2.123.

of the two legions sent from Caesar's army, which were stationed at Capua.[109] Of course, Caesar had not yet made a move to invade Italy, and was still waiting for word about his proposals and for an update on the political situation. Curio soon left Rome and brought Caesar a report in person, announcing that the hard-liners had ignored the will of the Senate and people, and that a handful of senators had effectively declared Rome to be at war with Caesar.[110]

Marcellus had several motives for calling on Pompey to defend the state in direct opposition to the apparent will of the Senate.[111] First, Marcellus and his supporters needed to force Pompey to break openly with Caesar and publicly announce his support for the Senate and its optimate leadership. Until that point, Pompey had been evasive about where his true loyalties lay, no doubt because he had hoped to maintain his alliance with Caesar while simultaneously building new alliances with the *optimates*. Since the *optimates* could not hope to challenge Caesar without Pompey's military resources, it was essential to coerce Pompey into severing his alliance with Caesar once and for all, and this was deftly arranged by the Senate's full embrace of Pompey as their leader—a voluntary approbation and recognition from Rome's most esteemed men, which Pompey had long desired.[112] Second, this effort to rally the Senate behind Pompey was no doubt intended to break the neutrality of those senators who had thus far avoided choosing a side. By (independently) declaring that Caesar was an enemy of the state, Marcellus and his supporters created a "with us or against us" atmosphere in which it would have been difficult for others not to declare for Pompey and the *optimates*. Third, by forcing Pompey and the Senate to come together in preparation for war, the *optimates* no doubt hoped to frighten Caesar into compliance.[113] Although they were intent on destroying Caesar politically, many—especially Cato—probably did not expect that Caesar would actually fight if confronted with united opposition. To this end, the anti-Caesarians were working very hard to create a senatorial consensus (or at least the appearance of consensus) in order to increase pressure on Caesar.

---

109. Plut. *Pomp.* 59.1–2, App. *BC* 2.31, Dio 40.66.1–3.

110. App. *BC* 2.31. Gelzer (1968) 187, "the situation had become very serious through the arbitrary action of the consul and his followers."

111. Raaflaub ([1974a] 40–5 and 78) examines Marcellus's motives in detail.

112. Raaflaub (1974a) 40–44.

113. Raaflaub (1974a) 55 emphasizes Appian's statement (*BC* 2.31) that Pompey accepted the commission "unless a better way could be found," which Raaflaub takes to indicate that Pompey was looking to put pressure on Caesar.

As events would soon prove, Cato did not want a civil war, but his personal feud with Caesar over the past fifteen years had convinced many of his supporters that Caesar needed to be destroyed at all costs, even if it meant fighting a civil war. Cato did not feel the same, but his sustained efforts to brand Caesar as a tyrant had taken root in many *optimates* who did not share his abhorrence of civil war, especially in the up-and-coming senators who saw Caesar as a threat to their own ambitions. Cato and those around him had steadily increased their rhetoric and adopted more aggressive measures to marginalize Caesar and to push the senators to oppose him. Although biased, Caesar (and his lieutenant Aulus Hirtius) saw these efforts by Cato and his allies clearly: he describes them as working to put forward "the greatest necessities by which the Senate could be forced to approve what they had already decided," and portrays them as trying to bully the Senate into supporting their strategy of intractable opposition to him: "the weaker were terrified, the hesitant were encouraged, and the ability to consider the matter freely was ripped away entirely from the majority."[114] By forcing a conflict that pitted Pompey and the *optimates* against Caesar, the hard-liners sought to eliminate the middle path and force all senators to choose a side. This was a daring and risky tactic, but the leading *optimates* at this time were relatively inexperienced and had not participated in the events leading up to the bloody civil war between Marius and Sulla a generation earlier, so they tended to be more aggressive in their handling of powerful commanders.[115] Whereas the previous generation of *optimates* such as Catulus, Hortensius, and Metellus Pius knew the horrors of civil war directly, and so had tread more carefully around the ambitions of Pompey and Crassus, the cohort of *optimates* in 50 BC were more eager to push for confrontation as a political strategy. Indeed, they were following the very same aggressive style of politics that Cato had championed and modeled throughout his career. By forcing a fight between Pompey (lionized as the defender of the Republic and freedom) and Caesar (branded as a tyrant), they expected that most senators would assess the situation and calculate that their interests lay in supporting Pompey and the *optimates*. Cato hoped that Caesar would fold under the pressure of a united Senate, but many of his allies were eager to bring about a war and to crush Caesar on the battlefield. While Cato had been instrumental in organizing and building the anti-Caesar movement, therefore, his allies would

---

114. Caes. *BG* 8.53, *BC* 1.3.

115. Gruen ([1974] 57) points out that they "were too young to have engaged in a meaningful way in the civil wars of the 80s or to have felt the insecurities of men in power during the decade after Sulla's death. They inherited a going concern; they could afford the luxury of a more flexible attitude and a more aggressive politics."

take control of their coalition and would expand their goals to include war with Caesar.

Returning to Italy from Cilicia, Cicero reports discussions with numerous senators and equestrians who disapproved of the push toward war, and Pompey himself admitted to Cicero that Marcellus's instructions to mobilize military forces were far more likely to trigger a war than to force Caesar to stand down.[116] Although Pompey had previously hoped for a peaceful arrangement in which he could keep Caesar as a useful (but weaker) political ally, he had come to realize that Marcellus's move had made war inevitable, and that Caesar would not submit to compulsion and give up his provinces and legions upon demand.[117] On December 6, Caesar's envoy Hirtius had come to Rome to discuss the situation with Pompey and Scipio, but left without seeing either man, which Pompey took as a sign that reconciliation was impossible.[118] Cicero's letters reveal that very few senators were truly desirous of war, and that most preferred giving Caesar the concessions he desired, but the anti-Caesarian minority was steadily pushing the state to war. On December 9, Cicero wrote that he intended to urge Pompey to make peace with Caesar, noting that "Caesar's side lacks only a cause, but overflows with all other resources. Here people are choosing all other courses of action except war, the results of which are always uncertain, and even now the worst result is most feared."[119] An ominous sign occurred on December 10: Curio fled north to Caesar when his term as tribune expired, indicating that he did not feel safe remaining in Rome as a private citizen.[120] Around December 13 Cicero wrote that Pompey had been convinced that war was coming, although Cicero himself did not believe that Caesar would cause a disturbance if given the second consulship he desired—he still saw room for compromise.[121] A few days later he said that even the best men (the *boni*) were split, and many were critical of Pompey, and around December 18 he wrote that "thus far I have found scarcely anyone who does not agree that giving Caesar what he demands is better than fighting. The demand itself is certainly shameless, but it is better than expected."[122] And on

---

116. Cic. *Att.* 7.5.4, 7.8.4.

117. Cicero would try to change Pompey's mind, but to no avail: Cic. *Att.* 7.3.4–5, *Marc.* 14, *Phil.* 2.24. Raaflaub ([1974a] 52–3) demonstrates that Pompey was not necessarily eager for this war.

118. Cic. *Att.* 7.4.2–3.

119. Cic. *Att.* 7.3.5.

120. App. *BC* 2.31, Dio 40.66.5.

121. Cic. *Att.* 7.4.3.

122. Cic. *Att.* 7.5.4 and 7.6.2 (quoted).

December 19 he argued against war because it would bring no advantage, even if the *optimates* won.[123] On the other hand, Cicero met with Pompey on December 25 at Formiae and discussed the political situation for hours, and in that conversation Cicero could not find even the desire for peace.[124] Clearly, a core of anti-Caesarian senators had Pompey's ear. Pompey was opposed to allowing Caesar a second consulship, and he assumed that Caesar would abandon that goal and focus on keeping his provinces and legions once he learned of the forces Pompey was preparing for war. Despite this conversation, however, Cicero continued to believe that Caesar would lay down his army if allowed to stand for the consulship on his terms, although he admitted that "as some people think, nothing is more fearful to us than Caesar becoming consul."[125] The phrase "some people" (*quidam*) seems pointed, and reveals Cicero's dread that things had moved beyond the Senate's ability to control, and that it was only this small group that was preventing the possibility of peace. Cicero recognized that war could be avoided, and that Caesar would lay down his army and enter peacefully upon the consulship if allowed to do so by his political opponents, but he recognized that Pompey and the hard-liners would not permit this peaceful solution to happen. Indeed, they thought Cicero was timid and weak.[126]

Pompey, Cato, and their anti-Caesarian allies refused to contemplate any concession to Caesar, but this does not seem to have been the opinion of the majority in the Senate. As the preceding letters from Cicero make clear, most senators were willing to compromise with Caesar, and many thought his demands were not particularly burdensome. Despite the inflexible position being pushed by Cato and other hard-liners, the Roman Senate was long accustomed to making concessions to great commanders, so Caesar's requests—although perhaps irksome—were not out of line with conventional practice.[127] Indeed, many probably thought that Caesar was only asking for the same types of privileges that had already been granted to Pompey. This neatly points to the hypocrisy of Pompey's position: in

---

123. Cic. *Att.* 7.7.7.

124. Cic. *Att.* 7.8.4–5.

125. Cic. *Att.* 7.9.3.

126. Cic. *Fam.* 6.6.5.

127. Shackleton Bailey ([1965] 3.302) made this point in his commentary on Cicero's letter from December 18: "the public opinion which C[icero] describes as favouring concession may have thought Caesar's claims not more but less exorbitant than might have been anticipated. Alarmist reports of his intentions had been current in Rome in the latter half of the year. . . . Evidently it was widely expected that he might return to Rome after the fashion of Marius and Sulla. But now lovers of peace could tell themselves that Caesar was only asking what might easily have been granted to Pompey in 52."

his lifetime, he had—with an army at his back—made tremendous demands of the Senate, and his entire career had been built on extraordinary commands.[128] The Senate had granted all of those concessions, choosing to compromise rather than fight the ambitions of a capable general. Caesar was asking for less, and he was trying very hard to give his requests the appearance of legitimacy through the "law of the ten tribunes." Cicero is surely right, therefore, that the vast majority in the Senate were willing to give Caesar what he wanted, but they were prevented from doing so by the hard-liners, who had adopted Cato's stance of preventing compromise and pushing for aggressive steps to strike at Caesar. To this end, the circulation of false rumors that Caesar was already marching on Rome was no doubt intended to frighten the senators, to convince them that compromise was no longer possible, and to drive them to huddle together for safety behind the anti-Caesarian consuls. Cato had used similar tactics back in the Catilinarian debate, and knew that the senators were unlikely to take an aggressive stance unless forced by fear for their own interests.

As a result of their tactics, Pompey and the hard-liners had a strong grip on the Senate as 49 BC began. Caesar had succeeded in getting two of his men elected to the tribunate (M. Antony and Q. Cassius), and they were aggressively opposing the actions of the hard-liners and painting Pompey as the real threat to the survival of the Republic, but the *optimates*—with Pompey's support—had secured the election of C. Claudius Marcellus (the brother of M. Marcellus, the consul of 51 BC) and L. Cornelius Lentulus Crus, both of whom were fierce critics of Caesar.[129] These consuls had no interest in negotiating with Caesar; as consuls-elect they had supported authorizing Pompey to begin mobilizing troops, and once they entered office they were hostile to Caesar's tribunes. In the Senate meeting on January 1, they did their best to prevent Antony and Cassius from reading aloud a letter from Caesar, and when the tribunes used the sacrosanctity of their office to ignore this obstruction and read it anyway, the consuls refused to permit any discussion of the letter by the senators.[130] It is not clear why discussion

---

128. In 77 BC, Pompey had encamped his army outside of Rome to pressure the Senate into giving him a proconsular command in Spain (Plut. *Pomp* 17.3–4), and in 71 BC he again used his army as leverage to win a consulship despite being ineligible (Plut. *Pomp.* 21.3–5, App. *BC* 1.121, 3.88). He was a private citizen when he arranged to receive his piracy command through the *lex Gabinia* in 67 BC, and he used the tribunician *lex Manilia* to take over Lucullus's eastern command in 66 BC (*MRR* 2.144–5 and 153).

129. Caes. *BG* 8.50. This C. Claudius Marcellus is a different person from the homonymous consul of the previous year.

130. Caes. *BC* 1.1, Plut. *Caes.* 30.3, *Ant.* 5.3–4, Dio 41.1.1–3. See Seager (2002) 148 and Pelling (2011) 306–8 for discussion.

was prohibited; Cicero says the letter was sufficiently threatening that it gave offense to some, but it must have contained further offers for peace that the consuls
did not want deliberated in the Senate House, such as a reiteration of Curio's
proposal.[131] On the other hand, Plutarch says that Caesar's letter "changed the
thinking of many men, who thought from what he wrote that he was expecting
just and moderate things," and Dio says the letter summarized all the benefits
Caesar had performed for the state and rebutted all the charges that had been
brought against him.[132] This suggests that the consuls prevented discussion because they feared that an open debate would undercut their efforts and increase
support for a compromise with Caesar. The consuls raised the question of what
should be done with Caesar's command, and there seems to have been considerable hesitation to take any step that might antagonize him. This widespread desire
to de-escalate the growing tensions was expressed well by the senator M. Calidius,
who suggested that Pompey should leave Italy and go to his Spanish command,
thereby relieving Caesar of the fear that Pompey would use force against him.[133]
Several years later in 46 BC, Cicero would write that he also urged Pompey to
leave for Spain in order to remove the threat of war.[134] This suggestion implies his
confidence that Caesar would not have resorted violence except in self-defense.
Yet the consuls and their supporters would not allow a discussion of Calidius's
motion, and they put the senators under great pressure to adopt an aggressive
posture, going so far as to threaten that Pompey would abandon them entirely
if they refused to stand up to Caesar now (a threat that only had teeth if the
senators were already convinced that Caesar was a greater threat to them).[135] Thus
coerced, the Senate approved a measure promulgated by Metellus Scipio, that
Caesar should be instructed to lay down his provinces and legions and return to
Rome by a particular date, or else should be proclaimed a public enemy.[136] The
date was probably the day by which candidates for the consulship of 48 BC had
to make their *professio* in Rome.[137] Since the *professio* generally had to be made at
least three weeks before the July elections, this would mean that Caesar was being

---

131. Cic. *Fam.* 16.11.2.

132. Plut. *Ant.* 5.3 (cf. *Caes.* 31.1 and *Pomp.* 58.3) and Dio 41.1.3–4.

133. Caes. *BC* 1.2.

134. Cic. *Fam.* 6.6.5. In July of 51 BC Cicero had been against Pompey leaving Italy for Spain
(*Att.* 5.11.3).

135. Caes. *BC* 1.1–2.

136. Caes. *BC* 1.2, Plut. *Caes.* 30.4–5.

137. Raaflaub (1974a) 56 n. 219.

instructed to return to Rome in less than six months without his legions. Caesar's tribunes (Antony and Cassius) immediately vetoed this measure, blocking the effort.[138] Several of Caesar's enemies seem to have spent time in the Senate debating what to do with the tribunician veto, but nothing was decided by the time the meeting ended for the day.

To keep the pressure on the senators, Pompey summoned them that night to meet with him outside of the city, since he could not cross the *pomerium* and enter the city without forfeiting his *imperium*. He praised those who supported him and castigated those who were reluctant, and tried to encourage them all by pointing out his military preparedness. Caesar wrote that this private meeting was used to browbeat and even terrify wavering or uncertain senators, which sounds like exaggeration and yet fits the tactics some of the hard-liners were using.[139] Despite this show of confidence, the censor L. Calpurnius Piso (Caesar's father-in-law, the consul of 58 BC) and the praetor L. Roscius requested that any decision be delayed six days so they could travel to Caesar and see if some arrangement might be reached, and other senators supported the proposal that envoys should be sent to discuss the matter with Caesar.[140] Those making and supporting this proposal were shouted down by the consul Lentulus, by Metellus Scipio, and by Cato. According to Caesar, Lentulus and Metellus Scipio were motivated by the hope that they would profit from a war, but Cato was motivated by his old feud with Caesar and by his anger at having lost his bid for the consulship.[141] This description attributes highly improper motives to Lentulus and Scipio, but the explanation of Cato's opposition was less critical, since personal feuds had long been an accepted part of Roman politics. Yet Cato's appearance here demonstrates his constant presence in the opposition to Caesar—he did not hold consular rank as did Lentulus and Scipio, but he is found in the middle of a heated senatorial debate, shouting down those seeking to lessen the pressure on Caesar. Episodes such as this reveal how Cato worked to stiffen the resolve of those opposing Caesar, to suppress the activities of those seeking to accommodate him, and in particular to make sure Pompey did not try to come to an individual

---

138. Caes. *BC* 1.2, Dio 41.3.1.

139. Caes. *BC* 1.3.

140. Caes. *BC* 1.3. Piso had entered the censorship the previous year, but it was an eighteen-month term in office. See von Fritz (1941) 125–56 and Shackleton Bailey (1960) 80–3.

141. Caes. *BC* 1.4 (*Catonem veteres inimicitiae Caesaris incitant et dolor repulsae*). Seneca (*Ep.* 71.11) believed that Cato did not feel shame or rejection at his electoral loss, but Seneca also attributed to Cato the *apatheia* of a Stoic sage that he probably did not merit (see later discussion). Yates ([2011] 161–74) discusses this passage in detail.

understanding with his former co-triumvir.[142] In this case, his forceful intervention may have been necessary because Cicero returned to Rome on January 4,
and was trying very hard to convince Pompey (and others) to de-escalate tensions
and find a peaceful solution.[143] Cato may not have wanted war, but he pushed
Pompey to maintain an uncompromising and unyielding stance in the hope that
Caesar could be forced to back down. Cato was certainly not alone in driving
Pompey to reject Cicero's efforts to find peace through compromise, but few
voices could have been as authoritative, influential, and forceful.

The messengers who had brought Caesar's letter to the January 1 meeting
of the Senate appeared again at its next meeting (probably sometime between
January 4 and 7) with a different offer.[144] They now proposed that Caesar lay
down Transalpine Gaul and all but two of his legions, and when Pompey and
his supporters received this coldly, Caesar's agents suggested that he retain only
one legion.[145] This satisfied previous demands that Caesar give up command of
Transalpine Gaul (where all of his campaigning took place), and yet kept him
safe from physical and legal attacks until he could step into the consulship.[146]
Cicero actively advocated for Caesar's offer, but found that his efforts to prevent
civil war were blocked at every turn, and he complained that "I long to remedy
the situation and I believe I am able to do so, but the objectives of certain men
have become an obstacle for me, since there are those on both sides who are eager
to fight."[147] Other sources suggest the identity of these obstacles, explaining
that Pompey was inclined to accept Caesar's proposal, but Cato and Lentulus
attacked him for this and scolded him for blundering and allowing himself to
be deceived, and so the offer was rejected.[148] The treatment of this proposal is
revealing. Pompey was probably inclined to accept the deal because it gave him
military superiority over Caesar, and this latest proposal could be presented as

---

142. Caes. *BC* 1.4, Vell. 2.49.3, Plut. *Pomp.* 59.4, *Cat. Min.* 51.5. See Pelling (2011) 311.

143. Cic. *Fam.* 6.6.5, 6.21.1, 16.12.2, Plut. *Caes.* 31.1–2 and *Pomp.* 59.3.

144. Raaflaub ([1974a] 66–8) believes that this meeting took place between January 4 and 7,
and that Caesar's messengers had been empowered to bring forth the second proposal if the
first was rebuffed (which it was).

145. Vell. 2.49.4, Suet. *Iul.* 29.2, Plut. *Caes.* 31.1–2, *Pomp.* 59.3–4, App. *BC* 2.32.

146. Pelling ([2011] 369) gives a discussion and references of how serious the threat of prosecution was for Caesar.

147. Cic. *Fam.* 16.11.2 (cf. Cic. *Fam.* 16.12.2).

148. Plut. *Caes.* 31.2, *Pomp.* 59.4, App. *BC* 2.32. Pompey initially did not support the proposal,
but was won over when Caesar offered to keep only one legion. See Gelzer (1968) 191–2 and
Raaflaub (1974a) 66–7.

a concession that proved Pompey's superiority and preeminence. It would have been a small victory, but it probably would have satisfied Pompey and would have enabled him to save face without resorting to war. Cato and Lentulus, on the other hand, rejected the proposal because it would allow Caesar to escape prosecution in the courts by stepping from his proconsulship to a second consulship. If Caesar's own assessment (noted in the preceding) is correct, Lentulus and Cato may have wished to see Caesar destroyed in different ways (Lentulus wanted to crush him on the battlefield, Cato in the law courts), but both were determined to block any concession or negotiation that prevented Caesar's ruin. While Cato was no longer Caesar's most obvious and visible opponent, therefore, he was certainly still a key influence on political decisions, pushing his old policy of no concessions, no negotiations.

On January 7 another meeting of the Senate was held, and the senators had been sufficiently inspired, frightened, and/or browbeaten by the hard-liners that a majority were willing to pass a *senatus consultum ultimum* authorizing the consuls, the praetors, the tribunes, and the proconsuls near to city to take necessary steps to defend the state.[149] Whereas the earlier charge given to Pompey by the consuls to defend the state against Caesar had not been a law or *senatus consultum*, this *senatus consultum ultimum* conferred the Senate's approval on the action. Why the Senate was now willing to take this decisive step against Caesar when it had previously avoided such provocative action is not certain, but the propaganda of Cato and his allies—now including Pompey—seems to have persuaded many that Caesar had already begun an invasion of Italy or would do so imminently. In the previous year the consul C. Marcellus is said to have justified ignoring the Senate and calling on Pompey by falsely claiming that Caesar was invading Italy, and many such rumors continued to spread, certainly aided by those seeking to turn public sentiment against Caesar.[150] Despite the fear inspired by those false reports, the majority of senators had been very reluctant to support the *senatus consultum ultimum*, no doubt because they did not want war with Caesar.[151] Many probably hoped that passing the *senatus consultum ultimum* would be the final move that would break Caesar's resolve and force him to heed the instructions of the Senate. Based on his later reaction to the outbreak of the war, Cato was among those who believed that issuing the Senate's final

---

149. Caes. *BC* 1.5, Cic. *Phil.* 2.51, Livy *Per.* 109. Dio (41.3.2–3) says the tribunes were driven out of the city before the passage of the decree.

150. Cic. *Att.* 6.8.2, 6.9.5, 7.1.1, App. *BC* 2.31.

151. See Seager (2002) 150–1 and Raaflaub (1974a) 78–80 and 324 for discussions of the senators' motives.

decree would overwhelm Caesar's defiance of the Senate, and would force him to comply. This strategy was also likely predicated on the assumption that Caesar's soldiers would not follow him in a civil war and that—if enough pressure were brought to bear—Caesar's support would crumble. Of course, this strategy was based upon the false rumors of low morale in Caesar's army, probably spread by *optimates* trying to push Pompey to war. Despite his propaganda to the contrary, therefore, Cato did not think that Caesar would choose civil war, and therefore he kept increasing the pressure on Caesar, backing him into a corner where he could choose only civil war or political annihilation. Cato had used similar tactics against Caesar, Pompey, and Crassus years earlier, building up enough senatorial support to back each man into a corner, but this time Caesar was isolated. To be sure, several of Cato's allies wanted war with Caesar, and they were confident that, with Pompey's support, they would crush Caesar in the field, but given his efforts to make peace once the war began, it seems clear that Cato expected Caesar to choose political defeat before war.[152]

Caesar's tribunes (Antony and Cassius) surely interposed their veto once again to block the *senatus consultum ultimum*, but their veto was ignored. Some of the sources suggest that *optimates* threatened the tribunes with violence in order to drive them from the city and thereby prevent any obstruction of the decree, but the tribunes may have interpreted the passage of the decree in defiance of their veto to be an attack on their inviolability, and so they departed the city without waiting for a direct threat.[153] The truth is not clear. Cicero claimed that they were expelled without violence, but Dio notes that "Lentulus advised them to escape before the votes would make the difference," which if true certainly seems like a threat.[154] Whichever the case, this action gave Caesar the justification that he needed and that Cicero had feared: claiming that he had been unfairly attacked and that the ancient rights of the tribunes had been abused in a gross violation of tradition, Caesar crossed the Rubicon ahead of his thirteenth legion and began his conquest of Italy. Cato's thoughts about the flight of the tribunes are not recorded, but ignoring their veto was a tremendous contravention of the ancestral customs that Cato claimed to champion. It is possible that he had not intended for the tribunes to be threatened, and had not been a part of it, or he may have thought that the passage of the *senatus consultum ultimum* was the essential final ingredient that would compel Caesar to yield, and therefore he was willing to

---

152. See Tatum (2010) 207.

153. Caes. *BC* 1.5, Plut. *Caes.* 31.2, *Ant.* 5.4, Dio 41.3.2. See Gelzer (1968) 192 on the tribunes interpreting the disregard of their veto as an attack.

154. Cic. *Fam.* 16.11.2 and Dio 41.3.2.

overlook a violation of tradition if it achieved his higher priority of defending the state as he knew it. Given his role in preventing Pompey from compromising, there can be little doubt that Cato was among those who pushed for the decree. The flight of the tribunes provided Caesar with the propaganda he needed to cast the *optimates* as tyrants who were transgressing the traditional rights of the people (and their tribunes), and his invasion demonstrated the error of those who thought he could be compelled to give up.

What Caused the Civil War?

The first true act of war was Caesar's crossing of the Rubicon, probably during the night of January 10/11 in 49 BC. Commanders returning to Rome from their provinces were expected to dismiss their soldiers upon entering Italy, and under no conditions were they to approach Rome at the head of an army. In this respect, one can say that Caesar started the war by marching on Rome. But what degree of responsibility should be attached to his political opponents in Rome, including Cato? The question could be asked another way: was Caesar's invasion of Italy indefensible, or would a neutral spectator have judged that Cato and his supporters forced Caesar into a corner from which his decision to cross the Rubicon seemed predictable, necessary, and even defensible according to contemporary standards? Given that the majority of senators long supported compromise and negotiation with Caesar, and resisted moves that they feared would push him to war, how should one judge those hard-liners who ignored the will of the majority? Cato may not have expected that Caesar would resort to civil war, but if so, he made a catastrophic mistake, because most senators seem to have realized that Caesar would fight rather than allow himself to be destroyed, and so they had long resisted the pressure of the minority to move against him.

When Caesar marched on Rome, he did so believing that Cato and his circle had already violated the accepted parameters of Roman politics; they had "broken the rules" in their efforts to humble Caesar, and in his mind this justified and even demanded that he defend his social, political, and legal rights. For this reason, he appealed to his soldiers to defend his honor and *dignitas*—strong traditional values—rather than the laws of the state.[155] From Caesar's perspective, his actions throughout his public career had been legally correct, had good precedents, and were in keeping with the prevailing practices of his day. This is not to say that he was above reproach; he had taken full advantage of the entire range of political tactics an ambitious aristocrat could use to get ahead in Rome,

---

155. Caes. *BC* 1.7.

but he did nothing that others had not done before him. It was not Caesar's political tactics that made him unusual, but rather his considerable and even remarkable success at using those tactics, the scale of his execution of those tactics, his boldness in taking risks that more cautious senators would not take, and his deft skill in getting those risks to pay off. Although his use of force as consul to pass legislation had been unusual and deeply unpopular, he could claim that he only used the authority and prerogatives invested in his office to serve the will of the people, which had been wrongly blocked by the unprecedented and untraditional obstruction of Cato's filibusters (he could disavow the actions of the mobs). And although he had defeated his political enemies by making alliances to get his legislation passed through the popular assemblies, his victories—although humiliating to his opponents—had been perfectly legal.[156] Caesar's ambition was vast, but it did not set him apart from other Roman senators. Rather, it was his ability to achieve his ambitions that made him exceptional and frightening.

In comparison with Pompey (the current darling and eventual champion of the *optimates*), Caesar's career had been conventional and based on sound precedent. Pompey had come to power by raising a private army while still too young to hold office; he had used that army to intimidate the Senate and to demand extraordinary military commands despite being a private citizen; he had skipped most of the *cursus honorum* and had acquired his military reputation by slaughtering fellow citizens in civil war; he had stolen military commands and glory from leading senators; and he had held commands of unprecedented size and scope. Compared to this, Caesar's career had been unremarkable: his command in Gaul was no greater than the Eastern command held first by Lucullus and then by Pompey; his use of bribery was extensive, but followed normal practices (even Cato had approved the use of bribery for Bibulus's campaign); most of his legislation was excellent and built on established practices; and even his use of *popularis* politics had been far less threatening to the authority of the Senate than had been the legislation of earlier populist politicians. Indeed, as consul he first tried to move his legislation through the Senate in an optimate fashion, and only turned to *popularis* methods after Cato and small minority blocked his *lex agraria* despite seeing no fault in the bill. In hindsight, Caesar's career may appear to foreshadow his march on Rome, but he could fairly claim that—until he crossed the Rubicon—all of his actions had precedents, and that

---

156. Gruen (2009) 35, "Caesar's career through 59 had observed the normal conventions and pursued the customary goals of ambitious aristocrats, but with an astuteness and deliberation that put most of his contemporaries in the shade. . . . Caesar operated largely within traditional modes of political behavior. And he promoted policies and principles that others too had embraced. He was simply better at it than anyone else."

he was only seeking the types of accommodations that the Senate had already given other great men, including their current champion Pompey.

While Caesar's goals to reach the consulship, hold a great command, and achieve tremendous glory were normal and even praiseworthy for ambitious members of the senatorial order, the vigorous challenges he faced from the outset of his career by Cato and others seem unusual and out of keeping with conventional practices. While personal feuds were common enough in Roman politics, there is no clear explanation for Cato's extraordinary animosity toward Caesar, except perhaps his conviction—from an early date and without clear evidence—that Caesar would aim at a tyranny. Cato began attacking Caesar aggressively and without obvious explanation early in their careers, and these attacks were extreme: in 63 BC he tried to get Caesar condemned and executed alongside the Catilinarian conspirators even though Caesar had actually *helped* Cicero to build his case against them; as tribune in 62 BC he did his best to block Caesar's initiatives as praetor; in 60 BC he prevented the Senate from granting Caesar's request to stand for the consulship *in absentia* (which was not unreasonable or unprecedented), unnecessarily forcing him to choose between his praetorian triumph and standing for the consulship of 59 BC; he refused to allow the Senate even to consider Caesar's *lex agraria* in spite of the fact that he had no complaint against the bill; he had proposed handing Caesar over to his German enemies when the rest of Rome was celebrating Caesar's victory; he repeatedly accused Caesar of seeking tyranny and conspiring against the state; his allies falsely claimed that Caesar was marching on Rome to frighten the Romans into declaring Caesar an enemy; and time after time, Cato sought to prevent votes on Caesar's initiatives and stop the wheels of government by launching into filibuster speeches, thereby denying the Senate and/or people their right to vote as they wished. This last point is particularly significant, because Cato's extensive use of obstruction was in sharp conflict with the *mos maiorum*—it was a tactic employed by radical tribunes more than by conservative senators, and as such it was unconventional and contrary to tradition.[157] The Senate and the Roman people as a whole had normally found ways to work together in the past, but Cato's tactics prevented Caesar and the Senate from finding a workable solution, thereby breaking with tradition and pushing both sides toward confrontation.[158] When he reached the consulship, Caesar tried to act like a traditional magistrate and follow conventional procedures, but his efforts were repeatedly stymied by Cato,

---

157. Flower (2010b) 32, 138, and 144–5.

158. Raaflaub ([1974a] 113–52 and 182–92) argued that Caesar's various enemies had pushed him to war.

whose antagonism seems as radical as it was extreme. Plutarch wrote that Cato was thought peevish and meddling before the civil war, and only afterward was recognized as wise, suggesting that he saw and understood the coming disaster but could not prevent it.[159] Upon reviewing the evidence, however, one might fairly ask whether Plutarch's statement attempts to relieve Cato of responsibility for a war he helped create. Was he a wise third party who foresaw a destined conflict that he could not stop, or did he help create a series of events that led Rome into civil war? Is Cato credited with foreseeing a crisis that—in fact—he himself had helped to create?

Cato had not intended his feud to lead to a civil war, but his success in labelling Caesar a tyrant and alienating him from the Senate influenced many of the new generation of senators to take up his aggressive opposition to Caesar, although they may have had a range of motives for doing so. According to Velleius Paterculus, Cato insisted that the *optimates* fight to the death rather than allow the Republic to receive a dictate from a single citizen.[160] This hyperbole is unlikely to reflect Cato's true feelings, since he was horrified by the civil war and lamented the loss of Roman lives, but it conveys the power and relentless nature of his rhetoric, which hammered the senators with accusations that Caesar wished to make himself a tyrant over Rome and destroy their *libertas*. For this reason, several scholars have recognized Cato's important role in creating the political atmosphere that made civil war possible.[161] Plutarch highlights his relentless antagonism, explaining how Cato continued blaming and attacking Pompey for his role in elevating Caesar, even when they were working together against Caesar.[162] After crossing the Rubicon, Caesar (although biased) pointed specifically to Cato's unreasonable and unfair opposition as the injustice that brought about the civil war, showing that he recognized how Cato's accusations had prevented the Senate from finding a peaceful resolution with him.[163] All of this shows how Cato—starting early in their careers—had worked relentlessly to label Caesar as

---

159. Plut. *Caes.* 13.6.

160. Vell. 2.49.3. See Raaflaub (1974a) 64–8 for discussion.

161. Fantham ([2003] 103) suggested that Cato was primarily responsible for organizing the senatorial resistance that drove Caesar to cross the Rubicon, and Raaflaub ([2003] 43) noted that "Cato's harsh and uncompromising insistence on what he perceived as right drove his opponents to extreme reactions." Syme ([1939] 49) argued that Cato's vehement opposition to Caesar foolishly pushed the *optimates* to war for bad reasons: "a small faction misrepresented the true wishes of a vast majority in the Senate, in Rome, and in Italy. They pretended that the issue lay between a rebellious proconsul and legitimate authority."

162. Plut. *Pomp.* 60.5.

163. Caes. *BC* 1.32.

a public enemy, and how his success helped drive many senators to war against Caesar.

Any informed senator contemplating the situation at the end of 50 BC might have paused to consider who was really to blame for pushing Rome to the brink of civil war. While Caesar's ambition was great and his requests for special treatment were irksome, he was still acting within established precedents, following the letter of the law, and usually making his requests in a respectful manner. It is true that he used his extensive resources and talents to get laws passed that favored him and advanced his interests, but even so, he was following the rules of the political game that already existed when he started his career. Cato and the men around him, on the other hand, seem to have become so frustrated by their constant losses to Caesar that they decided to break those rules: the consul C. Marcellus ignored the overwhelming vote (370 to 22) in the Senate that Caesar and Pompey should both lay down their commands, and he exceeded the authority of his office by instructing Pompey to mobilize forces against Caesar, effectively (but not legally) declaring him an enemy of the state; the consuls M. Marcellus and L. Lentulus falsely reported that Caesar was marching on Rome in order to intimidate Romans into declaring Caesar an enemy; and Lentulus had the Senate pass a *senatus consultum ultimum* that ignored the "law of the ten tribunes" (which was illegal, since *senatus consulta* did not have legal weight, and could not override *leges*) and may have used the passage of the *senatus consultum ultimum* to threaten the sacrosanct tribunes Antony and Cassius with violence if they exercised their legal right of veto. These were tremendous violations of Roman tradition and the *mos maiorum*, emphasizing that the opposition to Caesar had little to do with traditional Roman values. This gross transgression of the ancient rights of the tribunes gave Caesar the moral high ground to pose as the champion of tradition, which was the justification that Cicero had earlier identified as the only thing Caesar's side lacked.[164] Indeed, on December 27 Cicero had stated plainly a fact that was obvious to him (and presumably to many others): any violence used against Caesar's tribunes would absolutely drive Caesar to war.[165] He and many others in the Senate thought the anti-Caesarians were going too far in their efforts to defeat Caesar, and that these efforts were much more likely to start a civil war than prevent one. Indeed, whenever it looked likely that a compromise might be in reach, Cato and his allies invariably blocked any possible accord and drove Pompey to follow a strategy that gave Caesar no

---

164. Caes. *BC* 1.5 and 1.7, Cic. *Att.* 7.3.5. See Hölkeskamp (2013) 14–15.

165. Cic. *Att.* 7.9.2.

choice other than civil war or personal ruin.[166] As late as December 27, 50 BC, Cicero could imagine several different possible resolutions to the conflict that would avoid war, but the hard-liners would not allow any such compromise.[167] Whereas Romans had long worked together to build compromises, Cato and the hard-liners ignored this, and instead presented absolute integrity and inflexible application of law as being the truest value of Rome's ancestors. In doing this, they gave legitimacy to a policy of obstruction and lack of compromise, which contributed to building a political crisis. Caesar certainly was not above reproach, and he was in large part responsible for the outbreak of civil war, but he at least was putting forward workable compromises that protected everyone's status (especially his own), whereas Cato and his allies would accept nothing short of Caesar's utter destruction.

---

166. Senators in favor of compromise: Cic. *Att.* 7.3.5–7, 7.4.2, 7.6.2, 7.8.4–5, 7.9.3. See Raaflaub (1974a) 262–90 and (2003) 46–7, and Fehrle (1983) 239–40.

167. Cic. *Att.* 7.9.2.

8

Civil War

Caesar's Invasion of Italy

Cato was shocked when Caesar crossed the Rubicon and began his invasion of Italy. Although most were stunned by Caesar's speed and daring in launching his attack, Cato seems to have been surprised that he actually resorted to war. Pompey, Metellus Creticus, and others among the hard-liners had probably expected that their efforts would drive Caesar to war, but Cato seems to have been truly surprised that Caesar invaded Italy, and he quickly began advocating for peace rather than war. According to Plutarch, from the moment Caesar crossed the Rubicon, "Cato did not cut his hair or trim his beard, nor did he wear a garland. Both in victory and in defeat, he maintained to the very end a singular bearing of grief, dejection, and burden over the misfortunes of the country."[1] Cato and his supporters had worked tenaciously to push Caesar into a corner where his only choices were civil war and political ruin, but now that they had succeeded and had compelled Caesar to choose, Cato seems to have been surprised and depressed by the consequences of his political strategy. In the face of his miscalculations, he would soon be found saying that peace was worth making concessions to Caesar, and throughout the war he would work to preserve the lives of his fellow Romans. Yet Cato's famous determination and uncompromising nature did not abandon him: he carried out every responsibility given him in the war to the best of his ability, and he maintained the struggle against Caesar as long as he could, which was longer than Pompey's other allies. His idealism in opposing Caesar to the bitter end would become celebrated, but one can

---

1. Plut. *Cat. Min.* 53.1.

only wonder whether he felt any personal responsibility for driving Caesar to war in the first place.[2]

Caesar's enemies drove the Senate to pass its *senatus consultum ultimum* on January 7, and in the following days they published further resolutions authorizing the recruitment of soldiers and the assignment of provinces. Caesar was at Ravenna in Cisalpine Gaul with a single legion when he received word of the Senate's decree. Realizing that further negotiation was impossible, and that his enemies would accept no alternative but his own destruction, he began his invasion of Italy—probably on January 10—with lightning strikes at Ariminum and Arretium, which he took and followed up with further victories.[3] The news of his invasion reached Rome on January 17, surprising and demoralizing everyone, most especially the *optimates*, who had believed that Pompey's experience and military preparations would prevent Caesar from invading Italy so quickly.[4] Indeed, Pompey had famously bragged that he had only to stomp his foot on the ground and soldiers would spring up to serve him, but when it became clear that he was unprepared for Caesar's assault, Cato's ally Favonius taunted Pompey for this boast, suggesting that it was time for him to start stomping.[5] Cato was less witty; he simply reminded everyone that he had warned Pompey about the danger of Caesar.[6] Although caught unprepared, Pompey had a good plan: he ordered the evacuation of Rome, and was even willing to evacuate Italy if necessary, to make time for his Spanish and eastern legions to arrive, and with those legions and his control of Rome's fleet, he intended to contain Caesar in Italy.[7] Despite the strategic sense of this plan, the abandonment of Rome weighed heavily on the *optimates*, and Pompey was blamed for not being able to stop Caesar immediately, as he had been expected to do.[8]

Bolstered by the early successes of his invasion, Caesar continued sending messages to Pompey and to many other senators, seeking a peaceful resolution. Attempting to recapture the moral high ground that he had forfeited by invading

---

2. This chapter is not intended to give a full description of the civil war, but rather to explore Cato's role and activities during the war. For a full discussion of the many stages of the war, see Gelzer (1968) 195–302, Seager (2002) 152–168, Tatum (2010) 190–211, Welch (2012) 43–91.

3. On the date of Caesar's crossing the Rubicon: von Fritz (1941) 127–9 and Gelzer (1968) 192.

4. Cic. *Att.* 7.11.1–3, 7.12.2, 7.13.2, 7.15.3, 7.20.1, *Fam.* 16.12.2, Plut. *Pomp.* 60.3–5.

5. Plut. *Pomp.* 57.5, 60.4–5, *Caes.* 33.5, App. *BC* 2.37.

6. Plut. *Pomp.* 60.5.

7. Welch ([2012] 43–91) gives a detailed discussion of Pompey's strategy.

8. Cic. *Att.* 7.21.1 (cf. 7.15.3).

Italy, on January 23 he essentially accepted the Senate's resolution of January 1: he was willing to lay down his provinces and armies, and to set aside the "law of the ten tribunes" and appear in Rome to stand for the consulship, but in return he insisted that Pompey dismiss his army in Italy, that he go to Spain and assume personal command of his provinces there, and that the regular government of Rome be restored, which presumably meant rescinding the *senatus consultum ultimum*.[9] This should have been a significant victory for the *optimates*, whose main goal had long been to bring Caesar back to Rome—without his legions—to stand for elections in the city (not *in absentia*). Indeed, if Cato had been solely in charge, he probably would have accepted Caesar's terms: on January 26, Cicero wrote that Cato had begun advocating that any peace terms were preferable to war, and he insisted on being present with Pompey's council when Caesar's offer was discussed.[10] The fact that Favonius, who had always emulated Cato in all things, remained staunchly opposed to offering any concessions to Caesar illustrates how far Cato had departed from his traditional posture; Favonius continued to maintain the trademark Catonian inflexibility, but Cato himself had changed in the face of Caesar's invasion. This sudden reversal in his famously resolute attitude was unexpected, and highlights his surprise that his provocations had actually driven Caesar to war. In essence, Caesar had raised the stakes of their conflict beyond what Cato was willing to risk—the Republic itself. According to Cicero, therefore, Cato quickly began advocating for slavery over war, but by that point in the conflict, he may not have exercised much influence in the war council, where the hawks were taking charge.[11] Pompey and the *optimates* refused to take any step until Caesar removed himself and his army from Italy.[12] This was obviously a play for time, intended to force Caesar to give up his gains while Pompey's legions converged on Italy, but it shows that the *optimates* were no longer willing to deal with Caesar in any peaceful or civilian manner. The *optimates* believed that overall they had the stronger position for war, and they refused to adopt Cato's

---

9. Caes. *BC* 1.9, Cic. *Fam.* 16.12.3, *Att.* 7.14.1. See Shackleton Bailey (1980) 80–2, Fehrle (1983) 245, Raaflaub (1974a) 265–7 and (1975) 251, 261–3, and Seager (2002) 154.

10. Cic. *Att.* 7.15.2 (*Cato enim ipse iam servire quam pugnare mavult*). Lintott ([1971] 499) suggests that Cato's reluctance was a literary fabrication of later authors who wanted to lionize him. This is possible, but the events of his life support the idea that Cato was opposed to civil slaughter, so it is more likely that his nobility was merely exaggerated (but not fabricated).

11. Cic. *Att.* 7.15.2.

12. Cic. *Att.* 7.14.1, 7.15.2–3, 7.17.2, *Fam.* 16.12.3, Caes. *BC* 1.10. See Raaflaub (1974a) 268–70 and (1975) 272.

(reported) belief that any peace was better than civil war.[13] Cato had wanted Caesar vulnerable in a court of law, but those who sided with him—including Pompey—now wanted Caesar vulnerable on a battlefield. Whether Cato had lost control of his own political allies, or whether he had not recognized their desire for war, the terms he and his allies had sought on January 1 were no longer acceptable to Pompey and his allies. Caesar understood their intent, and continued his invasion.

Another sign that Cato may have lost his leadership role with the outbreak of the war appears in the conflict over Pompey's status as leader of the "state" forces against Caesar. Back in December of 50 BC the consul C. Marcellus had given Pompey a sword and had asked him to take command of the two legions in Capua to defend the state, but Marcellus had no authority to do this at the time, and consular edicts did not extend to granting provinces and armies. Pompey was already invested with *imperium* and a command in Spain, but he did not have the legal authority to claim supreme command over any other campaign.[14] When the war finally broke out, therefore, Cato urged the Senate to give Pompey supreme command of the war against Caesar, perhaps in the belief that Pompey would be the best commander, and would care for the Romans better than some of the others who were eager for war. Instead, the Senate shared out commands and armies among a number of *imperium*-holders.[15] The rejection of Cato's demand was a tremendous blunder, because it meant that those fighting against Caesar were not unified under a single strategy, but instead each commander could follow his own instincts. The consuls soon wrangled with Pompey over leadership, and several other *optimates* refused to heed Pompey's instructions, with disastrous consequences. For example, the consul Lentulus failed to carry out Pompey's instructions to secure the money in Rome's treasury, with the result that the entire treasury fell into Caesar's hands, providing him with the funds to pay and supply his soldiers.[16] Domitius Ahenobarbus provides an even better example: he had raised a strong army in Corfinium, but refused to follow Pompey's

---

13. Cicero (*Fam.* 16.12.4) thought that any peace was better than war, but he believed that Caesar could still be beaten.

14. On the importance of provincial assignment to determine priority of command in the Roman Republic, see Drogula (2015) 131–61.

15. Plut. *Pomp.* 61.1–2, *Cat. Min.* 52.2, *Mor.* 810C, App. *BC* 2.36. See Seager (2002) 153. Welch ([2012] 58–9) has suggested that Cato and Pompey were allies in the civil war, and this seems very plausible. Although Cato had bitterly opposed Pompey earlier, he had clearly decided that supporting Pompey was a reasonable means to destroy Caesar. Yet even Pompey worried that Cato's cooperation was only temporary (see later discussion).

16. Cic. *Att.* 7.15.3, 7.21.2, Caes. *BC* 1.14, Dio 41.6.3–6.

urgent instructions to march this army south, where he could join up with Pompey's forces. Refusing to acknowledge Pompey as his superior, Domitius ignored his strategically wise instructions, and was soon trapped and defeated by Caesar's army.[17] Caesar released him to fight another day, but Domitius's soldiers happily abandoned their defeated leader to join the victorious army, and as a result of this loss, any chance Pompey had of holding Italy was lost. Despite Cato's urging, the *optimates* would not cooperate and recognize Pompey as their sole commander-in-chief, and they wrangled with him and rebelled against his authority.[18] Furthermore, while Cato took the high moral ground and urged Pompey not to plunder cities or put any Roman to death except in battle, their allies took a brutal approach, threatening cities and towns throughout Italy that they would be treated as enemies unless they pledged loyalty to Pompey's side.[19] Cato was also surely repulsed by the fact that many *optimates* were pleased to use the civil war as an excuse to enrich themselves by pillaging their fellow citizens.[20] While Cato had seen the threat of war as a political tactic to force Caesar to back down, many of his fellow *optimates* seem to have been eager for war as a means to profit and to acquire individual glory—Cicero lamented the immoral lust for civil war that many on Pompey's side demonstrated.[21] Just as Sulla's lieutenants had made fortunes during the civil war a generation earlier (much to the young Cato's horror), many of these hard-liners must have hoped for profit by going to war against Caesar.[22] To such men, Cato's high-minded principles were not attractive. He was a useful and influential figurehead in civilian politics, but the *optimates* were not inclined to heed his old-fashioned principles in times of civil war.

The Civil War in Sicily, Greece, and Africa

As reinforcements from Caesar's Gallic legions began arriving in Italy, and since the legions under Domitius had been lost to Caesar, Pompey and the majority

---

17. Cic. *Att.* 7.23.1 and 3, 8.12A.1, 8.12C.1–2, 8.12D.1–2, Caes. *BC* 1.19–22, App. *BC* 2.38. For more on Caesar's defeat of Domitius, see Shackleton Bailey (1956) 56–64 and Burns (1966) 84.

18. In Greece, the *optimates* serving in Pompey's army accused him of purposefully delaying the war because he enjoyed holding power too much (Plut. *Caes.* 41.2, *Pomp.* 67.3).

19. Cic. *Att.* 11.6.2 and 6, *Fam.* 4.9.2–3, 4.14.2, Plut. *Cat. Min.* 53.4, *Pomp.* 65.1, Suet. *Nero.* 2.3.

20. Caes. *BC* 3.82–83, Cic. *Fam.* 7.3.2.

21. Cic. *Fam.* 16.12.2, *Att.* 11.6.2.

22. Caesar (*BC* 3.83) writes that, during the civil war, several of Cato's friends regularly quarreled over which of them would receive Caesar's priesthood (he was *pontifex maximus*).

of the *optimates* abandoned Italy and left for Greece. This was not a simple retreat: Pompey intended to concentrate his forces in Greece and use Rome's fleet
to contain Caesar in Italy, where he hoped a shortage of supplies would enfeeble
his army and turn the vast population of Rome against Caesar.[23] To achieve this
strategy, Pompey needed to control the key islands around Italy to block shipping
lanes, most especially Sicily, which was also a critical source of grain for Rome.
Pompey had wanted to send Cicero to take command of the island, since he had
extensive connections there and was already in possession of *imperium* from his
Cilician command, but he declined the offer, saying he had no legal authority
to assume command of a province not properly assigned to him by the state.[24]
This refusal emphasizes Cicero's disappointment in the policies that had pushed
Rome to civil war, but his legal objection was also valid, although most of those
around Pompey overlooked such strict observance of the law in their eagerness
to hold a command.[25] Pompey selected Cato as a second choice to control Sicily,
which demonstrates confidence in Cato's abilities, but it may also reveal a desire
to remove him (and Cicero) from the main army. Neither Cicero nor Cato was
known as a military man, and both were advocating for peace with Caesar, so
Pompey's selection of them to go to Sicily may have been more political than
military. That is, Cato's gloomy attitude toward civil war may have led Pompey
to send him to Sicily, where he would be useful organizing ships and recruits, but
would be too far away to interfere with the bloody business of the legions. Cato
dutifully accepted the assignment, but when he realized that he might miss important meetings of Pompey's war council, he refused to leave Italy until he had
participated in the discussions about Caesar's proposals. What he intended to
say in such a discussion is not clear, but Cicero thought that he would only get
in the way.[26] A certain Postumius was supposed to accompany Cato to Sicily, but
he refused to leave Italy without Cato, so another senator (C. Fannius) had to be
dispatched quickly to take command of the island until Cato was ready to leave,
which he did sometime after January 26.

These events make it seem that Pompey no longer valued Cato highly, but
another interpretation is possible. Kathryn Welch has argued that Pompey originally intended to use his available legions and Rome's navy (which he controlled)

---

23. Welch ([2012] 43–62) gives a discussion, with full references, of Pompey's strategy to fight
Caesar.

24. Cic. *Att.* 7.7.4.

25. Caes. *BC* 1.6. See discussion in Drogula (2015) 110.

26. Cic. *Att.* 7.15.2. Taylor ([1949] 165) suggests that Cato was afraid that Caesar would make a
new alliance with Pompey and turn him once more against the *optimates*.

to trap and contain Caesar in Italy, and with this done, he planned to block all grain shipments to Italy in the expectation that famine would cause the civilian population to turn against Caesar, giving Pompey a bloodless victory.[27] This plan became impossible after Domitius lost his army to Caesar in late February, but it may be that—at the time that Cato was appointed and dispatched—he was to play an important role in Pompey's naval strategy, since the control of Sicily would have been vital to the plan. If this reconstruction is correct, Cato may have had a strong influence on Pompey's intention to win a bloodless war. On the other hand, Pompey does not seem to have given much thought to Cato once he was gone: Cato received little aid while on Sicily, he was not recalled after Domitius's defeat ruined any entrapment strategy, and he does to seem to have been highly valued when he rejoined Pompey in Greece (see later discussion). The truth may be somewhere in the middle of these positions: Pompey and the *optimates* may have grown weary of Cato's moralizing and wanted him out of their war council, so they honored him by giving him a command in which his undoubted skills for organization would be put to good use. So Cato was invested with *imperium* and sent to Sicily *pro praetore* (a lower rank for a commander), although the legitimacy of his authority was questionable, since it was conferred through untraditional means (normally, *imperium* was conferred after religious ceremonies held in Rome, which Caesar now held).[28] He left Italy with only twelve slaves—which was a paltry entourage compared to other senators in Pompey's circle—and apparently very little money, such that he would be obliged to borrow money from Lucullus's son later while they were in Greece.[29] Perhaps this was simply an example of Cato's continued austerity even in civil war, but more likely he did not expect the war to last as long as it did.

Arriving in Sicily with a moderate force, he threw himself into preparations. According to Caesar, he set about repairing old warships and requisitioning new ones, and recruiting infantry and cavalry from the cities on the island.[30] While Cato was making these preparations, however, Caesar's legate Asinius Pollio landed on the island at Messana with an advance force. According to Plutarch, Cato wrote to Pollio asking about his legal authority to be on the island, which seems a very strange question to ask during a civil war.[31] He may have been

---

27. Welch (2012) 43–6.

28. See Drogula (2015) 105–10.

29. Cic. *Att.* 13.6.2, Val. Max. 4.3.12.

30. Caes. *BC.* 1.30. Welch ([2012] 58–9) discusses Cato's activities on Sicily.

31. Plut. *Cat. Min.* 53.1–2 (cf. App. *BC* 2.40). See Fehrle (1983) 249.

prepared to fight Pollio for control of the island, but learning of Pompey's departure for Greece, and that a larger Caesarian force was coming to Sicily under Curio, he decided to abandon the island altogether. According to Caesar, Cato publicly blamed Pompey for failing to send reinforcements and other resources necessary to hold the strategically critical island, but Plutarch says that he simply advised the Syracusans to seek their own safety by joining the winning side, while Dio records that he left Sicily to spare the cities there from needless danger.[32] It is a bit surprising that Caesar gives the most sympathetic portrayal of Cato's activity, describing him as one who performed his duties well, but had been abandoned by Pompey. This may indicate that Caesar did not return Cato's intractable hatred, or more likely he sought to make his chief rival Pompey look like an unworthy commander who did not support his lieutenants.[33] Cicero, on the other hand, actually blamed Cato for failing to hold Sicily, complaining that he had sufficient resources to defend the island, which would have been an important resource and rallying point for Pompey's forces. Of course, this negative assessment may also be the product of Cicero's own frustration with Cato and the hard-liners who had forced the conflict with Caesar. Cato abandoned the island on April 23, but he did not leave the war.[34]

It is difficult to know what to make of Cicero's censure of Cato for losing Sicily. Caesar suggested that Cato was preparing ships and other forces to defend the island, but Cicero treats with skepticism a report that the inhabitants of Sicily supported Cato.[35] He had very little experience in command, but the same could be said of most Roman commanders. He was no coward, so it may well be that he lacked the resources necessary to hold the island, or he may have thought it more useful to take what resources he had to Pompey rather than lose them in an unwinnable battle, as Domitius had done. Yet the abandonment of Sicily was a serious loss for Pompey, since it ruined any hope of controlling the seas. It handed over one of Rome's chief sources of grain to Caesar, and it provided him with whatever navy was still stationed on the island.[36] The loss of Sicily (and eventually Sardinia as well) gave Caesar a strong base in Italy, and meant the civil war would be decided by a massive battle in Greece. Realistically, Cato—who was a good soldier but had no experience in senior command—probably had little hope

---

32. Caes. *BC* 1.30, Plut. *Cat. Min.* 53.3, Dio 41.41.1.

33. See Raaflaub (2009) 188 and Yates (2011) 166–8.

34. Cic. *Att.* 10.16.3.

35. Caes. *BC* 1.30, Cic. *Att.* 10.12.2.

36. Welch (2012) 47.

of holding the island once Curio had arrived with significant forces, so taking what resources he could salvage to Pompey was a prudent decision. Another man might have tried to hold Syracuse or some other part of the island as a stronghold, but Cato never displayed much desire to observe (much less lead) the mutual slaughter of his fellow citizens.

Retreating from Sicily, Cato sailed to Greece and joined Pompey at Dyrrhachium. What kind of reception he received is unknown, but Plutarch says he spent his time looking for ways to put off a decisive battle, hoping that some end might be found that did not involve a bloody contest between citizen armies.[37] He also continued to urge the Pompeians not to sack any neutral city or kill any Roman except in battle, which was tantamount to urging his allies not to profit from the war or seize the opportunity to settle old scores. These were surely unwelcome admonitions to many senators around Pompey, who had looked forward to civil war as an opportunity for both plunder and revenge. Plutarch gives an illuminating detail: when Cicero arrived at Dyrrhachium, Cato blamed him for joining Pompey's side:

> Cato faulted Cicero greatly for siding with Pompey. For while it had not been morally possible for Cato to forsake the political order that he had embraced from the beginning, Cicero had unreasonably and unnecessarily made himself Caesar's enemy and had come to them to share in such great danger, when he would have been more useful to his country and to his friends if—remaining neutral—he had adapted himself to events there.[38]

If accurate, this reflects how much Cato had been changed by the outbreak of the civil war. Whereas he had previously worked to push and bully senators into opposing Caesar at every turn, he is now found suggesting that moderate voices like Cicero's were needed for the good of the state. Cato himself was not one of these, and could not "adapt himself" to the current course of events, but he seems to have recognized that the state needed men who could work without taking a hard line on either side. On previous occasions he had shouted down attempts by moderates to compromise in the Senate, but now he regretted that Cicero was not in Rome to help broker a peace. His distress at the consequence of his own

---

37. Plut. *Cat. Min.* 53.3–4. See Fantham (2003) 104, "Cato, although of fighting age, did not take part in the military engagements, and perhaps he had told Pompey that he would not do so."

38. Plut. *Cic.* 38.1.

hard-line policies (and those of other anti-Caesarians) may have been weighing heavily on him.

Perhaps for this reason, Pompey soon dispatched Cato to Asia Minor to aid in the collection of transport ships, but arriving and finding that the local commanders had no need of him, Cato went to Rhodes and convinced the islanders to take Pompey's side, after which he left his half-sister Servilia and her son (by Lucullus) on the island for safety and returned to Pompey.[39] Back in Dyrrhachium, Pompey is said to have considered placing Cato in command of his entire fleet, but gave the command instead to Bibulus when friends warned him that Cato might turn the fleet against them once Caesar had been defeated.[40] This also seems unrealistic, and perhaps was tainted by Caesar's later propaganda, although Cato's recent performance on Sicily and his grave misgivings about fighting his fellow citizens may have persuaded Pompey to exclude him from further important command positions.[41] It is also possible that Cato refused the offered naval command on the grounds that his friend and son-in-law Bibulus was available for the position and had a higher claim on it because he had achieved consular status, whereas Cato was only of praetorian status (Cato would later decline command of the Pompeian army in Africa on similar grounds—see later discussion). Bibulus did indeed receive command of the fleet, and if Pompey had misgivings about Cato's loyalty, he surely would have refrained from giving the fleet to Cato's close friend and son-in-law.

While Pompey probably did not fear Cato, he does seem to have kept him at a distance following the loss of Sicily. Cato was and always had been an inspiring figure to the *optimates*, but his deeply felt convictions had always made him a difficult and occasionally unpredictable ally. This seems to have been the case during the Battle of Dyrrhachium, which was a victory for Pompey, albeit an indecisive one. Before the battle Cato demonstrated his value as an inspirational figure, motivating the soldiers better than any of Pompey's other commanders. Recounting to them "all of the fitting sayings from philosophy about freedom and moral excellence and death and glory," he was able to cast the upcoming battle in the best light.[42] After the battle, however, he could not restrain his remorse at seeing so many Romans killed by their fellow citizens. While Pompey's

---

39. Plut. *Cat. Min.* 54.1–3. Servilia's presence with Cato is strange, and Plutarch may be correct that she remained with her half-brother to erase her bad reputation for immorality, since there is no reason to think she was in any particular danger in Rome.

40. Plut. *Cat. Min.* 54.3–5. See Pelling (2011) 353.

41. On this, see Lintott (1971) 495–500 and Welch (2012) 68.

42. Plut. *Cat. Min.* 54.5–6.

army celebrated its (indecisive) victory, Cato "wailed loudly for his country, and seeing so many good citizens killed by one another, he lamented the destructive and miserable lust for power."[43] This outpouring of grief and lamentation in the moment of Pompey's much-needed victory once again demonstrated that Cato was a difficult ally. His misery at the fate of his country was a complete rejection of Stoic *apatheia*, but was entirely proper and appropriate for one dedicated to Roman values and to the Republic. Amid Pompey's first and desperately needed victory against Caesar, therefore, Cato's behavior made him a wet blanket casting a funereal pall over what should have been a celebration to cheer the men.

Cato was also sneered at for being the only senator to support Pompey's caution in pursuing Caesar's army. After the indecisive battle, Caesar withdrew his army from Dyrrhachium in search of supplies and better territory for fighting, but the men in Pompey's council thought Caesar was defeated and on the run, and urged Pompey to attack immediately, heaping insults upon him for his hesitation. Cato was the only member of Pompey's council to support this caution, although he reportedly did so primarily to spare the lives of the Romans in Caesar's army: "Cato alone advised the sparing of fellow citizens, and indeed, seeing even those of the enemy who had died in the battle, a group of one thousand men, he walked away covering his face and lamenting loudly."[44] This great sorrow at the death of his countrymen was probably exaggerated by the later legends about Cato that took hold after his death, but it is consistent with his repeated disinclination to engage in—or even be present at—battles between Roman armies; not only had he abandoned Sicily rather than fight to hold it (or even a part of it), but he would also be absent from the decisive battles at Pharsalus and Thapsus. Furthermore, Cicero reports that Cato was deeply disturbed by predictions made by a certain oarsman in the Rhodian fleet that Greece would soon be bathed in blood, and that Dyrrhachium would be pillaged.[45] Such susceptibility to rumor hardly seems typical of Cato, and reflects a man deeply disturbed by the tremendous carnage of Roman soldiers around him. He may even have felt sorrow and deep guilt for his role in driving the events that had led to war.

When Pompey moved his army inland to face Caesar at Pharsalus, he decided to leave Cato in charge of the camp at Dyrrhachium. This was an important assignment, because Cato had command of fifteen cohorts and was charged with protecting the army's supply depot, as well as acting as a rearguard against attacks

---

43. Plut. *Cat. Min.* 54.7.

44. Plut. *Caes.* 41.1–2.

45. Cic. *de Div.* 1.68.

by native tribes or Caesarian reinforcements.[46] His reliability and talent for organization made him the perfect man for this assignment, but it is also likely that Pompey did not want him present at Pharsalus. Not only had Cato made his horror at civil slaughter clear, but Plutarch also suggests that Pompey was afraid of what Cato might do should the Pompeians be victorious at Pharsalus.[47] Pompey must have known that the *optimates* were honoring him because they needed him to defeat Caesar, and that—once this victory was achieved—Cato and the others would swiftly turn on him, as they had back in 61 and 60 BC. Indeed, many were already chafing under Pompey's leadership, and many were complaining that he was delaying the war simply to maintain his command over them, which was an ominous sign for his position as commander. Plutarch writes, "all the others reproached Pompey's avoidance of battle, and calling him 'Agamemnon' and 'King of Kings' they provoked him as one not planning on laying down his sole command, but glorifying in having so many commanders attached to him and coming to and from his tent."[48] Thus Pompey surely feared that his position would swiftly change once Caesar was gone. Of all the *optimates*, Cato had been Pompey's most consistent political opponent until the fear and hatred of Caesar had driven him to tolerate an alliance, so Pompey may have thought it wiser to leave Cato at Dyrrhachium, where he would be a reliable and cautious commander of the rearguard, but would not be present to influence the events immediately following the battle should Pompey be victorious. Plutarch notes that Pompey left several other prominent men with Cato at Dyrrhachium—including Cicero, who was ill at the time—so it could be that he was trying to sequester his most vocal critics (or potential critics) in hopes that he would have time to plan his next move after the battle.[49]

The Battle of Pharsalus was fought on August 9, 48 BC, and Pompey was defeated utterly and driven to flight. Many *optimates* fell on the battlefield, although large numbers took advantage of Caesar's famous clemency and were permitted to surrender and return to Rome unharmed. One of these was Cato's nephew, M. Junius Brutus, who returned to Rome, where he would participate in the plot to assassinate Caesar four years later. Others refused to surrender and fled to Africa and elsewhere. Several days after the battle, T. Labienus—Caesar's chief lieutenant in Gaul who had defected to Pompey at the start of the civil

46. Plut. *Cat. Min.* 55.1, *Pomp.* 67.2, Dio 42.10.1. See Fehrle (1983) 257 and Welch (2012) 69.

47. Plut. *Cat. Min.* 55.1–2.

48. Plut. *Caes.* 41.2–3 (cf. *Pomp.* 67.3).

49. Plut. *Cat. Min.* 55.2.

war—brought news of the defeat to Dyrrhachium.[50] Panic took hold of the men, but Cato maintained control and moved the camp and its supplies to the nearby island of Corcyra, which he could protect with the fleet under his control while his forces regrouped and waited for news of Pompey.[51] At this point, and in spite of their past differences, Cato asked Cicero to take command of the Pompeian forces on the island. He may have believed that Cicero should assume command because he held consular status, whereas Cato was only a former praetor.[52] He may also have felt that Cicero was a more legitimate commander, since he had received his *imperium* in the proper manner in Rome, whereas Cato's own grant of *imperium* had been irregular because of the outbreak of the war. Finally, Cato's heart may not have been in this campaign anymore. According to Plutarch, he had decided that—if Pompey were still alive—he would join him and continue fighting the war, but if Pompey was dead, Cato intended to send his men back to Italy and live the rest of his own life in exile, as far away as possible from Caesar.[53] He was willing to continue fighting the war so long as there were credible leadership and a chance of winning, but he did not relish expending Roman lives needlessly in an unwinnable war. He may also have believed that Cicero was the only other available senator who would prioritize the good of the Republic over the drive for personal profit and vengeance. Cicero refused to take over the Pompeian force, preferring to return to Rome rather than continue fighting a war that he had never wanted and that he had worked strenuously to prevent.[54] Pompey's hot-headed son Gnaeus was with them on Corcyra, and he verbally assaulted and threatened Cicero for wanting to leave the Pompeian cause, but Cato intervened and allowed him and many others to leave Corcyra peacefully.[55] In doing this, Cato was far more generous and humane than other *optimates* had been at the start of the war: whereas they had declared in 49 BC that those who remained neutral would be treated as enemies, Cato now allowed his own allies to leave his army, quit the war, and return to Rome unharmed if they wished. Still, Cicero realized that those he was abandoning would bear a grudge for this abandonment, and expected to be ill-treated by them in the future, but he was relieved

---

50. Cic. *Div.* 1.68–9.

51. Plut. *Cat. Min.* 55.2–3, App. *BC* 2.87, Dio 42.10.1–2.

52. Fantham ([2003] 104) suggests that Cato made this offer out of protocol only, and that he did not really want or expect Cicero to accept.

53. Plut. *Cat. Min.* 55.2.

54. Cic. *Att.* 11.7.3.

55. Plut. *Cat. Min.* 55.3, *Cic.* 39.1–2, Dio 42.10.2–3.

to be away from them.[56] Cato went into deep mourning after Pharsalus, refusing to recline except in sleep, and so taking all of his meals in a sitting position (rather than reclining as usual), but he could not bring himself to leave the Pompeian army without a leader.[57]

After failing to convince Cicero to assume command, Cato could not in good conscience abandon his soldiers while Pompey was still alive. There is no indication that he considered giving up and returning to Rome as Cicero and others had done, perhaps because this may not have been an option for him: Caesar had instructed Mark Antony to prevent any Pompeian aristocrats from returning to Italy unless given Caesar's express permission.[58] There is little chance that Cato would have sought such permission from his archenemy, but neither did he settle on exile as he might have done. Instead, he remained in command and continued to receive Pompeians in flight from Pharsalus, but when he learned that Pompey had gone to Africa, he loaded his entire force onto the ships in his care and set sail for Egypt.[59] Discovering en route that Pompey had been murdered by the king of Egypt (who hoped to gain Caesar's favor), and that Egypt was not safe for Pompeian forces, Cato instead landed his army in Cyrene, where he seems to have remained for some time. While there, some of the senators in his group—including C. Cassius, the future assassin of Caesar—decided that Pompey's death had ended the war, and they returned to Rome to seek Caesar's pardon. Cato still refused to do this, either from his hatred of Caesar or because he could not bring himself to abandon those who remained loyal to Pompey's cause.[60] Learning that the province of Africa was still in the hands of Pompey's lieutenant Attius Varus, and that Metellus Scipio had gone there from Pharsalus, Cato resolved to join this Pompeian stronghold. According to Dio, he transported his army there by sea using the fleet they brought from Corcyra, but Plutarch suggests that the arrival of winter had made sailing unsafe, so Cato led his force on a very difficult seven-day march to the province of Africa.[61] This was an arduous journey, and he provided for his men by acquiring as many pack animals, cattle, and chariots as possible, and even brought along a group of natives skilled in curing snakebites.

---

56. Cic. *Att.* 11.6.2, 11.7.3–6.

57. Plut. *Cat. Min.* 56.3–4.

58. Cic. *Att.* 11.7.2.

59. Plut. *Cat. Min.* 56.1, Dio 42.13.1–5. Dio (42.13.3) records that Cato attempted to capture Patrae on the way, but was repulsed by one of Caesar's lieutenants.

60. Dio 42.13.4.

61. Plut. *Cat. Min* 56.3–4, Dio 42.13.4. See Fehrle (1983) 260–1.

Plutarch mentions that Cato walked the entire journey at the head of his column, neither riding on a horse nor using a pack animal himself.

Arriving in Africa, Cato found Attius and Scipio squabbling over which of them should exercise supreme command over the Pompeian forces. Both were appealing to King Juba of Numidia for support, and Cato was incensed to see two Roman commanders kowtowing to a foreign ruler. At their first public meeting, therefore, he took decisive action. Discovering that Juba had placed his own chair in the central position between the chairs reserved for Cato and Scipio (thereby indicating the king's superiority over the Romans), he abruptly moved his own chair so it was next to Scipio's, thereby making Scipio the central figure of the meeting.[62] Afterward, Cato reconciled the two Roman commanders, who immediately asked him to assume supreme command over their joint forces.[63] This was a considerable display of their respect for Cato's moral authority, especially since he and Scipio had been bitter rivals years earlier for the hand of Aemilia Lepida. Yet Cato still had no desire for command, and he argued that Scipio should have the command for two reasons: because he held consular *dignitas* and *auctoritas* whereas Cato and Attius had only reached the praetorship, and because the famous Scipio name would better inspire their soldiers, especially since two previous *Cornelii Scipiones* had celebrated tremendous victories fighting in Africa.[64] One can only wonder whether Cato reflected on the fact that the *Cornelii Scipiones* had been his great-grandfather's most bitter political enemies. By urging Scipio to take command, Cato was observing the *mos maiorum* by deferring to Scipio's greater status, but it is also unlikely that he wanted the command for himself. As he had displayed on Sicily and at Dyrrhachium, Cato was not as eager as his aristocratic colleagues for command, and he probably had no stomach for fighting against his countrymen, however much he disliked Caesar. This was another episode in which Cato's personal virtue ended up hurting his long-term goals and his allies, however, since Scipio would make several critical missteps that enabled Caesar's victory.[65]

---

62. Plut. *Cat. Min.* 57.1–3. See Fehrle (1983) 263.

63. Plut. *Cat. Min.* 57.3, App. *BC* 2.87, Dio 42.57.2–3.

64. Plut. *Caes.* 52.4, *Cat. Min.* 57.3, Suet. *Iul.* 59.1, Dio 42.57.2–5. P. Scipio Africanus (cos. 205 and 194 BC) had defeated Hannibal and the Carthaginians at the Battle of Zama in 202 BC, and P. Scipio Aemilianus (cos. 147 and 134 BC) had sacked and destroyed Carthage in 146 BC. See Fehrle (1983) 267. As I argue elsewhere (Drogula [2015] 206–9), neither Cato nor Scipio had been assigned the command of Africa by the Roman state, so neither had the legal grounds to claim precedence of command over the other. Lacking a legal basis for determining seniority, Cato followed custom by willingly deferring to Scipio, who as a consular held higher status.

65. Duff (1999) 154.

Despite handing over authority, Cato continued to have a strong influence. Pompey's son Cn. Pompeius was present in Africa, and Cato joined with Scipio in encouraging the young man to take their fleet to Spain to make that province another Pompeian stronghold against Caesar.[66] Spain was still inclined toward the Pompeians, and Pompey's son would assemble a powerful army that nearly defeated Caesar at the Battle of Munda in 45 BC. This was a good strategic move for continuing the war effort, but Cato also continued to argue against any unnecessary bloodshed: the city of Utica had supported Caesar, and Scipio planned to punish it by massacring all of its inhabitants and razing the city to the ground, but Cato decried the suggestion and argued in their military council until Scipio relented.[67] Scipio put Cato in command of the city, primarily to maintain it as a supply depot for Scipio's army, although he may have wanted some distance from Cato's moralizing. Cato did not harm the untrustworthy citizens of Utica (those who had favored Caesar), but he forced them to exit the city and encamp outside the city walls as a precaution against treachery.[68] He threw himself into improving the fortifications, digging new trenches, raising troops, and laying in a large supply of provisions to support Scipio's army and, if necessary, to withstand a siege.[69] He also gathered together a number of the city's elite men and, together with the Pompeians who had fled to Africa, he formed them into a "new Senate" that gave some semblance of Republican governance to his operation.[70] Once again, Cato preferred—and perhaps was better suited for—the responsibilities of a quartermaster to those of a general.

Scipio and Cato had plenty of time to prepare for Caesar's inevitable arrival. After the Battle of Pharsalus in August of 48 BC, Caesar spent a year campaigning in the East, and after briefly returning to Rome, he set out for Africa in December of 47 BC. During this time, Cato's disillusionment with—and bitterness over—the civil war continued to grow, and he became estranged from Scipio. He seems to have become increasingly displeased with Scipio's management of Africa and his disregard for ancestral tradition, and he grew afraid that Scipio would not behave with moderation if victorious over Caesar.[71] In Scipio's defense, it appears that Cato offered much unwanted advice, and was resentful when Scipio did not

66. Luc. 9.84–96, Caes. *BAfr*. 22–3, Dio 42.56.4.

67. Plut. *Cat. Min*. 58.1, Dio 42.57.4.

68. Caes. *BAfr*. 87.

69. Plut. *Cat. Min*. 58.2–3.

70. Plut. *Cat. Min*. 59.2, App. *BC* 2.95.

71. Vell. 2.54.3, Plut. *Cat. Min*. 58.4–6.

take it. For example, hoping that Caesar's army would collapse under the strain of campaigning in Africa, Cato urged Scipio to avoid battle altogether. He had already laid in a large store of supplies in Utica, and he thought he could win a waiting game with Caesar, whose army would soon be weakened and demoralized by a lack of supplies in a hostile environment.[72] This was probably sound tactical advice, and it also suited his desire to limit the Roman causalities in the war, but Scipio did not agree, and he called Cato a coward for hiding in Utica instead of risking battle against Caesar with their soldiers.[73] Cato tried to clear himself of his charge by declaring that he was ready to take his soldiers and invade Italy immediately, and thereby divert Caesar from invading Africa, but Scipio dismissed this offer as an insincere jest. In consequence of this, Cato is said to have told his friends that the war was hopeless, and that he would abandon Rome no matter which side prevailed, since he thought Scipio and his supporters would be just as harsh and cruel as Caesar.[74] After a lifetime of championing Roman tradition and urging others to do the same, Cato's experience in the war and in Africa seems to have convinced him that the Republic as he conceived of it was gone. In his view, the defenders of the Republic had become as bad as the would-be tyrant, and nowhere was the *mos maiorum* to be found. It had been hard enough for Cato to lend his support to Pompey, whom he had despised and tried to destroy in the late 60s BC, but now he could see no other commander who would serve his cause. He had spent his life fighting for his vision of a traditional (perhaps antiquated) Republic, and during his long wait for Caesar to arrive in Africa, he may have mulled over the fact that very few Romans had ever shared his particular vision.

Caesar finally landed in Africa in late December of 47 BC, and after an initial victory over some Pompeian forces under his old legate Labienus early in January 46 BC, he and Scipio spent several months maneuvering their armies in accordance with their own strategies. Cato had urged Scipio to avoid a decisive battle and to delay, so that the winter months and shortage of supplies could eat away at Caesar's army and starve it into bloodless submission, but this advice was ignored.[75] On April 6 Scipio engaged Caesar in the decisive battle near the city of Thapsus. Caesar's soldiers were victorious, and in their fury they ignored their orders to spare those who surrendered, instead slaughtering all they encountered

---

72. Pelling (2011) 402 and Welch (2012) 94–5.

73. Plut. *Cat. Min.* 58.4.

74. Plut. *Cat. Min.* 58.6.

75. Plut. *Cat. Min.* 58.3–4. See Welch (2012) 94.

and destroying Scipio's entire army.[76] It took three days for the survivors to reach Utica, and their reports of the staggering loss threw the city into a panic. Cato retained his composure and did his best to calm the citizens and prepare for Caesar's imminent arrival.[77] He received separate letters from Scipio and from King Juba, both of whom had escaped from the battle and were waiting to see what Cato would do with the stronghold of Utica.[78] Although he seems briefly to have considered trying to hold the city that he had fortified and provisioned well, he perceived that the local inhabitants were likely to go over to Caesar, so he advised Scipio and Juba to stay away from the city and concentrated his efforts on evacuating by sea those Roman citizens who wished to flee.[79] In this way, Plutarch portrays a magnanimous Cato who felt no grudge against either the citizens who fled or against those who would go over to Caesar. This is consistent with Cato's previous attempts to preserve Roman life at Dyrrhachium and Pharsalus, but the particular emphasis on Cato's calm and detached acceptance of Caesar's victory may be the product of later authors who would recast Cato's legacy. Yet saving a fellow citizen's life in war had always been an outstanding act of Roman virtue, and merited one of Rome's highest military awards, so Cato was simply displaying his true Roman values.[80] He had long ago realized that the Rome he was fighting for was gone, and that the leaders of the Pompeian cause lacked legitimacy, so his magnanimity may also have been recognition of the futility of the situation.

   While Cato was occupied with the evacuation, a large unit of Scipio's cavalry that had escaped from Thapsus arrived at Utica. The author of the *African War* (attributed to Caesar, but not written by him) writes that these horsemen began to vent their rage by slaughtering the pro-Caesar citizens of Utica, whom Cato had forced to camp outside the city walls.[81] Unable to stop the slaughter any other way, Cato and Faustus Sulla paid the horsemen one hundred sesterces each to leave the city, and they rode off to Juba's kingdom. Yet Plutarch tells this story differently, saying the horsemen came to Utica peacefully but divided in purpose, some wanting to flee to Juba, some wanting to serve under Cato, but all

76. Caes. *BAfr*. 85, Plut. *Caes*. 53.1–7, App. *BC* 2.97, Dio 43.9.1.

77. Plut. *Cat. Min*. 58.7, App. *BC* 2.98.

78. Plut. *Cat. Min*. 60.3.

79. Plut. *Cat. Min*. 62.1, Dio 43.10.1. See Fehrle (1983) 267–8.

80. Polybius (6.39.6–8) discusses the importance in Roman culture of saving the life of a citizen or ally in war.

81. Caes. *BAfr*. 87.

very nervous about entering the city, which they expected to go over to Caesar.[82] They demanded that Cato drive out or kill all the inhabitants of Utica before they would enter and defend the city. He refused, but he prevailed upon them to stand guard long enough for him to arrange transport vessels and to embark the majority of the Romans. As the panic grew, Cato had to intercede personally to prevent these cavalrymen from looting the city, and finally they left ahead of Caesar's advance. So the author of the *African War* demonizes Pompey's soldiers and makes Cato look weak (he needed to buy the loyalty of his own soldiers), whereas Plutarch's account shows Cato to be a man of principle.

One of Caesar's relatives, Lucius Caesar, was among the Pompeians at Utica, and he volunteered to lead an embassy to Caesar seeking mercy for himself and for all the Romans in the city. Cato instructed his son and companions to accompany L. Caesar when he went, and to seek mercy from the conqueror, but Cato refused to go himself, nor would he allow anyone to intercede with Caesar on his behalf.[83] He understood his old adversary well and knew that Caesar was very eager to pardon him, but he had no interest in prolonging his life if it meant giving Caesar the satisfaction of bestowing clemency. He had pursued a personal feud with Caesar for seventeen years or more, so the very idea of yielding to his nemesis was untenable—Dio writes that Cato believed it would be easier to die than to endure being the recipient of Caesar's mercy.[84] Plutarch says that he instructed his son never to engage in politics, since it was no longer possible to do so in a manner worthy of their family name, but Dio gives him a longer exchange with his son, explaining that it was appropriate for the boy to seek mercy and live because he was young and accustomed to living as a slave in a tyranny, but because Cato was older and knew what it was to live in a free Republic, it would be impossible for him to live under Caesar's tyranny.[85] This speech was probably a later literary creation to celebrate the ideal Republican that Cato became in legend, but it also reflects well his attitude over the past two years: following the defeat of Pompey at Pharsalus, Cato seems to have lost hope and no longer saw a path back to the Republic he wanted.

Cato carried out to the end his responsibilities to his fellow Romans and to the citizens of Utica. After arranging all other matters, he conveyed all remaining

82. Plut. *Cat. Min.* 62.1–65.4.

83. Caes. *BAfr.* 88, Plut. *Cat. Min.* 66.1–3, App. *BC* 2.98, Dio 43.10.1–5. Caesar would indeed pardon Cato's son and allow him to inherit his father's property, but four years later the young man would die fighting with Brutus and Cassius at the second Battle of Philippi.

84. Dio 43.10.3, τοῦ τε θανάτου πολὺ τὸν παρὰ τοῦ Καίσαρος ἔλεον χαλεπώτερον ἡγεῖτο εἶναι.

85. Plut. *Cat. Min.* 66.3, Dio 43.10.4–5.

funds to the inhabitants of the city, along with his accounts and a careful record
of his administration, and he continued to monitor the progress of the evacuation of the city.[86] With these things done, he began preparing himself for death.
The accounts of Cato's suicide—Plutarch's in particular—are probably as much
fiction as fact, ornamented later by those who admired Cato and wanted to present his suicide as the final act of a true philosopher who refused to live under the
conditions in which he found himself. Indeed, it is Cato's death that begins the
transformation of his legend. The epilogue will examine the literary tradition of
Cato's suicide in detail, but Plutarch—who gives the fullest account—was primarily interested in exploring Cato's moral character, and so went out of his way to
link him to Socrates, whose own death was famous among educated readers.[87] It
is all but certain, therefore, that Plutarch shaped his account of Cato's death to fit
his own preconceived notion of what Cato represented or should represent, thus
creating the famous suicide that has been preserved in literature.

After bathing, Cato dined with friends, and then sat up drinking and discussing
literary and philosophical subjects with them.[88] While discussing the Stoic idea
that only the good man is truly free, while all bad men are slaves, Cato defended
this point with such force and conviction that his entourage soon realized that he
intended to end his life and thus free himself from his concerns. At the end of the
evening, he embraced his son and friends longer than usual, and then retired to his
chambers to read Plato's *Phaedo*, the philosophical dialogue set in the final hours
of Socrates's life.[89] While reading, he noticed that his sword was missing from
his room, and when his servants could not (or would not) produce it, he grew
angry, struck a slave hard enough to bruise his own hand, and began shouting so
loudly that his son and others came running into the room, begging him not to
kill himself. After calming them and receiving his sword, he dismissed his son and
friends with calm reassurances. He read the *Phaedo* a second time and then slept a
while longer, but awoke around midnight and consulted with his servants about
the progress of the evacuation of the city. Satisfied that all ships had left or were
on the verge of doing so, he instructed his servants to be on watch for ships that
were forced to return on account of bad weather, and then retired again to his
room. Taking his sword, he stabbed himself in the stomach, but his aim was poor
and the blow was not immediately mortal. His son and friends heard the noise

---

86. Plut. *Cat. Min.* 70.2–3, App. *BC* 2.98, Dio 43.11.1.

87. Duff (1999) 131–60, esp. 135 and 156.

88. Plut. *Cat. Min.* 66.4–67.2 (cf. App. *BC* 2.98, and Dio 43.11.2–3)

89. Plut. *Cat. Min.* 68.1–2, App. *BC* 2.99, Dio 43.11.2.

and discovered him dazed and not responding, and so they summoned a doctor who stitched the wound. Awaking in the middle of the operation, Cato shoved the doctor away and ripped open his wound, tearing at his own organs until he died. Caesar arrived at Utica the next day, having hastened his approach in the hopes of taking Cato alive. When he discovered his old rival dead, he declared that he was angry to have missed the opportunity of pardoning him.[90] There can be no doubt that Caesar had hoped to have the pleasure of hearing him ask for clemency, but he can hardly have been surprised that the famously inflexible Cato had refused to yield.

---

90. Val. Max. 5.1.10, Plut. *Caes.* 54.1–2, *Cat. Min.* 72.1–2, App. *BC* 2.99, Dio 43.11.3–12.1.

Epilogue

CATO THE STOIC

IT IS UNFORTUNATE that Cato's suicide is his most famous and celebrated deed. His common identification as "Cato Uticensis" indicates that his suicide in Utica in 46 BC became the defining action of his life. His death was very Roman and fit within a long Roman tradition of suicide, but Cato's personality, his implacable opposition to the now-victorious Caesar, and his refusal to continue living under Caesar's domination all combined to give his death special meaning to those who survived the war. Within months of his death, Cicero and Brutus were writing eulogies of him, and Cicero in particular draped his death in a Stoic mantle. Like many Romans, Cato had been interested in Stoicism during his life, but in death he became identified as a great Stoic philosopher by those who wanted to see in him a symbol for the lost Republic. A century later, Stoics finding life intolerable under Nero's reign would admire Cato as the quintessential Stoic hero; they interpreted and described his suicide through Stoic lenses, and imitated his example and built his legacy as an outstanding philosopher. In this way, he was transformed in his afterlife from a man into a philosophical ideal, but this is not the real man, the real Cato who had been the greatest champion of the *mos maiorum*.

While Cato's reputation as a great exemplar of Stoic virtue seems solid, the arguments and observations made in the preceding chapters suggest that a review of this idea is merited. Some scholars have pointed out that Cato's identification as a Stoic philosopher is problematic, but the majority accept the testimony of ancient authors who refer to him as a great Stoic.[1] Yet these

---

1. For example, Russo ([1975] 95–6) suggested that Cato's character derived more from his natural temperament than from his studies in philosophy, but Morrell ([2017] 98–128) has argued that Cato was a genuine Stoic, and that his philosophical beliefs shaped his views of Roman policies.

references are not as clear as they may seem. Plutarch does refer to Cato as a philosopher in his biographies of Cato the Elder, Pompey, and Brutus, but he conspicuously fails to recognize him as a philosopher in his biography of Cato himself, where the greatest attention and care are given to explaining Cato's nature and character.[2] Instead, Plutarch there identifies him first and foremost as a statesman.[3] Similarly, Cicero refers to Cato as a "most perfect Stoic" (*Cato perfectus, mea sententia, Stoicus*), but he does this in the opening of his *Paradoxa Stoicorum*, where his main point is that Cato does *not* speak like a Stoic—his behavior does not reflect his philosophical study.[4] Plutarch records that Cato studied with prominent Stoic philosophers such as Antipater and Athenodorus, but this was not unusual for an elite Roman, and it is hardly sufficient to turn him into a Stoic philosopher.[5] Indeed, Cato is also known to have studied with the Epicurean Philostratus and the Peripatetic Demetrius, suggesting a more general interest in philosophy rather than a specific dedication to Stoicism.[6] In Cicero's *Brutus*, Cato is referred to as a Stoic, but mainly so the other characters can discuss how Cato was so *unlike* a Stoic in his rhetoric and oratory—Cicero even emphasizes that Cato took what he wanted from Stoicism, but sought other types of training as well.[7] Similarly, in his *Pro Murena* Cicero attacks and ridicules Cato's presentation of Stoic principles, and even encourages Cato to improve his understanding of philosophy, while in his *De Finibus* he portrays Cato several times actually disagreeing with mainstream Stoic thought.[8] Mark Morford argued that Cato never obtained

---

2. Plut. *Cat. Mai.* 27.5, *Brut.* 2.1, and *Pomp.* 40.1. Duff ([1999] 156) notes, "Plutarch is reticent about stating explicitly that Cato was a Stoic. . . ."

3. Swain ([1990] 192–203) developed this argument well.

4. Cic. *Parad.* Pro. 1–3.

5. Plut. *Cat. Min.* 4.1–2, 10.1–2, 16.1 (cf. Strabo 14.5.14). Rome's elite had been deeply interested in Greek philosophical training since at least 155 BC, and by the first century BC Rome itself had become a leading center for philosophical thought. See Hadot (1987), Frede (1999), Sedley (2003), Ferrary (2007), Warren (2009) 29–30.

6. Plut. *Cat. Min.* 57.2, 65.5, 67.2, 69.1, 70.1. Fantham ([2003] 99) also refers to Cato's adherence to philosophers of the Academy.

7. Cic. *Brut.* 119. See van der Wal (2007) 189.

8. See Chapter 2 on the *Pro Murena*, and see Morrell (2017) 104–5 on the *De Finibus*. In a letter to Atticus (13.19.4), Cicero even remarks that for his *De Finibus* he specifically chose men who were already dead to be his representatives of the philosophical schools, so that none of his friends would be jealous. Cato's recent death, rather than his mastery of Stoicism, was the key criterion.

any kind of formal education in philosophy, and that his knowledge of it was informal and unshaped.[9]

The decisive influence in Cato's life was not Greek philosophy, but Rome's ancestral heroes, and in particular his great-grandfather, who had climbed to the pinnacle of the *cursus honorum* by promoting himself as an *exemplum* of old-fashioned values. Cato the Elder had been a great scourge of Greek philosophers, and had meditated on the achievements of earlier Roman heroes who had lived in a simpler, most austere time.[10] Far from embracing Greek philosophical thought, the elder Cato reviled philosophers and philosophy: when the famous philosophers Carneades and Diogenes came to Rome with an Athenian delegation in 155 BC, Cato urged the Senate to drive them out of town lest they enfeeble and waste the Roman youth.[11] He spoke publicly against philosophy and philosophers, and taught his son to hate them, and even prophesied that the study of Greek would ruin Rome's empire.[12] It is a contradiction that Cato the Younger would become a devotee of Stoicism while simultaneously mimicking his great-grandfather, whose opposition to Greek philosophy was one of his most famous and recognizable traits.

It was easy to misidentify Cato the Younger as a Stoic, because Greek Stoic principles were not much different from Cato's own austere interpretation of traditional Roman values; they overlapped to a significant degree, and so were similar without being the same. To the casual eye, Cato the Elder—who spectacularly hated Greek philosophy—could easily be misidentified as a Stoic: he lived a simple and austere life, was famously self-controlled, was devoted to law and justice, and fought against the opulence and luxury that he saw in Rome. So old-fashioned Roman simplicity and self-control could easily be misidentified as Stoic *apatheia*, especially if one was predisposed to look for Stoic qualities. The same was true of Cato the Younger, whose frugality, self-discipline, and honesty were intended to display his uniformity with the *mos maiorum*, but his early biographers—most of whom were philosophers—were inclined to look at the world through Stoic lenses, and so misinterpreted his behavior as deriving from Stoic *apatheia* rather than from the Roman *mos maiorum*.[13] But Cato was not

---

9. Morford (2002) 47–8.

10. Plut. *Cat. Mai.* 2.1. The elder Cato modeled himself after Manius Curius—the three-time triumphator—whose small farm and humble cottage were near Cato's home.

11. Plut. *Cat. Mai.* 22.1–3.

12. Plut. *Cat. Mai.* 23.1–3.

13. Syme (1939) 57, "the Stoic teaching, indeed, was nothing more than a corroboration and theoretical defense of certain traditional virtues of the governing class in an aristocratic and

trying to live like a Stoic; he was trying to live like his own conception of what an authentic, conservative Roman should be, and later authors mischaracterized his behavior.

As the preceding chapters have shown, Cato's unusual behavior was intended to display his adherence to Roman tradition. His archaic style of clothing was adopted from old statues he saw around Rome, his scrupulous observance of the law and his campaigns against corruption reflected his view of how traditional Romans had lived, as did his extraordinary refusal of military honors and his habit of walking on long journeys rather than riding on a horse or in a litter. Furthermore, Cato pursued many goals that were inconsistent with Stoic principles, but entirely acceptable for a Roman senator. He sought status by standing for offices as soon as he was eligible, and he did his best to increase his glory and fame whenever possible, even arranging a magnificent triumphal entry to Rome from Cyprus. He defended his glory jealously, repelling any attempt to annul or minimize the fame of his Cyprian mission, and he shared the Roman passion for wealth: although his finances were fairly modest (for a senator) early in his life, he did not spurn the considerable wealth that came his way during his career. And Cato's disregard for Stoic *apatheia* is obvious: he was bitterly resentful at the loss of his fiancée Aemilia Lepida and lashed out in poetic verses; his grief at the death of his half-brother Caepio was tremendous and unrestrained; he approved the use of bribery to defeat Caesar in elections; and he regularly engaged in politics with extreme *animus* and *pathos*. Cicero—who was himself a philosopher and knew Cato well—once observed that the Caesarians needed to be faced with either his own *stomacho* or with Cato's *animo*, indicating that Cato was known more for his zealous and fiery spirit, rather than the cool and calm tolerance of Cicero.[14] In all of these actions, Cato continually ignored fundamental Stoic ethics, but never the boundaries of traditional Roman behavior.

Even Cato's suicide—which is often seen as the most important proof of his Stoicism—seems less the act of a philosopher than it was the act of a proud Roman senator who had lost his war. Plutarch gives the fullest account, and he gives the death a veneer of philosophic significance: the ritual bathing, the long dinner

---

republican state. Hellenic culture does not explain Cato, and the *virtus* about which Brutus composed a volume was a Roman quality, not an alien importation." For the overlap between Stoicism and traditional Roman values, see also Oost (1955) 108, Gill (2003) 57–8, and Connolly (2012) 122–3.

14. Quint. *Inst.* 6.3.112. Almost a century later, Seneca (*Ep.* 14.12–13)—who thought of Cato as a Stoic—remarked that Cato's behavior sharply deviated from the calmness and moderation expected of Stoic philosophers.

conversation about philosophy in which Cato insists that only the good man is free, the reading of Plato's *Phaedo* twice before going to bed, and the calm and brave way he reassures his son and convinces his friends of the rightness of his action.[15] Much of this philosophic flavor surely comes from Plutarch's sources, especially descriptions given by the philosopher Thrasea Paetus, whose own writings about Cato were probably based on the work of the philosopher Munatius Rufus, although he may also have used the writings of Cicero and Brutus, both of whom were extensively trained in philosophy.[16] All of these authors—culminating in Plutarch's account—were predisposed to think of Cato's suicide as a Stoic act, and saw him as an exemplar of philosophic virtue, much like Socrates, who famously accepted death in a calm and noble fashion. Yet beneath the philosophic veneer, several details of Cato's suicide undermine the idea that he was a Stoic: his forceful and heated insistence on the argument that only the good man is free, which was sufficiently violent and uncontrolled to alarm his friends; his wrathful outburst when he discovers that his friends had removed his sword from his room; and his enraged striking of a slave's mouth, which was so fierce that it wounded Cato's own hand.[17] And whereas Socrates's passing had been fairly peaceful, Cato's death was extremely gruesome and bloody, stabbing himself in the stomach with a sword, and later ripping open the wound and tearing at his own entrails.[18]

This death was not about Stoic acceptance of fate, but about heroic and superhuman endurance of pain. Plutarch even suggests that Cato's decision to commit suicide may have been motivated by sheer spite, to deny Caesar the opportunity to claim a reputation for clemency by sparing the defeated Cato.[19] Many scholars have noted that these violent and unrestrained aspects of his suicide simply do

---

15. But see Edwards ([2006] 205–6), who argues that Plato's *Phaedo* was usually seen as arguing against suicide, and that Cato's long death speech was probably added to the story decades later by Seneca.

16. Plutarch cites Thrasea Paetus as a source (*Cat. Min.* 25.1, 37.1), and explains (37.1) that Paetus followed the account of Munatius Rufus. See Geiger (1979) 48–72 for discussion.

17. See Plutarch *Cat. Min.* 67.1–4 and 68.5. Zadorojnyi ([2007] 216–30) discusses these points in detail, and remarks (218–19) "the picture of Cato punching the slave . . . is particularly damning, since punishment of slaves in anger was regarded as precisely the kind of error a philosophical individual must aim to avoid." Duff ([1999] 151) also notes that Cato's violent outbursts—during this episode, but also earlier in his life—contradict the norms of Stoicism.

18. Plut. *Cat. Min.* 70.5–6. Duff ([1999] 141–5) discusses Plutarch's efforts to connect Cato to Socrates.

19. Plut. *Cat. Min.* 72.2.

FIGURE E.I. *The Death of Cato*, Pierre Narcisse Guérin (1744–1833). 1797, Ecole nationale supérieure des Beaux-Arts, Paris.
Source: Art Resource.

not fit the Stoic ideal of *apatheia*.[20] Even on the surface, therefore, Cato's suicide violates traditional Stoic values.

A Roman without a predisposition toward philosophical thinking might look at Cato's suicide very differently, especially if he was steeped in the history and traditions of the Republic. Roman legend was full of noble suicides that had nothing to do with philosophy: Lucretia committed suicide to preserve her honor and reputation; in 450 BC Ap. Claudius the *decemvir* killed himself rather than face the wrath of the people for his misdeeds; in 362 BC the young Marcus Curtius hurled himself into a chasm that had opened up in the Roman Forum in order to save the state; in 340 BC P. Decius Mus gave his life to save his army through the practice of *devotio* (his son did the same in 295 BC).[21] In more recent

20. For example, Griffin (1986) 202, Goar (1987) 71 n. 64, and Zadorojnyi (2007) 219. Indeed, Cato is made to look like such a bad Stoic in this scene that Trapp ([1999] 496–7) suggested that Plutarch was deliberately trying to undermine the Roman tradition of Cato as a true Stoic.

21. Lucretia: Livy 1.58.1–12; Ap. Claudius: Livy 3.58.6; M. Curtius: Livy 7.6.1–6; Decius Mus (father and son) *MRR* 1.135 and 177. See Grisé (1982) 16–17.

times, P. Licinius Crassus Dives Mucianus—having been captured by the enemy
in 130 BC—committed suicide rather than face the shame of defeat; C. Papirius
Carbo committed suicide rather than face condemnation in the courts in 119 BC;
in 102 BC the young M. Scaurus killed himself rather than live with his father's
disapproval; in 87 BC L. Cornelius Merula and Q. Lutatius Catulus committed
suicide to avoid the indignation of being murdered by Marius's henchmen; in 66
BC C. Licinius Macer killed himself to avoid condemnation for extortion; in 63
BC L. Sergius Catilina—with his insurrection against Rome facing utter defeat—
killed himself through a suicidal charge into the ranks of the enemy; and in 42 BC
Brutus and Cassius both killed themselves after their respective military defeats
by the Caesarians.[22] Even humbler Romans might prefer suicide to accepting defeat in battle: in 217 BC Roman soldiers at Lake Trasimene took their own lives
rather than allowing themselves to be slaughtered by Hannibal's army; the same
happened in the winter of 54/53 BC when several of Caesar's soldiers killed themselves rather than die at the hands of their enemies; and during the civil war in
49 BC, a cohort of Caesar's soldiers and their military tribune C. Vulteius Capito
preferred a pact of mutual murder-suicide rather than surrender to Pompey's
forces.[23] Pompey was said to have deeply respected the bravery of these soldiers,
just as Sallust spoke respectfully of the brave way the traitor Catiline brought
about his own death.[24] A brave death was not uniquely, or even especially, a Stoic
action; it was every bit a Roman action, and one that had a distinguished place in
Rome's long history.

In this light, Cato's decision to commit suicide in 46 BC can be seen as a sol-
idly traditional and praiseworthy *Roman* action. Caesar's victory over Metellus
Scipio at Thapsus signaled—at least for Cato—the collapse of the Republican
cause, and even of the Republic itself. Although it was open to him to surrender and return to Rome, he decided that it was preferable to die, much like
the legendary Lucretia who died for her reputation. Faced with unacceptable
alternatives, it is not at all surprising that a proud Roman would take his own life,
especially if doing so delivered a final insult to a hated enemy. Metellus Scipio
did the same—he tried to escape by sea after his defeat at the Battle of Thapsus,

---

22. Mucianus: Val. Max. 3.2.12; Carbo: Cic. *Brut.* 103; Scaurus: Val. Max. 5.8.4, Auct. *Vir. Ill.*
72.10, Front. *Strat.* 4.1.13; Merula and Catulus: Val. Max. 9.12.4–5; Macer: Val. Max. 9.12.7;
Catiline: Sall. *BC* 60.7; Brutus and Cassius: *MRR* 2.360–1.

23. Polyb. 3.84.10, Caes. *BG* 5.37, Luc. 4.476–580.

24. Rauh ([2015] 383–410) argues that public shame may not have been a normal motive in
Roman military suicides, but he does not consider suicides before 264 BC because they slip
into the realm of folklore, and those legendary examples could be potent models for Romans,
especially for a person who followed tradition closely, such as Cato.

but being cut off by Caesar's forces, he committed suicide rather than humiliate himself by accepting Caesar's famous clemency.[25] His legate M. Petreius acted similarly, entering a suicide pact with King Juba after their defeat at Thapsus.[26] Few would have considered Scipio, Petreius, or Juba to be great Stoic sages for this action. There is no reason to doubt that the educated Cato was thinking about Socrates's death on the evening before his suicide, or that the teachings of the Stoics entered his mind and gave him comfort, but his lack of *apatheia* in the events leading up to his death, and the particularly gruesome and violent manner of his death—which showcased extreme bravery rather than acceptance of fate— suggest that his death was motivated by Roman tradition.

When Cato died, his contemporaries did not at first view his suicide as an outstanding example of Stoic fortitude, but simply as a Roman death. Shortly after learning of the news, Cicero called Cato's death honorable, but did not immediately attach much philosophical significance to it.[27] In fact, some of Cato's closest associates even disapproved of his suicide, and thought less of Cato for taking that course. According to Plutarch, Brutus "blamed Cato for killing himself, since it was an unholy and unmanly deed to try to escape from one's allotted fate, and not to accept fearlessly what comes, but to run away."[28] This description of Cato's death as unholy and unmanly does not portray Cato's suicide as something noble and praiseworthy, but as a morally wrong action that tainted—rather than exalted—his reputation. Rather than accepting fate without passion or distraction as a Stoic should, Cato had fled life in an attempt to escape the events that fate had produced. Brutus was very well trained in philosophical thought, and he knew his uncle as well as anyone, so the fact that he did not see in Cato's death a great Stoic *exemplum* undermines any notion that Cato intended his suicide to follow Stoic ideals.

Cato took his own life during the night between April 12 and 13 in 46 BC, and shortly after the man died, his legend began to grow. Cicero—now safely back in Italy—began contemplating Cato's life and death, and with the encouragement of Brutus he decided to write a eulogy praising Cato. This was potentially dangerous, since it was certain to anger the triumphant Caesar, who was now dictator and in control of Rome, and who had no interest in seeing his former

---

25. Livy *Per.* 114, Val. Max. 3.2.13, App. *BC* 2.100–101, Dio 43.9.5. As Griffin ([1986b] 194) argues, "these suicides fit into the pattern of those that had long been considered acceptable, namely those to escape the shame of defeat and surrender."

26. Caes. *BAfr.* 94, Livy *Per.* 114, App. *BC* 2.101, Dio 43.8.4.

27. Cic. *Fam.* 9.18.2.

28. Plut. *Brut.* 40.7.

rival or his ideas celebrated. Cicero expressed his concerns in a letter to Atticus, emphasizing that—if one focused solely on Cato's values and virtues, and thus avoided discussing his political career as Caesar's enemy—one would not understand the true Cato:

> Regarding the *Cato*, it is a problem for Archimedes. I cannot find a way to write something that your companions would be able to read with pleasure or even with an even temper. Because even if I avoided the opinions he pronounced in the Senate, and his entire inclination and the counsels which he held regarding the Republic, and I wished only to praise his seriousness and constancy, even this would be an unpleasant noise to them. But indeed, that man cannot be praised unless these things are included, because he saw the present and future situation, and he strove to prevent them from happening, and he abandoned his life so that he would not see them happen.[29]

Despite his misgivings, however, he began the work, and by July he was well on his way and pleased with his progress.[30] This work does not survive, so its content and structure are not known, but to avoid offending Caesar, Cicero seems to have focused his work on praising Cato's moral qualities.[31] In all likelihood, therefore, the eulogy emphasized Cato's morals and ideals, rather than his political career, and so it sidestepped the politically dangerous topic of his lifelong opposition to Caesar. In a passage preserved by Macrobius, for example, Cicero wrote of him: "the opposite of what normally happens in most people happened in him: that all things were greater in fact than in report; it does not often happen that expectation of someone is surpassed by knowing them, and that what one hears of a person is surpassed by what one sees."[32] Just as Cicero had once disguised his attack on Cato's prosecution of Murena with a discussion of Stoic ideas, he now disguised his praise of Cato's republicanism by presenting it in the guise of Stoic philosophy—instead of praising the man himself (which was risky),

---

29. Cic. *Att.* 12.4.2.

30. Cic. *Att.* 12.4.2, 12.5.2, *Fam.* 7.24.2, *Orat.* 35, cf. Cic. *Div.* 2.3, Plut. *Cic.* 39.5, *Caes.* 54.3, App. *BC* 2.99. See Kumaniecki (1970) 168–88 and Fehrle (1983) 285–92.

31. Russo ([1975] 93) argues that it primarily focused on his character and so was more philosophical in tone. Jones (1970) discusses the few fragments found in the works of other authors. See Goar (1987) 15 n. 6.

32. Macrob. *Sat.* 6.2.33, *contingebat in eo quod plerisque contra solet, ut maiora omnia re quam fama viderentur: id quod non saepe evenit, ut expectatio cognitione, aures ab oculis vincerentur.*

he praised Cato's philosophy (which was safe). Indeed, Christopher Jones has even suggested that the work took the form of a philosophical dialogue, which further removed the treatise from the political questions of the day.[33] As a consequence, talk about Cato would rapidly come to focus on his morals and virtues, rather than on his fierce republicanism that Caesar had defeated.[34] Furthermore, Cicero was himself a notable philosopher, and as he came to feel that Caesar's domination was leaving little room for personal freedom in the Republic, he began interpreting Cato's suicide through philosophic lenses.[35] For this reason, Cicero's descriptions of Cato became more laudatory after 46 BC, and it was his *Cato* more than anything else that presented—and therefore established—Cato as a Stoic sage.[36] Cicero had previously been a fierce critic of Cato's unyielding nature, but with Cato dead and Caesar ruling Rome, he could reinterpret that obstinacy as Stoic virtue. It was easier and safer to praise Cato as a philosopher rather than as a politician, so Cicero's *Cato* recast the man for later generations.

Nor was Cicero alone in eulogizing Cato in this way. By the following March (45 BC), Brutus had begun his own literary encomium also entitled *Cato*, and soon afterward Cato's friend Munatius Rufus and the senator Fabius Gallus had likewise started composing works to praise Cato.[37] Very little is known of these last two works, but Cicero comments on Brutus's work, since it clearly worried him. Brutus had always admired his uncle, and had even married Cato's daughter Porcia, so he may have seen himself as responsible for preserving and augmenting Cato's legacy.[38] In fact, Cicero felt that Brutus went much too far, and he complained to Atticus that Brutus was giving Cato credit for things he had not done. For example, he was shocked and offended to learn that Brutus was giving Cato the credit for being the first to propose capital punishment for the Catilinarian conspirators, and was presenting him (instead of Cicero) as being the driving force in the suppression of the conspiracy. He complained that Brutus was wrongly presenting Cato as the only senator who argued for

---

33. Jones (1970) 194–6.

34. Cic. *de Div.* 2.1–2, Plut. *Caes.* 54.5–6. Tacitus (*Ann.* 4.34) reveals that many decades later it was still dangerous to praise the political activities of Republican heroes too enthusiastically. See Goar (1987) 14 n. 4.

35. Cic. *Fam.* 4.9.2, 4.14.1, 9.16.3.

36. Goar (1987) 13–15. See also Jones (1970) 188–96, Morford (2002) 43, Stem (2005), Pelling (2011) 406, and van der Blom (2011) 569–70.

37. Brutus: Cic. *Att.* 12.21.1, 13.46.2; Munatius Rufus: Plut. *Cat. Min.* 37.1; Fabius Gallus: Cic. *Fam.* 7.24.2. See Pelling (2011) 407 for discussion.

38. Plut. *Cat. Min.* 73.4, *Brut.* 13.3 and 7, *Caes.* 62.1, App. *BC* 4.136, Dio 44.13.1.

harsh punishment of the conspirators, and to prove the point he provided a list of high-ranking senators who argued for the death penalty before Cato. Cicero attempted to set the record straight, but it is clear that he, Brutus, and others had already begun the process of idealizing—and even rewriting—aspects of Cato's character and political career.

None of these eulogies to Cato survive, but they were so laudatory that they quickly drew the displeasure of Caesar, who had no wish to see his most persistent political foe praised and glorified. Indeed, Tacitus would later write that Cicero's extravagant praise, which lauded Cato to the heavens, drove Caesar to respond.[39] While he praised Cicero's eloquent style of writing (which he said was better than Brutus's), he found the glorification of Cato and the embellishment of his reputation irksome and politically awkward, especially since he was entering his fourth dictatorship in April 45 BC, and wanted to leave his defeated enemies—and their accusations of his tyrannical ambitions—in the past. Although Caesar had been victorious in the civil war, many Romans still looked favorably on Cato and on the *mos maiorum* that had been crushed by Caesar's legions. In the previous year (46 BC), when Caesar was celebrating his four triumphs—one each over Gaul, Egypt, Pontus, and Africa—the Romans had taken offense at his inclusion in the fourth triumph of painted scenes depicting the suicide of important Romans. As Appian describes the triumph,

> [Caesar] avoided listing the names of Romans in his triumph, because it did not seem appropriate to him, and it would have been shameful and ill-omened to the Roman people, but he nevertheless displayed the men and all their sufferings in likenesses and in full color paintings, excepting only Pompey. For this man alone he avoided displaying, since he was still very much missed by everyone. Although they were afraid for themselves, the people still lamented these national evils, most of all when they saw the *imperator* Lucius Scipio stabbing himself in the chest and collapsing into the sea, and Petreius killing himself at the dinner table, and Cato tearing himself asunder like a wild beast.[40]

The portrayal of these suicides in his triumph was an unusual misstep for Caesar, and suggests that he had underestimated the depth of the Roman people's affection for Cato and his allies. He had omitted Pompey's image, demonstrating sensitivity to popular opinion, but the backlash against his inclusion of other

---

39. Tac. *Ann.* 4.34.4.

40. App. *BC* 2.101.

Romans, including Cato, seems to have come as a surprise.[41] The Roman citizens had been unwilling to emulate Cato's values in life, but in death they admired him as an *exemplum* of their noble past. It is possible that Caesar had only seen Cato as a difficult adversary, and had not fully appreciated the people's appreciation of his *exemplum*.

This respect for Cato implied a rebuke to Caesar, so the pamphlets that Cicero and Brutus composed extolling Cato and magnifying his values were very unwelcome, and Caesar determined to publish a counter-narrative that would criticize Cato's actions. The text of Caesar's *Anticato* is lost, and few specifics are known of its content, but it may have taken the form of a prosecutorial speech in which Caesar accused Cato of some crime, perhaps *maiestas* (treason).[42] In May 45 BC, Cicero received a pamphlet from Hirtius that may have been an early draft of the *Anticato*. It was very harsh and it detailed Cato's faults, but Cicero believed that Caesar and Hirtius had made a mistake in abusing Cato so severely, and so he urged the copying and circulation of the pamphlet, which he thought would increase Cato's reputation rather than squash it.[43] Little is known about the reception of the *Anticato*, but while it undoubtedly maligned Cato and exaggerated his faults, there may have been enough truth in the work to give it some weight. For example, the *Anticato* seems to have portrayed Cato as a drunk, but even Cato's friends admitted that he had always enjoyed drinking. Likewise, the *Anticato* portrayed Cato as using Marcia to obtain Hortensius's wealth, but no one could deny that his handing over of Marcia had been strange, as had been the fact that he took her back once Hortensius was dead and his wealth was in Marcia's hands. This was the start of the propaganda war over Cato's memory, which ultimately led to the transformation and idealization of his legacy.

In different times, Cato probably would have been remembered only as the man he had been, but Caesar's victory in the civil war and his sole domination over the empire led many Romans to begin thinking more ideologically about Caesar and his great opponent Cato. As Caesar the dictator was increasingly viewed as a tyrant by many of Rome's elite, his archrival Cato—who had often warned the Romans of Caesar's tyrannical aspirations, and who had died rather than live under Caesar's power—became the symbol of republicanism. In life,

---

41. For a discussion of Caesar's depiction of these suicides in this triumph, see Havener (2014) 170–2 and Östenberg (2014) 181–93.

42. Cic. *Att.* 12.41.4 and 13.50.1, Suet. *Iul.* 56.5, Tac. *Ann.* 4.34.4, Plut. *Caes.* 3.4, 54.6, *Cic.* 39.6, App. *BC* 2.99, Dio 43.13.4. Taylor ([1949] 170–1) suggests this format. For a discussion of when Caesar started the work, see Jones (1970) 194. For general discussion, see Gelzer (1968) 301–5, Russo (1975) 94, Tschieder (1981), Fehrle (1983) 293, Goar (1987) 17, and Pelling (2011) 408.

43. Cic. *Att.* 12.40.1, 12.41.4, 12.44.1, 12.45.2, 12.48.1.

Caesar and Cato had been mere aristocratic rivals, but after Cato's death in 46
BC (and Caesar's death two years later in 44 BC), their rivalry came to be seen
as a conflict of ideologies; the more Caesar and his successors came to be seen
as monarchs, the more Cato was lionized as a champion of republican virtues,
and of Stoic virtues as well.[44] This process probably did not take long: Caesar
was holding repeated dictatorships at the time, and in 44 BC received the title
of "dictator for life," and in the eyes of many his behavior was becoming increasingly autocratic.[45] As a result, Cato increasingly came to be seen as a hero of the
Republic, and—if nothing else—as the greatest opponent of Caesar.[46] In this
idealizing process, the men became archetypes of opposing political principles,
and as such they came to be ideas as much as men: Caesar became the conquering
general and tyrant, while Cato became the Stoic sage.[47] Cato had been a major
player in Roman politics during his life, but his passionate championing of the
mos maiorum—and his suicide in particular—took on tremendous symbolic importance under Caesar's dictatorship, and under later warlords such as Antony
and Octavian, who seemed more concerned about their own power than about
the Republic. As Cato's life and death became symbols of the dying Republic,
Cicero and others began to infuse them with new meanings and interpretations.

This idealization of Cato as a Stoic philosopher probably continued in another early account of his life and death, written by his friend the philosopher
Munatius Rufus.[48] Although this work does not survive, it was influential in
shaping Cato's legacy: the Stoic philosopher Thrasea Paetus used it in composing
his own encomium to Cato, and Plutarch relied on both works to produce his biography of Cato.[49] Caesar's assassination led Roman thinkers to begin developing

---

44. See Pelling (2002) 99.

45. Cic. *Fam.* 6.7.1–4, Suet. *Iul.* 76.1, Plut. *Caes.* 60.1–62.10.

46. Taylor (1949) 170, "the nobles were still permitted under Caesar's mild rule to talk and
write with relative freedom, and some of them were talking and writing of the republic, of the
old days of public responsibility or the body politic. And Cato's unconquered soul speedily
became identical with the republic and liberty."

47. Griffin ([1986b] 195–6) argues that Cicero made Cato a martyr by drawing comparisons of
his suicide to that of Socrates, while Van der Blom (2010) discusses Cicero's use of Cato's reputation in his philosophical writings, and Morford ([2002] 53) suggests that Cicero placed Cato
in his *de Finibus* as a memorial to the civil war dead. Taylor ([1949] 162–82) discusses the rise
of "Catonism and Caesarism."

48. Geiger (1979) 48–72, Zecchini (1980) 46–8, Swain (1990) 198, Zadorojnyi (2007)
220 n. 28.

49. Fantham ([2003] 98) noted, "Cato became by his suicide a saint and martyr, and the
single continuous life of Plutarch has preserved the essence of a hagiography by his confidant
Munatius, further developed by the Stoic Thrasea Paetus."

philosophical arguments justifying the slaying of a tyrant, and so the invocation to *libertas* as a political ideal came to be colored with Stoic elements and ideas as the empire developed.[50] Cato's very name became synonymous with *libertas*, so it should not be surprising that later authors imported all new meanings to his life and death.[51] His suicide was caught up in this new thinking about tyranny and liberty, and it was endowed with deep philosophical significance and meaning. Therefore, while Cato lived and ended his life according to his own understanding of Roman values, others viewed and presented his suicide as a philosophical act of great significance.

This becomes clear in Sallust's comparison of Caesar and Cato in his work on the Catilinarian conspiracy. This passage was quoted in full in the Introduction of this book, and it makes clear that the two men were already being cast as oppositional figures by the time Sallust wrote his account of the Catilinarian conspiracy in the years following Caesar's assassination.[52] In a sequence of comparisons, Sallust describes the men in very different terms: Caesar's generosity is contrasted to Cato's integrity; his clemency to Cato's severity; congeniality to honesty; Caesar is a shelter for the weak, while Cato is a bane to evildoers; and his courtesy is contrasted to Cato's constancy. In the end, Caesar wanted to win military glory through a great command, while Cato sought a reputation for severity, virtue, decency, and integrity. Sallust describes the two men not merely as political rivals, but as polar opposites. Just as Caesar represents the sheer power of the great commander and politician, Cato represents the traditional basket of republican virtues that Cicero, Brutus, Munatius Rufus, and others identified as Stoic.[53] Cato's suicide was central to this dichotomy: by taking his own life bravely and in defiance of Caesar, he provided the perfect and absolute rejection of Caesar.[54] As the victorious Caesar and his heirs claimed autocratic rule, Cato

---

50. See discussions in Pina Polo (2011) 76–80 and Arena (2007) 49–73.

51. Gowing (2005) 5–6.

52. Sall. *Cat.* 53.6–54.6. Goar ([1987] 20–1) provides a discussion of this comparison of Caesar and Cato, along with a discussion of previous scholarship.

53. Taylor ([1949] 178) says of Sallust's description: "already he is integrity, sternness, and steadfastness incarnate, the Cato of legend."

54. Hill ([2004] 71) makes this point well: ". . . so thoroughly had Cato identified with the Republican and aristocratic aesthetic that to look upon Caesar's victory filled him with a revulsion so intense that death was preferable to continued existence under an autocrat. It was Cato's undoubted *virtus*, however, his *constantia* and *incredibilis gravitas*, that allowed this perception to transcend the level of mere individual preference and revealed Caesar to be a tyrant before the eyes of the wider social audience. The self-killings of those possessed of a *lenior vita* ('more pliable life') or *mores faciliores* ('more flexible characters') might be misinterpreted or even condemned by others, but the rigidity of Cato's character meant that his voluntary death

became not only Caesar's greatest political opponent, but also the very antithesis of Caesarianism. Thus the preeminence of Caesar caused the elevation of Cato from a defiant Roman to a Stoic ideal.

Caesar's heir Augustus also participated in this recasting and use of Cato's legacy, seeking to secure and legitimize his own domination of the Roman Empire by draping his imperial monarchy in a veil of Catonian republicanism. The new emperor minimized the legacy of his controversial great-uncle, but celebrated and promoted the ideal of Cato as the champion of traditional Republican values.[55] Augustus even composed a work of his own on Cato that he read to his family, thus using—and no doubt adjusting—Cato's legacy to suit his own political agenda.[56] Augustan authors took their cue from their patron, and Cato rapidly became a sainted figure in Roman literature. Robert Goar has presented an excellent and detailed analysis of the treatment of Cato by Augustan authors, and shows that they continued to build his legacy not only as a great champion of republican virtues, but also that "the Stoic conception of Cato, created by Cicero, is still flourishing in an era which was perhaps more interested in rhetoric and literature than in philosophy."[57] When Virgil described the god Vulcan decorating a shield for Aeneas in the *Aeneid*, he noted that "he further adds to this the dwelling places in Tartarus, the tall doors of Dis, the punishments for crimes, and you—Catiline—hanging from a menacing crag and trembling at the mouths of the Furies. The good were separated, with Cato giving laws to them."[58] This is, of course, the idealized Cato; in reality, the Romans had been very unimpressed with Cato when he exercised jurisdiction as a praetor, and many thought he had degraded the majesty of his office with his outlandish style of dress.[59] Horace celebrates Cato's noble death (*Catonis nobile letum*) in his odes, but whereas Brutus had begun by thinking that suicide was improper and unworthy of so great man, Horace shows little doubt that Cato's suicide was the act of a stern and unconquered soul.[60] A little while later, Valerius Maximus would summarize Cato as a man of perfect virtue, whose very name had become a synonym

---

could only serve to demonstrate the absolute incompatibility of Caesar's rule with the ethical ideals of the Republic."

55. Syme (1939) 317–18 and Taylor (1949) 176–82.

56. Suet. *Aug.* 85.1.

57. Goar (1987) 23–31 (31 quoted).

58. Vir. *Aen.* 8.666–70.

59. Cic. *Att.* 2.1.8, Plut. *Cat. Min.* 44.1.

60. Hor. *Carm.* 1.12.35–6 (cf. 2.1.24).

for a venerable and extraordinary citizen.[61] As Cato became a symbol for the old Republic and for traditional Roman values, the original aspects and nuances of the real man became harder to see.

Cato's reputation as a great Stoic guru came to its full development under the reign of Nero. Although Augustus had tried to present his own rule as lying within the Catonian mantle of republicanism, his successors were far more blatant in their exercise of autocratic power, and many of Rome's elites found it increasingly difficult to live under their regime. As Robert Goar explained, "Cato was held in high esteem by Augustan writers and by Augustus himself, was revered by Velleius Paterculus and Valerius Maximus, and virtually deified by Seneca and Lucan. As the Julio-Claudian era wore on, thinking men and women who were forced to endure the terrors of Caligula or Nero naturally turned to the memory of Cato for comfort and inspiration."[62] Under Nero's reign, Stoics such as Seneca and Thrasea Paetus looked on Cato as a Stoic sage whose suicide provided an *exemplum* for those living under the tyranny of the emperors. When these men were condemned and forced to take their own lives, they deliberately modeled their own suicides after Cato's example, or at least, after the Stoic reconstruction of it.[63] Yet there was an important difference: whereas Cato chose willingly to commit suicide, people like Seneca and Thrasea were condemned to death and so killed themselves only under compulsion. Thus their admiration and emulation of Cato was out of necessity, and they focused on the manner of his death more than on his philosophical beliefs.[64] Thus the many aspects of Cato's life and death that violated Stoic beliefs could be minimized or even excised, and those facing their deaths could focus on Cato's brave suicide and see in it a Stoic ideal. Seneca, for example, was said to have admired not only Cato's decision to die, but also his endurance of pain during his particularly grisly death.[65] Thus it was not Cato's philosophical beliefs that were particularly admired by later Stoics, but his ability to endure pain bravely, which was as much a Roman virtue as a Stoic one.[66] Seneca wrote extensively on Cato, embellishing his memory and transforming his suicide from a violent and gruesome affair into a calm and

---

61. Val. Max. 2.10.8.

62. Goar (1987) 48.

63. See Zecchini (1980) 39–56, Hill (2004) 186–7.

64. See Griffin (1986a) 70 and Edwards (2006).

65. Edwards (2006) 206.

66. One need only consider the Roman hero Mucius Scaevola, who was said to have held his hand in a fire until it was ruined in order to prove his bravery and capacity to endure pain to King Porsenna in 508 BC (Livy 2.12.13–16).

serene Stoic example of *apatheia*, even composing fictional death speeches that enhanced the image of Cato as the true philosopher.[67] Such reworking of Cato's memory was not limited to his suicide: Seneca transformed Cato in several of his writings, perpetuating a very particular memory of him as a moral example, rather than as the hard-nosed politician he had been in life.[68] This emphasizes how Cato the Roman senator—who threw himself (often violently) into political battles, who tenaciously held the Senate floor filibustering legislation, and who struggled physically with hired ruffians to get his voice heard in public meetings—got lost in Neronian Rome, while Cato the philosopher emerged. This appropriation of Cato's memory continued with Seneca's nephew Lucan. According to Goar, in the lines of Lucan "the Cato legend reaches its apogee, that the man of Utica is canonized, even apotheosized."[69] To those educated elites who suffered and were condemned to death under the autocratic rule of the later Caesars, the Stoic legend of Cato—which offered individuals an attractive *exemplum* of how to live and die under a tyrant—became fixed in the Roman mind.

By the time Plutarch started his biography of Cato in the late first or early second century AD, Cato's memory had been substantially transformed. Working within the philosophic tradition of Cicero, Seneca, Lucan, Thrasea Paetus, and Munatius Rufus—and using their writings—Plutarch had little reason to question the idealized Cato that he received from them. Yet doing this must have raised problems, since Plutarch was attempting to place the idealized Cato back within the very real events of the late Republic. This explains why Plutarch's Cato is sometimes portrayed as the very essence of the Stoic philosopher, while at other times he seems to have little interest in the most basic Stoic doctrines; he shows remarkable self-control on some occasions, but on others he falls easily into wrath or misery.[70] In his *Precepts of Statecraft* in his *Moralia*, Plutarch states that Cato never allowed personal feeling or enmity to influence his political activity, but this is very clearly contradicted by any number of incidents in which Cato was

---

67. See Goar (1987) 37–40, Edwards (2006) 206, and Hammer (2014) 313.

68. Gowing (2005) 79.

69. Goar (1987) 41. See further discussion in Hill (2004) 222–36 and Gowing (2005) 94–6.

70. Duff ([1999] 131–60) has argued that Plutarch wrote this biography in part to explore the underlying question of the relationship of personal morality with public leadership, and that he often critiques Cato's tendency to allow his personal virtue to harm the Republic. Meanwhile, Cowan ([2015] 16) emphasized that Plutarch shaped his biographies to "map onto literary or historical paradigms, and indeed the life of Cato itself is carefully crafted to make him conform to the model of Socrates."

driven by feuds or even personal hatred.[71] These incongruities likely come from Plutarch's efforts to combine Cato the symbol with Cato the man.

Yet there were those who did remember Cato first and foremost as a patriot and a champion of tradition, and thought this commemoration as a Stoic philosopher absurd. The poet Martial was one of these. He was unimpressed with the growing practice of aristocratic suicide, and frequently criticized such deaths as mere pretension.[72] In one of his epigrams, Martial writes:

> You are doing what I would wish you to do, Decianus, because you follow the philosophical doctrines of the great Thrasea and the consummate Cato in this way, that you wish to be safe and not run against drawn swords with a bare breast. I do not like the man who purchases fame with easy blood; I like the man who is able to be honored without death.[73]

Martial was not only unfriendly to aristocratic suicide, but also to the use of Cato's memory to justify such action as a noble act of Stoic philosophy.[74] In another epigram, Martial compares the suicide of a friend Festus to Cato's death:

> When a wasting disease was pressing down on his undeserving throat, and black fluid spreading into his very face, Festus himself determined to go to the Stygian lake, with dry eyes giving courage to his weeping friends. He did not, however, pollute his pious mouth with dark poison or wrench a sad death from slow starvation, but instead he ended his venerable life with a Roman death, and released his soul with a more noble pyre. Fame is able to prefer this death to the fate of great Cato: Caesar was this man's friend.[75]

The allusion to Cato suggests that Festus killed himself with a sword, rather than the other forms of suicide often favored by Stoics of the time. Martial identifies this death by the sword—and therefore Cato's own suicide—as a particularly Roman death.

---

71. Plut. *Mor.* 809d.

72. See discussion in Hill (2004) 255.

73. Mart. 1.8.

74. As Griffin ([1986b] 194) suggests, "[Martial] was hostile to Cato or rather to what Cato had become, namely, the solemnly revered and much-imitated model of heroic Stoic suicide."

75. Mart. 1.78.

Nevertheless, Cato's reputation as an ideal Stoic became so entrenched that it formed the basis for his repudiation by later Christian thinkers. Christian doctrine condemned suicide and considered it a form of homicide, so Christian writers argued against the widespread belief in the nobility of Stoic suicide. Because Cato continued to be the great and admired *exemplum* of Stoic suicide, Christian writers such as Lactantius and especially Augustine condemned his death and argued for its immorality.[76] Augustine gives extensive treatment to this, showing that—in widespread opinion—Cato had become a representative for Stoic ideas.[77] In the pages of these Christian thinkers, therefore, Cato was remembered and discussed primarily as a philosopher, not as a politician.

Cato's life and legacy were dramatically recast in the years following his death, and the transformation was so fast that few other interpretations of his career survived. In life, Cato had joined other members of Rome's elite in studying several different schools of philosophy, but his outstanding and defining characteristic was his incredible dedication to traditional Roman values. The *mos maiorum*—or at least his interpretation of Rome's ancestral tradition—was his guiding principle and determined his outlook. This might have been better remembered if Pompey had won the Battle of Pharsalus, but Caesar's victories in the civil war ultimately led Cato to kill himself, both to spite his archenemy and to escape living a life contrary to his principles. In the years that followed, his suicide was reinterpreted, recast, and endowed with profound philosophical significance. The particulars of his life and death, and even more the changing nature of Rome—which was already beginning its transformation from a Republic into an imperial monarchy—made Cato a symbol in the eyes of those who survived him. His personal and political feud with Caesar was reinterpreted as a philosophical battle between freedom and tyranny, and the details of his career became less important than his symbolic representation of the philosophical values that later Romans ascribed to him and to the lost Republic. As his legacy was handed down to later generations, he became the archetype of the Stoic philosopher and the champion of freedom, and so he came to be remembered for his death more than for his life. In all likelihood, however, Cato would have resented this transformation of his legacy; he was not a sage of Greek philosophy, but a stern champion of ancient Roman custom.

---

76. Lact. *Inst. Diu.* 3.18.8–12, August. *De Civ. Dei* 1.23–4 and 19.4.

77. See Goar (1987) 77–100 for discussion.

Glossary of Terms

Ambitus	The legal charge of bribery
Academic	School of philosophical thought
Accusator	Plaintiff or prosecutor in a court case
Aedile	Magistrate responsible for policing Rome's markets and infrastructure and for organizing certain festivals (there were four each year)
Amicitia	'Friendship,' but also the usual term for a political alliance
Apatheia	Stoic value of emotional disengagement, freedom from passion
As	Roman coin of small value
Auctoritas	The moral authority wielded by men of great reputation
Augur	A Roman priesthood
Boni	'Good men,' term used to refer to senators who supported the traditional practice of politics
Campus Martius	'Field of Mars,' a space near the city, but outside the *pomerium*, where citizen assemblies could be held and where elections for consuls and praetors took place
Capitol	Hill in Rome, important religious site
Censor	Magistrate responsible for maintaining the role of citizens and the list of senators and equestrians, held by two men for eighteen month every five years
Centuria praerogativa	The first century (group of voters) to cast its ballot in an election or other voting matter, thought to be predictive of the outcome of the entire vote of all 193 centuries
Civil War	(1) The conflict between Marius, Sulla, and their supporters (87–81 BC); (2) the conflict between Caesar, Pompey, and their supporters (49–45 BC)
Clientela	Clientage, the clients one possessed
Clients	Roman citizens who had a moral obligation to another Roman (their *patron*)

Cognomen	A Roman man's third name, usually an inherited nickname
Comitia	One of Rome's citizen assemblies, in which laws were passed and (in some cases) elections were held
Consul	Rome's highest annual magistracy, responsible for presiding over the Senate and some assemblies and for military command; there were two consuls each year
Consulares	Senators who had held the consulship and constituted the Senate leadership
Constantia	Roman virtue of constancy
Contio	A public meeting to discuss an issue
Curia	The Senate House
Cursus honorum	Rome's political ladder, the 'race of honors'
Curule	Office invested with the regalia of Rome's ancient kings, Rome's highest and most prestigious magistracies
Decemvir	Member of a board of ten men; usually refers to ten men commissioned to write a code of law for Rome in the fifth century BC
Denarius	Roman coin of high value
Devotio	Devoting oneself to death (to the gods of the Underworld) in exchange for supernatural assistance, usually a magistrate who dies to save his army or the state
Dignitas	One's standing or status in society
Divisores	Officials who help with census; also refers to individuals used to distribute bribes
Epicurean	School of philosophical thought
Equestrian	Rome's highest census class based on wealth, originally Rome's cavalry, but in the late Republic, Rome's wealthy class
Exemplum	An example, usually a moral example of a type of behavior or value
Factio	'Faction,' negative term for a political alliance
Fasces	A bundle of rods that symbolizes the authority of a high magistrate, carried by lictors; magistrates with *imperium* inserted axes into the bundle of rods outside the *pomerium* to symbolize their military authority
Forum	The central open space for public business in the heart of Rome
Gens	Roman clan
Gratia	Moral obligation(s) owed to another citizen
Gravitas	Roman virtue of seriousness and moral weight

Imperator	'Commander,' also the honorific title given to a victorious military commander by his men after a great victory, which was usually a precondition to applying for a triumph
Imperium	Military authority, could not be possessed or used inside the *pomerium* (Rome's sacred boundary)
Intercalary month	The Romans used a lunar calendar, and so had to add an extra month at regular intervals to correct their calendar
Interrex	Special official appointed to hold elections when no consuls are available
Iudex quaestionis	Specially appointed judge
Legate	A high-ranking lieutenant in charge of a military unit or of an entire army
Lex, leges	Law
Lex curiata	Law that conferred *imperium* on a commander
Libertas	Roman value of personal and political freedom
Lictors	Special attendants that accompany some high magistrates
Maiestas	Legal charge of treason
Mos maiorum	Roman tradition, the 'custom of the elders'
Nobilis	A nobleman, one with an illustrious personal or family reputation, one who had held the consulship
Nobilitas	Nobility, status, and influence of those who had held the consulship, or whose family had held the consulship
Nomenclatores	Slaves who remembered people's names for their owners, particularly useful to men campaigning for political office
Novus homo	A 'new man,' one whose ancestors had not held the consulship
Obnuntiatio	Declaration by a qualified magistrate that he was watching for an omen from the gods, and so public business could not be held
Optimates	Senators who championed the traditional style of politics, which favored established aristocratic families with great influence and moral authority
Ornamenta	The regalia given to certain magistrates
Pater	'Father,' also a title for senators
Pater patriae	'Father of the Country,' an honorary title
Patrician	Roman citizen belonging to one of a handful of ancient families, conferred special social status
Patron	Roman citizen who did favors for other citizens
Peripatetic	School of philosophical thought
Pietas	Roman value of respect
Plebeian	Any Roman citizen who was not a patrician

Pomerium	The sacred boundary encircling the older parts of the city of Rome; military force was forbidden inside it
Pontifex maximus	High priesthood in Rome
Populares	Senators who used populist measures to gain personal influence over voters, often at the expense of the Senate as a whole
Praetor	Magistrate who presided over the major courts of Rome, who presided over the Senate and some assemblies in the absence of the consuls, and was responsible for less important provinces and military commands; after Sulla there were eight praetors each year
Proconsul	'In place of a consul,' usually a consul whose magistracy has expired but who has been authorized to continue exercising military command (outside of Rome) as if he were still a consul, usually a provincial governor
Professio	The official announcement of one's candidacy in an election
Propraetor	'In place of a praetor,' usually a praetor whose magistracy has expired, but who has been authorized to continue exercising military command (outside of Rome) as if he were still a praetor, usually used as provincial governors; Cato was given a similar title on his special commission to Cyprus in spite of the fact that he had not yet reached the praetorship
Publicani	Groups of wealthy men who join together into companies to bid for public contracts to collect taxes in Rome's provinces.
Quaesitor	Official who presides over a court
Quaestio	A law court
Quaestor	Magistrate assigned to a range of different responsibilities, including supervision of Rome's treasury and port, acting as quartermaster in a Roman army, and exercising some police functions in Rome; tenure of office conferred membership in the Senate; twenty elected each year after Sulla
Repetundae	The legal charge of extortion; provincial governors were the most common defendants
Senatus consultum	A senatorial resolution or decree, not legally binding but carried great influence and moral weight
Senatus consultum ultimum	'Final decree of the Senate,' the Senate's instructions that consuls and other magistrates should take whatever steps necessary to protect the state, not legally binding

Sestertius	Roman coin of medium value
Social War	Rome's war with its Italian allies (91–87 BC)
Stoicism	School of philosophical thought
Suo anno	Winning an office in the first year one is eligible, a special honor
Supplicatio	Public thanksgiving for divine intervention, usually a way of thanking the gods for a great military victory
Talent	Very large unit of money
Toga praetexta	The toga with a purple or crimson stripe worn by certain magistrates
Toga virilis	The plain white toga worn by citizen men after their coming-of-age
Tribune (military)	High-ranking officer in a Roman legion, some elected by people and others appointed by commanders
Tribune (plebeian)	Magistrate to protect common people (plebeians) from abuse by other magistrates; presided over plebeian assembly and so could propose legislation; held veto power over most any action, often used by *populares* to circumvent authority of Senate
Tribuni aerarii	A high category in the census based on wealth, below the equestrian order
Triumph	The victory parade through Rome that was granted to successful generals (consuls or praetors); had to be authorized by the state
Triumphator	One who celebrates a triumph
Triumvirate	A panel of three men appointed by the state to carry out some responsibility; also the common term to refer to the alliance between Caesar, Pompey, and Crassus
Veto	Magistrates could veto or obstruct actions by their colleagues (those who held the same office), while plebeian tribunes could veto or obstruct any public action
Vis	Legal charge of violence

Bibliography

Abbott, F. (1898) "The Chronology of Cicero's Correspondence during the Year 59 BC," *AJP* 19: 389–405.

Adcock, F. (1932) "The Legal Term of Caesar's Governorship in Gaul," *CQ* 26: 14–26.

Adcock, F. (1966) *Marcus Crassus, Millionaire*. Cambridge.

Afzelius, A. (1941) "Die Politische Bedeutung des jüngeren Cato," *C&M* 4: 101–203.

Alexander, M. (1990) *Trials in the Late Roman Republic, 149 BC to 50 BC*. Toronto.

Alexander, M. (2002) *The Case for the Prosecution in the Ciceronian Era*. Ann Arbor.

Alexander, M. (2010) "Law in the Roman Republic," in N. Rosenstein and R. Morstein-Marx (eds.), *A Companion to the Roman Republic*. Malden, MA: 236–55.

Allen, W. (1950) "The 'Vettius Affair' Once More," *TAPA* 81: 153–63.

Arena, V. (2007) "Invocation to Liberty and Invective of *Dominatus* at the End of the Roman Republic," *BICS* 50: 49–74.

Arena, V. (2012) *Libertas and the Practice of Politics in the Late Roman Republic*. Cambridge.

Arena, V. (2015) "Informal Norms, Values, and Social Control in the Roman Participatory Context," in D. Hammer (ed.), *A Companion to Greek Democracy and the Roman Republic*. Chichester, UK, and Malden, MA: 217–38.

Astin, A. E. (1958) "The *Lex Annalis* before Sulla," *Latomus* 17: 49–64.

Astin, A. E. (1964) "The Roman Commander in Hispania Ulterior," *Historia* 13: 245–54.

Astin, A. E. (1978) *Cato the Censor*. Oxford.

Ayers, D. M. (1954) "Cato's Speech against Murena," *CJ* 49: 245–53.

Badian, E. (1959) "Caesar's *cursus* and the Intervals between Offices," *JRS* 49: 81–9.

Badian, E. (1965) "M. Porcius Cato and the Annexation and Early Administration of Cyprus," *JRS* 55: 110–21.

Badian, E. (1974) "The Attempt to Try Caesar," in J. A. S. Evans (ed.), *Polis and Imperium: Studies in Honour of Edward Togo Salmon*. Toronto: 145–66.

Badian, E. (1996) "*Tribuni Plebis* and *Res Publica*," in J. Linderski (ed.), Imperium sine Fine: *T. Robert S. Broughton and the Roman Republic*. Stuttgart: 187–213.

Balsdon, J. P. V. D. (1939) "Consular Provinces under the Late Republic, I. General Considerations," *JRS* 29: 57–73.

Balsdon, J. P. V. D. (1962) "Roman History, 65–50 B.C.: Five Problems," *JRS* 52: 134–41.

Bauman, R. A. (1967) *The Crimen Maiestatis in the Roman Republic and Augustan Principate*. Johannesburg.

Beard, M. (2007) *The Roman Triumph*. Cambridge, MA, and London.

Beard, M., J. North, and S. Price. (1998) *Religions of Rome*. Two volumes. Cambridge.

Bellemore, J. (1995) "Cato the Younger in the East in 66 BC," *Historia* 44: 376–9.

Bellemore, J. (1996) "The Quaestorship of Cato and the Tribunate of Memmius," *Historia* 45: 504–8.

Bellemore, J. (2005) "Cato's Opposition to Caesar in 59 BC," in K. Welch and T. W. Hillard (eds.) *Roman Crossings: Theory and Practice in the Roman Republic*. Swansea: 225–57.

Bettini, M. (2000) "*Mos, mores* und *mos maiorum*: die Erfindung der 'Sittlichkeit' in der römischen Kultur," in M. Braun, A. Haltenhoff, and F.-H. Mutschler (eds.), "*Moribus antiquis res stat Romana. Römische Werte und römische Literatur im 3. und 2. Jh. v. Chr.* Munich and Leipzig: 303–52.

Billows, R. (2008) *Julius Caesar: The Colossus of Rome*. New York.

Bleicken, J. (1955) *Das Volkstribunat der klassischen Republik*. Munich.

Blom, H. van der. (2010) *Cicero's Role Models: The Political Strategy of a Newcomer*. Oxford.

Blom, H. van der. (2011) "Pompey in the *Contio*," *CQ* 61: 553–73.

Blom, H. van der. (2012) "Cato and the People," *BICS* 55: 39–56.

Blösel, W. (2000) "Die Geschichte des Begriffes *mos maiorum* von den Anfängen bis zu Cicero," in B. Linke and M. Stemmler (eds.), Mos Maiorum. *Untersuchungen zu den formen der Identitätsstiftung und Stabilisierung in der römischen Republik*. Stuttgart: 25–97.

Botermann, H. (1989) "Cato und die Sogenannte Schwertübergabe im Dezember 50 V. Christus. Ein übersehenes Zeugnis für die Vorgeschichte des Bürgerkrieges. Zum Gedenken an Helmut Dreitzel," *Hermes* 117: 62–85.

Brennan, T. C. (1989) "C. Aurelius Cotta *Praetor Iterum* (CIL I² 610)," *Athenaeum* 67: 467–87.

Brennan, T. C. (2000) *The Praetorship in the Roman Republic*. Two volumes. Oxford.

Broughton, T. R. S. (1951–52) *The Magistrates of the Roman Republic*. Two volumes. Cleveland.

Brown, R. D. (1991) "'*Catonis Nobile Letum*' and the List of Romans in Horace 'Odes' 1.12," *Phoenix* 45: 326–40.

Brunt, P. A. (1961) "The *Lex Valeria Cornelia*," *JRS* 51: 71–83.

Brunt, P. A. (1971) *Italian Manpower: 225 BC–AD 14*. Oxford.

Brunt, P. A. (1982) "*Nobilitas* and *Novitas*," *JRS* 72: 1–17.

Bücher, F. (2006) *Verargumentierte Geschichte: Exempla Romana im politischen Diskurs der späten römischen Republik*. Stuttgart.

Bucher, G. S. (1995) "Appian *B.C.* 2.24 and the Trial '*de ambitu*' of M. Aemilius Scaurus," *Historia* 44: 396–421.

Burckhardt, L. A. (1988) *Politische Strategien der Optimaten in der späten römischen Republik*. Stuttgart.

Burckhardt, L. A. (1990) "The Political Elite of the Roman Republic: Comments on Recent Discussion of the Concepts '*Nobilitas* and *Homo Novus*,'" *Historia* 39: 77–99.

Burns, A. (1966) "Pompey's Strategy and Domitius' Last Stand at Corfinium," *Historia* 15: 74–95.

Canfora, L. (2007) *Julius Caesar: The People's Dictator*. M. Hill and K. Windle, translation. Edinburgh.

Cantarella, E. (2002) "Marriage and Sexuality in Republican Rome: A Roman Conjugal Love Story," in M. C. Nussbaum and J. Sihvola (eds.), *The Sleep of Reason: Erotic Experience and Sexual Ethics in Ancient Greece and Rome*. Chicago and London: 269–82.

Carlsen, J. (2006) *The Rise and Fall of a Roman Noble Family: The Domitii Ahenobarbi 196 BC–AD 68*. Odense.

Churchill, J. B. (2001) "The Lucky Cato, and His Wife," *Phoenix* 55: 98–107.

Clarke, M. L. (2012) *Higher Education in the Ancient World*. London and New York.

Collins, J. (1955) "Caesar and the Corruption of Power," *Historia* 4: 445–65.

Connolly, S. (2012) "*Disticha Catonis Uticensis*," *CPh* 107.2: 119–130.

Cornell, T. J. (2013) *The Fragments of the Roman Historians*. Three volumes. Oxford.

Courtney, E. (1961) "The Prosecution of Scaurus in 54 BC," *Philologus* 105: 151–6.

Courtney, E. (1999) *Archaic Latin Prose*. Atlanta, GA.

Cowan, R. (2015) "On Not Being Archilochus Properly: Cato, Catullus and the Idea of *Iambos*," *Materiali e Discussioni per l'Analisi dei Testi Classici* 74: 9–52.

Craig, C. P. (1986) "Cato's Stoicism and the Understanding of Cicero's Speech for Murena," *TAPA* 116: 229–39.

Crawford, J. (1984) *The Lost and Unpublished Orations*. Göttingen.

Crawford, M. H. (1989) "The *lex Iulia agraria*," *Athenaeum* 67: 179–90.

Cristofori, A. (2002) "Grain Distribution in Late Republican Rome," in F. Petrucci (ed.), *The Welfare State: Past, Present, Future*. Pisa: 141–54.

Culham, P. (2004) "Women in the Roman Republic," in H. Flower (ed.), *The Cambridge Companion to the Roman Republic*. Cambridge: 139–59.

Dart, J., and F. J. Vervaet. (2014) "Claiming Triumphs for Recovered Territories: Reflections on Valerius Maximus 2.8.4," in C. H. Lange and F. J. Vervaet (eds.), *The Roman Republican Triumph beyond the Spectacle*. Rome: 53–64.

De Libero, L. (1992) *Obstruktion: Politische Praktiken im Senate und in der Volksversammlung der ausgehenden römischen Republik (70–49 v. Chr.)*. Stuttgart.

Dragstedt, A. (1969) "Cato's *Politeuma*," *Agon* 3: 69–96.

Drogula, F. K. (2011) "The Lex Porcia and the Development of Legal Restraints on Roman Governors," *Chiron* 41: 91–124.

Drogula, F. K. (2015) *Commanders and Command in the Roman Republic and Early Empire*. Chapel Hill, NC.

Drummond, A. (1995) *Law, Politics and Power: Sallust and the Execution of the Catilinarian Conspirators*. Stuttgart.

Duff, T. (1999) *Plutarch's Lives: Exploring Virtue and Vice*. Oxford.

Earl, D. C. (1965) "Appian *BC* 1.14 and '*Professio*,'" *Historia* 14: 325–32.

Ebel, C. (1976) *Transalpine Gaul: The Emergence of a Roman Province*. Leiden.

Edwards, C. (2006) "Modeling Roman Suicide? The Afterlife of Cato," *Economy and Society* 34: 200–222.

Eilers, C. (2002) *Roman Patrons of Greek Cities*. Oxford.

Epstein, D. F. (1987) *Personal Enmity in Roman Politics, 218–43 BC*. London.

Fantham, E. (1975) "The Trials of Gabinius in 54 B.C.," *Historia* 24: 425–43.

Fantham, E. (2003) "Three Wise Men and the End of the Roman Republic," in F. Cairns and E. Fantham (eds.), *Caesar against Liberty?: Perspectives on His Autocracy*. Cambridge: 96–117.

Fantham, E. (2005) "Liberty and the People in Republican Rome," *TAPA* 135: 209–29.

Fantham, E. (2013) *Roman Literary Culture: From Plautus to Macrobius*. Baltimore.

Fehrle, R. (1983) *Cato Uticensis*. Darmstadt.

Ferrary, J.-L. (2001) "La legislation *de ambitu* de Sulla à Auguste," in J.-L. Ferrary (ed.), *Iuris vincula. Studi in onore di Mario Talamanca*, vol. III. Naples: 161–98.

Ferrary, J.-L. (2007) "Les philosophes grecs à Rome," in A. M. Ioppolo and D. N. Sedley (eds.), *Pyrrhonists, Patricians, Platonizers: Hellenistic Philosophy in the Period 155–86 BC*. Naples, 9–46.

Ferrill, A. (1978) "The Wealth of Crassus and the Origins of the 'First Triumvirate,'" *AncW* 1: 169–77.

Flower, H. (1996) *Ancestor Masks and Aristocratic Power in Roman Culture*. Oxford.

Flower, H. (2010a) "Rome's First Civil War and the Fragility of Republican Political Culture," in B. Breed, C. Damon, and A. Rossi (eds.), *Citizens of Discord*. Oxford: 73–86.

Flower, H. (2010b) *Roman Republics*. Princeton, NJ, and Oxford.

Fraschetti, A. (2001) *Roman Women*. L. Lappin, translation. Chicago and London.

Frede, M. (1999), "On the Stoic Conception of the Good," in K. Ierodiakonon (ed.), *Topics in Stoic Philosophy*. Oxford: 71–94.

Frost, B.-P. (1997) "An Interpretation of Plutarch's *Cato the Younger*," *HPTh* 18: 1–23.

Gehrke, H.-J. (2000) "Marcus Porcius Cato Censorius—ein Bild von einem Römer," in K.-J. Hölkeskamp and E. Stein-Hölkeskamp (eds.), *Von Romulus zu Augustus. Große Gestalten der römischen Republik*. Munich: 147–58.

Geiger, J. (1970) "M. Hortensius M. f. Q. n. Hortalus," *CR* 20: 132–4.

Geiger, J. (1971) *A Commentary on Plutarch's* Cato Minor. Diss. Oxford University.

Geiger, J. (1979) "Munatius Rufus and Thrasea Paetus on Cato the Younger," *Athenaeum* 57: 48–72.

Geiger, J. (2000) "Plutarch on Late Republican Orators and Rhetoric," in L. van der Stockt (ed.), *Rhetorical Theory and Praxis in Plutarch*. Louvain: 211–23.

Gelzer, M. (1934) "Cato Uticensis," *Die Antike* 10: 59–91.

Gelzer, M. (1949) *Pompeius*. Munich.

Gelzer, M. (1968) *Caesar: Politician and Statesman*. Cambridge, MA.

Gelzer, M. (1969) *The Roman Nobility*. R. Seager, translation. New York.

George, D. B. (1991) "Lucan's Cato and the Stoic Attitudes to the Republic," *CAnt* 10: 237–58.

Gildenhard, I. (2007) *Paideia Romana: Cicero's Tusculan Disputations*. Oxford.

Gill, C. (2003), "The School in the Roman Imperial Period," in B. Inwood (ed.), *The Cambridge Companion to the Stoics*. Cambridge: 33–58.

Girardet, K. M. (2000) "Imperium 'maius': Politische und verfassungsrechtliche Aspekte. Versuch einer Klärung," in A. Giovannini and B. Grange (eds.), *La Révolution Romaine après Ronald Syme*. Genève: 167–227.

Girardet, K. M. (2000a) "Caesars Konsulatsplan für das Jahr 49: Gründe und Scheitern," *Chiron* 30: 679–710.

Goar, R. (1987) *The Legend of Cato Uticensis from the First Century B.C. to the Fifth Century A.D.* Brussels.

Goldsworthy, A. (2008) *Caesar: Life of a Colossus*. New Haven, CT.

Goodman, R., and J. Soni. (2012) *Rome's Last Citizen: The Life and Legacy of Cato, Mortal Enemy of Caesar*. New York.

Gordon, H. L. (1933) "The Eternal Triangle, First Century B.C.," *CJ* 28: 574–8.

Gowing, A. M. (2005) *Empire and Memory: The Representation of the Roman Republic in Imperial Culture*. Cambridge.

Gray, E. W. (1969) "The End of the Roman Republic," *CR* 19: 325–30.

Green, P. (1993) *Alexander to Actium: The Historical Evolution of the Hellenistic Age*. Berkeley.

Griffin, M. T. (1968) "Seneca on Cato's Politics: Epistle 14.12–13," *CQ* 18: 373–5.

Griffin, M. T. (1986a) "Philosophy, Cato, and Roman Suicide: I," *G&R* 33.1: 64–77.

Griffin, M. T. (1986b) "Philosophy, Cato, and Roman Suicide: II," *G&R* 33.2: 192–202.

Grisé, Y. (1982) *Le suicide dans la Rome antique*. Montreal and Paris.

Gruen, E. S. (1968) *Roman Politics and the Criminal Courts, 149–78 BC*. Cambridge, MA.

Gruen, E. S. (1969) "Notes on the 'First Catilinarian Conspiracy,'" *CP* 64: 20–4.

Gruen, E. S. (1970) "*Veteres Hostes, Novi Amici*," *Phoenix* 24: 237–43.

Gruen, E. S. (1971) "Pompey, Metellus Pius, and the Trials of 70–69 BC: The Perils of Schematism," *AJP* 92: 1–16.

Gruen, E. S. (1974) *The Last Generation of the Roman Republic*. Berkeley.

Gruen, E. S. (1992) *Culture and National Identity in Republican Rome*. Ithaca and London.

Gruen, E. S. (2009) "Caesar as a Politician," in M. Griffin (ed.), *A Companion to Julius Caesar*. Malden, MA: 23–36.

Hadot, P. (1987) "Théologie, exégèse, révélation, écriture, dans la philosophie greque," in M. Tardieu (ed.), *Les règles de l'interpretation*. Paris: 13–34.

Hallet, J. P. (2014) *Fathers and Daughters in Roman Society: Women in the Elite Family*. Princeton, NJ.

Hammer, D. (2014) *Roman Political Thought: From Cicero to Augustine*. Cambridge.

Harders, A.-C. (2007) "Die verwandtschaftlichen Beziehungen der Servilia, Ehefrau des L. Licinius Lucullus: Schwester oder Nichte des Cato Uticensis?" *Historia* 56: 453–61.

Harders, A.-C. (2010) "Roman Patchwork Families: Surrogate Parenting, Socialization, and the Shaping of Tradition," in V. Dasen and T. Späth (eds.), *Children, Memory, and Family Identity in Roman Culture*. Oxford: 49–72.

Harris, W. (1985) *War and Imperialism in Republican Rome*. Oxford.

Havener, W. (2014) "A Ritual against the Rule? The Representation of Civil War Victory in the Late Republican Triumph," in C. H. Lange and F. J. Vervaet (eds.), *The Roman Republican Triumph: Beyond the Spectacle*. Rome: 165–79.

Hayne, L. (1974) "The Politics of M'. Glabrio, cos. 67," *CP* 69: 280–2.

Hellegouarc'h, J. (1963) *Le vocabulaire Latin des relations et des partis politiques sous la République*. Paris.

Heyworth, S. J., and A. J. Woodman. (1986) "Sallust, *Bellum Catilinae* 50.3–5," *LCM* 11: 11–12.

Hill, T. (2004) Ambitiosa Mors: *Suicide and Self in Roman Thought and Literature*. New York and London.

Hillman, T. P. (1993) "When Did Lucullus Retire?" *Historia* 42: 211–28.

Hillman, T. P. (1996) "Plutarch and Dio on the Postponed Consular Elections for 61," *Hermes* 124: 313–20.

Hölkeskamp, K.-J. (2004) Senatus Populusque Romanus: *Die politische Kultur der Republik—Dimensionen und Deutungen*. Stuttgart.

Hölkeskamp, K.-J. (2010a) *Reconstructing the Roman Republic*. Princeton, NJ, and Oxford.

Hölkeskamp, K.-J. (2010b) "Self-Serving Sermons: Oratory and the Self-Construction of the Republican Aristocrat," in C. Smith and R. Covino (eds.), *Praise and Blame in Roman Republican Rhetoric*. Swansea: 17–34.

Hölkeskamp, K.-J. (2012) "Im Gewebe der Geschichte(n): *Memoria*, Monumente und ihre mythhistorische Vernetzung," *Klio* 94: 380–414.

Hölkeskamp, K.-J. (2013) "Friends, Romans, Countrymen: Addressing the Roman People and the Rhetoric of Inclusion," in C. Steel and H. van der Blom (eds.), *Community and Communication*. Oxford: 11–28.

Hopkins, K. and G. Burton (1983) "Ambition and Withdrawal: The Senatorial Aristocracy under the Emperors," in K. Hopkins (ed.), *Death and Renewal*. Cambridge: 120–200.

Jackson, J. (1978) "Cicero, *Fam.* 1.9.9, and the Conference of Luca," *LCM* 3: 175–7.

Jameson, S. (1970) "Pompey's *Imperium* in 67: Some Constitutional Fictions," *Historia* 19: 539–60.

Jameson, S. (1970a) "The Intended Date of Caesar's Return from Gaul," *Latomus* 29: 638–60.

Jehne, M. (1995) "Die Beeinflussung von Entscheidungen durch 'Bestechung': Zur Funktion des Ambitus in der römischen Republik," in M. Jehne (ed.), *Demokratie in Rom? Die Rolle des Volkes in der Politik der römischen Republik.* Stuttgart: 51–76.

Jehne, M. (1999) "Cato und die Bewahrung der traditionellen res publica. Zum Spannungsverhältnis zwischen *mos maiorum* und griechischer Kultur im zweiten Jahrhundert v. Chr.," in F. Voight-Spira and B. Rommel (eds.), *Rezeption und Identität. Die kulturelle Auseinandersetzung Roms mit Griechenland als europäisches Paradigma.* Stuttgart: 115–34.

Jehne, M. (2016) "The Senatorial Economics of Status in the Late Republic," in H. Beck, M. Jehne, and J. Serrati (eds.), *Money and Power in the Roman Republic.* Bruxelles: 188–207.

Jones, C. P. (1970) "Cicero's 'Cato,'" *RHM* 113: 188–96.

Kaster, R. A. (2006) *Marcus Tullius Cicero: Speech on Behalf of Publius Sestius.* Oxford.

Kay, P. (2014) *Rome's Economic Revolution.* Oxford.

Keaveney, A. (1992) *Lucullus: A Life.* London and New York.

Keaveney, A. (2005) *Sulla: The Last Republican.* Second edition. London.

Kenty, J. (2016) "Congenital Virtue: *Mos Maiorum* in Cicero's Orations," *CJ* 111: 429–62.

Kierdorf, W. (1978) "Ciceros 'Cato': Überlegungen zu einer verlorenen Schrift Ciceros," *RhM* 121: 167–84.

Knapp, R. (1980) "Cato in Spain, 195/194 BC: Chronology and Geography," in C. Deroux (ed.), *Studies in Latin Literature and Roman History II.* 21–56.

Kumaniecki, K. (1970) "Cicero's Cato," in W. Wimmel (ed.), *Forschungen zur römischen Literatur, Festschrift zum 60. Geburtstag von Karl Büchner.* Wiesbaden: 168–88.

Lacey, W. K. (1961) "The Tribunate of Curio," *Historia* 10: 318–29.

Lazenby, J. F. (1959) "The Conference at Luca and the Gallic War: A Study in Roman Politics, 57–55 BC," *Latomus* 18: 67–76.

Leach, J. (1978) *Pompey the Great.* London.

Lehmann-Hartleben, K. (1938) "*Maenianum* and *Basilica*," *AJP* 59: 280–96.

Levene, D. S. (2000) "Sallust's 'Catiline' and Cato the Censor," *CQ* 50: 170–91.

Levick, B. (2015) *Catiline.* London.

Lewis, M. (1955) *The Official Priests of Rome under the Julio-Claudians.* Rome.

Linderski, J. (1965) "Constitutional Aspects of the Consular Elections in 59 BC," *Historia* 14: 423–42.

Linderski, J. (1966) "Were Pompey and Crassus Elected in Absence to Their First Consulship," *Mélanges offerts à Kazimierz Michalowski*, 523–6. Warsaw.

Linderski, J. (1971) "Three Trials in 54 B.C.: Sufenas, Cato, Procilius and Cicero, 'ad Atticum,' 4.15.4," in *Studi in onore di Edoardo Volterra*, vol. 2. Milan: 281–302.

Linderski, J. (1972) "The Aedileship of Favonius, Curio the Younger and Cicero's Election to the Augurate," *HSCP* 76: 181–200.

Linderski, J. (1985) "Buying the Vote: Electoral Corruption in the Late Republic," *AncW* 11: 87–94.

Linderski, J. (1986) "The Augural Law," *ANRW* 2.16: 2146–2312.

Linderski, J. (1995) "Ambassadors Go to Rome," in E. Frezouls and A. Jacquemin (eds.), *Les Relations Internationales: Actes de Colloque de Strasbourg, 15–17 juin 1999*. Paris: 453–78.

Lintott, A. (1968) *Violence in Republican Rome*. Oxford.

Lintott, A. (1970) "The Tradition of Violence in the Annals of the Early Roman Republic," *Historia* 19: 12–29.

Lintott, A. (1971) "Lucan and the History of the Civil War," *CQ* 21: 488–505.

Lintott, A. (1981) "What Was the 'Imperium Romanum'?" *G&R* 28: 53–67.

Lintott, A. (1981) "The *Leges de Repetundis* and Associate Measures under the Republic," *ZSav.* 98: 162–212.

Lintott, A. (1990) "Electoral Bribery in the Roman Republic," *JRS* 80: 1–16.

Lintott, A. (1992) *Judicial Reform and Land Reform in the Roman Republic*. Cambridge.

Lintott, A. (1993) *Imperium Romanum*. London and New York.

Lintott, A. (1999a) *The Constitution of the Roman Republic*. Oxford.

Lintott, A. (1999b) *Violence in Republican Rome*. Oxford.

López, C. R. (2010) *La corruption à la fin de la République romaine (IIᵉ–Iᵉʳ s. av. J.-C.)*. Stuttgart.

Luibheid, C. (1970) "The Luca Conference," *CP* 65: 88–94.

Lundgreen, C. (2014) "Rules for Obtaining a Triumph: The *ius triumphandi* Once More," in C. H. Lange and F. J. Vervaet (eds.), *The Roman Republican Triumph beyond the Spectacle*. Rome: 17–32.

MacDonald, C. (1977) *Cicero Orations*. Cambridge, MA.

Magie, D. (1950) *Roman Rule in Asia Minor*. Two volumes. Princeton, NJ.

Marin, P. (2009) *Blood in the Forum: The Struggle for the Roman Republic*. London and New York.

Marshall, A. J. (1972) "The *lex Pompeia de provinciis* (52 BC) and Cicero's *imperium* in 51–50 BC: Constitutional Aspects," *ANRW* 1.1: 887–921.

Marshall, B. A. (1975) "Q. Cicero, Hortensius and the *lex Aurelia*," *RhM* 118: 136–52.

Marshall, B. A. (1976) *Crassus: A Political Biography*. Amsterdam.

Marshall, B. A. (1978) "Problems in the Career of Crassus," *LCM* 3: 159–64.

Marshall, B. A. (1985) *A Historical Commentary on Asconius*. Columbia, MO.

May, J. (1988) *Trials of Character*. Chapel Hill, NC, and London.

McDermott, W. C. (1949) *"Vettius Ille, Ille Noster Index,"* *TAPA* 80: 351–67.

McGushin, P. (1977) *C. Sallustius Crispus, Bellum Catilinae: A Commentary*. Leiden.

McGushin, P. (1987) *Sallust: The Conspiracy of Catiline*. London.

Means, T., and S. K. Dickison. (1974) "Plutarch and the Family of Cato Minor," *CJ* 69: 210–5.

Meier, C. (1961) "Zur Chronologie und Politik in Caesars erstem Konsulat," *Historia* 10: 68–98.

Meier, C. (1966) Res Publica Amissa: *Eine Studie zu Verfassung und Geschichte der späten römischen Republik*. Wiesbaden.

Meier, C. (1995) *Caesar: A Biography*. London.

Meyer, E. (1922) *Caesars Monarchie und das Principat des Pompeius*. Stuttgart.

Millar, F. (1964) "The *Aerarium* and Its Officials under the Empire," *JRS* 54: 33–40.

Miller, J. (2009) *Apollo, Augustus, and the Poets*. Cambridge.

Mitchell, R. E. (1986) "The Definition of *Patres* and *Plebs*," in K. A. Raaflaub (ed.), *Social Struggles in Archaic Rome: New Perspectives on the Conflict of the Orders*. Malden, MA: 130–74.

Mitchell, T. N. (1971) "Cicero and the *Senatus 'consultum ultimum*,'" *Historia* 20: 47–61.

Mitchell, T. N. (1975) "*Veteres Hostes, novi amici* (Cic. *fam*. V. 7,1)," *Historia* 24: 618–22.

Mitchell, T. N. (1979) *Cicero: The Ascending Years*. New Haven, CT, and London.

Mitchell, T. N. (1991) *Cicero: The Senior Statesman*. New Haven, CT.

Moreau, P. (1982) *Clodiana religio: Un procès politique en 61 av. J.-C*. Paris.

Morford, M. (2002) *The Roman Philosophers: From the Time of Cato the Censor to the Death of Marcus Aurelius*. London and New York.

Morrell, K. (2014) "Cato and the Courts in 54 B.C.," *CQ* 64: 669–81.

Morrell, K. (2015) "Cato, Caesar, and the Germani," *Antichthon* 49: 73–93.

Morrell, K. (2017) *Pompey, Cato, and the Governance of the Roman Empire*. Oxford.

Morrell, K. (2018) "Cato, Pompey's Third Consulship, and the Politics of Milo's Trial," in C. Steel, H. van der Blom, and C. Gray (eds.), *Institutions and Ideology in Republican Rome: Speech, Audience and Decision*. Cambridge: 165–80.

Morstein-Marx, R. (2004) *Mass Oratory and Political Power in the Late Roman Republic*. Cambridge.

Morstein-Marx, R. (2007) "Caesar's Alleged Fear of Prosecution and His *Ratio Absentis* in the Approach to the Civil War," *Historia* 56: 159–78.

Mouritsen, H. (2001) *Plebs and Politics in the Late Roman Republic*. Cambridge.

Münzer, F. (1999) *Roman Aristocratic Parties and Families*. Baltimore, MD, and London.

Nelson, H. (1950) "Cato the Younger as a Stoic Orator," *Classical Weekly* 44: 65–9.

Nicolet, C. (1980) *The World of the Citizen in Republican Rome*. P. S. Falla, translation. Berkeley and Los Angeles.

Nicolet, C. (1991) *Space, Geography and Politics in the Early Roman Empire*. Ann Arbor.

Odahl, C. M. (2010) *Cicero and the Catilinarian Conspiracy*. New York and London.

Olson, K. (2017) *Masculinity and Dress in Roman Antiquity*. London and New York.

Oost, S. I. (1955) "Cato Uticensis and the Annexation of Cyprus," *CPh* 50.2: 98–112.

Oost, S. I. (1956) "The Date of the *Lex Iulia de Repetundis*," *AJP* 77: 19–28.

Östenberg, I. (2014) "Triumph and Spectacle: Victory Celebrations in the Late Republican Civil Wars," in C. H. Lange and F. J. Vervaet (eds.), *The Roman Republican Triumph: Beyond the Spectacle*. Rome: 181–93.

Paterson, J. (2009), "Caesar the Man," in M. Griffin (ed.), *A Companion to Julius Caesar*. Malden, MA: 126–40.

Pecchuira, P. (1965) *La Figura di Catone Uticense nella Letteratura Latina*. Torino.

Pelling, C. (1985) "Plutarch and Catiline," *Hermes* 113: 311–39.

Pelling, C. (1986) "Plutarch and Roman Politics," in I. S. Moxon, J. D. Smart, and A. J. Woodman (eds.), *Past Perspectives: Studies in Greek and Roman Historical Writing*. Cambridge: 159–87.

Pelling, C. (2002) *Plutarch and History*. London.

Pelling, C. (2011) *Plutarch, Caesar*. Oxford.

Pina Polo, F. (2004) "Die nützliche Erinnerung: Geschichsschreibung, 'mos maiorum' und die römische Identität," *Historia* 53: 147–72.

Pina Polo, F. (2006) "The Tyrant Must Die: Preventive Tyrannicide in Roman Political Thought," in F. M. Simón, F. Pina Polo, and J. R. Rodríguez (eds.), *Repúblicas y ciudadanos: Modelos de participación cívica en el mundo antiguo*. Barcelona: 71–101.

Pina Polo, F. (2011) "Public Speaking in Rome: A Question of *Auctoritas*," in M. Peachin (ed.), *The Oxford Handbook of Social Relations in the Roman World*. Oxford: 286–303.

Pina Polo, F. (2016) "Magistrates-Elect and Their *potestas contionandi* in the Late Roman Republic," *Historia* 65: 66–72.

Raaflaub, K. A. (1974a) Dignitatis contentio: *Studien zur Motivation und politischen Taktik im Bürgerkrieg zwischen Caesar und Pompeius*. Munich.

Raaflaub, K. (1974b) "Zum politischen Wirken der caesarfreundlichen Volkstribunen am Vorabend des Bürgerkriegs," *Chiron* 4: 293–326.

Raaflaub, K. (2003) "Caesar the Liberator? Factional Politics, Civil War, and Ideology," in F. Cairns and E. Fantham (eds.), *Caesar against Liberty?: Perspectives on His Autocracy*. Cambridge: 35–67.

Raaflaub, K. (2009) "*Bellum Civile*," in M. Griffin (ed.), *A Companion to Julius Caesar*. Malden, MA: 175–91.

Ramsey, J. T. (2009) "The Proconsular Years: Politics at a Distance," in M. Griffin (ed.), *A Companion to Julius Caesar*. Malden, MA: 37–56.

Ramsey, J. T. (2016) "How and Why Was Pompey Made Sole Consul in 52 BC?" *Historia* 65: 298–324.

Rauh, S. (2015) "The Tradition of Suicide in Rome's Foreign Wars," *TAPA* 145: 383–410.

Reay, B. (2005) "Agriculture, Writing, and Cato's Aristocratic Self-Fashioning," *ClAnt* 24: 331–61.

Rickman, G. (1980) *The Corn Supply of Rome*. Oxford.

Rising, T. (2013) "Senatorial Opposition to Pompey's Eastern Settlement. A Storm in a Teacup?" *Historia* 62: 196–221.

Robb, M. A. (2010) *Beyond* Populares *and* Optimates: *Political Language in the Late Republic*. Stuttgart.

Rosenstein, N. (2010) "Aristocratic Values," in N. Rosenstein and R. Morstein-Marx (eds.), *A Companion to the Roman Republic*. Malden, MA: 365–82.

Rotondi, G. (1912) *Leges publicae populi Romani*. Milan.

Rundell, W. M. F. (1979) "Cicero and Clodius: The Question of Credibility," *Historia* 28: 301–27.

Russo, P. M. (1975) *Marcus Porcius Cato: A Political Reappraisal*. Diss. Rutgers University, New Brunswick, NJ.

Ryan, F. X. (1993) "Ψευδοκάτων," *Glotta* 71: 171–3.

Ryan, F. X. (1994a) "Senate Intervenants in 50 B.C.," *CQ* 44: 542–4.

Ryan, F. X. (1994b) "The Praetorship of Favonius," *AJP* 115: 587–601.

Ryan, F. X. (1995) "The Tribunate of C. Memmius L. F.," *Hermes* 123: 293–302.

Ryan, F. X. (1998) *Rank and Participation in the Republican Senate*. Stuttgart.

Salmon, E. T. (1935) "Catiline, Crassus, and Caesar," *AJP* 56: 302–16.

Salmon, E. T. (1970) *Roman Colonisation under the Republic*. London.

Santangelo, F. (2014) "Roman Politics in the 70s BC: A Story of Realignments?" *JRS* 104: 1–27.

Schiller, A. A. (1978) *Roman Law: Mechanisms of Development*. The Hague.

Schonfield, M. (1999) *Saving the City: Philosopher-Kings and Other Classical Paradigms*. London and New York.

Sciarrino, E. (2011) *Cato the Censor and the Beginnings of Latin Prose*. Columbus.

Scott, W. C. (1969) "Catullus and Cato (c. 56)," *CP* 64: 24–9.

Seager, R. (1964) "The First Catilinarian Conspiracy," *Historia* 13: 338–47.

Seager, R. (1965) "Clodius, Pompeius and the Exile of Cicero," *Latomus* 24: 519–47.

Seager, R. (1989) "Caesar's Political System," *CR* 39: 84–6.

Seager, R. (2002) *Pompey the Great: A Political Biography*. Malden, MA.

Sedley, D. (2003) "The School, from Zeno to Arius Didymus," in B. Inwood (ed.), *The Cambridge Companion to the Stoics*. Cambridge: 7–32.

Shackleton Bailey, D. R. (1956) "*Expectatio Corfiniensis*," *JRS* 46: 56–64.

Shackleton Bailey, D. R. (1960) "The Credentials of L. Caesar and L. Roscius," *JRS* 50: 80–3.

Shackleton Bailey, D. R. (1965–70) *Cicero's Letters to Atticus*. Six volumes. Cambridge.

Shackleton Bailey, D. R. (1980) *Cicero: Select Letters*. Cambridge.

Shatzman, I. (1975) *Senatorial Wealth and Roman Politics*. Bruxelles.

Siani-Davies, M. (2001) *Pro Rabirio Postumo*. Oxford.

Sklenár, R. (1998) "La République des Signes: Caesar, Cato, and the Language of Sallustian Morality," *TAPA* 128: 205–20.

Smith, R. E. (1966) *Cicero the Statesman*. Cambridge.

Smith, R. E. (1977) "The Use of Force in Passing Legislation in the Late Republic," *Athenaeum* 55: 150–74.

Southern, P. (2014) *Augustus*. London and New York.

Spielvogel, J. (1993) *Amicitia und Res Publica: Ciceros Maxime während der innenpolitischen Auseinandersetzungen der Jahre 59–50 v. Chr.* Stuttgart.

Stanton, G. R., and B. A. Marshall. (1975) "The Coalition between Pompeius and Crassus 60–59 BC," *Historia* 24: 205–19.

Stanton, G. R. (2003) "Why Did Caesar Cross the Rubicon?" *Historia* 52: 67–94.

Staveley, E. S. (1954) "The Conduct of Elections during an 'Interregnum,'" *Historia* 3: 193–211.

Staveley, E. S. (1955) "*Provocatio* during the Fifth and Fourth Centuries BC," *Historia* 3: 412–28.

Steel, C. (2012) "The *lex Pompeia de provinciis*: A Reconsideration," *Historia* 61: 83–93.

Steel, C. (2013) "Cicero, Oratory and Public Life," in C. Steel (ed.), *The Cambridge Companion to Cicero*. Cambridge: 160–70.

Stem, R. (2005) "The First Eloquent Stoic: Cicero on Cato the Younger," *CJ* 101: 37–49.

Stemmler, M. (2000) "*Auctoritas exempli*: zur Wechselwirkung von kanonisierten Vergangenheitsbildern und gesellschaftlicher Gegenwart in der spätrepublikanischen Rhetorik," in B. Linke and M. Stemmler (eds.), Mos Maiorum: *Untersuchungen zu den Formen der Identitätsstiftung und Stabilisierung in der Römischen Republik*. Stuttgart: 141–205.

Stockton, D. (1971) *Cicero: A Political Biography*. Oxford.

Stroup, S. C. (2010) "Greek Rhetoric Meets Rome: Expansion, Resistance, and Acculturation," in W. Dominik and J. Hall (eds.), *A Companion to Roman Rhetoric*. Malden, MA: 23–37.

Sumner, G. V. (1963) "*Lex Aelia, Lex Fufia*," *AJP* 84: 337–58.

Swain, S. (1990a) "Plutarch's Lives of Cicero, Cato, and Brutus," *Hermes* 118.2: 192–203.

Swain, S. (1990b) "Hellenic Culture and the Roman Heroes of Plutarch," *JHS* 110: 126–45.

Stanton, G. R., and B. A. Marshall. (1975) "The Coalition between Pompeius and Crassus 60–59 B.C.," *Historia* 24: 205–19.

Steel, C. E. W. (2001) *Cicero, Rhetoric, and Empire*. Oxford.

Steel, C. E. W. (2009) "Friends, Associates, and Wives," in M. T. Griffin (ed.) *A Companion to Julius Caesar*. Oxford: 112–25.

Stem, R. (2005) "The First Eloquent Stoic: Cicero on Cato the Younger," *CJ* 101.1: 37–49.

Stone, A. M. (2005) "*Optimates*: An Archaeology," in K. Welch and T. W. Hillard (eds.), *Roman Crossings: Theory and Practice in the Roman Republic*. Swansea: 59–94.

Stover, T. (2008) "Cato and the Intended Scope of Lucan's '*Bellum Civile*,'" *CQ* 58: 571–80.

Sumi, G. (2005) *Ceremony and Power: Performing Politics in Rome between Republic and Empire*. Ann Arbor.

Swain, S. (1990) "Plutarch's Lives of Cicero, Cato, and Brutus," *Hermes* 118: 192–203.

Syme, R. (1939) *The Roman Revolution*. Oxford.

Syme, R. (1964) *Sallust*. Berkeley.

Syme, R. (1986) *The Augustan Aristocracy*. Oxford.

Syme, R. (1987) "M. Bibulus and Four Sons," *Harv. Stud.* 91: 185–98.

Szymanski, M. (1997) "Who Is Who in Cato's Progeny?" *Hermes* 125: 384–6.

Tannenbaum, R. F. (2005) "What Caesar Said: Rhetoric and History in Sallust's *Coniuratio Catilinae* 51," in K. Welch and T. W. Hillard (eds.), *Roman Crossings: Theory and Practice in the Roman Republic.* Swansea: 209–23.

Tansey, P. (2013) "Marcia Catonis and the *Fulmen Clarum*," *CQ* 63: 423–6.

Tatum, W. J. (1999) *The Patrician Tribune: Publius Clodius Pulcher.* Chapel Hill, NC, and London.

Tatum, W. J. (2008) *Always I Am Caesar.* Malden, MA.

Tatum, W. J. (2010) "The Final Crisis (69–44)," in N. Rosenstein and R. Morstein-Marx (eds.), *A Companion to the Roman Republic.* Malden, MA: 190–211.

Taylor, L. R. (1949) *Party Politics in the Age of Caesar.* Berkeley, Los Angeles, and London.

Taylor, L. R. (1960) *The Voting Districts of the Roman Republic.* Rome.

Taylor, L. R. (1968) "The Dating of the Major Legislation and Elections in Caesar's First Consulship," *Historia* 17: 173–93.

Toher, M. (2009) "Augustan and Tiberian Literature," in M. Griffin (ed.), *A Companion to Julius Caesar.* Malden, MA: 224–38.

Trapp, M. B. (1999) "Socrates, the *Phaedo*, and the *Lives* of Phocion and Cato the Younger," in A. Pérez Jiménez et al. (eds.), *Plutarco, Platón y Aristóteles. Actas del V Congreso Internacional de la I.P.S.: Madrid-Cuenca 4–7 de Mayo de 1999.* Madrid: 487–99.

Treggiari, S. (2002) *Roman Social History.* London and New York.

Treggiari, S. (2003) "Ancestral Virtues and Vices: Cicero on Nature, Nurture and Presentation," in D. C. Braund and C. Gill (eds.), *Myth, History and Culture in Republican Rome: Studies in Honour of T. P. Wiseman.* Exeter: 139–64.

Tschieder, H. J. (1981) *Caesars Anticato. Eine Untersuchung der Testimonien und Fragmente.* Darmstadt.

Ungern-Sternberg, J. von (1998) "Die Legitimitätskrise der römischen Republik," *HZ* 266: 607–24.

von Fritz, K. (1941) "The Mission of L. Caesar and L. Roscius in January 49 BC," *TAPA* 72: 125–56.

Wal, R. L. van der. (2007) "'What a funny consul we have!' Cicero's Dealings with Cato Uticensis and Prominent Friends in Opposition," in J. Booth (ed.), *Cicero on the Attack: Invective and Subversion in the Orations and Beyond.* Swansea: 183–205.

Wallace-Hadrill, A. (2008) *Rome's Cultural Revolution.* Cambridge.

Ward, A. M. (1970) "The Early Relationships between Cicero and Pompey until 80 B.C.," *Phoenix* 24: 119–29.

Ward, A. M. (1972) "Cicero's Fight against Crassus and Caesar in 65 and 63 B.C.," *Historia* 21: 244–58.

Ward, A. (1977) *Marcus Crassus and the Late Roman Republic.* Columbia, MO, and London.

Ward, A. M. (1978) "Problems in the Career of Crassus," *LCM* 3: 147–57.

Ward, A. M. (1980) "The Conference of Luca: Did It Happen?" *AJAH* 5: 48–63.

Warren, J. (2009) "Socratic Suicide," *JHS* 121: 91–106.

Weinrib, E. J. (1968) "The Persecution of Roman Magistrates," *Phoenix* 22: 32–56.

Weinrib, E. J. (1970) "*Obnuntiatio:* Two Problems," *ZSS* 87: 395–425.

Welch, K. (2012) Magnus Pius: *Sextus Pompeius and the Transformation of the Roman Republic*. Swansea.

White, P. (1997) "Julius Caesar and the Publication of the *Acta* in Republican Rome," *Chiron* 27: 73–84.

Williams, R. S., and B. P. Williams. (1988) "Cn. Pompeius Magnus and L. Afranius: Failure to Secure the Eastern Settlement," *CJ* 83: 198–206.

Williamson, C. (2005) *The Laws of the Roman People*. Ann Arbor.

Wistrand, M. (1979) *Cicero Imperator*. Göteborg.

Woodman, A. J. (1983) *Velleius Paterculus: The Caesarian and Augustan Narratives (2.41–93)*. Cambridge.

Woolf, G. (2000) *Becoming Roman: The Origins of Provincial Civilization in Gaul*. Cambridge.

Yakobson, A. (1999) *Elections and Electioneering in Rome*. Stuttgart.

Yakobson, A., and H. Horstkotte. (1997) "'Yes, Quaestor': A Republican Politician versus the Power of the Clerks," *ZPE* 116: 247–8.

Yates, D. C. (2011) "The Role of Cato the Younger in Caesar's *Bellum Civile*," *CW* 104: 161–74.

Zadorojnyi, A. V. (2007) "Cato's Suicide in Plutarch," *CQ* 57.1: 216–230.

Zecchini, G. (1980) "La morte di Catone e l'opposizione intellettuale a Cesare e ad Augusto," *Athenaeum* 58: 39–56.

Index

Printed in the USA
CPSIA information can be obtained
at www.ICGtesting.com
CBHW070907250624
10593CB00002B/5

9 780197 604373